THE

OF

MARY RUSSELL MITFORD,

AUTHORESS OF "OUR VILLAGE, &c."

𝕿𝖔𝖑𝖉 𝖇𝖞 𝕳𝖊𝖗𝖘𝖊𝖑𝖋 𝖎𝖓 𝕷𝖊𝖙𝖙𝖊𝖗𝖘 𝖙𝖔 𝕳𝖊𝖗 𝕱𝖗𝖎𝖊𝖓𝖉𝖘.

EDITED

BY THE REV. A. G. K. L'ESTRANGE.

IN TWO VOLUMES.

VOL. II.

NEW YORK:

HARPER & BROTHERS, PUBLISHERS,

FRANKLIN SQUARE.

1870.

CONTENTS OF VOL. II.

LIFE AND LETTERS

OF

MARY RUSSELL MITFORD.

CHAPTER I.

LETTERS FOR 1823.

To SIR WILLIAM ELFORD, *Bickham, Plymouth.*

Three-mile Cross, Feb. 28, 1823.

MY DEAR FRIEND,—I have no frank, but I have at last the pleasure of being able to give you good news; and I think you would rather pay postage than not hear it. After a degree of contention and torment and suspense such as I can not describe, one of my plays—my last and favorite play—is, I do really believe, on the point of representation, with my favorite actor for the hero. He (Mr. Macready) read it in the green-room on Wednesday, and I suppose it will be out in ten days or a fortnight. Mr. Kemble behaved very fairly and honorably—has given Macready full power in getting up the play; and, with that admirable actor (certainly the best since Garrick) and this play (certainly worth a thousand of "Foscari") we can do very well without him. "Julian," or "The Melfi" (for I really don't know which they call it), is a tragedy on a fictitious story. I am afraid to tell you what the critics say of it—but not afraid to stake on it my dramatic hopes. Mr. Macready will be supported by Mr. Bennett (the new actor), Mr. Abbott, Miss Lacy, and Miss Foote. So you must write to your play-going friends; for I am sure that ardent spirit, Macready, will drive the matter on. It is odd enough that I and this zealous friend of mine have never met! He is just such another soul of fire as Haydon—highly edu-

A 2

cated, and a man of great literary acquirements—consorting entirely with poets and young men of talent. Indeed it is to his knowledge of my friend Mr. Talfourd that I owe the first introduction of my plays to his notice.

Forgive this short note. I have many letters to write, and have been for the last fortnight exceedingly unwell; but this news would cure me if I were dying. *I know* that I shall be quite well to-morrow.

Ever most affectionately yours,   M. R. M.

[On the second Saturday of March, 1823, " Julian " was performed, with Mr. Macready as the principal character. It was successful. Miss Mitford went to town for a few days on a visit to Mrs. Hofland, in Newman Street, to witness its first representation and to enjoy her triumph.]

Copy of a letter to WILLIAM MACREADY, ESQ.

Three-mile Cross, April, 1823.

MY DEAR SIR,—Do not fancy yourself engaged in another " Mirandola " office, when I take the great liberty—too great, perhaps—of requesting you to read over the enclosed scheme of a play on the story of Garzia de Medici, and to tell me if you think it be worth attempting—in one word, Yes or No! The subject first struck me in the " Life of Benvenuto Cellini;" and on reperusing while in town the intense but terrible tragedy of " Alfieri," I was still more caught by the contrast of character which it offers, and the dreadful truth of the catastrophe. I have somewhat injured the collision of various characters in one family, which is so striking in his play. I have omitted one of the brothers, which seemed necessary to disencumber the plot : but he could be restored, if necessary. Altogether, I do not like the subject so well as not to be very ready to abandon it if I could find a better. Procida *is* a better, but then—would that be quite right? Well, you will tell me what their " Procida " is ; and perhaps we may find out the real author.* If it be by a woman—really a woman, and writing for money—Heaven forbid that I should jostle with her ! If it be Mr. Milman, I should not mind taking the field—Francesca da Rimini—beginning with

* Mrs. Hemans. It was produced under the name of " The Sicilian Vespers."

the scene of Phædra from Euripides, and making the brother
—I forget his name, Paola—quite unconscious of his love till
it bursts on him suddenly in reading with her the old romance.   That would be very fine, if we had a great actress
—but Miss Lacy!   Oh! Rienzi?   I don't think you like Rienzi; and perhaps Gibbon has done too much for the story,
and it might be censured as too political.   The temptation is,
that there exists, or that I have fancied, some slight resemblance of character and history between him and Napoleon.
Both were of obscure birth—both governing by force of mind
—both driven headlong to ruin by an indomitable self-will—
rising by liberty and falling by ambition.   Surely there is
enough resemblance to justify an attempt to portray the man
who, with all his faults, has possessed my imagination all my
life long!   But I am afraid of the attempt.   It would be an
over-excitement—I should get nervous and fail.   Massaniel-
lo, the fisherman of Naples—is he promising?   Am I likely
to find any thing to the purpose in Froissart?   I have not
seen that delightful book for many years, but I remember a
romantic story of the Count of Orthes and his son; I don't,
however, think it would do for tragedy, though the old chroni-
cler is full of high and chivalrous incident.   I must read him
for that.   I am half afraid of attacking Greek or Roman story;
because women, from mere want of learning, from the absence
of real depth, are always pedantic, and spread their thin gold
leaf over an immense quantity of surface.   And yet history
is best, for a thousand reasons.   Well, if I were wise I should
form a strong resolution to conquer my besetting sin of idle-
ness—to renounce " le délicieux far niente," as Rousseau calls
it, and work hard this summer, so as to produce two or three
tragedies from which you might choose, if any were worthy
of your choice, and throw the others into the fire.

My father, who would go to town, tells me, as your dear
sister does, that "Julian" went splendidly on Wednesday,
and not amiss, considering the wet night, on Friday, and that
you think it rising.   But you must not perform that fatiguing part again when you are not well—no, not for all the Ju-
lians in the world.   I have implored your sister not to let
you.   Are you amenable to this sort of management?   By
the way, if the play do reach the ninth night, it will be a very
complete refutation of Mr. Kemble's axiom that no single per-

former can fill the theatre; for, except our pretty Alphonso,[*] there is in " Julian" one, and only one. Let him imagine how deeply we feel his exertions and his kindness! Have you seen the attack upon *us* in the "London?" Can you guess the author? It is evidently one who does not understand, who has never felt, the pleasure of gratitude—the delight of being thankful; but I hope that it is not—that it can not be —no, I will not suspect that a man of genius could write that sneering and heartless article. To make amends, Mr. Haydon writes me word that Mr. Hazlitt has applied to Mr. Jeffrey for his sanction to review " Julian " in the " Edinburgh." This is a great compliment, and will be, if the request be granted, a great advantage; he will do it so well. Of course this is quite in confidence.

I am frightened to look at the length of this letter. I may say, with Anacreon's dove, " I have chattered like a jay." Pray forgive it, and believe me always, my dear sir, most sincerely yours,   M. R. MITFORD.

To SIR WILLIAM ELFORD, *Bickham, Plymouth.*

Three-mile Cross, April 25, 1823.

MY DEAR FRIEND,—I am but just returned from town, whither I have been led by one of the evil consequences of dramatic authorship—that is to say, a false report—and lose not a moment in writing to thank you for your zealous kindness.

I have no time to tell you the story of the strange mistake which led me to London, and really my soul sickens within me when I think of the turmoil and tumult which I have undergone, and am to undergo, for Charles Kemble will not suffer me to withdraw my tragedy of " The Foscari," and threatens me with a lawsuit if I do. In the mean time I am tossed about between him and Macready like a cricket-ball —affronting both parties and suspected by both, because I will not come to a deadly rupture with either. Only imagine what a state this is, for one who values peace and quietness beyond every other blessing of life! In the mean time, they have stopped " Julian " at the end of the eighth night, though it was going brilliantly to brilliant houses, and (but this is quite between ourselves) have not paid me for the

* Miss Foote.

third and sixth nights.* To be sure, I have Charles Kemble's personal word, and I believe him to be an honest man; but to undergo all this misery, and not get my money, would be terrible indeed! To crown all, Mr. Hamilton, of the "Lady's Magazine," has absconded above forty pounds in my debt. Oh! who would be an authoress! The only comfort is, that the Magazine can't go on without me; and that the very fuss they make in quarreling over me at the theatre proves my importance there; so that, if I survive these vexations, I may in time make something of my poor, poor brains. But I would rather serve in a shop—rather scour floors—rather nurse children, than undergo these tremendous and interminable disputes, and this unwomanly publicity.

Pray forgive this sad no-letter. Alas! the free and happy hours, when I could read and think and prattle for you, are past away. Oh! will they ever return? I am now chained to a desk, eight, ten, twelve hours a day, at mere drudgery. All my thoughts of writing are for hard money. All my correspondence is on hard business. Oh! pity me, pity me! My very mind is sinking under the fatigue and the anxiety. God bless you, my dear friend! Forgive this sad letter. Ever most faithfully yours, M. R. Mitford.

To Sir William Elford, *Bickham, Plymouth.*

Three-mile Cross, May 13, 1823.

The kind interest which you are so good as to take in me, my dear and true friend, is a great consolation. That Macready likes me I know; but I have perhaps suffered even more from his injustice and prejudice and jealousy than from the angry attacks of the Kembles. Do not misunderstand me: our connection is merely that of actor and author; but his literary jealousy, his suspicion and mistrust have really the character of passion. And yet he is a most ardent and devoted friend; and it seems ungrateful in me to say so much, even to you, with whom, I know, it will remain sacred. I intend, if Macready remains in Covent Garden (remember that this is most strictly confidential), to write a tragedy on a very grand historical subject (Rienzi, *vide* Gib-

* Miss Mitford received £200 for "Julian" from Covent Garden—£100 cash on the 9th of May, and £100 by bill payable on the 12th of October.

bon, vol. xi. or xii.), and send it to him to bring out without a name.

Mr. Davison has taken to the "Lady's Magazine," and promises, if not "indemnity for the past, security for the future." I told you, I believe, that the late editor had run away upward of forty pounds in my debt, after having, chiefly by my articles, increased the sale of the magazine from two hundred and fifty to two thousand. However, I hope Mr. Davison will go on, for he is sure pay; and that sort of drudgery is heaven when compared with Covent Garden. In the mean time there is one thing which, to so old and kind a friend, I venture to mention. My father has at last resolved—partly, I believe, instigated by the effect which the terrible feeling of responsibility and want of power has had on my health and spirits—to try if he can himself obtain any employment that may lighten the burden. He is, as you know, active, healthy, and intelligent, and with a strong sense of duty and of right. I am sure that he would fulfill to the utmost any charge that might be confided to him; and if it were one in which my mother or I could assist, you may be assured that he would have zealous and faithful coadjutors. For the management of estates or any country affairs he is particularly well qualified; or any work of superintendence which requires integrity and attention. If you should hear of any such, either in Devonshire or elsewhere, would you mention him, or at least let me know? The addition of two or even one hundred a year to our little income, joined to what I am, in a manner, sure of gaining by mere industry, would take a load from my heart of which I can scarcely give you an idea. It would be every thing to me; for it would give me what, for many months, I have not had—the full command of my own powers. Even "Julian" was written under a pressure of anxiety which left me not a moment's rest. I am, however, at present, quite recovered from the physical effects of this tormenting affair, and have regained my flesh and color, and almost my power of writing prose articles; and if I could but recover my old hopefulness and elasticity, should be again such as I used to be in happier days. Could I but see my dear father settled in any employment, I know I should. Believe me ever, with the truest affection, very gratefully yours,   M. R. M.

P.S.—The Duke of Glo'ster went once, if not twice, to see "Julian." You know him, I believe.

To B. R. HAYDON, ESQ.

Three-mile Cross, May 29, 1823.

MY DEAR SIR,—I have no words to say how deeply we feel your situation. Oh! it is a dishonor to the age and to the country, as well as a grief to you and to those who love you. But it can not last—that, thank Heaven! is impossible. Parliament, or the king, or the public, must do the duty which they owe to the great artist, the excellent man, whose pure and admirable character has never given them an excuse for the neglect of his genius. Be assured that it can not last. Have you thought of my proposal of an appeal to the king? It can do no harm; and eloquently as you write, I am sure that it would touch him. Pray think of this. It is terrible to think of you amongst these men, bearing, as you say, "the mark on their countenance." It is like an imprisoned antelope—a caged eagle. But it can not last, thank Heaven! And you will come out a free and a happy man, with fresh cause to love your sweet wife and your noble art. Pray try the king; I have great confidence in his kindly nature. Surely Sir W. Knighton, your townsman, can not refuse to present an appeal to him. Do try.

I am inclosing a number of notes for the twopenny post to a friend in Parliament, and shall add this. The direction is heartbreaking.* but it can not last, I am sure of that. Pray let me know how you are, and, above all, the moment that any thing is done for your release. God bless you, my dear friend! Most faithfully and admiringly yours,

MARY RUSSELL MITFORD.

To SIR WILLIAM ELFORD, *Bickham, Plymouth.*

Three-mile Cross, August 21, 1823.

I hasten, my dear and kind friend, to reply to your very welcome letter. I am quite well now, and if not as hopeful as I used to be, yet less anxious, and far less depressed than I ever expected to feel again. This is merely the influence of the scenery, the flowers, the cool yet pleasant season, and

* The direction was, "B. R. Haydon, Esq., Historical Painter, King's Bench Prison."

the absence of all literary society; for our prospects are not otherwise changed. My dear father, relying with a blessed sanguineness on my poor endeavors, has not, I believe, even inquired for a situation; and I do not press the matter, though I anxiously wish it, being willing to give one more trial to the theatre. If I could but get the assurance of earning for my dear father and mother a humble competence I should be the happiest creature in the world. But for these dear ties I should never write another line, but go out in some situation as other destitute women do. It seems to me, however, my duty to try a little longer; the more especially as I am sure separation would be felt by all of us to be the greatest of all evils.

My present occupation is a great secret. I will tell it to you *in strict confidence*. It is the boldest attempt ever made by woman, which I have undertaken at the vehement desire of Mr. Macready, who confesses that he has proposed the subject to every dramatic poet of his acquaintance—that it has been the wish of his life—and that he never met with any one courageous enough to attempt it before. In short, I am engaged in a grand historical tragedy on the greatest subject in English story—Charles and Cromwell. Should you ever have suspected your poor little friend of so adventurous a spirit? Mr. Macready does not mean the author to be known, and I do not think it will be found out, which is the reason of my requesting so earnestly your silence on the subject. Macready thinks that my sex was, in great part, the occasion of the intolerable malignity with which " Julian " was attacked. They, at least, can not call this a melodrame. My wish is to do strict poetical justice, in the best sense of the word, to both the men and both their causes. What is your opinion of Cromwell? Mine is, that he was a man acting under an intense conviction of the justice of his cause, and little scrupulous as to the means employed in its furtherance. His domestic character appears, in the old memorials and letters and State papers which I have been consulting, to have been delightful and amiable past expression. I shall give only the short time of Charles's being in town before his execution, not at all varying from history, except by bringing in the queen and giving Cromwell a Royalist daughter. Do you think I shall succeed? Macready says he is sure of it. But I fear, I greatly fear. He himself will probably have no power at all next season, since I find they have engaged Mr. Young.

Pray, my dear friend, if you should hear of any situation that would suit my dear father, do not fail to let me know, for that would be the real comfort, to be rid of the theatre and all its troubles. Any thing in the medical line, provided the income, however small, were certain, he would be well qualified to undertake. I hope there is no want of duty in my wishing him to contribute his efforts with mine to our support. God knows, if I could, if there were any certainty, how willingly, how joyfully, I would do all; but that there is not. Pray forgive this long detail, and the apparent vanity with which I have spoken of my tragedies, casting off all the usual circumlocutions, and writing my very thoughts; but I have learned to know myself too well for vanity—my weakness, my impatience, my many faults. If I were better, more industrious, more patient, more consistent, I do think I should succeed; and I will try to be so. I promise you I will, and to make the best use of my poor talents. Pray forgive this egotism; it is a relief and a comfort to me to pour forth my feelings to so dear and so respected a friend; and they are not now so desolate, not quite so desolate, as they have been. God grant me to deserve success! Ever, my dearest and kindest friend, most gratefully and affectionately yours,

M. R. MITFORD.

Pray forgive the sad stupidity of this letter. Since I have become a professed authoress, woe is me! A washerwoman hath a better trade. I am but a shabby correspondent. Pray forgive it, and continue to think of me with your old invaluable kindness.

To B. R. HAYDON, Esq., *Paddington Green.*

Three-mile Cross, August 24, 1823.

Pray are you a cricketer? We are very great ones—I mean our parish, of which we, the feminine members, act audience, and "though we do not play, o'erlook" the balls. When I wrote to you last I was just going to see a grand match in a fine old park near us, Bramshill, between Hampshire, with Mr. Budd, and All England. I anticipated great pleasure from so grand an exhibition, and thought, like a simpleton, the better the play the more the enjoyment.   Oh, what a mistake ! There they were—a set of ugly old men, white-headed and bald-headed (for half of Lord's was engaged in the combat, players and gentlemen, Mr. Ward and Lord Frederick, the veterans of the green), dressed in tight white jackets (the Apollo Belvedere could not bear the hideous disguise of a cricketing jacket), with neckcloths primly tied round their throats, fine japanned shoes, silk stockings, and gloves, instead of our fine village lads, with their unbutton-ed collars, their loose waistcoats, and the large shirt-sleeves which give an air so picturesque and Italian to their glow-ing, bounding youthfulness: there they stood, railed in by themselves, silent, solemn, slow—playing for money, making a business of the thing, grave as judges, taciturn as chess-players—a sort of dancers without music, instead of the glee, the fun, the shouts, the laughter, the glorious confusion of the country game. And there were we, the lookers-on, in tents and marquees, fine and freezing, dull as the players, cold as this hard summer weather, shivering and yawning and trying to seem pleased, the curse of gentility on all our doings, as stupid as we could have been in a ball-room.   I never was so much disappointed in my life.   But every thing is spoilt when money puts its ugly nose in.   To think of playing cricket for hard cash ! Money and gentility would ruin any pastime under the sun.   Much to my comfort (for the degrading my favorite sport into a "science," as they were pleased to call it, had made me quite spiteful), the game ended unsatisfactorily to all parties, winners and losers. Old Lord Frederick, on some real or imaginary affront, took himself off in the middle of the second innings, so that the two last were played without him, by which means his side lost, and the other could hardly be said to win.   So be it al-ways when men make the noble game of cricket an affair of bettings and hedgings, and, may be, of cheatings.

And now God bless you ! Kindest regards and best wishes from all.   Ever yours,   M. R. MITFORD.

To B. R. HAYDON, Esq., 8 *Paddington Green.*

[*Fragment.*]

October, 1823.

I have a sneaking kindness for portraits.   I do not mean

the faces on the Royal Academy walls, but those portraits which *escaped* from the great painters, Titian, Rubens, Rembrandt; and that is the way that yours will be considered, not only by posterity, but by that near part of posterity, the next generation, the Englishmen of twenty years hence. Paint plenty of portraits and plenty of humorous pictures. It is your peculiar talent, and do tell me what this one is about. I am so stupid that I have not been able to guess.

CHAPTER II.

LETTERS FOR 1824.

To SIR WILLIAM ELFORD, *Bickham, Plymouth.*

Three-mile Cross, Jan. 18, 1824.

MY DEAR FRIEND,—I should have written to ask after you all had I not been for nearly six months very much and very painfully engrossed. My dear mother has had an attack of that terrible complaint, the spasmodic asthma, which continued for several months. The spasms came on every night at twelve or one o'clock, and continued for three or four hours with such violence that I have feared, night after night, that she would die in my arms. At last, the very great skill of a medical gentleman in this neighborhood relieved her; though the remedies were so severe that for months she continued as weak as an infant, and the very first day that she thought herself well enough to venture to church she took cold, and the tremendous disorder reappeared, if possible with greater violence and greater obstinacy. At last, I thank God! she is again convalescent; and as we have her now fast prisoner by the fireside, and do not mean to let her peep out till the sun shines on both sides of the hedges, I humbly trust that this invaluable parent and friend may yet be spared to me. But you must imagine how much we have all suffered. My dear father's anxiety, great as it was, did not, however, incapacitate him from being the kindest and most excellent of nurses. He was a thousand times more useful than I; for the working of this perpetual fear on my mind was really debilitating, almost paralyzing, in its effect. We are now happy amidst all our cares and poverty, and feel as if a hundredweight of lead had been taken from our heads by her recovery. God grant that it may be permanent! You may imagine that this has been no slight interruption to my business. Nevertheless, I am hoping to get out a little volume of very playful prose ("You will like it, I promise you," as Mr. Haydon said to me, a week ago, about his picture of "Silenus and Nymphs") some time this season. It would have been out before now if I had been able to go to London and arrange matters with my friend and bookseller, George Whittaker. This young and dashing friend of mine (papa's godson, by-the-by) is this year sheriff of London, and is, I hear, so immersed in his official dignities as to have his head pretty much turned topsy-turvy, or rather, in French phraseology, to have lost that useful appendage; so I should not wonder now, if it did not come out till I am able to get to town and act for myself in the business, and I have not yet courage to leave mamma. It will be called—at least, I mean it so to be—"Our Village;" will consist of essays and characters and stories, chiefly of country life, in the manner of the "Sketch Book," but without sentimentality or pathos—two things which I abhor—and will be published with or without my name, as it shall please my worshipful bibliopole. At all events, the author has no wish to be *incognita ;* so I tell it you as a secret to be told.

I wish you had seen my friends Mr. Macready and his sister, for she is traveling with him. You would have been pleased with both; and Miss M. would have had one point of sympathy with you in her exceeding passion for my letters. (N.B.—I have not written her a line since September.) They are very fascinating people, of the most polished and delightful manners, and with no fault but the jealousy and unreasonableness which seem to me the natural growth of the green-room. I can tell you just exactly what Mr. Macready would have said of me and of "Julian." He would have spoken of me as a meritorious and amiable person, of the play as a first-rate performance, and of the treatment as "infamous!" "scandalous!" "unheard of!"—would have heaped every phrase of polite abuse which the language contains on the C. G. managers; and then would have concluded as follows:—"But it is Miss Mitford's own fault—entirely her own fault. She is, with all her talent, the weakest and most feeble-minded woman that ever lived. If she had put matters into *my* hands—if she had withdrawn "The Foscari"—if she had threatened the managers with a lawsuit—if she had published her case—if she had suffered me to manage for her; she should have been the queen of the theatre. Now, you will see her the slave of Charles Kemble. She is the weakest woman that ever trod the earth."

This is exactly what he would have said; the way in which he talks of me to every one, and most of all to myself. "Is Mr. Macready a great actor?" you ask. I think that I should answer, "*He might have been a* VERY GREAT *one.*" Whether he be now I doubt. A very clever actor he certainly is; but he has vitiated his taste by his love of strong effects, and been spoiled in town and country; and I don't know that I do call him a very great actor. Kean is certainly more intense; but I doubt very much if there be really a great actor now alive, except Liston. At least, I am sure I never saw one who came up to my conception of any of Shakspeare's characters. I have a physical pleasure in the sound of Mr. Macready's voice, whether talking, reading, or acting (except when he rants). It seems to me very exquisite music, with something instrumental and vibrating in the sound, like certain notes of the violoncello. He is grace itself; and he has a great deal of real sensibility, mixed with some trickery. But having seen him in "Virginius," the best of his parts, you are aware of his merits.

By the way, that play seems to me a very fine one (does it to you?) though the curtain ought certainly to have dropped at the end of the fourth act.

You are very good and kind and flattering in what you say of publishing my letters; but, if there were no other reason against that measure, think how freely I have spoken of contemporary authors, and remember that I am a writer of plays, and that the slightest enmity may be vented on me fatally. Besides, I would not for the world hurt people's feelings.

When you see "Our Village" (which, if my sheriff be not bestraught, I hope may happen soon), you will see that my notions of prose style are nicer than these galloping letters would give you to understand. No; our correspondence

must wait for half a century* (like the hoards in Horace
Walpole's box), and then be edited by your great-grand-
son. . . . . I could not help indulging myself with writing
to you, though I ought to have been otherwise busy; but I
will make up for it. God bless you, my dear friend!

Always most affectionately yours,　　M. R. MITFORD.

To B. R. HAYDON, 51 *Sovereign Terrace, Connaught Place.*

Three-mile Cross, Monday night, Feb. 9, 1824.

MY DEAR SIR,—I have to congratulate you most heartily
on your escape from two such disagreeable oddities as your
late landlord and landlady, and to wish you all prosperity
in your new abode. I do not wish you happiness, for you
have it. With such a wife and such a boy, and such a consciousness of those blessings, I do really think you the happiest man in the world.

I found in the "New Monthly," in one of Mr. Hazlitt's delightful Table Talks, the terrible story of Mr. Wordsworth's
letter to you, which spoils his poetry to me; for there was
about his poetry something personal. We clung to him as
to Cowper; and now—it will not bear talking of. The article on "Jeremy Bentham" is also, I think, by Mr. Hazlitt.
I wonder if he ever heard a story told to me by your countryman Mr. Northmore, a great Devonshire reformer, one
of the bad epic poets and very pleasant men in which that
county abounds. He said that Jeremy Bentham being on a
visit at a show house in those parts, at a time when he was
little known, except as a jurist, through the translations of
M. Dumont—certainly before the publication of the Church
of Englandism, or any such enormities—Mrs. Hannah More,
being at a watering-place in the neighborhood, was minded
to see him, and availed herself of the house being one which
was shown on stated days, to pay a visit to the philosopher.

He was in the library when the news arrived; and, the
lady being already in the antechamber and no possible mode
of escape presenting itself, he sent one servant to detain her
a few minutes, and employed another to build him up with
books in a corner of the room. When the folios and quartos
rose above his head, the curious lady was admitted. Must
it not have been a droll scene? The philosopher playing at

* That half-century is well-nigh over.

bo-peep in his intrenchment, and the pious maiden, who had previously ascertained that he was in the room, peering after him in all the agony of baffled curiosity !

Your Frank must be a charming little fellow. Give my love to him and his dear mother. How well I can fancy you darting about in your half-furnished house, doing half every body's work with your own rapid hands ! No wonder that when the bustle was over you should feel a little languid, like a young lady after a ball. All happiness be with you and yours ! Ever very sincerely,

M. R. MITFORD.

To SIR WILLIAM ELFORD.

Three-mile Cross, March 5, 1824.

MY DEAR FRIEND,—In spite of your prognostics, I think you will like " Our Village." It will be out in three weeks or a month ; and it will be an obligation if you will cause it to be asked for at circulating libraries, etc. It is not one connected story, but a series of sketches of country manners, scenery, and character, with some story intermixed, and connected by unity of locality and of purpose. It is exceedingly playful and lively, and I think you will like it. Charles Lamb (the matchless " Elia " of the " London Magazine ") says that nothing so fresh and characteristic has appeared for a long while. It is not over modest to say this ; but who would not be proud of the praise of such a *proser?* And as you, in common with all sensible people, like light reading, I say again that you will like it.

Pray have you read the American novels ? I mean the series by Mr. Cooper—" The Spy," etc. If you have not, send for them, and let me hear the result. In my mind they are as good as any thing Sir Walter Scott ever wrote. He has opened fresh ground, too (if one may say so of the sea). No one but Smollett has ever attempted to delineate the naval character ; and then he is so coarse and hard. Now this has the same truth and power, with a deep, grand feeling. I must not overpraise it, for fear of producing the reaction which such injudicious enthusiasm is calculated to induce ; but I must request you to read it. Only read it. Imagine the author's boldness in taking Paul Jones for a hero, and his power in making one care for him ! I envy the Americans

their Mr. Cooper. Tell me how you like "The Pilot."
There is a certain Long Tom who appears to me the finest
thing since Parson Adams. God bless you, my dear friend !
Ever very sincerely yours,   M. R. MITFORD.

One can not help regretting the destruction of Lord Byron's Memoirs; though, from what the "Examiner" says of
his feelings (and on this point the "Examiner" is, I suppose, good authority), it might not perhaps have been quite
proper to publish them at present without great omissions.
My friend, Mrs. Franklin (I mean Miss Porden "that was,"
as Richardson would say), the epic poetess, and wife of the
man of the North Pole—my friend Mrs. Franklin, who lives
in an atmosphere of Albemarle Street gossip, wrote me an
account of these Memoirs which I will transcribe for you *ver-
batim*. "On inspection they were found so disgraceful in
every way that they could not be published, either on his
account or that of his readers. A friend of mine, who was
at Naples when he gave them to Moore (a whole sackful of
detached papers), and who read them in the carriage as they
afterward traveled through Italy together, told me at the
time that if ever they met the public eye it must be with
such changes and curtailments as would almost destroy their
authenticity. No one whom he ever met, if but once and in
the most casual manner, seems to have escaped vituperation
in his black journal; and his pen was always dipped in the
deepest gall when writing of those who at the moment were
his greatest intimates—Hobhouse, for instance !"
Now, if this be at all true (and Mrs. Franklin is undoubtedly a person of veracity), it is certainly a very good reason
for not publishing what would give so much pain to many
unoffending individuals. But there must be parts that are
harmless; why not publish them ? And why utterly destroy
the last relics of so remarkable a man ? But that little
man-milliner of a poet seems to me to have a sort of design
of turning good as he grows old; witness his attack on
Rousseau. Shall I confess to you, that except his *jeux d'é-
sprit*, which are capital, I am no admirer of that dandy song-
writer. And—I am half afraid to say it—but I was no very
ardent enthusiast for Lord Byron. I admit his stupendous
powers—his exquisite *morceaux;* but he was too melancholy

—too morbid—too sneering. He attacked Napoleon; he failed in the drama, and did not find out that he had failed. And the want of purity! God forbid that I should be a canter; but the want of purity—the harm that both he and Mr. Moore have done to the young men and women of the day—must not be overlooked, though I trust it is forgiven. After all, it is a great light that is quenched*—a most powerful instrument for good and for evil; and the evil will pass away, and the good will remain. Peace to his spirit!

Adieu, my dear friend. I trust that you are going on well with your sitters. They who come to you now are persons of taste. In a very short time it will be the fashion to come, and therefore no criterion.

Always most sincerely yours,   M. R. MITFORD.

[Sir William Elford, in answering this letter, expressed his opinion that the sketches of rural life given in " Our Village" would have been better written in the form of letters.]

To SIR WILLIAM ELFORD, *Bickham, Plymouth.*

Three-mile Cross, June 23, 1824.

MY DEAR FRIEND,—I am quite delighted that you like my book. Your notion of letters pleases me much, as I see plainly that it is the result of the old prepossessions and partialities, which do me so much honor and give me so much pleasure. But it would never have done. The sketches are too long, and necessarily too much connected, for *real* correspondence; and as to any thing make-believe, it has been my business to keep that out of sight as much as possible. Besides which, we are free and easy in these days, and talk to the public as a friend. Read "Elia," or the "Sketch Book," or Hazlitt's "Table Talk," or any popular book of the new school, and you will find that we have turned over the Johnsonian periods and the Blairian formality to keep company with the wigs and hoops, the stiff courtesies and low bows of our ancestors. In short, my dear friend, letters are nowadays more the vehicles of kindness, and less of wit, than they used to be. It was very convenient, when people who wrote books were forced to put stiff stays on them, to

* Lord Byron had died in the preceding April.

VOL. II.—B

have a sort of dishabille for the mind as well as for the body, and to write a letter as they put on a *robe de chambre*.   But now the periodical press takes charge of those bursts of gayety and criticism which the post was wont to receive ; and the public—the reading public—is, as I said before, the correspondent and confidant of every body.

Having thus made the best defense I can against your criticism, I proceed to answer your question, " Are the characters and descriptions true ?"   Yes ! yes ! yes !   As true as is well possible.   You, as a great landscape painter, know that in painting a favorite scene you do a little embellish, and can't help it ; you avail yourself of happy accidents of atmosphere, and if any thing be ugly, you strike it out, or if any thing be wanting, you put it in.   But still the picture is a likeness ; and that this is a very faithful one, you will judge when I tell you that a worthy neighbor of ours, a post-captain, who has been in every quarter of the globe, and is equally distinguished for the sharp look-out and the *bonhomie* of his profession, accused me most seriously of carelessness in putting "The Rose " for "The Swan," as the sign of our next-door neighbor ; and was no less disconcerted at the *misprint* (as he called it) of B for R in the name of our next town.   *A cela près*, he declares the picture to be exact.   Nevertheless, I do not expect to be poisoned.   Why should I ?   I have said no harm of my neighbors, have I ?   The great danger would be that my dear friend Joel might be spoiled ; but I take care to keep the book out of our pretty Harriette's way ; and so I hope that that prime ornament of our village will escape the snare for his vanity which the seeing so exact a portrait of himself in a printed book might occasion.

By the way, the names of the villagers are true—of the higher sketches they are feigned, of course.   But I will give my dear Miss Elford, who seems interested in knowing the exact state of the case, a key.   Her note is charming.   I never saw a more beautiful simplicity ; and when she speaks of her sister, it is quite enchanting to see how the love breaks out.   Yes ! I shall give her the key, and will only thank you, in the first place, for promoting the sale ; and tell you, in the second, that it sells well, and has been received by the literary world, and reviewed in all the literary papers, etc., better than I, for modesty, dare to say.* God bless you, my dear friend! Always most sincerely and affectionately yours,

M. R. MITFORD.

To MISS JEPHSON, *at the Rev. G. Smith's, Castle Martyr, Ireland.*

Three-mile Cross, July 10, 1824.

We have a pretty little pony-chaise and pony (oh! how I should like to drive you in it!), and my dear father and mother have been out in it three or four times, to my great delight; I am sure it will do them both so much good. My great amusement is in my garden. I am so glad you have a little demesne of your own too; it is a pretty thing to be queen over roses and lilies, is it not? My nook of ground is very beautiful this year, rosy as one of the poems in "Lalla Rookh," crammed with all sorts of flowers, and parted from, or joined to, the long open shed where we sit, and which Harriette and mamma call the arcade, by a double row of rich geraniums. I look at them now without any tender fears, because Mrs. Reeve has promised to house them for me during the winter—a very precious piece of hospitality. By the way, Mrs. Reeve, besides bringing her charming self to Whitley (the only thing that could have consoled me for the loss of our dear friends), has also imported a most valuable and faithful female servant—a warmhearted Irishwoman, who loves every body that her mistress loves; so that, with old faithful Rainer at the gate with his face of welcome, hers at the door, and her mistress's in the parlor, Whitley is quite itself again. Nevertheless, I never go to it without wishing for our dear friends.

Being a good deal unhinged by the anxiety I suffered during my dear father's illness, and therefore unfit for writing (though not at all ill, and now getting the better even of that nervousness), I have been reading an immense number of books, old and new, good and indifferent. Will you have a specimen of the brief one-, two-, or three-word character with which I put them down in a catalogue which I keep of works as I read them?

* Mrs..Hall writes: "My 'Sketches of Irish Character,' my first dear book, was inspired by a desire to describe my native place, as Miss Mitford had done in 'Our Village;' and this made me an author."

Captain Hall's "South America" (the Loo-Choo man excellent).

Landor's "Imaginary Conversations" (very, very good—very, very bad).

"Captain Rock" (witty and tiresome—is it true?).

Charles Lamb's Works (for the third time—and that is saying enough).

"Redgauntlet" (for the first, and I fear the last).

"The Inheritance" (clever—too clever—but not genial—not amiable—written by one who sees faults too plainly by half).

"Wilhelm Meister's Apprenticeship" (Mignon a gem—the setting rather German).

"Letters to and from Lady Suffolk" (very particularly naughty—especially the maids of honor).

"Travels," I forget where—by, I forget whom—just exactly nothing at all.

Are you not glad that I am come to an end of my list and my letter?—come to the thousand loves and good wishes that attend you from all here? Adieu! M. R. MITFORD.

To B. R. HAYDON, ESQ., 8 *Paddington Green.*

Three-mile Cross, July 11, 1824.

MY DEAR FRIEND,—I like to hear of your painting ex-mayors (corporate bodies are generally generous), and eating corporation dinners. I shall have a respect for the aldermen of Norwich as long as I live, for their choice of a painter. Is it possible that the Exhibition has closed and "Silenus" not been sold?

You will be glad to hear that my dear father continues to recover, although he has not yet got up his strength. My mother is better too. Some little hay was got in in a magical sort of way between the showers. The Northumberland people have an idiom of "*saving* hay" for making hay"—which is exceedingly proper for this year, when all hay not spoilt by the wet may literally be said to be saved. I tell you all these little pieces of good fortune, because, as I generally trouble you with my bad news, it seems but fair to give you a glimpse of the sun when it does peep out for a minute between the showers. I should not omit, when reckoning up my felicities just now, to tell you that my little garden is a perfect rosary—the greenest and most blossomy nook that ever the sun shone upon. It is almost shut in by buildings; one a long open shed, very pretty, a sort of rural arcade, where we sit. On the other side is an old granary, to which we mount by outside wooden steps, also very pretty. Then, there is an opening to a little court, also backed by buildings, but with room enough to let in the sunshine, the north-west sunshine, that comes aslant in summer evenings, through and under a large elder-tree. One end is closed by our pretty irregular cottage, which, as well as the granary, is covered by cherry-trees, vines, roses, jessamine, honeysuckle, and grand spires of hollyhocks. The other is comparatively open, showing over high pales the blue sky and a range of woody hills. All and every part is untrimmed, antique, weather-stained, and homely as can be imagined—gratifying the eye by its exceeding picturesqueness, and the mind by the certainty that no pictorial effect was intended—that it owes all its charms to " rare accident." My father laughs at my passionate love for my little garden—and perhaps you will laugh too; but I assure you it's a " bonny bit " of earth as ever was crammed full of lilies and roses, to say nothing of a flourishing " green ——.

[*The rest is wanting.*]

To the Rev. WILLIAM HARNESS, *Hampstead.*

Three-mile Cross, July 29, 1824.

MY DEAR FRIEND,—Do you think you have interest enough with Mr. Campbell* to get an engagement for a sort of series—"Letters from the Country," or something of that sort—altogether different, of course, from " Our Village " in the scenery and the *dramatis personæ*, but still something that might admit of description and character, and occasional story, without the formality of a fresh introduction to every article. If you liked my little volume well enough to recommend me conscientiously, and are enough in that prescient editor's good graces to secure such an admission, I should like the thing exceedingly.

Mr. Talfourd urges me to write a novel. Do you think I could ? I beg a thousand pardons for tormenting you with

* Thomas Campbell, author of "The Pleasures of Hope," and at that time editor of the " New Monthly Magazine."

my poor concerns; but I have an entire reliance on your kindness, and to get money, if I can, is so much my duty, that that consciousness takes away at once all the mock modesty of authorship, for the display of which the rich have leisure. I write merely for remuneration; and I would rather scrub floors, if I could get as much by that healthier, more respectable, and more feminine employment.

Give my very best love to your sister—our very best love—and accept my father's and mother's best regards. Ever, my dear friend, your obliged and affectionate

M. R. MITFORD.

What you say of Haydon's picture grieves me much. Some parts of his other pictures (I have not seen this) always seemed to me very, very fine—the head of Lazarus, for instance; and he himself—oh! how you would like him!—is a creature of air and fire; the frankest, truest man breathing; absolutely free from pretense or trickery. There are three moderate wishes that I should like to see realized; you—a bishop (how should you like the wig?); Mr. Talfourd—Attorney-General; and Mr. Haydon—President of the Royal Academy. The middle wish, if not to the letter, will yet, I think, come true in the spirit; for he is getting on incredibly, and will be the Mr. Scarlett of twenty years hence; the other two will, I hope, follow in order. Once again, good-bye. My postscript threatens to be longer than my letter—but you know by experience that a woman's pen, like a woman's tongue, is a difficult thing to stop. Have we any chance of seeing you in Berkshire?

For the last time, good-bye!

To MISS JEPHSON, *Castle Martyr, Ireland.*

Three-mile Cross, August 28, 1824.

MY DEAR EMILY,—I thank you most heartily for your very welcome letter.

My dear mother continues better, and is, of course, not so close a prisoner as in the winter; but she has not yet ventured so far as Silchester, and, indeed, I am half afraid to propose so long an excursion. She has only once been in Reading, and generally speaking, goes nowhere but to Whitley, and then only for an hour, on some fine morning, when there is neither sun, nor wind, nor dust. It is impossible to be more delicate than she is. My dear father, too, I am sorry to say, continues poorly. He can not bear exercise or exertion of any kind; and yet the activity of his mind continuing undiminished, there is all the difficulty on earth to keep him quiet. They both send their most affectionate love to you, and talk of you and think of you very often indeed.

You are very good in inquiring into my plans. I write as usual for magazines, and (but this is quite between ourselves —a matter strictly confidential) I have a tragedy, which will, I may say, certainly—as certainly as one can speak of any thing connected with the theatre—be performed at Drury Lane next season. It is on the story of Rienzi, the friend of Petrarch; the man who restored for a short time, and in so remarkable a manner, the old republican government of Rome. If you do not remember the story you will find it very beautifully told in the last volume of Gibbon, and still more graphically related in L'Abbé de Sade's "Mémoires pour la Vie de Petrarque." We do not speak of it, because Mr. Macready talks of bringing it out as written by a man, to avoid the great annoyance of newspapers, etc., so unpleasant to a female writer. This is my first sheet anchor, of course; but I am also pressed to try a novel, by almost every one who has read my little volume—more especially by Mr. Milman, who (by the way) has just married and brought home a very beautiful wife. But I am half afraid of a novel, and more inclined to try a second volume of "Our Village," for which there are plenty of materials close at hand. What do you advise? There is great danger of falling off always in continuations; but I am so afraid of a novel. After all, I suppose the bookseller is, in this respect, the best counselor.

I have been much occupied lately by a friend who has resided for the last six years in Paris, and can not help telling you a story illustrative of the state of society there.

A lady of her intimate acquaintance was about to open her house for company—that is to say, to give *soirées*, once a week. On this being known, she was waited upon by an agent of the police, who requested to see a list of the persons invited, as it was necessary that some friend of Government should be amongst them.

" Really, sir," said the lady, " I would rather relinquish the thing altogether than introduce a spy amongst my guests."

" Just let me see the list, Madame," retorted the policeman; and having looked at it, continued, "You need not trouble yourself—neither need I; for there are four or five of us invited already !"

Better be at Three-mile Cross, my dear Emily, or in your wilder and more beautiful country, than in that polished prison—that Ear of Dionysius.

What weather for the seaside ! How you must enjoy it ! We almost see the corn ripen before our eyes.

God bless you, my dear friend ! Do not fail to write to me, and to talk to me of all that interests you ; it will all interest and gratify me, especially all that tends to make you happy. Ever most sincerely yours,   M. R. M.

To B. R. HAYDON, ESQ., *Paddington Green.*

Three-mile Cross, Sept. 23, 1824.

MY DEAR FRIEND,—Your last charming letter was delivered to me by my friend Mr. Monck, at a large dinner-party, where he knew he should meet me. I put it in my little bag till I could steal away to read it after dinner.

Before that opportunity arrived, a friend of mine, who resides in Paris, but has been on a visit in this neighborhood, asked me if I could furnish her with any autographs of celebrated persons, for the widow of Bernardin St. Pierre.

" I want more than the signature," continued my unconscionable friend; " the mere handwriting will not do—something characteristic."

When I went to her room to read your letter after dinner, imagine how I was struck with the glorious conclusion—the three last lines :—"For my part, I love my country, and would lay my head on the block to insure her advancement in art.—B. R. HAYDON." They seemed to me the very motto to your character—the very inscription to put under a picture or a bust of you. So, as my friend assured me that the name and sentiment would be prized as they ought to be, I even cut them off for Madame St. Pierre.

What are you about? Portraits? I ought to be very busy, for my bookseller has sent to me for two volumes

more of our " Our Village;" and then a novel! Oh! dear
me!

God bless you, my dear friend! Love to dear Mrs. Haydon. Ever most sincerely yours,   M. R. MITFORD.

To MISS JEPHSON, *Castle Martyr, Ireland.*

Three-mile Cross, Friday, Oct. 22, 1824.

MY VERY DEAR EMILY,—We are just recovering from a
dramatic crisis in Reading. Dr. Valpy's triennial Greek play
has been represented, last week and this, with splendid success. It was the "Alcestis" of Euripides, a drama which
has, you know, great extrinsic interest; embodying a lovely
trait of female devotedness; alluded to by Milton in that
sonnet of which I remember our talking together in this very
room; mentioned still more finely by Wordsworth in the
"Laodamia;" and, finally, being that identical play which
Charles Fox was found reading when he had lost his whole
fortune at a gaming table, and his friends were fearful of his
committing suicide. In spite of all this, the play is not so
fine as I thought it when it was acted here fifteen years ago,
and the world of the Greek drama were fifteen years young
er with me. I should have been quite out of humor at the
destruction of the illusion which I had entertained respecting it in my own mind, had not the admirable acting of one
boy given me a delight such as I never thought to feel from
any thing theatrical again. It was the mean, selfish, odious
part of Admetus, which he made exquisitely noble by an exhibition of passion the most natural and consummate that I
ever beheld. He is about sixteen, short and fair, the son of
a dancing-master of the name of Richardson. They talk of
bringing him up to the bar, but I want him for the stage.
His talent is altogether dramatic—peculiar, distinctive, nothing but dramatic. And the stage is fame and fortune—the
bar is starvation and obscurity.

Little Richardson is quite a Macready in embryo. I said
to him one evening, behind the scenes, " Well, you have the
principal part." " I don't know," answered he; " there is a
great deal to say, and that is all you can say for it. Alcestis
is the heroine, and, if there be a hero, it is Hercules. He is
the only one who does any thing but talk." "At all events,
you have a magnificent dress." " Dress!" rejoined my grum-

B 2

bler, pointing to the splendid god of the silver bow—" dress! Look at Apollo!" These plays would have annoyed me exceedingly on these accounts but for the interest I took in this boy.

I had a letter from Mr. Haydon yesterday, containing an anecdote of Sir Walter Scott, which I will transcribe for you in the very words of our great painter. "A friend of mine has been spending some time with Sir W. Scott. He (Sir Walter) is liable to perpetual intrusion of every kind. A stupid chattering fellow got at him by a letter and staid a week. He was a sad bore, and my friend and another young dog were obliged to retire to a window to avoid laughing. Sir Walter hobbled up to them and said, ' Come, come, young gentlemen, I assure you it requires no small talent to be a *decided bore*. Be more respectful!' I like this; there is the geniality of the Unknown in it." I like it too, and so I hope will you, although it has hardly left me room to say that my father and mother are both better, and both send their kindest remembrances. Adieu, my very dear friend.

Believe me always, most affectionately yours,

M. R. MITFORD.

Fragment of a letter to R. B. HAYDON, ESQ., 8 *Paddington Green.*

Three-mile Cross, Oct. 28, 1824.

No! no! no! not wild about all those boys, only about one of them. The boys generally did the thing surprisingly well. We had a pretty Alcestis, and a very magnificent Hercules, but it was Admetus only that showed such extraordinary genius. The part, you know, is odiously mean and selfish, and cowardly and complaining; every thing that a woman likes least. The boy is not at all handsome—pale and short, and fair and old-looking—not at all the lad to catch a woman's eye. Nothing but genius, that life-pulse genius, could have inspired me with the enthusiasm which I did feel, and do feel, on his account. Some of the things which he did (things which, to my certain knowledge, nobody there could have taught him) were as grand and fine as any thing that Kean does in Othello, perhaps finer, for they were as passionate, as intense, but more chaste. He is unspoilt by the exaggeration of a great theatre. I am sure of his being so very great, not only by the impression which he made on me and Mr. Talfourd, but by the dissimilar effect on some wiseacres of my acquaintance, whose blame is praise. It is a fine thing to have two or three fools of whose folly one is so certain that it is a standard. Say the reverse of what they say, and you must be right. I wish you had seen this boy Richardson.

I heartily agree with you in admiration of the "Agamemnon" of Æschylus. He was perhaps the most wonderful of the three great poets, although Sophocles seems to me the most perfect. His "Philoctetes," besides the fine romance of the first scene, moves one to deeper pity and livelier indignation than any play I ever read out of Shakspeare. One hates Ulysses with a heartiness that does one good, but he is a very detestable person always, even in Homer. Euripides has exquisite scenes, but only scenes—no whole play, like the "Philoctetes," or the "Œdipus," or the "Antigone," —nothing that approaches in situation to the "Prometheus." Yet there are beautiful scenes, too, in "Euripides," especially those two of Phædra in the "Hippolitus."

I once thought of writing a tragedy on the story of Francesca of Rimini, and using those two scenes, and I still would do so if we had a great tragic actress—one who could give an intense and fervid personification of passionate, unhappy, but yet pure love. All this seems very blue, but although I have no knowledge of Greek, I have read these plays very often in translations, both French and English. And, setting aside the immense power of that most extraordinary language, whose *interfusing* quality seems quite unapproached by any modern tongue—setting this aside, I do not hesitate to say that there is more in one scene of Shakspeare than in all the Greek drama put together. And yet there is more in the Greek drama than in the French, the Italian, the Spanish, or (setting aside Shakspeare) the English.

To Sir William Elford, *Bickham, Plymouth.*

Three-mile Cross, Nov. 9, 1824.

I begin my answer, my dear and valued friend, as soon as I receive your welcome letter, although I may probably not have an opportunity of sending it off for some days. My father and mother, to commence with that which, as most interesting to me will be most acceptable to you, are better than they have been. *He* is much older for his terrible illness, but otherwise quite recovered, and my dear mother has had a cold, but has not suffered another attack of her dreadful complaint. This has set me a little free from the nervousness which used to beset me whenever a breath of air blew upon her, to her great annoyance. I am most grateful for these blessings, as you may well believe.

First, let me tell you that I am very much gratified by your kind friend Mr. Cranstoun's approbation, and that I will take heed, if I write another volume—if I Our-Village-it again—I will try to profit by his criticism.

By the way, you will be glad to hear that our dear friend Mr. Haydon has now made up his mind to portrait painting, has plenty of employment, and is going on well. He has sold his "Silenus," and, in short, will prosper now, I trust in God ! He is a most delightful person, and, above all, a capital correspondent, writing me two or three letters for one tiny note.

We have a dispute respecting Lord Byron and Wordsworth which is of great use in these communications. Nothing like a good standing quarrel to which people may fall ding-dong. These two poets are cut and come again, like a goose pie at Christmas. You will guess, of course, that he is all for Byron, I all for Wordsworth. And truly this last book ("The conversations of Lord Byron," as collected by Captain Medwin) gives me no small cause to crow. His infamous libertinism, his intolerable effeminate vanity, his utter want of taste—Wordsworth, Milton, Shakspeare cried down —Dr. Johnson's criticisms, Moore's songs, and his own plays (about the three worst things of their sort in the language) cried up ! Truly my dear and very clever adversary is put to his trumps, and forced to say that "I am a woman, and therefore—." I have never had any respect for Lord Byron's talents since he failed so egregiously in the drama, and did not find it out. Scott failed in the drama too, but then he made the discovery and drew back, and, accordingly, nobody remembers "Halidon Hill," and every body adores the novels.

Friday, I don't know the day of the month,⎱
but the last Friday in November. ⎰

Since writing the inclosed I have been to town; and am, and have been, hard at work altering a play which I hope to get out within a month at Drury Lane. It is on the subject of Rienzi. Macready is with me heart and soul. His new wife is a pretty, little, gentle creature—very young and very timid. Kindest regards from all. Say every thing for me to dear Miss Elford. Always most affectionately yours,

M. R. MITFORD.

To B. R. HAYDON, Esq., 58 *Connaught Terrace, Portman Square.*

Castle Street, Saturday evening, Dec. 20, 1824.

MY DEAR FRIEND,—I am commissioned by Mr. Talfourd to tell you, with his very best compliments, that next Tuesday is fixed for Miss Foote's trial; and that, if you will come here at eight o'clock precisely on that morning in a coach, he will equip you in a spare wig and gown of his own, and take you with him to the court. You had better come in an *old* black coat and waistcoat,—old, observe, because the powder of the wig will spoil them. Mr. Talfourd could supply you with these articles also, if you think you could get into them. I don't—he being a delicate, womanly man, and you a sort of lesser Hercules. If you dislike the masquerade, which I think will be capital fun, he will do all he can to get you in *in propriâ personâ.* But the court is so small and expected to be so crowded with barristers, that, as the greatest painter in Europe and nothing else, you are likely to be turned out; whereas, as a mere trumpery lawyer whom no one knows, you are safe. At all events you must be here precisely at eight. I am so sorry that I shall not see this famous frolic, being engaged on Monday to dine and sleep at Hampstead; but you must come back in your legal costume, that I may see you. It would be too bad to be in a position in which I should at once lose the personal participation of the fun, and the almost equal gratification of your account of it, which, if I were actually in the country, you would infallibly send me. Ever yours, M. R. M.

CHAPTER III.

LETTERS FOR 1825 AND 1826.

To B. R. HAYDON, ESQ., *Connaught Terrace.*

Three-mile Cross, Feb. 3, 1825.

MY DEAR FRIEND,—If you see Mr. Young, do say how much I am flattered at his ready acceptance of the part, and that it was not withdrawn owing to any disrespect toward him. You may send letters to me through Mr. Monck always. He talks of taking the liberty to call and look at my picture. I am sure you will, if you see him, be pleased with his frankness and originality. He is a great Grecian and a great political economist—a sort of Andrew Marvel in Parliament; living in a lodging close to the House, with an old woman, who cooks him alternately a beefsteak, a mutton chop, or a veal cutlet: he does not indulge in a lamb chop till after Easter. He votes sometimes with one party and sometimes with another, as he likes their measures; respected by all, notwithstanding his independence; and idolized here in the country for his liberality, his cheerfulness, his good-humor, and his unfailing kindness.

God bless you all, my dear friend! Say every thing for me to your loveliest wife, and believe me always, most faithfully yours,   M. R. MITFORD.

To SIR WILLIAM ELFORD, *Bickham, Plymouth.*

Three-mile Cross, Feb. 19, 1825.

MY VERY DEAR FRIEND,—I believe that if I could conquer my own predilection for the drama I should do wisely to adhere to the booksellers; for the little prose volume has certainly done its work, and made an opening for a longer effort. You would be diverted at some of the instances I could tell you of its popularity. Columbines and children have been named after Mayflower; stage-coachmen and postboys point out the localities; schoolboys deny the possibility of any woman's having written the cricket-match without schoolboy help; and such men as Lord Stowell (Sir

William Scott—the last relique, I believe, of the Literary Club) send to me for a key. I mean to try three volumes of tales *next* spring—having given over the intention of a second volume, in which there is always danger of falling off. Heaven knows how I shall succeed !

If you can think of a pretty story, do send it me; for that is my want. Of course I shall copy as closely as I can Nature and Miss Austen—keeping, like her, to genteel country life; or rather going a little lower, perhaps ; and, I am afraid, with more of sentiment and less of humor. I do not *intend* to commit these delinquencies, mind. I *mean* to keep as playful as I can; but I am afraid of their happening in spite of me. Pray, talking of tales, have you seen Mrs. Opie's "Lying ?" She is all over Quakerized, as you of course know—to the great improvement, as I hear (for I have not seen her) of her appearance. It is certainly a pretty dress. She *thee's* and *thou's* people; calls Mr. Haydon "friend Benjamin ;" and directs to the Rev. William Harness after the same fashion, "William Harness, Hampstead." With all this, she is just as kind and good-humored as ever; and Mr. Haydon told me that, in about a quarter of an hour's chat, she forgot her *thee's* and *thou's*, and became altogether as merry as she used to be. She has really sacrificed upward of a thousand pounds copy-money for a novel, which she had contracted for; and yet I believe there are difficulties still as to her admission to the sisterhood. You also may have heard say that a certain Mr. Gurney is in some sort the cause of this conversion, and that there are difficulties there also; but of this *I* say nothing.

Whilst in town, I put myself in the way of a conversion of another sort, by going to hear Mr. Irving. Did you ever hear him ? If not, do; he is really worth a little trouble. I had read a hundred descriptions of him, and seen half a score prints, which I took for caricatures, till I saw him; and then he seemed to me a caricature of his portraits—more tall, more squinting, more long black-haired, more cadaverous, more like Frankenstein. His sermon, too, was even odder than I expected, in matter and manner; the *latter* seems to me as good as possible, the *former* sometimes good, but full of pretension and affectation of every sort. I have no doubt whatever but that the Rev. Edward Irving is the vainest person that lives at this moment; and I that say so have got the honor of being acquainted with divers actors and sundry poets. I could not have conceived so much quackery possible in the pulpit. A small adventure befell me which I can not help telling you. I went with an old lady, who, at the end of two hours and a half, was really ill with the heat and crowd, and asked me to go out with her. Of course I complied. When we got to the door we found a gentleman with his back planted against it, who point blank refused to let us out. Heard ever any one of being shut into a chapel! Mr. Milman says an action would lie for false imprisonment; and, being in a barrister's house, I might have had law cheap. My poor old friend, however, was suffering; and I was not quite young enough in the world to be taken in. I therefore turned to the loiterers in the aisles, and picking out my man— a fine spirited-looking person, the most anti-puritanical that you can imagine—I said to him, " Sir, this lady is indisposed, and that gentleman—" " G— d—n me, madam," exclaimed my hopeful ally, " this is some d—d whim of Dawkins's—I'll let you out." And forthwith he and another young man of his sort sprang at once on the luckless Dawkins (an elder of the congregation)—displaced him *par voie du fait,* and gave us free egress from the Caledonian Church, under the very nose of the pastor.

On telling this story the next day to Charles Lamb, he told me that a friend of his, having sat through two hours of sermon walked off in the same way ; but, just as she was leaving the church, Mr. Irving himself addressed her in a most violent manner from the pulpit, whereupon she turned round, smiled, nodded, courtesied, and then walked off. I certainly could not have done that, nor was it right, although Mr. Irving himself has turned the house of worship into a mere public place—a Sunday theatre—where he delivers orations half made up of criticism and abuse, and preaches for five hours a day such sermons as never were called sermons before. If you have not heard him you will accuse me of levity ; but I assure you the most scrupulous people speak of him as I do—every body, indeed, except the select few who compose his exclusive admirers—and even they praise him just as they praise an orator, and cry up his discourses just as they cry up a clever article in a magazine. I am sorry for this; for the man, in spite of his execrable taste, has power—great power. He fixes the attention, provokes you very much by the most inconceivable bombast, but never wearies you. He certainly has power, and if he should have the good luck to go so completely out of fashion as neither to be followed, praised, nor blamed, which is likely enough to happen in a year or two, I should not wonder to find him become a great orator.

Adieu, my very dear friend. This is something like my old budget of sauciness—in length at least—and I am afraid in carelessness and illegibility; but I am quite sure of your indulgence, and of that of your kind family. Say every thing for me to them all, especially to Miss Elford. Ever most gratefully yours,   M. R. M.

To B. R. HAYDON, ESQ., *Connaught Terrace, Portman Square.*

Three-mile Cross, March 3, 1825.

MY DEAR FRIEND,—Pray should you like to be an M.P.? Did the thing ever take your fancy? I can not understand the charm at all; but a charm there must be, notwithstanding, and a very strong one. What a prodigious sensation you would make in the House! Good Lord, how they would stare! Our friend Mr. Talfourd will be there some day or other, beyond a doubt—and he will make a sensation too. He has just made a most splendid display at the Berkshire Assizes; I wish you had heard him. I was in court one day, during which he *led* in every cause—all of them interesting; two prosecutions for maltreating a negro boy, and one defense for libel. They were of the highest local importance— one of them a special jury cause, and the court (a very large one) was crammed to suffocation, including all the first people in the county. He spoke in the libel case for an hour and a half; and really I never before witnessed such an exhibition of high and passionate eloquence; quite different from the ordinary eloquence of the bar, from its being far finer and purer in kind, as well as mightier in power. No cant, no commonplace, no claptraps, no bitterness; appealing to the highest and loftiest feelings, the deepest and noblest sympathies of our nature! Such eloquence is a grand and glorious thing. He swayed the multitude as a steed is swayed by its rider. You might have heard a pin drop, till he ceased; and then the irrepressible applause was so tumultuous that it was not for a long time that the judge could get the court quiet enough to be heard, when he threatened to send the clappers to gaol; confessing, at the same time, that he did not wonder at the plaudits bestowed on the young and most eloquent pleader, only they had chosen a wrong place. You may imagine that this was a very proud day for Mr. Talfourd and for his friends. We dined together at Dr. Valpy's after the court closed; and I never remember being so much excited and gratified in my life. He spoke of you with great enthusiasm—and has quite recanted about Kean; disgusted, of course, at the quantity of cant that has been written about him.

Have you read Dr. Antommarchi's account of the last days of Napoleon? It appears clearly to me that the exceeding ignorance of that Italian co-operated with the climate and the gaoler in killing him. Only think of never giving calomel till the two or three last days! The effect that it had, even then, proves what it might have done if administered sooner. My father says that he has no doubt but the accumulation of acrid bile in the stomach produced the ulcer. But foreign physicans are old women. Altogether it is a very painful book to read, and yet one that I could not help reading. Every thing about that great man has for me a charm absolutely inexpressible. I rejoice that you do not mean to paint Mrs. Haydon in lace and velvet; they are too poor, too millinery for her. She is a creature of poetry. The only costume I could fancy for her would be Oriental—rich and splendid as her matchless beauty. Kindest love to her and the dear little ones. God bless you, my dearest friend! Ever most faithfully yours,   M. R. MITFORD.

To the Rev. WILLIAM HARNESS, *Hampstead.*

Three-mile Cross, April 22, 1825.

MY DEAR FRIEND,—Many thanks for your kindness about Mr. Campbell. I have sent him two articles to the care of Mr. Colburn. In future, I will send them to his house, when I can get a frank or a private hand. My little book is in a third edition, which is encouragement for a novel. Do you know who wrote the critique in the " Quarterly," which has certainly done me so much good? Now for the plot of my

novel, although I am so afraid of the undertaking, that I am
quite persuaded it will never be good for any thing. I mean
to take a whole village—one of those islands of cultivation
and habitancy which are found amidst the downs of Wiltshire, or the vale of Berkshire—that which is called in these
parts the low country. There I mean to place an old and
splendid, but nearly deserted residence, belonging to an impoverished nobleman, whose park, etc., are rented by a Mrs.
Ellis, widow of a rich farmer—a comely, kindly dame, with
one very pretty, spoilt, romp of a daughter, about sixteen.
The book shall open with a letter to Mrs. Ellis from a lawyer
in London, informing her that an old stockbroker, her great
uncle, whom she had never seen in her life, is dead, having
left a miser's fortune between her and the descendant of some
other niece then abroad. The lawyer, who is also the agent
for the nobleman her landlord, informs her that the mansion
and estate, part of which she rents, are to be sold, and advises
her to purchase them. In the course of further communications he makes an offer, on the part of the old lord, of his only
son to her only daughter. Mrs. Ellis catches eagerly at the
proposal, and requests the lawyer's lady to provide a governess forthwith for her Kate. Accordingly a lady-like young
woman of three or four and twenty, a Miss Clive, arrives;
and, shortly afterward, come the nobleman and his son—apparently to finish the sale, but in reality to commence the
courtship. The father is much more anxious for this match
than the son; and gradually it shall ooze out that there had
been an old attachment between the latter and Miss Clive,
the governess, whose father had been an officer in the same
regiment; that it had been broken off by the remonstrances
of Lord N. (I have not named him yet) with Miss Clive;
and still more gradually it shall be felt, that the old love is
reviving—interrupted, of course, by the proper quantity of
hopes and fears, and a good deal of the usual coquetry on the
part of the pretty little Kate, who, herself in love with a
scapegrace nephew of Lord N.'s, takes no small pleasure in
perplexing her lover and all about her. At length, things
come to a crisis; Kate declares to her mother that she will
not have the man selected for her, and he, on his part, affirms
to his father that he will marry none but Augusta Clive.
Lord N. reproaches Miss Clive with breaking her promise to

him. At last it is discovered that Augusta is herself the heiress to the other half of the miser's property; and that, finding both her name and person unknown to Mrs. Ellis, she has availed herself of her sending for a governess to make, under that title, an interest in the affections of her relations, and perhaps to examine into the faith of her lover. Of course all parties marry and are happy as usual.

This is a very rough sketch; but I send it to a master, whose fancy can easily supply the lights and shades and the coloring. Is the story, do you think, sufficiently original? It is free from vice and pecuniary evil (both of which are so unpleasant in books); and the conclusion will be comfortable and satisfactory. I see that I must not make too much perplexity about nothing (that provoking fault of Madame D'Arblay's novels), and that I must get as much incident and character as I can. Do tell me any thing you think might mend it. But I shall finish "Charles" first. Most gratefully and affectionately yours,   M. R. MITFORD.

To SIR WILLIAM ELFORD, *Bickham, Plymouth.*

Three-mile Cross, May 21, 1825.

MY DEAR FRIEND,—I thank you for remembering my request, although it is with sincere regret that I read your opinion. To me, Dr. Darling* seemed a fine portrait, both as to expression and color. As to myself,† it seemed a strong unflattered likeness—one that certainly would not be very calculated to feed a woman's vanity, or to cure the public of the general belief that authoresses are and must be frights. But really I don't think it much uglier than what I see every day in the looking-glass; and I especially forbid you from answering this observation by any flattery, or any thing whatsoever.‡

I am sorry that the portrait is not more complimentary; because it vexes my father to hear it so much abused, as I must confess it is, by every body except Miss James, and the artist, who maintain that it is a capital likeness—quite a woman of genius, and so forth. Now, my dear friend, I en-

---

* Portrait by Haydon.   † Haydon's portrait of her.

‡ The fault of the portrait was, that every thing was larger than life. It represented a Brobdignagian fat woman seated in a bower of Brobdignagian honeysuckles.

treat and implore you not to mention to any one what I say. I would not have Mr. Haydon know it for worlds. It was a present, in the first place, and certainly a very kind and flattering attention; and, in the second, my personal feelings for him would always make the picture gratifying to me for his sake were it as ugly as Medusa. He is a most admirable person, whose very faults spring from that excess of brilliancy and life with which, more than any creature that ever lived, he is gifted. I never see him without thinking of the description of the Dauphin's horse in "Henry the Fifth"—all air and fire—the duller elements have no share in his composition. You know, I suppose, that he has a commission for an historical picture.

Pray write again soon. God bless you, my very dear friend! Ever yours, M. R. M.

To Miss Jephson, *Bath.*

Three-mile Cross, May 27, 1825.

My dear Friend,—We rejoice to hear that you are well and in England, and with friends whom you love so much. Oh! how I wish you were passing near us! I have been sitting all the morning in my little garden, with its roses and stocks of all kinds; and rich peonies and geraniums; and purple irises and periwinkles; and yellow laburnums and globe anemones; and greens vivid and beautiful even as flowers, making altogether the finest piece of color I ever saw—and I really yearned after you—you would have liked it so much. It is provoking to show such a thing to common eyes, which go peeping about into the detail, pulling the effect to pieces as children do daisies. Besides the nightingale and the scent of lilies of the valley, my garden, on which my father rallies me so much, is my passion. But you will forgive me for overrating it. It is, at least, a mistake on the right side, to be too fond of one's own poor home—and no mistake at all to wish you in it.

I am now busy finishing a tragedy on the story of Charles and Cromwell for Covent Garden next season; after which I shall set to work at the "Heiress" ding-dong. One alteration I have made in the plan; Augusta shall not know that she is entitled to a share in the property. I shall give my miser an involved pedigree, and make a difficulty on all sides in tracing the descent; which will give rise to some good comic scenes, and will give to the whole work something of interest independent of love. After all, I am really and unfeignedly afraid of my power in this line of composition.

Your story of Carlo is very pretty. May has puppies: we had seven-and-twenty applications; and, as poor May has only eight, were obliged, keeping one, to refuse twenty friends. The one kept is a little white beauty—May in miniature. It fell down the other day and hurt—almost dislocated—its hip. We picked it up, poor little thing, and rubbed it with camphorated spirits of wine, during which operation it lay in my lap quite quiet and patient, whilst May sat close by, shivering and whining and moaning at every touch, just as if it had been her limb that was hurt, and not the puppy's. The scene was really affecting.

Pray excuse this blotted scrawl—for which I have no other excuse than that of being a blotter by profession. I wish I could write tidily! My father and mother join in most affectionate remembrances—and I am ever, my own dear Emily, most faithfully yours,   M. R. M.

To Sir William Elford, *Bickham, Plymouth.*

Three-mile Cross, June 23, 1825.

My dear Friend,—I write to you *de provision*, as Madame de Sevigné says, although I have no M. P. under hand; but I am tired to death—I have been all the morning talking, entertaining morning visitors (the deuce take 'em)—and all the afternoon gardening, planting, and watering flowers (deuce—no, not deuce take them—I love them too well); and so, being fairly worn off my feet and off my tongue, it has occurred to me out of my great friendship and affection to bestow the bloom of my weariness, the first moments of yawning and grumbling on you. Are you not exceedingly obliged to me.

My mother is so well as to be staying with a relation in Hampshire, so that my father and I are left to keep house together. *He* is housekeeper—mamma thinks him the trustier of the two—so she left those ensigns of authority, the keys, in his possession; and they are only lost fifty times in an hour. We were in great danger of going without dinner, because such a thing was not thought of till it was wanted to be eaten; but we have dressed a great bit of beef, and now we are independent. All these troubles amuse us excessively, and I can't tell you which is the most in fault of the two—only I rather think I am. Dear me, if mamma knew the disorderly life we lead, what would she say!

Good-bye, my dear Sir William, for to-night. Next time I am thoroughly done up I shall write to you by way of resting myself. Most affectionately yours,   M. R. M.

To B. R. Haydon, Esq., *Connaught Terrace.*

Three-mile Cross, July 18, 1825.

My dear Friend,—I have just received your hot-weather letter, which I could return point by point—only that the country is the country, and London is London; and that we have a long shed open to the north, which runs along one side of my little garden, where we live entirely, looking out upon that bright piece of color, my flower-beds. *Your* verses amused me exceedingly. I do think they are yours—at least they might be; for there is the very mixture of honest fun and strong humor and fine high fancy which you would put into such a subject. I have a theory, very proper and convenient for an old maid, that the world is over-peopled, and always hear with some regret of every fresh birth. I hold old maids and old bachelors—especially old maids, for an obvious reason—to be the most meritorious and patriotic class of his Majesty's subjects; and I think the opinion seems gaining ground. Three persons in this neighborhood especially, all friends of mine, are staunch in the creed; only, unluckily, their practice does not quite accord with their principles. The first, an old maid herself, I caught last week in the act of presiding over a dozen of country-town ladies, cutting out baby-linen for a charity—"The Maternal Society," save the mark! Bounties upon babies! The second, an admiral of the last edition, called on me on Saturday with a very rueful face to announce the birth of a daughter (he has a pretty young wife and six children under eight years old). —"Well," said I, "it must be endured." "Yes," said he, "but who would have thought of its being a girl!" The third, a young married woman, was brought to bed this very morning of twins—a catastrophe which I have been predicting to her this month past. Never fear for dear Mrs.

Haydon — there is a wonderful providence in such cases. Besides, there is a purity of health about her; and she is so loving and so precious that she will be taken particular care of—depend upon it.

When I last saw my portrait it seemed to me as like as what I see every day in the looking-glass; and even if it were as ugly as Medusa I should always think it the greatest honor of my life that it was painted. There is a long letter from me to you somewhere on the road. God bless you, my dear friends! Believe me always, most affectionately yours,

M. R. MITFORD.

To B. R. HAYDON, ESQ., *Connaught Terrace.*

Three-mile Cross, Aug. 11, 1825.

I congratulate you on your boy Frank not being prematurely clever! We have a precocious child here, the daughter of a dear friend, and the heiress of ten thousand a year, who frightens me for her own destiny and her mother's happiness. She is like a little old fairy; with eyes over-informed, preternatural in their expression. She really startles me. If there be one thing that I deprecate more than another, it is that precociousness. You know who says

"At Christmas I no more desire a rose
Than wish for snow in May's new-fangled shows;"

and a wiser thing even he never said.*

I have just been reading Mr. Combe's and Mr. Deville's books on phrenology. Really I half believe. The names of the organs are most absurd — most unphilosophical—most un-English. If they were altered I believe a great deal of the objection against the science would disappear. It is at all events an interesting pursuit, taken moderately. God bless you, my very dear friends! Ever most faithfully yours,

M. R. MITFORD.

To the Rev. WILLIAM HARNESS, *Hampstead.*

Three-mile Cross, Wednesday, Oct. 9, 1825.

MY DEAR FRIEND,—Although I have no member under hand, I write without waiting the uncertain chance of meeting with one—first, to thank you for your very kind atten-

* Shakspeare. The lines are in "Love's Labor Lost," Act i. scene 1.

tion about the money—secondly, to give you all the information I myself possess respecting the play. Mr. Kemble found "Charles" on his table on his return from abroad—read it immediately—thought it "admirable though somewhat dangerous"—and sent it at once tò the licenser. For three weeks we heard nothing of it. At last came a note from Mr. Colman to say "that, in consequence of the exceedingly delicate nature of the subject and incidents of "Charles the First," he had received instructions to send the MS. to the Lord Chamberlain, that he might himself judge, on perusal, of the safety of granting a license." Accordingly the piece is gone to the Duke of Montrose, who is in Scotland. And there we stand. Is not this very strange and unusual?

Have you read Pepys's Memoirs? I am extremely diverted by them, and prefer them to Evelyn's, all to nothing. He was too precise and too gentlemanly and too sensible by half;—wrote in full dress, with an eye, if not to the press, at least to posthumous reputation. Now this man sets down his thoughts in a most becoming dishabille—does not care twopence for posterity; and evidently thinks wisdom a very foolish thing. I don't know when any book has amused me so much. It is the very perfection of gossiping—most relishing nonsense.

How long do you stay at Hampstead? I shall tell you the fate of "Charles" as soon as I know it. Do let me know what you think of Mr. Fitzharris. Kindest love to dear Mary. Mamma's to all of you. Ever, my dear friend, most sincerely yours,   M. R. MITFORD.

To the Rev. WILLIAM HARNESS, *The Deepdene, Dorking.*

Three-mile Cross, Oct. 30, 1825.

MY DEAR FRIEND,—You are the only friend whose advice agrees with my strong internal feeling respecting the drama. Every body else says, Write novels—write prose? So that my perseverance passes for perverseness and obstinacy, which is very discouraging. There is a most splendid subject for historical tragedy which has taken great hold of my imagination:—Henry the Second—introducing, by a pardonable anachronism, the whole story of Becket, Eleanor, and Rosamond, and the rebellious sons. I should only take the best and worst of these, Henry and Geoffrey—Richard and

VOL. II.—C

John being too familiar to the stage; and the death of Prince Henry would supply, what in the story of so long-lived a monarch is very material, a good conclusion. This would certainly be a fine subject, and quite untouched. But the licenser! The chief temptation is of course Thomas à Becket, whom I should make as like as I could to what he was—a mixture of prelatic haughtiness and personal austerity—the haircloth peeping under the prince's robes; and the great scene would be an excommunication, not of the king, but of the ministers and the nation; certainly a fine thing to do: but the licenser! Henry, an enlightened prince, at least two centuries before his age, must have the better of the argument. But may we touch the subject? And Eleanor and Rosamond, odious as the queen was and must be—would that do?

I have a good mind to write to Mr. Colman and ask. I would, if I knew any way of getting at him. Certainly I mean no harm—nor did I in " Charles ;" and the not licensing that play will do great harm to my next, by making me timid and over careful. Let me know what you think about Henry the Second.

You can not imagine how perplexed I am. There are points in my domestic situation too long and too painful to write about. The terrible improvidence of one dear parent—the failure of memory and decay of faculty in that other who is still dearer, cast on me a weight of care and of fear that I can hardly bear up against. Give me your advice. Heaven knows, I would write a novel, as every one tells me to do, and as, I suppose, I must do at last, if I had not the feeling of inability and of failure so strong within me that it would be scarcely possible to succeed against such a presentiment. And to fail there would be so irremediable! But it will be my lot at last.

God bless you, my dear friend! Kindest love to dear Mary. I hope we shall see you here, or at least at Reading. Pray, pray contrive it. Ever most gratefully yours,

M. R. MITFORD.

Yes! I have read Madame de Genlis with great amusement. What a delightful mixture of cant and affectation and shrewdness and vanity she is! I had a peculiar pleasure in reading these volumes, as they completely justified the contempt I had always entertained for the authoress; a contempt chiefly grounded on her *good* characters, of which the exaggerated and morbid virtues proved so decidedly a defective moral sense.

To the Rev. WILLIAM HARNESS, *Hampstead.*

Three-mile Cross, Dec. 1, 1825.

MY DEAR FRIEND,—I followed your advice, and requested Mr. Rowland Stephenson to ask Mr. Colman if the " Charles " could not be altered so as to be licensable, and to-day's post brought me a packet from Miss Stephenson, enclosing the following from Mr. Colman to her brother-in-law. I transcribe it word for word :—

" *Private.*

"28th Nov., 1825, Brompton Square.

" MY DEAR SIR,—It is much to be regretted that Miss Mitford has employed her time unprofitably, when so amiable a motive as that of assisting her family has induced her to exercise her literary talents; but it would be idle and ungenerous to flatter her with hopes which there is no prospect of fulfilling.

"My official opinion of her tragedy is certainly unfavorable to the author's interests. I was, however, so far from wishing it to prejudice the Lord Chamberlain, that the play was submitted to his perusal at my suggestion. He therefore formed his own judgment upon it, and decidedly refused to license its performance.

"As to alterations—the fact is, that the subject of this play and the incidents it embraces are fatal in themselves—they are an inherent and incurable disease—the morbid matter lies in the very bones and marrow of the historical facts, and defies eradication. Indeed it would be a kind of practical bull to permit a detailed representation of Charles's unhappy story on a public stage, when his martyrdom is still observed in such solemn silence that the London theatres are actually closed and all dramatic exhibitions whatever suspended on its anniversary.

"I give Miss Mitford full credit for the harmlessness of her intentions, but mischief may be unconsciously done, as a house may be set on fire by a little innocent in the nursery. Believe me, my dear sir, most truly yours, G. COLMAN.

" Rowland Stephenson, Esq., Lombard Street. "

Now, is not this a precious *morceau?* But there is no use in contending.

Poor mamma's failure of faculty is very peculiar. You might see her twenty times for twenty minutes, and yet not perceive it; or, on the other hand, she might in one twenty minutes show it a hundred times. She mistakes one person for another—one thing for another—misjoins facts—misreports conversations—hunts for six hours together after a pin-cushion which she has in her pocket, or a thimble on her finger—and is totally absorbed in the smallest passing objects. *This* is, in one respect, fortunate, since it prevents her from foreseeing greater evils. But then again, it deters her from supporting me in any effort to mitigate them. So that, from her incapacity, and the absolute inertness of my father in such matters—an obstinacy of going on in the same way which I can not describe—I find myself compelled to acquiesce in a way of living which, however inexpensive, is still more so than we can afford, for fear of disturbing, and perhaps killing her. If she were herself she would rather live on dry bread in a garret than run in debt; and so would I, merely as a question of personal comfort.

Well, it is very wrong to worry you with these grievances, which must have their course, especially now, that you are yourself tormented about the church. You can not imagine how sorry we all are for that sad affair.

I have not yet written to Mr. Campbell, but I certainly shall. It is the best way. I am quite delighted with your edition of Shakspeare. It must do. The Life is like the portrait prefixed to it; the old beloved well-known features, which we all have by heart, but inspired with a fresh spirit. I did not think it possible to make a scanty narrative seem so full. Only I have a favor to beg; in the next edition leave out the latter part of Malone's ill-natured note on Milton's verses. I don't think that Milton did mean to speak ill of Shakspeare; and, at all events, there is no need to dwell on a slight offense toward the memory of Shakspeare in such a man as Milton—his worthiest admirer and most exquisite eulogist. You, especially, who have so admirably vindicated Ben Johnson from such a charge, ought not to admit Mr. Malone's sour observation into your pages, of which the tone is, generally speaking, so genial. Ever most gratefully and affectionately yours, M. R. MITFORD.

To B. R. HAYDON, ESQ., *Connaught Terrace.*

Three-mile Cross, Dec. 18, 1825.

MY DEAR FRIEND,—I heartily agree with you about Sheridan and about Moore. *Wits* (for neither of them are in the true sense *Poets*) are essentially of a lower order of mind. Better have written any comedy of Shakspeare than "The School for Scandal." Better have written "The Merry Wives of Windsor" than all other comedies put together. Notwithstanding the marvelous variety of character in that delicious piece, there is a harmony which pervades it and prevents any feeling of discrepancy—all is in keeping. And "As You Like It" and "Much Ado About Nothing"—what exquisite things are these! The notion of any body being jealous of Shakspeare! I have never thoroughly liked Scott since the passage in "Kenilworth" where he is introduced as a player, with an intentional degradation. Have you seen Mr. Harness's new edition of Shakspeare? The Life is very spirited and good, and there is a delightful portrait, which one is sure is like.

How very unlucky I am! Only to think of George Whittaker's having stopped payment! It was lucky that I had not parted with the copyright of my little book; but there are the profits of my last large edition unaccounted for, and other trifling things—more than we can afford to lose. I have been so urged by friends and importuned by booksellers (amongst others by Longman's house), that I have at last actually begun a novel. Wish me success! It is a tremendous undertaking, for I write with extreme slowness, labor, and difficulty; and, whatever you may think, there is a great difference of facility in different minds. I am the slowest writer, I suppose, in England, and touch and retouch perpetually.

Adieu, my dear friend. Kindest regards from my father and mother. Ever most truly yours,   M. R. M.

[The following is in answer to a letter from Miss Mitford, requesting Charles Kemble to produce "Foscari."]

"Dec. 20, 1825.

"MY DEAR MADAM,—I am fearful that I shall not be able to comply with your request. My word is already pledged to the production of so much novelty of one kind or another, that, were there no other reasons against "Foscari's" being acted, I might almost say it is impossible. It is, I hope, unnecessary for me to say that I shall be happy of any opportunity of being useful to you, or to assure you that I am, with great sincerity, your faithful servant,

"CHARLES KEMBLE."

1826.

[Miss Mitford went up to town in the beginning of this year in the greatest hurry, to collect, if possible, money due to her from publishers and booksellers. She staid at Mrs. Hofland's for some days, but seems to have received little from her debtors beyond invitations and compliments.]

To the REV. WILLIAM HARNESS, *Hampstead.*

Three-mile Cross, March 4, 1826.

MY DEAR FRIEND,—Your kind letter has given me the greatest possible relief. To have been—however unintentionally—the cause of serious annoyance to you, would have been insupportable.

How very striking that circumstance of Mr. Deville and little N——u* is ! I really think there is a great deal of truth in the system. What a pity that they have not amongst them some accurate writer, who knows the power of *words*, and would sweep away the strange jargon which has crept amongst them from the cockneyism of Deville and the Germanism of Spurzheim ! Mr. Combe's book is the best on the subject. Have you seen it ?

I inclose my charades, which in all but their faults might more truly be called *yours.* If you think the thing will remain intact till next year (for I am sure that my novel can not appear before), then it would be better to suppress them, and insert one therein, more carefully written and *àpropos* to the story ; but if it seems to you probable that some will

* The boy was about five years old. His father was an Englishman, his mother a Portuguese. Of this Deville was perfectly ignorant ; but his words, on feeling the boy's head, were : "A wonderful development ! I never found the *perceptive* organs so strong in any English head, nor the *reflective* organs so strong in any foreign head before."

make their appearance before (and really one wonders that the idea has not been seized), then these might be sent to a magazine.* Do as you judge best. Ten guineas a sheet is very bad pay for a magazine in double columns like " Blackwood;" I have twelve for those of which the printing is so much opener, and after the rate of twenty or thirty from the annual publications; but that I should not mind. It could not make much difference.

By the way, I wrote about " Rienzi," as it was right to do. You and I were talking of Mrs. Radcliffe's Romances. Mr. Talfourd gave me the other day a very interesting account of her posthumous works,† containing a real genuine ghost-story—a *bonâ fide* ghost—simple in its construction, but excessively powerful whenever the supernatural agency is introduced, and full of remarkable felicities of expression. The scene is at Kenilworth, in the reign of Henry the Third. But Mr. Talfourd says that by far the finest things he has seen of hers are her manuscript notes on different journeys in England—simple, graphical, without a single word to spare—and with a Cobbett-like power of putting a scene before your eyes. Some few of these will be incorporated in the Memoirs, but not nearly all. Her biographer says that the trouble of drawing up this life, under the jealous supervision of Mr. Radcliffe, exceeds any thing that can be imagined; to use his own illustration, it is worse than drawing an affidavit, from the fidgety scrupulousness he shows about things of no manner of consequence. Considering the lies we have to encounter, it is something to find that there is any body left in the world who cares for truth, however unimportant. Mr. Radcliffe is an old gentleman, quite of the old school; who—notwithstanding he has since her decease married his housekeeper—retains the fondest affection for his more illustrious wife—calls her the dear deceased, and cries whenever she is mentioned.

Have you heard any thing of Sir Walter Scott's affair lately? Mr. Haydon wrote me word, a day or two ago, that he had had a letter from him, in which he said that he had lost a large fortune, but that he should have a competence

---

* They were published with others in Blackwood. Mr. H. gave Miss Mitford the plans for the three first of the series.

† Mr. Radcliffe, after his wife's death, placed her MSS. in Mr. Talfourd's hands to be edited.

left. When does your church open? Make our kindest
regards to dear Mary. God bless you, my dear and kind
friend! Ever most sincerely yours,   M. R. MITFORD.

To the REV. WILLIAM HARNESS, *Hampstead.*

Three-mile Cross, March 23, 1826.

MY DEAR FRIEND,—I write, although I have no frank, because an idea has just taken such possession of me that I
can not rest without asking your advice and co-operation
concerning it. I want to write a grand opera on the story
of " Cupid and Psyche," with Weber's music. It has been
done as a ballet, I know, and I think there is a French play
on the subject, by Molière, but I know nothing of the sort
in English, or in great music. Do you? Just look at the
story, and see how dramatic it is—how full of situation and
variety, both for dialogue and poetry, for music and scenery;
the response of the oracle—the funeral procession—then the
Cupid part—then the labors—the hell—the apotheosis; and,
moreover, I am quite sure that I could give it a strong *human*
interest, by plunging myself into the beautiful story and entirely forgetting the allegory. I wish with all my heart you
would ask Mr. Kemble whether, if I were to put all my
strength into such an opera, he could get Weber to compose
the music, and whether Weber would like the subject. It
has seized my imagination most strongly, and there would
be no fear of the licenser in this case, I suppose. Do pray
ask. I am *sure* that I could do my part satisfactorily. Kindest love from all here. Ever most gratefully yours,

M. R. MITFORD.

To the REV. WILLIAM HARNESS, *Hampstead.*

Three-mile Cross, April 3, 1826.

MY DEAR FRIEND,—I am quite delighted with Mr. Blackwood's approbation of the charades, and still more so, infinitely more so, with yours. Pray write some, and send to
" Blackwood," and let us come out together afterward in a
joint volume. You can't think how much I shall like to
Beaumont-and-Fletcher it with you. I have sent him two
more—" Match-lock " and " Block-head." After writing the
first (which is quite a little drama of the Commonwealth
days), it occurred to me to look for the word. Accordingly,

I searched in one folio Johnson, and in half a dozen small dictionaries, and no such word! Was not this a most absurd difficulty? To have written a charade upon a non-existing word! However, in Todd's Johnson, at last I found it. So that trouble is happily over.

April 16.

This note has been awaiting a letter from you, and I hasten to reply to your very kind one received yesterday. I have written, but not sent, another charade on "Messmate." I tell you this to avoid any awkward jostling of words. I quite long to see your story. I shall like it I am sure. Let me know, as soon as you hear any thing of Psyche. It might make an exquisite opera, and I do think that I could manage it.

Mrs. Trollope, who has been reading " Rienzi," and who is a most kind and warm-hearted person, has set her heart on getting it out either with Kean or Macready. I don't know how she may succeed with the former; but I think I know enough of the latter worthy, to predict her non-success. Mr. Milman—induced, I believe, by her praises—also wished to read it, and has written me a most kind and gratifying letter respecting it, with excellent criticisms. He likes the play; and I am myself quite sure that, with a great actor, it could not fail. But I am so unlucky—am I not? I have not yet begun the Pysche, having been engaged in preparing another volume of "Our Village," which I think of bringing out. Does Apuleius say what oracle they consulted? And what was the mode of consulting an oracle—the ceremony? Was there a sacrifice? I wish with all my heart that Mr. Kemble may take the opera. I think of writing another charade on "Black-wood"—a good local subject. You'll find writing charades ·very amusing. I like nothing else. Poor mamma has been very unwell, but is much better. Kind love from all. Ever yours most sincerely,

M. R. M.

To the REV. WILLIAM HARNESS, *Hempstead.*

Three-mile Cross, May 2, 1826.

I thank you heartily, my dear friend, for your kind letter. My father went to London Monday morning and returned Tuesday night, having settled the business of my second

C 2

volume, I think, very fairly. George Whittaker buys that and the copyright of the first volume for £150, or rather his brother-in-law buys the work for him. I might certainly have got £200 elsewhere, but I think the price fair, considering the extreme depression of the trade. Don't you? Last year it would have been worth £300 at least. Blackwood sent me the magazine, with a most handsome letter, requesting a continuance of my contributions, and begging me to accept of an order on Messrs. Cadell for £10 10s., as a retaining fee. This is pleasant, and quite explains why his magazine is so good. Liberal men are sure to have things well done. He spoke of you most handsomely. By the way, I begged to reserve the copyright.

I must read the "Martyr" as soon as possible. She is a glorious woman—a great and delicious poet; but certainly not dramatic in any of her doings. She always wanted spontaneity—vividness—presentness, if I may use such a word. It was that want which made her plays—full as they are of the noblest thoughts and the most racy diction—altogether unfit for the stage. There must have been a want, when we have seen the majestic " Jane de Montfort "* fail in the hands of Mrs. Siddons, who seemed born to embody that grand conception of genius. Macready used to say that it was want of passion. But there is passion—high passion, both in De Montfort and Basil. What they want is *life*.

A thousand thanks for the " Oracle," and best love from all. Ever yours,   M. R. M.

.   *To* B. R. Haydon, Esq., *Connaught Terrace.*

Three-mile Cross, May 4, 1826.

My dear Friend,—I am always delighted to hear from you, but never in a fuss if I do not, because I am so sure of your kindness that I only think you are busy. The " Alexander " must be a fine thing. I quite agree with you; he is the man for my money. It is the *doers* of the world—the Alexanders and Cromwells and Napoleons—that are the materials of painting and poetry, and not the mere talkers and thinkers and writers. I shall long to see it. I hear from Hannah Rowe, who is here, that you are as well and as brilliant as ever.

* By Mrs. Joanna Baillie.

Poor Sir Walter Scott! Captain Kater told me, when I was in town, that he had heard, from undeniable authority that a letter had been sent to him, signed only with a single initial, authorizing him to draw for £30,000 on a particular banker. A most noble gift! But, still, Sir Walter must feel it very hard to be deposed, at his time of life, from the station which he held in the world, as well as in literature; the more especially as the great falling-off in the late works rendered it desirable for his fame that he should cease writing. But what is his reverse of fortune compared with Napoleon's! I hope your patron will soon be able to cash his bills. Most fervently I hope this on your account, and also on his. I rejoice to hear so good an account of your invalids! God bless you all! Ever yours,

M. R. MITFORD.

To B. R. HAYDON, ESQ., *Connaught Terrace.*

Tuesday morning, 11th July, 1826.

MY DEAR FRIEND,—I should be delighted to take in your article on the rabbit, only my second volume is printed and ready for delivery—and has been for these three weeks, but is kept back by the booksellers till the election flurry subsides. But you must keep it for me; I shall have another volume probably in the spring.

It's very delightful to hear that Sir Walter's loss is only forty thousand pounds, which can not affect his comfort or even the prospects of his children, vexatious as it must be. I confess to you, my dear friend, that with every respect for the genius of Scott, I am one of those who think that he has had his reward both in fame and money. I have been credibly informed that he received eight thousand guineas for "Woodstock!" Now, just look at "Woodstock," and tell me if the author who receives eight thousand four hundred pounds for that book has any reason to complain? I do not say that so delightful a writer—so great a one as he has been, so pleasant a one as he is—is overpaid, but simply that he is well paid and can afford a few remarks from the good-natured world.

Have you read Cooper's novel, "The Last of the Mohicans?" I like it better than any of Scott's, except the three first and the "Heart of Mid-Lothian;" and it interests me

more even than those, as giving a true and new picture of
a new and great people. How wonderfully America is rising in the scale of intellect! A friend lent me lately an
essay on Milton's life and writings by Dr. Channing, of
Boston, compared with which Macaulay's article in the "Edinburgh," that was so puffed and cried up, is mere drivel-
ing.

If you have not read the American novels, do. Depend
on it that America will succeed us as Rome did Athens;
and it is a comfort to think that by their speaking the same
beautiful language, Shakspeare and Milton will not be buried
in the dust of a scholar's library, but live and breathe in after ages as they do now to us.

This weather is dreadful. My garden, which a week ago
was really like a bit of Paradise, so far as flowers and beauty go, is now so scorched and withered that it is a grief to
look at it. My father has been poorly. My mother, thank
Heaven! keeps tolerably well, and so am I, when I am quiet.
I wish, heartily, we had any chance of seeing you. I trust
you keep well. God bless you all, my dear friends! Ever
yours,   M. R. M.

To the REV. WILLIAM HARNESS, *Heathcote Street, London.*

Three-mile Cross, August 26, 1826.

MY DEAR FRIEND,—After my last good-for-nothing, pet-
tish, and suspicious letter (which pray burn), I have been
made quite ashamed of myself by receiving the following
most kind one from Mr. Kemble:

"Since the receipt of yours of the 28th of July, I have
been troubled with many cares, or I would have attended
more promptly to the questions it contained. To your first
question—'Do you think that Mrs. Radcliffe's posthumous
romance would answer as a drama?' I answer that not
having read it I am unable to say whether it would or not.
To your second question—'Have you employed any one to
dramatize it?' I answer, No. You surely must be as good
a judge of the fitness of the subject for the stage as any one;
and if you set about it, let me warn you that it will not be a
great success unless you contrive to introduce some good
comic character into the story. A comedy! a comedy! still
a comedy! say I, and without songs, or at most with not

above two. It is in vain to write tragedies till we have an actress to give proper effect to them.

"From what you say respecting the little time that would be requisite for you to arrange 'Gaston de Blondeville,' you might perhaps finish that and a comedy too. The last time I spoke with Mr. Young on the subject of 'Rienzi,' he seemed to me to have changed his opinion in some measure with regard to it. Have you read the French tragedy of that name, which was acted last winter in Paris with great success? I shall be in London in the course of a week or ten days, and am ever, dear madam, etc.,   C. KEMBLE.

"Harrogate, 22d August."

Now this letter is enough to make me hate myself, when I think with how much suspicion and mistrust I had been led to regard this kind person. I don't quite know what he means about the "Rienzi."

How shall I excuse my pestering you with all my dramatic hopes and fears ?—all my sins of thought and weaknesses of character ? But you are so very, very kind. Have we any chance of seeing you here ? Mr. Milman made a great display last Wednesday at the Bishop's Visitation, preaching a sermon which I was so unlucky as not to hear, but which every body speaks of as a most splendid piece of oratory—on the Philosophy of Preaching. I hope he'll print it.

I hope you are getting a great deal of money at your church, I mean that you have the rents from the pews, so that your popularity may be profitable as well as pleasant to you. It's one of the worst results of being poor, that it makes one think of nothing but money, whether for one's self or one's friends.

God bless you, my dear friend ! Kindest regards from my father and mother. Ever most gratefully yours,

M. R. MITFORD.

To the REV. WILLIAM HARNESS, *Deepdene, Dorking.*

Three-mile Cross, Oct. 27, 1826.

MY DEAR FRIEND,—I am very troublesome to you, but it is all your own fault ; be less kind, and you'll get rid of the torment. I have no frank, but I can't help answering your

most welcome note; the more especially as I had before
written to you a letter, which you had not received when
that note was written, requesting you to forward our dividend in two half notes;* whereas I have now to request you
to keep the money till my father and you meet, which will
very probably be almost immediately on your arrival in
town.

I suppose that I must be in town next Wednesday or
Thursday; I don't at present know where, but incline to take
a lodging near the theatre, with my father, for a week; and
perhaps if Mary be returned (I depend on you for not hur-
rying her back before the time she would otherwise come),
and you are sure that I should not occasion you any inconvenience, I may be tempted to accept your most kind invitation for a day or two, after that period. It would be such
an indulgence! such a holiday! But it must depend on two
circumstances; the success of the play (for if that fail I shall
scud away home like a rabbit to its burrow), and my dear
mother's health. I have promised also to spend a day, or
perhaps two, in case all be favorable, with Mrs. Trollope, of
Harrow, who is so good as to make a great point of it; so
that my visit to Heathcote Street might be made to suit
your convenience, before or after that.

Perhaps if there be really any chance of " Gaston " (which
Mr. Kemble has not read yet), I had better come to you then.
But we shall meet, at all events, on Saturday night; for
whether in good or evil fortune, you are amongst the few
whom I must see on that eventful evening. You can not
imagine how nervous I am! So much seems to hang on it;
" Gaston;" the American plays,† which the success of " Foscari " would certainly bring forward; and a volume of " Dramatic Scenes," which I have long intended to publish, and
which a really successful tragedy would undoubtedly sell.
By the way, my second volume is published at last, and I
hope waiting for you in Heathcote Street—at least I desired
it to be sent there.

---

* The dividend on the small sum in the funds still remaining of Mrs. Mitford's fortune, was received by the Rev. W. Harness as executor to his father, who was Mrs. Mitford's trustee.

† " Rienzi " and " Charles the First," which had gone to America with
Macready.

"Gaston" is a mere melodrama—but, Mr. Talfourd says, a singularly good one—intended to *act* and not to *read*. I thought of nothing but effects from beginning to end. Well, I have tired you of my doings.

Kindest love from my dear mother. Ever yours,

M. R. MITFORD.

There are no words for Mr. Kemble's kindness from the beginning of this affair to the end.

To MRS. MITFORD, *Three-mile Cross.*

London, 45 Frith Street, Nov. 2, 1826.

MY DEAR GRANNY—I got here quite safe and well, and you will be delighted to hear that Drum* is looking extremely well, and the apartments are delightful. We all went to the play last night, Betsey and all, to see "Clari," the new farce, and "Charles the Second." Charles Kemble is very great indeed in "Charles the Second," and Farren in the farce, and Miss Paton in "Clari." I saw none of my people except Mr. Serle and Miss Henry. Miss Henry is very pretty, and Mr. Serle well-looking and pleasant-spoken. Charles Kemble is at present as hoarse as a crow, but it's to be hoped he'll get better before Saturday. I understand that they are all as sanguine as possible, and that Mr. Young is more zealous than any one. This is very pleasant. Mr. Warde is also all zeal. I am expecting him every moment, as he appointed to be here this morning. Mr. St. Quintin breakfasted with us; he is looking well, but old. Mrs. St. Q. has sent you a beautiful cap of her work, which I shall bring you down. Mr. Talfourd joined us at the play; he is very sanguine, and much struck with Mr. Young's acting. William Ogbourn has also been here to-day, and he is also sanguine. Betsey was prodigiously pleased. Mrs. Hofland, whom I saw yesterday, has quite lost her voice; both she and her husband are looking more deplorable than ever. My gown does capitally, and is just what they wear. We are in a great fright about the Duke of York, who is worse again. Heaven grant he may live over next week! There was a report last night that he was dead, but that is not so. He is alive this morning, but very ill.

* Pet name for Dr. Mitford.

I hope you got both dear Drum's letter and the " Times " newspaper, which I sent by the boy, and that you have by this time received the new number of " Blackwood," in which I am very pleasantly mentioned in the last article, the " Noctes Ambrosianæ." This will do good. Drum wrote yesterday to Newberry to let you have five pounds, which I hope you have received by this time. If he does not send it to you, send Will with a note to him for it. And pray, my dearest dear, take great care of yourself, and be sure to let me hear exactly how you are; and give my love to poor dear Molly and the owl. God bless you, my very dearest ! I shall leave Drum to finish. Ever your own,

M. R. M.

To Mrs. Mitford,* *Three-mile Cross.*

45 Frith Street, Saturday night, Nov. 5, 1826.

I can not suffer this parcel to go to you, my dearest mother, without writing a few lines to tell you of the complete success of my play. It was received, not merely with rapturous applause, but without the slightest symptom of disapprobation, from beginning to end. We had not a single order in the house, so that from first to last the approbation was sincere and general. William Harness and Mr. Talfourd are both quite satisfied with the whole affair, and my other friends are half crazy. Mrs. Trollope, between joy for my triumph and sympathy with the play, has cried herself half blind. I am, and have been, perfectly calm, and am merely tired with the great number of friends whom I have seen today. Mrs. Story has been here the greater part of the morning—kinder and warmer-hearted than any one that ever lived, except dear, dear Mrs. Trollope, who has also been with me most part of the day; Mrs. Morgan, Hannah Rowe, and my own darling Marianne, who staid with me during the whole of the time that the play was acting, which I passed at George Robins's; and men innumerable. Marianne is going with me on Monday to the tragedy. Of course I shall now stay rather longer than I intended; having the copyright of the play and a volume of " Dramatic Sketches " to sell, if I can. We shall probably take these very comfortable lodgings for another week, but certainly not longer.

* This was addressed outside, " Mrs. Mitford, *Good News.*"

I quite long to hear how you, my own dearest darling, have borne the suspense and anxiety consequent on this affair—which, triumphantly as it has turned out, was certainly a very nervous business. They expect the play to run three times a week till Christmas. It was so immense a house that you might have walked over the heads in the pit; and great numbers were turned away, in spite of the wretched weather. All the actors were good; but it was a great thing for Mr. Serle and Mrs. Sloman, who made each what is called a hit. Mr. Young gave out the tragedy amidst immense applause.

God bless you, my dearest mother! Papa is quite well, and happier than you can imagine. He had really half a mind to go to you, instead of writing—so much do both of us wish to share our happiness with you. But I knew that you would be sorry that he should encounter so much fatigue. God bless you, once more, my dearest! Let dear Mrs. Fielde know how well all has gone. Ever most fondly your own, M. R. M.

[The agreement between the theatre and Miss Mitford for "Foscari" was £100 on the third, the ninth, the fifteenth, and the twentieth nights. The copyright, together with a volume of "Dramatic Sketches," was sold to Whittaker for £150.]

To SIR WILLIAM ELFORD, *Oakampton Hall, Wivilscombe, Somerset.*

Three-mile Cross, Nov. 17, 1826.

I thank you most sincerely, my dear Sir William, for your congratulations. Hitherto the success has been very brilliant. We can hardly expect it to last—since to continue to pull people so thoroughly undramatic as we English are become to a theatre in this deadest of dead seasons, to witness the representation of a quiet tragedy, would be next to a miracle. But great good has been done, if (which Heaven avert!) the tragedy stop not to-night. A real impression has been made, and a reputation of the highest order established—to say nothing of that which with me is now every thing, the money. My second volume, having been out only a fortnight, has again gone to press. A strange thing to say, that little volume has done real mischief to my tragedy. . You can not have lived so long in the world without finding that people will never allow any body the power of doing two things well; and, because it is admitted that I can write playful prose, there be many who assume that I can not write serious verse. Let them go and cry at " Foscari " (if " Foscari " continue)—for I assure you that during two acts the white handkerchief is going continually, to my great astonishment.

I am just returned from passing a brilliant fortnight in London, where I saw Mr. Haydon and the picture that he is painting for Lord Egremont—"Alexander Taming Bucephalus;" and heard a great deal more literary news than I have head to remember or time to tell. For, alas! my dear Sir William, the holiday time of our correspondence is past. I am now a poor slave of the lamp, chained to the desk as the galley slave to his oar, and am at present triply engaged; for the monthly periodical publications, which I have been too much engaged to supply; to the annual books, which to my sorrow are just on, and have begun dunning me again; and to my own bookseller, who has bought a volume of "Dramatic Scenes," which I have still to finish.

Adieu, my dear friend. Kindest respects to all your family, especially to my dear friend and correspondent, Miss Elford. Always most affectionately yours,

M. R. MITFORD.

I don't wonder at what you tell me about Hazlitt. If you won't quote me as an authority (for one had as soon provoke Satan as that man, being, as I am, a dramatic writer), I'll tell you a good story about him. My friend, Archdeacon Wrangham, who is a thorough-paced bibliomaniac—a complete collector of scarce books, and never purchases any other—bought the Sally-Walker book (the "Modern Pygmalion," was not it called?)* on speculation—it being so exceedingly *bad*, that he was sure it would soon become *scarce.* I think this an admirable piece of anticipation.

* The title of the book was "Liber Amoris."

CHAPTER IV.

LETTERS FOR 1827 AND 1828.

To SIR WILLIAM ELFORD, *Totnes, Devon.*

Three-mile Cross, March 5, 1827.

I THANK you very sincerely for your most kind note, my dear friend, which afforded us all the greatest pleasure, from the proof that it contained of your good health and good spirits—your unchangeable vigor of mind and of hand. Mr. Jones* is very good—very kind. There is no love lost; I was delighted with his pictures and his conversation. He is certainly out of health, and complained to me of being obliged to leave the high classical and romantic style, in which he delights, and of which he has so many splendid sketches, for the battle-pieces, of which he is weary, and the old Flemish and German towns, which employ his hand rather than his imagination; but of which two kinds his commissions mainly consist. He complained also of the *number* of commissions, being overworked. But, after all, that's a very good misfortune for an artist nowadays. He had a scheme of making drawings from Sophocles, as Flaxman has done from Homer and Æschylus, which, as he only deferred it out of compliment to that fine veteran, he will, I hope, now that he is gone, carry into speedy effect. Sophocles deserves to be so illustrated. I have an enthusiasm for his plays only second to that which I entertain for Shakspeare. Did I tell you (*à propos* of art) that William Havell, who went out with Lord Amherst to China, and has remained ever since in India, is now returned—much improved as an artist, and with a most rich collection of drawings. He writes as well as he paints; so I suppose we shall have a splendid work on Ellora, his attention having been mainly directed to that remarkable spot, of which we know just enough to wish to know more. What a stupendous labor those caverns must have been! The Pyramids seem to me less wonderful.

* The Royal Academician.

Say every thing for me to your dear daughters. My father and mother join in kindest remembrances, and I am always, my dear Sir William, most affectionately yours,

M. R. M.

To the REV. WILLIAM HARNESS, *Heathcote Street.*

Three-mile Cross, March 30, 1827.

MY DEAR FRIEND,—Your most kind letter and my little note crossed as usual; but my father, who gives a delightful account of you and dear Mary and your pretty house, says that you would like to hear my scheme for "Inez;" so I shall write it as carelessly as usual, trusting to your quickness for comprehending and your indulgence for forgiving my puzzle-headed way of telling the story. There are two French plays, one English, and one Spanish, on the subject, but I follow none of them; my plot is my own, and closer to the narrative given in an old Portuguese chronicle—lent by Mrs. Maria Graham (now Mrs. Callcott) to Miss Skerrett for my use—than any of the other dramas. This is not of much consequence, one way or the other, so that the play be interesting; but if one can get effects in the history, it's as well.

The play opens with a scene of courtiers, etc., who speak of the arrival of an ambassador from Castile at the Court of Lisbon, to enforce the immediate union of the Princess Constance, sister of the King of Castile, to Don Pedro, Infant of Portugal, she having been a long time resident there, and her brother thinking her trifled with. The king, Alphonso (Young), and Don Manuel, his minister (Warde), enter and receive the ambassador. The king agrees that he is right, and sends for Don Pedro to inform him that the marriage shall take place forthwith. Pedro (C. Kemble) enters, equipped for hunting; answers decidedly "No!" and after a short skirmish with his father (sufficiently respectful and rather gay), a fiery defiance to the ambassador, and a contemptuous scoffing at Don Manuel, goes out. The king and his minister are left together, and Don Manuel insinuates that the Infant's repugnance to the marriage results from his attachment to Donna Inez de Castro, the maid of honor who had accompanied the Infanta from Spain. The king disbelieves the charge, which he places to the account of Manuel's jealousy, who had been a rejected lover of Inez. Manuel asks his leave to try an experiment, and they go out. Then a short scene with Inez and Pedro; he tells her that he has got quit of the ambassador and his proposal, and conjures her to renew her vow to him not to suffer any circumstance to induce her to reveal a secret which subsists between them. She promises, and goes out with him, or promises to go to a certain window to see him mount his steed, and he proceeds to the chase. Then a scene between the king, Constance, Manuel, Inez, etc.,—the court of the princess. The king soothes Constance with the assurance of a speedy union, and invites the ambassador and the whole train to a nuptial banquet that evening. Some one rushes in with an account that Pedro is killed or dangerously hurt in hunting; the princess, deeply offended, is cold and haughty; the king, who knows the tale to be false, is almost passive, or only engaged with Manuel in watching Inez, who is in an agony of fear, urging one and another to go or send, until she hears him approaching, rushes toward him, and falls fainting with suppressed joy. (Now this will require a very fine actress, and if well done, will be a great hit. Can Miss Jarman do it, do you think?) Inez is removed; Pedro tries to explain away her agitation; the king is stern; the princess haughty; and Manuel throws out so many sarcastic hints that Pedro, wrought up to a pitch of passion, challenges him to fight in a wood without the town that very evening. In a scene between the king and Manuel, Manuel works up the king to propose that, as the only way to remove Inez from the Infant, she and Manuel should be married that night, taking advantage of the prince's absence on the challenge that he had given, and Manuel consenting not to meet him. Then the banquet; and the king, princess, and ambassador all announce to Inez that she must immediately marry Don Manuel—a very passionate scene of entreaty and struggle on her part. Just as they are forcing her to the altar, Pedro rushes in and claims her as his wife—his wedded wife. "That is high treason on her part by the law of the land," says Manuel; "she will not say so." "I do! I do!" replies Inez; and she is borne away to prison. In the next scene she is arraigned before the king and council, Pedro being present, and condemned to death. She is taken away, and a very passionate scene ensues between the king and Pedro, he imploring his father not to sign the sentence—which the king at last does—and his son leaves him renouncing his father, and swearing that Inez shall not die. In the next scene it is understood that Pedro is rousing the troops and the people, by whom he is much beloved, to revolt. The princess enters, and begs Inez's life. The king himself becomes much softened, and sends Manuel to her with commission that, if she will sign an act of divorce, she shall live. Then the prince, who has stormed and taken the palace, comes in at the head of a body of people to demand Inez. The king refuses to speak with him until the troops be dismissed. They are sent off, and a tender scene of reconciliation between the father and son takes place, the king consenting to forgive Inez unconditionally, and even holding out hopes of confirming their marriage. "But where is Inez?" says Pedro; "let me fly to her!" and he goes out. Then Manuel is discovered with Inez in her prison, trying to persuade her not only to sign the divorce but to fly with him and become his wife, telling her that Pedro is in arms, that he must be taken, and that it is the only means to save his life. She remonstrates passionately, and Pedro is heard approaching, when Manuel catches her in his arms, stabs her, and delivers her dead or dying to her husband, who loudly demands her, declaring that so, at least, he makes her his own.

Now, if you dislike any part of this, tell me, for there are not ten lines written. Pedro's part will be very fine—fiery and tender. The king will be good, too; and Manuel's villainy shall, if I can contrive it, be somewhat redeemed by sarcasm and subtlety, and excused by his violent passion for Inez, whose character ought to have a great actress. . . .

God bless you, my dear friend! Kindest love from all here to you and to dear Mary. Ever most gratefully and affectionately yours,   M. R. MITFORD.

What fools the Whigs are not to join Canning! He's a greater man than all of them put together, and that, I suppose, is the reason they hang back.

To ——.

Sunday, June, 1827.

If my truest and most affectionate sympathy can be any consolation to you, my dear friends, be assured that you pos-

sess it. I can think of nothing else. Would to God that
I had any thing more available to offer, but we are as poor
as poor can be—have only received one hundred pounds
yet from the theatre—and are ourselves living on credit.
Heaven protect and bless you all, is the earnest prayer of
your affectionate friend,   M. R. MITFORD.

To SIR WILLIAM ELFORD, *Totnes, Devonshire.*

Three-mile Cross, June 20, 1827.

Have you heard of Mr. Lough, the new sculptor? Mr.
Haydon says nothing like his model of "Milo" (eight feet
high) has been seen since the Phidian age. His account of
him personally is very interesting. He is the son of a small
farmer in Northumberland, and two years ago was sheaving
corn. A few months ago a friend of Mr. Haydon's found him
in his obscure lodging in London, tearing up his shirts for
rags to keep his clay model moist. For three months he
went without animal food, having spent all his money for materials for his great work; and it being winter, and he without a fire in the same room with a damp clay figure, he used
(to borrow his own words) "to go to bed and shiver asleep."
That is now past, and I trust forever. The "Milo" is exhibit-
ing. Five or six persons have put down their names for
eighty guineas each to have it done in marble, and more will
probably follow their example. Mr. Brougham and Sir John
Paul have each given him a commission for five hundred
pounds, and the former left fifty pounds on his table; and
the exhibition is clearing fifty pounds a week. I may as
well add, for it is to their great honor, that the present subscribers to the "Milo" are the Duke of Wellington, the Duke
of Northumberland, Lord Egremont, Lord Rivers, and Mr.
Sotheby. Mr. Lough is said to be a fine creature, full of simplicity, modesty, and ardor.

[The end of this letter is lost.]

To B. R. HAYDON, ESQ., *Connaught Terrace.*

Friday evening, Sept. 27, 1827.

MY DEAR FRIEND,—I was quite certain when we parted
that the "Mock Election" would be done, and more than
half converted to the belief of its being an excellent subject.

The hold that it has taken of your fancy is almost a pledge for your success. So I have only to say *Vogue la galère.*

I have liked my little garden the better ever since you honored it by your presence—you came among the flowers quite like a sunbeam. I never can see you without feeling assured that you are born for good fortune—born " to leave many people in your debt," as the gypsy woman said. How high has the subscription mounted? If both the " Eucles " and the " Mock Election " sell as they ought, you will have the comfort and blessing of money beforehand—the greatest happiness, I should think, that there is in the world. How large is the King's Bench picture to be? Finish very highly. Humor depends almost wholly on things being clearly made out; and don't care about morality and pathos —stick to fun.

Adieu, my dear friend. Kindest love from all to all. Ever yours,   M. R. MITFORD.

A propos of Art, we have an artist here taking views of the village in order to bring out a series of illustrations of my book. They are to be executed in a newly-invented sort of lithography on transfer paper which is said to have nearly the effect of line engraving, and will, I should think, answer well.

To the REV. WILLIAM HARNESS, *Heathcote Street, London.*

Oct. 16, 1827.

No, my dear friend, I did not write the " Chapters on Churchyards." I am quite ashamed of being ten pounds in Mr. Blackwood's debt—I mean ten pounds' worth of articles; but I firmly mean to pay him the moment " Inez " is put out of hand. If you write to him say so. I have been torn to pieces by the animals, who will have at least twenty articles of mine amongst them. How capital " Reverses "* was ! I don't know when I have been so delighted with any thing. The tone of fashion, and the little air of laughing at fashion even whilst adopting it, were admirable, and you and your books done to the life—only you should not have thought of shooting the Newfoundland. But the conclusion makes amends for all, and is so like your own real manner, that I should have known it for yours any where.

* A tale in " Blackwood's Magazine."

Adieu, my dear friend. Kindest love to dear Mary and to yourself from all. Ever most affectionately yours,

M. R. MITFORD.

1828.

To the REV. WILLIAM HARNESS, *Heathcote Street, London.*

Three-mile Cross, Jan. 6, 1828.

MY DEAR FRIEND,—Have you a mind to see a picture of me which is going to be engraved by Mr. Cousins—young Cousins, who did the print of young Lambton? It will be for the whole of next week at the artist's, Mr. Lucas's, lodgings (No. 3 Newland Terrace, Kensington), and if you should be going that way I really wish you would call and see it. I want your opinion. To me, and to every body here, it seems a really fine work of art, and has an elegance which you are especially likely to value. But I know my own enthusiasm, and am so much caught by the young man's personal character, that I have a laudable distrust of my own judgment, so far as he is concerned. He is only twenty-one, was bound to Reynolds, the engraver, and practiced the art which he was resolved to pursue, secretly, in his own room, and in hours stolen from sleep and needful exercise, and minutes from necessary food. Last July he became his own master, and since then he has regularly painted. Every body almost that sees his pictures desires to sit, and he is already torn to pieces with business. In short, I expect great things of him. But what I especially like is his character. I have seen nothing in all my life more extraordinary than his union of patience and temper and rationality, with a high and ardent enthusiasm. Moreover, my good friend, he puts me exceedingly in mind of you. He has your " Yeses," and " Noes," and your *piano* manner exactly ; and, as far as a young man of one-and-twenty and very thin, can resemble a not thin gentleman a few years older, he is like you in countenance. I want you to meet astonishingly. You will understand that he will be very clever—very. His quickness of observation and nicety of tact surpass all that I have met with. At present he has of course to struggle against an imperfect education, a mind engrossed by

VOL. II.—D

his art, and a delicate sensitiveness which keeps him back
for the moment, but which will blend finely with a firm and
manly character hereafter.

I believe it is having seen so much of Mr. H——'s violence
that leads me so greatly to value the patient ardor (if I may
be allowed such a phrase) of this most amiable young man,
of whom (in the close intimacy which must exist between
the inmates of the same house, in the country, and in winter) I have seen and known so much, and all so good. It is
a woman's delicacy and kindness with a man's spirit and
bravery. He sings exquisitely simple ballads, without ac-
companiment, and with a voice and taste and pathos that
make them equal to the finest recitation (I wonder what a
musical professor would say to such praise—but you know
what I mean)—a dangerous talent for most young men; but
I think he may be trusted, for he has a constitutional tem-
perance that will preserve him from coarse temptations.*

[*The rest is wanting.*]

To B. R. HAYDON, Esq.

[*A Fragment.*]

Three-mile Cross. No date.

History never will sell so well as more familiar and smaller subjects. I want you to try large, merry, rustic groups.
I could make twenty pictures (only that I can neither paint
nor draw), full of fun and incident and character, and with
infinitely more of color and beauty, as well as of grace and
richness in the accessories, than any town scene can have;
a fair, with all its sights and shows; the same at night,
lighted up; a statute or hiring fair, with its pretty lasses and
awkward bumpkins; a Revel—a Maying—Hop-picking—
Harvest Home. These are subjects, in which even daubers
please; they are so genial and so English! Only think
what *you* would make of them!

To Dr. MITFORD, *Old Betty's Coffee-house, behind the new church, Strand.*

Three-mile Cross, Thursday, Feb. 15, 1828.

Nothing, my own dearest, was ever more comfortable and

* Some additional particulars concerning Mr. Lucas will be found in a
letter dated Oct. 27, 1842.

satisfactory than the manner in which you have managed this affair. Pray write to George Whittaker directly. Of course we must not take a farthing less than one hundred and fifty pounds, when we are sure of it from such a respectable quarter as Longman's. I never had the slightest hesitation in my liking for that house, except their name for *closeness;* but certainly this offer is very liberal. You have done the business most excellently—just as I thought you would. God grant you an equal success with the dramatic affair! I am not the least afraid of your management there. I'll never write a play again, for I dare say Longman's people would give a good price for a novel.

If you can without inconvenience, will you bring me a bottle of eau de Cologne? this is a piece of extravagance upon the strength of the fifty pounds; but don't buy any thing else. And pray, my darling, get quit of the dogs. I have had a most delightful letter from Miss North—no letter for you. I suppose the "Belvidera" on Monday night at Covent Garden made no hit, or we should have heard of it—or rather, with a great actress, they would not hesitate an hour about "Inez." We are pretty well; and the gown gets on famously, and will be beautiful. Ever your own,

M. R. M.

[The volume referred to in the next letter was the third volume of "Our Village." A note in the pocket-book of Mrs. Mitford says: "The third volume, taken by Whittaker at one hundred and thirty pounds, which Mr. Orme, with unheard-of-generosity makes up to one hundred and fifty pounds—one hundred in the course of this month and fifty within two months."]

From G. B. WHITTAKER *to* Dr. MITFORD, *Old Betty's Coffee-house, Strand.*

Manchester, Feb. 22.

MY DEAR SIR,—You will perceive by a letter annexed for Miss M. that although distant I was not forgetful. That was written with an intention on Tuesday next to forward it with other letters to London in a parcel; and, on my arrival here this afternoon, I lose no time in sending it by a parcel in hopes of saving Saturday night's London mail, as none from here could reach you until Tuesday.

I am willing to do what is correct, and shall not, from correctness of principle, let the next volume slip through my hands. My only motive for not saying yes to your offer is that, owing to my present circumstances, I wish to make a calculation, and also to make an arrangement with some friend to carry the thing into effect, and which I shall have no difficulty in doing. I have now clearer prospects before me than when I last saw you. Believe me yours very truly,

G. B. WHITTAKER.

P.S.—Be easy on the subject.

N.B.—If they had told you Liverpool instead of Manchester, an answer would have been sent by return of post.

To the REV. WILLIAM HARNESS, *Heathcote Street.*

Three-mile Cross, Monday, March 31, 1828.

They say in the papers that there is a Miss B—— learning to be an actress at the manager's expense. I confess that it seems to me a sad blow on the respectability of that profession of which Mrs. Siddons was once the ornament. If actresses are bad, no manager can help it; but to take pains to turn a bad woman into an actress is another matter. I hope this announcement is a mere newspaper report. They say that she was brought up to be a rich man's mistress, upon sale, unhappy wretch! like a Georgian woman—and did live with somebody or other. Now *can* such a person as that think and feel as a high tragic actress ought to do? Honor, virtue, fidelity, love must be worse than words to her; she must have been used to consider them as things to spurn and laugh at. Besides, they say that she is as impudent in look and air as her sister.

Adieu, my very dear friend. Kindest regards from my father and mother to yourself, and dear Mary. Ever most faithfully yours, M. R. MITFORD.

To DR. MITFORD, *Old Betty's Coffee-house, Strand.*

Wednesday, April 17, 1828.

MY DEAR FATHER,—I can not bear this suspense. I have written to Mr. Kemble to say that I shall be in town to-morrow at half-past twelve, and will drive immediately to Soho Square—where, if he can not see me then, I have requested

him to leave word when and·where he will see me.   I only
wish I had done this last Thursday.

Mamma is still mending.   No news whatever.   God bless
you, my dearest!   Ever your own,   M. R..MITFORD.

I shall come by the seven o'clock coach.   Of course you
will meet me in Piccadilly.

To B. R. HAYDON, ESQ., 4 *Burwood Place, Edgware Road.*

Three-mile Cross, Tuesday, April 22, 1828.

A thousand and a thousand congratulations, my dear friend,
to you and your loveliest and sweetest wife!   I always liked
the king, God bless him!   He is a gentleman—and now my
loyalty will be warmer than ever.   What has he given for
the picture?*   Where is it to be?   This is fortune—fame you
did not want—but this is fashion and fortune.   Nothing in
this world could please me more—not even the production
of my own "Rienzi."   To see you in your place in Art, and
Talfourd in his in Parliament, are the wishes next my heart,
and I verily believe that I shall live to see both.   Are you
likely to know the king personally?   If you are, I'm sure
you'll take his fancy.   How should you like to be "Sir Benjamin?"   *She* would become the "Lady," would she not?

God bless you, my dear friends!   And God save the
king!   M. R. MITFORD.

My father and mother are as happy and as loyal as I am.
Once again, Long live the king!   Thank you so much for
letting me know.

To SIR WILLIAM ELFORD, *Washbourne House, Totnes.*

Three-mile Cross, Sept. 23, 1828.

MY DEAR FRIEND,—My tragedy of " Rienzi " is to be produced at Drury Lane Theatre on Saturday, the 11th of October; that is to say, next Saturday fortnight.   Mr. Young
plays the hero, and has been studying the part during the
whole vacation; and a new actress makes her first appearance
in the part of the heroine.   This is a very bold and hazardous
experiment, no new actress having come out in a new play
within the memory of man; but she is young, pretty, unaffected, pleasant-voiced, with great sensibility, and a singularly
pure intonation—a qualification which no actress has possess-

* "The Mock Election."

ed since Mrs. Siddons. Stanfield* is painting the new scenes, one of which is an accurate representation of Rienzi's house. This building still exists in Rome, and is shown there as a curious relique of the domestic architecture of the Middle Ages. They have got a sketch which they sent for on purpose, and they are hunting up costumes with equal care; so that it will be very splendidly brought out, and I shall have little to fear, except from the emptiness of London so early in the season. If you know any one likely to be in that great desert so early in the year, I know that you will be so good as to mention me and my tragedy. I do not yet know where I shall be. I think of going to town in about a fortnight, and, if the play succeeds, shall remain there about the same time.

Adieu! Ever very affectionately yours,

M. R. MITFORD.

To SIR WILLIAM ELFORD, *Washbourne House, Totnes.*

London, Oct. 5, 1828. }
5 Great Queen Street, Lincoln's Inn. }

MY DEAR FRIEND,—Our success last night was very splendid,† and we have every hope (in the theatrical world there is no such word as "certainty") of making a great hit. As far as things have hitherto gone, nothing can be better—nothing. Our new actress‡ is charming. We shall not keep her long, for she'll be in the peerage before two years are over, and is just fit for such a destiny both in mind and manner. Mr. Young is also admirable; and, in short, it is a magnificent performance throughout. God grant that its prosperity may continue, and these are not words, of course, but a prayer from my inmost soul, for on that hangs the comfort of those far dearer to me than myself.

Your last letter was delightful to me in every way—quite delightful—full of heart and head and youthfulness. I am proud of your good opinion, my dear Sir William, but prouder still of the kind mistake by which you are led to overrate me.

Make my very best and kindest love to both your daughters, and forgive my mistakes and blunders. I have twenty

---

* He first came into notice as a scene painter.
† The first performance of "Rienzi."
‡ Miss Phillips.

people in the room at this moment, all talking, not to each other, but to me.   God bless you all!   Ever most faithfully yours,   M. R. MITFORD.

To the REV. WILLIAM HARNESS, *Heathcote Street, Mecklen-burgh Square.*

5 Great Queen Street, Lincoln's Inn, Oct. 13, 1828.

MY DEAR FRIEND,—After consulting Mr. Talfourd and (between ourselves) Mr. Young, I have finally *determined* not to let "Inez" be done at Covent Garden at present, and accordingly I have dispatched a note, of which the following is a copy, to Charles Kemble:

"MY DEAR SIR,—Having heard from our mutual friend Mr. Harness that you some days ago expressed to him a wish to produce 'Inez de Castro' at Covent Garden, I think it right to tell you frankly and at once that, with reference to my own future prospects and the state of both theatres, it is my desire that that play should not be performed at present at either—that it should, in short, lie by for a while."

Now I hope I have not committed a breach of confidence in this.   If I have, forgive me.

Miss Phillips *is* only sixteen — was born in 1812; and really, when one remembers that, she is very wonderful, and of very great promise indeed.   Kindest love to all of you. Ever most faithfully yours,   ·   M. R. MITFORD.

To SIR WILLIAM ELFORD, *Washbourne House, Totnes.*

Three-mile Cross, Monday, Oct. 20, 1828.

MY DEAR FRIEND,—I seize the very first moment after my return home to thank you for your most kind and gratifying letter.   "Kind" is too cold a phrase; both yours and your daughter's had a glow of affection in them which went to my very heart.   Tell her how sincerely I thank and bless you both.

Hitherto the triumph has been most complete and decis-ive—the houses crowded—and the attention such as has not been known since Mrs. Siddons.   You might hear a pin drop in the house.   How long the run may continue I can not say, for London is absolutely empty; but even if the play were to stop to-night, I should be extremely thankful—

more thankful than I have words to tell; the impression has
been so deep and so general. You should have been in London, or seen the newspapers as a whole, to judge of the exceedingly strong sensation that has been produced by the
tragedy.

I breakfasted one day with your friend Mr. Jones, who
spoke of you with warm regard. He is painting a very fine
naval battle—that incident of the battle of St. Vincent where
Lord Nelson boarded one ship over the deck of another. It
will be very splendid; but I prefer his "Esther"—which is
full of expression and beauty and mind, as well as color—to
any thing that I have ever seen of his. He is a very elegant
and delightful person.

Adieu, my very dear friend. My father and mother join
in all that is truest and kindest, and I am always and unal-
terably your affectionate friend,   M. R. MITFORD.

To the REV. WILLIAM HARNESS, *Heathcote Street, London.*
Wednesday, Oct. 22, 1828.

MY DEAR FRIEND,—All that you say of "Rienzi" is deeply gratifying to me. Mr. Dyce's approbation is a very high
honor; and I had sooner be praised by you than by any body
under the sun—my oldest friend, and the person with whose
taste mine has always had all the accordance that is compatible
with frankness, independence, and individuality. I had rather
you liked my play than any body. It is selling immensely,
the first very large edition having gone in three days.

I am very glad that Mrs. D—— and Dora have called on
dear Mary; love her they must, and she will love them—
they are so good, so true, such gentle women, and have always been so very kind to me. Besides, they speak good
English, which Mary says is a rarity in your quarter. Kindest love to you all. How very quick and clever Henry is!
Love from all to all. Ever most affectionately yours,
M. R. MITFORD.

To the REV. ALEXANDER DYCE, *Welbeck Street, ·Cavendish*
Square.
Three-mile Cross, near Reading, Oct. 27, 1828.

MY DEAR SIR,—Accept my very sincere thanks for your
kind letter and your delightful books, which would have been

most valuable to me even if I had not the additional gratification of receiving them from the editor, and of reckoning him amongst my acquaintance—may I say, amongst my friends? I am sure his kindness gives me cause to think him such.

Of Peele I have only yet read "The Old Wives' Tale," a most striking and imaginative drama, and doubly interesting when one considers the impression that it must have made on Milton. Was his imitation of that play, and of "The Faithful Shepherdess," conscious or not? "That is the question," and a very curious question it is. A critic would answer "Yes!" at once; a poet, who knows how strongly memory and invention are intertwined and interwoven, would hesitate. Any way, all lovers of high poetry are much indebted to you for the reprint. I must just say that it is the only edition of old plays that I have ever seen in which the notes are a positive good; generally they are a positive evil.

The authoress book is quite delightful;* not only for the various specimens preserved from scarce works, but for the taste and candor of the latest selections, and of the characters of the writers. For instance, you are the only man I ever met with who did full justice to Charlotte Smith's fine and close observation of nature. Both her prose and her verse are full of nice and delicate touches of landscape painting; and, as far as trees and flowers are concerned, she has a mastery of the subject, and a truth and vividness of expression, second only to Cowper.

May I trouble you to let Mr. Harness have the inclosed letter? There is no hurry about it at all. I take it for granted that two persons so well suited to each other meet frequently. And it is only to thank him for a fresh demonstration of the kindness which he has been showing me all his life long. But you know William Harness!

If ever you pass near us I trust that you will honor our poor cottage by a call. Ever, my dear sir, very sincerely yours,   M. R. Mitford.

To B. R. Haydon, Esq., *Buckwood Place, Edgware Road.*

Sunday, Nov. 3, 1828.

My dear Friend,—I am now going to tell you something which I earnestly hope will neither vex nor displease you;

* "Selections from the Female Poets," by the Rev. A. Dyce.

D 2

if it do I shall grieve most heartily—but I do not think that it will. The patron of a young artist of great merit (Mr. Lucas) has made a most earnest request that I will sit to him. The picture is for a friend who wants one. He comes here to paint it—and there is a double view; first to get two or three people hereabout to sit to him; next to do him good in London, by having in the Exhibition the portrait of a person whose name will probably induce people to look at it, and bring the painting into notice. The manner in which this was pressed upon me by a friend to whom I owe great gratitude was such as I really could not refuse—especially as it can by no accident be injurious to your splendid reputation, that an ugly face which you happen to have taken, should be copied by another. There is a project of having the portrait engraved, which would increase the benefit that they anticipate to Mr. Lucas, and would be so far satisfactory to us, as it would supersede a villainous print out of some magazine, from a drawing of Miss Drummond's, which is now selling in the shops.

I have not yet been in Reading, but I hope to see the boys soon. I wish Simon were at sea, for school is a sad expensive place. The carelessness you speak of is quite characteristic of a sailor. God bless you all, my very dear friends! Ever most sincerely yours,   M. R. M.

To the REV. WILLIAM HARNESS, *Heathcote Street.*

Three-mile Cross, Saturday, Nov. 17, 1828.

MY DEAR FRIEND,—I am going to write another play, on a German story—a man under the ban of the Empire and succored by his daughter. I took the notion from a faint recollection of a play called "Otto of Wittelsbach." According to my recollection, there is no daughter in the German play, and I believe that my piece will be altogether different —though I should like to see the old "Otto."

Marianne Skerritt once thought of writing a tragedy on the subject, and her programme, which she sent me, is quite unlike both, and would take, I should think, a week in acting. Her first act had ten long scenes! There's an old German story-book, called "The Emperor Philip and his Daughters," which also tells the same history, with variations; for there Otto is represented as a very young man. But that I have not seen either. I suppose it will end in my working up the story as well as I can in my own way. William Farren is to have a principal part at Mr. Young's especial desire, and I believe at his own.

Adieu, my very dear friend. My father and mother join in all that is kindest to you and Mary—and I am always most gratefully yours, M. R. MITFORD.

To SIR WILLIAM ELFORD, *Washbourne, Totnes.*

Three-mile Cross, Dec. 16, 1828. (My birthday.)

Thinking over those whom I love and those who have been kind to me, as one does on these annual occasions, it occurred to me, my dear friend, that I had most unkindly checked your warm-hearted interest in my doings. I was very busy —not quite well—and overwhelmed, beyond any thing that can be conceived, by letters and visits of congratulation. I am now quite well again; and though still with much to do —much that I ought to have done to make up—yet, having fairly stemmed the tide of formal compliments, I steal a moment to tell you and your dear circle that "Rienzi" continues prosperous. It has passed the twentieth night, which, you know, insures the payment of four hundred pounds from the theatre (the largest price that any play can gain); and the sale of the tragedy has been so extraordinary, that I am told the fourth edition is nearly exhausted—which, as the publisher told me each edition would consist of at least two thousand, makes a circulation of eight thousand copies in two months. You may imagine that I am heartily thankful for this success.

Did you ever see or hear of Mr. Haydon's portrait of me? It was so exaggerated, both in size and color, that none of my friends could endure it. My father declared he would not have it home, and I believe it is now quite demolished. We are not the less good friends, for certainly he did not mean to produce a caricature; but such I believe it was. This gave me an aversion to the idea of sitting for a portrait; but we have been prevailed upon to suffer a young artist of high talent (a Mr. Lucas) to paint me. He was to have taken me a month ago; but I was so poorly at that time that I could not sit. So we introduced him to some friends of ours, who sat to him; and his pictures of them are so fine, and sitting for one's portrait is so catching, that I am quite sure he may, if he pleases, paint half Berkshire.

Have you read Mr. Smith, of the Museum's, "Life and Times of Nolleken's," the sculptor? It is a strange slip-slop style; but the matter is entertaining, and would be interesting to you who have lived so much amongst artists.

God bless you, my very dear friend! All good wishes, of this season and of every season, to you all. Kindest regards from my father and mother. Ever most affectionately yours,

M. R. MITFORD.

To SIR WILLIAM ELFORD, *Washbourne House, Totnes.*

Three-mile Cross, Dec. 26, 1828.

The payment of which you speak* has been done away with these thirty years; and the sum that I have received is probably the largest given to any tragic author during the present century. I have no reason to complain. The play has been most eminently successful, and will undoubtedly be a stock piece. Heaven grant I may ever do as well again! I shall have hard work to write up to my own reputation, for certainly I am at present greatly overrated.

Now for my young artist. I should greatly have wondered, my dear Sir William, if you had heard of him, for he has only just sprung to light. He is not a Berkshire man. He became known to me through a mutual friend—Mr. Milton, of the War Office—author of a very clever work on the pictures in the Louvre, and one of the best judges of art in England. He fell in with young Lucas, employed him to paint two of his own children (twins), and was so enchanted with the portrait, that he immediately determined to make me sit to him, by way of bringing him into notice. Mr. Milton is a lively, agreeable, enthusiastic person, who always carries things his own way; and, being sure that he would not propose an inadequate artist, I consented. Accordingly Mr. Lucas arrived to paint me. On that very morning, however, I was taken ill; and, instead of bringing him here, my father (who had gone to Reading to meet him) conveyed him to the house of a friend in the neighborhood, who wished for portraits of some of his family, hoping that by the time

* The old mode of paying dramatic authors in the last century, which was, the entire receipt of the house for the third, sixth, and ninth nights.

they were done I might be well enough to sit. Whilst there he painted two portraits—one of a venerable clergyman of seventy-six, the other of a lovely woman of twenty-eight; and then, I being still too unwell to sit, he was obliged to return to town to fulfill some other engagements. Last Monday he returned here; and in that time, such was the sensation caused by his previous pictures, that almost every one who had seen them wished to be portrayed by the same hand. At present, however, he only means to do my friend, the wife of the old clergyman, and myself. He will return in the summer to take Mr. Walter's (of the "Times") children; and, I hope and believe, *our* friend, Lady Madalina, and one or two other people of connection and consequence. But you may depend upon it that he is not likely to prove a provincial painter. London is his place, and that you will find. Several judges have seen these pictures—amongst them Mr. Barnes, the editor of the "Times;" and every body feels assured that this young man (he is only one-and-twenty) will be eminent in his art. There is nothing wild, or odd, or eccentric, or over-ambitious about his paintings. They are carefully finished, firmly painted, charmingly colored, and the strongest and pleasantest likenesses that I ever beheld. There is an ease about them—"a masterly *handling*" (I think that is the painter's phrase)—that is equivalent to great fluency of style and felicity of phrase in writing. When you look at them they seem so natural, so alive, that it is more like looking at a face in a looking-glass than one in a picture. My portrait, on which he is depending so very much, will be a great contrast with the cook-maid thing of poor dear Mr. Haydon. I have given him three very long sittings; and I think you will like it, though even the head is not finished yet. I am sure that you will like the style of the picture, which is exceedingly graceful and lady-like. It is of the kit-kat size, dressed in a high black gown and Vandyke collar, and a black velvet hat with white feathers—younger and fairer than I am, certainly, but, they say, very like. My father says so; and I am sure that to his fondness no flattery would compensate for the absence of likeness.

I earnestly hope we may meet in the spring. Most affectionately yours,   M. R. MITFORD.

CHAPTER V.

Letters for 1829.

To Sir William Elford, *Washbourne, Totnes.*

Three-mile Cross, Jan. 7, 1829.

A THOUSAND and a thousand thanks, my dear friend, for your most kind and cordial letter. I have told Mr. Lucas your kind order for a proof of the print,* which he will transmit to Mr. Cousins. The portrait, now just finished, is said by every body to be a very splendid work of art. It is certainly a most graceful and elegant picture—a very fine piece of color, and, they say, a very strong likeness. It was difficult, in painting me, to steer between the Scylla and Charybdis of making me dowdy, like one of my own rustic heroines, or dressed out like a tragedy queen. He has managed the matter with infinite taste, and given to the whole figure the look of a quiet gentlewoman. I never saw a more lady-like picture. The dress is a black velvet hat, with a long, drooping black feather; a claret-colored high gown; and a superb open cloak of gentianella blue, the silvery fur and white satin lining of which are most exquisitely painted, and form one of the most beautiful pieces of drapery that can be conceived. The face is thoughtful and placid, with the eyes looking away—a peculiarity which, they say, belongs to my expression.

He will be exceedingly clever generally, as well as in his art. I caution him (am I not right?) against two perils, matrimony and historical painting. He must neither fall in love nor paint history until he has made money enough by portraits to afford the indulgence. He is at present full of employment, and has a copy to make of my portrait for a female friend, in addition to his other commissions.

Adieu, my very dear friend. All the good wishes of this season, and of every season, to you and yours. Ever your faithful and affectionate friend,   M. R. MITFORD.

* The print of Miss Mitford, from Lucas's portrait.

To the REV. WILLIAM HARNESS.

Three-mile Cross, 3 o'clock Sunday morning, }
Jan. 19, 1829. }

MY DEAR FRIEND,—Three hours ago I received your book, my father, who dined at Coley, having brought it from Mr. Milman; and I have since read it through—the second part twice through. That second sermon would have done honor to Shakspeare, and I half expected to find you quoting him. There would be a tacit hypocrisy, a moral cowardice, if I were to stop here, and not to confess, what I think you must suspect, although by no chance do I ever talk about it—that I do not, or rather can not, believe all that the Church requires. I humbly hope that it is not necessary to do so, and that a devout sense of the mercy of God, and an endeavor, however imperfectly and feebly, to obey the great precepts of justice and kindness, may be accepted in lieu of that entire faith which, in me, *will not* be commanded. You will not suspect me of thoughtlessness in this matter; neither, I trust, does it spring from intellectual pride. Few persons have a deeper sense of their own weakness; few, indeed, can have so much weakness of character to deplore and to strive against.

Do not answer this part of my letter. It has cost me a strong effort to say this to you; but it would have been a concealment amounting to a falsity if I had not, and falsehood must be wrong. Do not notice it; a correspondence of controversy could only end in alienation, and I could not afford to lose my oldest and kindest friend—to break up the close intimacy in which I am so happy and of which I am so proud. Do not notice what I have said, and yet write soon. There is no cause why you should not. I occasion no scandal either by opinions or by conduct. The clergyman of our parish and his family are my most intimate friends. They render me their kindest services, their truest sympathy, and —which is more, far more—they ask for my poor service and my honest sympathy when they are in difficulty or in affliction. Write very soon—of any thing or every thing—of the bar, of the empire, of my picture, or of my young friend, Mr. Lucas. By the way, the picture will be with him all next week. I have been interrupted, and the postman is at the door. Ever yours,   M. R. MITFORD.

To SIR WILLIAM ELFORD, *Washbourne House, Totnes.*

Tuesday, March 2, 1829.

MY DEAR FRIEND,—You must forgive a short note in answer to your very kind and very delightful letter. I fear that, unless at Somerset House, where I hope it will find a place, my picture can not be visible this year. Mr. Lucas made me promise not to ask admission to Mr. Cousins's, even for myself. The reason is, that Sir Thomas Lawrence makes a great mystery of those pictures of his, which Mr. Cousins is engraving; does not like the prints in hand to be known or talked about until they come out; and therefore, for fear of offending him, Mr. Lucas particularly wishes no application to be made for entrance to Mr. Cousins's engraving-room. He says that Sir Thomas is at once so particular about this concealment, and yet so unwilling for people to know of this secrecy, which he insists upon, that an engraver who works for him has the most difficult course to steer that is possible. Of course I must beg you not mention this to him or to any one. It is a hundred to one but, if in town, you will be there at the time of the Exhibition, and then you would, of course, see the picture at the Royal Academy—in company, I hope, with the landscape, which I rejoice to hear you are painting.

I do not myself think that I shall be in town this year, having finally decided that I can not, without undue haste, complete my tragedy for this season. . . . I am delighted at this affair* of the Catholics; it will be a means of pacification in Ireland, and every where, when once the question is settled.

Kindest regards to all from all here. Ever, my dear friend, most affectionately yours,   M. R. MITFORD.

To the REV. WILLIAM HARNESS, *Heathcote Street, London.*

Three-mile Cross, Tuesday, May 20, 1829.

Once again, my dear friend, a thousand thanks for your great and constant kindness. Pray come and see us as soon as you can, and stay as long. Come on Monday morning, and stay till Saturday afternoon, as you do at Deepdene; and be sure and come *soon*, or *they* will be in the country,

* Emancipation.

and we shall have no chance. I really think that you would
not dislike our poor cottage; or, rather, I am sure that you .
would like my garden, where we live now all day, having
got the great comfort of a long, cool, dark shed on one side
—a sort of rustic arcade—and a light, sunny, cheerful room
which serves for a winter greenhouse and a summer parlor
on the other. And there is a clean, airy room at the little inn
opposite, at which my little artist felt himself very comfortable, and with which Miss James herself was satisfied.

I have been exceedingly worried by Mr. Haydon, who has
taken some affront at I know not what, and sent me a message a month ago to say that a print from *his* portrait of me
would be out in a day or two. This, if it had been so, would
have been most shameful, inasmuch as he knew, before my
sitting to Mr. Lucas, that I meant to do so for the purpose
of an engraving. I told him myself, and hoped he would
not be offended, and he said not at all, and that he should be
glad to be of use to Mr. Lucas, or of any service to the print
—for which civility I duly thanked him; so that his message
appears incredible. I wrote to tell him so, begging him, at
the same time, to let me know; and at the end of a few days
wrote again to the same effect. He has not thought proper
to answer either letter. But, as I hear no announcement of
such a print, and as the principal printsellers know nothing
of it, I begin to think that it is merely a coarse and ill-natured joke. If he had had the picture engraved, it would
have worried me much, not merely because it is unpleasant
to have a disagreeable portrait multiplied and perpetuated,
but on account of our very amiable young friend, who has
taken so much pains with *his* picture, and to whom I hope
the sale of the print will be of some advantage. I could not
help telling you this grievance, but pray don't mention it,
for that might make Mr. Haydon do the thing.

Pray don't forget to come to us. It will be such a treat!
I'll try if Mr. Milman will meet you here some day at dinner; I should think he would not refuse. And you must let
us know the day and the hour when you come, that my
father may meet you in Reading—for we have an old gig
and an old horse, and can take you about. You don't know
how often I have longed to press you to come to us, but have
always been afraid; you are used to things so much better,

and I thought you would find it dull; but now I really think that the calm and the country will pass us off—and it will be so great a treat, so great a comfort!

Kind regards from my father and mother to you and to dear Mary. Ever yours,   M. R. MITFORD.

To SIR WILLIAM ELFORD, *Washbourne House, Totnes, Devonshire.*

Three-mile Cross, May 29, 1829.

MY DEAR FRIEND,—Your last delightful letter was just as convincing a proof to me as your picture was to Mrs. Jones, that age only mellows the strong rich wine of your fancy. You are *young*, my dear Sir William, in spite of the register, and long may you continue so!

You will be glad to hear that "Rienzi" has been received rapturously all over America. No play, I am told, has ever produced such an effect there. I gain nothing by this; but one likes that sort of rebound of reputation—that traveling along with the language. I suppose the republican sentiments had something to do with it. . . . I hope soon to be able to resume my labors, which have necessarily been suspended: but I am still very nervous and languid, and quite unfit for the work which I must do. It is very strange that, ever since my great success, I have been more than ever low-spirited. But this I *must* conquer, and I will try to do so, and hope to succeed.

Adieu, my very dear and kind friend. Most faithfully yours,   M. R. MITFORD.

To the REV. WILLIAM HARNESS, *Heathcote Street, London.*

Three-mile Cross, June 20, 1829.

MY DEAR FRIEND,—There is nothing I would not do to assist Mr. Cathcart* in his difficulties. He is a man of genius, and worthy in every respect. If he thinks, and you think, that I can be of service to him, I will go to London, see Mr. Price, and do all that I can to forward his wishes. But—to you—I confess that this measure would be attended with great personal difficulty. My father—very kind to me in many respects, very attentive if I'm ill, very solicitous that my garden should be nicely kept, that I should go out with

* An actor of whom Miss Mitford entertained a high opinion.

him, and be amused—is yet, so far as art, literature, and the
drama are concerned, of a temper infinitely difficult to deal
with. He hates and despises them, and all their professors—
looks on them with hatred and scorn; and is constantly
taunting me with my "friends" and my "people" (as he
calls them), reproaching me if I hold the slightest intercourse
with author, editor, artist, or actor, and treating with frank
contempt every one not of a certain station in the county.
I am entirely convinced that he would consider Sir Thomas
Lawrence, Sir Walter Scott, and Mrs. Siddons as his inferiors.
Always this is very painful—strangely painful; but sometimes, in the case of the sweet young boy Lucas, for instance,
and in this of Mr. Cathcart, it becomes really hard to bear.

Since I have known Mr. C. I can say with truth that he has
never spoken to me or looked at me without ill-humor;
sometimes taunting and scornful—sometimes more harsh
than you could fancy. Now, he ought to remember that it
is not for my own pleasure, but from a sense of duty, that I
have been thrown in the way of these persons; and he should
allow for the natural sympathy of similar pursuits and the
natural wish to do the little that one so poor and powerless
can do to bring merit (and that of a very high order) into
notice. It is one of the few alleviations of a destiny that is
wearing down my health and mind and spirits and strength
—a life spent in efforts above my powers, and which will end
in the work-house or in a Bedlam, as the body or the mind
shall sink first. He ought to feel this; but he does not.

I beg your pardon for vexing you with this detail. I do
not often indulge in such repining. But I meant to say that
it will be a scene and an effort to get to town for this purpose. Nevertheless, *if you think I could do good I would
most assuredly go.* God bless you! Ever yours,

M. R. M.

To the REV. WILLIAM HARNESS.

Three-mile Cross, Thursday, Sept., 1829.

MY DEAR FRIEND,—I need not, I hope, tell you how delighted we shall be to see you at the time proposed, or at any
time, and for as long as your own convenience or your own inclination may induce you to give us the pleasure of your company. My mother, whom few things touch now, is particu-

larly pleased. I lament only that my garden will have lost
its bloom and the days their length. But you must try us
now at our worst; and then, if you like us, come next summer, when the roses and the sun may make us more tempting. You can not think how deeply I feel your kindness in
coming at all.

I have got the " Bann of the Empire "—the real words in
German and English; and, after the great chain of literary
connection that has been set in motion on this question, the
libraries that have been ransacked, the German historians and
law professors that have been written to, the document has
been discovered and sent to me by a Westminster school-boy!
Perhaps you know his mother, and I am indebted after all for
it to you. She is a Mrs. Hutchinson Simpson, living at Frog-
nal, Hampstead, and the youth, my friend, is her only child
by a former husband, a boy of the name of Cotton.* Do you
know them? The letters both of mother and son (of whom
I never heard before) are very interesting; hers, especially,
remind me much of Mrs. Hemans. The lad heard that I
wanted the document from "a friend," and sent me first the
Ecclesiastical Bann which he found in a French book. When
I told him, with many thanks, that that was not the thing
wanted, he set about learning German, and, by the help of a
Saxon friend, who was recently drowned in the Ganges, has
actually sent me the undiscoverable prize, as I have told you.
We shall hear of that youth himself in literature some day
or other. In the mean while I am more touched and pleased
by the interest which he has evinced in the matter than I
have ever been by any compliment in my life. Is it not
striking and interesting?

After I have finished this detestable play (which is as yet
sadly little advanced, I feeling within myself the certainty—
though I must not say so—that Young can't act it)—when
I have done this job I have another affair in contemplation
that I must have some talk with you about. Do you know
Mr. Jephson's plays? They are now so scarce that even his
grand-niece, Emily Jephson, has only seen three of them. She
is a very particular friend of mine, and has been staying for
some weeks about twelve miles off with Lady Sunderland

* George Edward Lynch Cotton; he became Bishop of Calcutta, and was
recently drowned in the Ganges.

and Miss Malone, the sister-in-law and sister of Edmund Malone, your brother editor of Shakspeare. We have ferreted out an immense number of Mr. Jephson's letters amongst Mr. Malone's papers, and find that there is a MS. play—a translation of Metastatio's "Vitellia," with a new last act—which we have no doubt of finding amongst Mr. Jephson's own papers, as well as other letters and *jeux d'esprit* (he being a man of great wit and living amongst the highest people, English and Irish), and Emily wants me to get up an edition of his dramatic works and some of the letters, and a critical and biographical preface, and so forth. Certainly I should like any fair opportunity of putting forth my own notions on the drama; the object which has employed my thoughts during my whole lifetime, and which I have never yet seen treated to my satisfaction.

Among the letters there is a most diverting quarrel between Jephson and Horace Walpole about the placing a statue on the stage in the representation of the "Count de Narbonne." The author, being in Dublin, had unluckily left to Mr. Walpole the charge of bringing out the play. Horace, with his antiquarianism, had laid the statue sprawling on its back on a tomb, instead of having it standing upright in the middle of the scene, to the utter ruin of the poor dramatist's *effect* and the great benefit of his correspondence; for I think the three or four letters about that subject are the most natural, characteristic, and comical that I ever read in my life. You must remember Mr. Jephson. He was a furious Anti-Jacobin, wrote a fine poem called "Roman Portraits," and a book called "The Confessions of Jean Baptiste Couteau," in ridicule of the French Republicans. Our plan is as yet only in embryo, but I thought you would like to hear of it. Ever most gratefully and affectionately yours,

M. R. MITFORD.

To the Rev. WILLIAM HARNESS, *Heathcote Street, London.*

Three-mile Cross, Sept. 9, 1829.

MY DEAR FRIEND,—We have had a sad check in the Jephson correspondence. Emily's chief reliance for materials was on a Mr. Baker (his nephew), whose address she had lost, but whom she was sure of getting at through their mutual friend Mr. Luttrell. Mr. Luttrell, in answer to her letter, says

that, six weeks ago, Mr. Baker died suddenly of apoplexy,
and that he can not point out any one likely to give us the
information we require. This is very shocking. Perhaps I
like Mr. Jephson's poetry the better from being so very fond
of his grand-niece, who is one of the most cultivated women
that I have ever known, with a sweetness and simplicity of
character, a charm of mind and manner, which really makes
one forget how very clever she is.   She is pretty, too, about
seven-and-twenty, well-born, well-connected, quite independent, and with four hundred a year; in short, after all my dis-
clamations of match-making, I very sincerely wish that Emily
Jephson were your wife. This wish (although a great compliment to your reverence) is the more absurd, as she was
going out of the neighborhood before you were expected in
it, and lives generally between Bath and Ireland; so that
you are not at all likely to meet anywhere but in my imagination.

I think more highly of Mr. Jephson's plays than you do,
perhaps, because I prefer *eloquence* in the drama to poetry,
and because I set a higher value on situation and effect.
Just look at the effects of Shakspeare, the great master of
dramatic situation, and tell me if they be not the finest parts
of the plays in which they occur; the play scene in "Hamlet"—the banquet scene in "Macbeth"—the quarrel in
"Julius Cæsar"—the trial in the "Merchant of Venice;"—
what are these but effects? And in what do they depart
from Nature and from pathos? It is all very well for those
who can not write acting tragedies to declaim against situation; but rely upon it that the thing is an essential part
of the drama in its very highest sense. The Greek tragedies are full of situation; so is Alfieri—so is Schiller—so is
Corneille—so are all the greatest tragic writers of all nations.

Of course I don't mean processions and pageants—the trash
of Reynolds or the bombast of Morton; but such effects as
arise from story and construction, skillful surprises and unexpectedness of fortune. One might as well exclude contrast
from painting as effect from the drama. There is no little
cant in the contempt for situation which infests the criticism
of the day, and I think that you are in some measure caught
by it. Tell me more of young Cotton. How old is he?

And ask, if you see him, in what book he found the "Bann."
God bless you, my dear friend! Ever yours,

M. R. MITFORD.

To Miss Jephson, *Binfield Park.*

Three-mile Cross, Friday night,
Oct. 3, 1829.

My own dear Emily,—A thousand thanks for the nativity.
You shall have it safe back. I think that I should like a copy
of Lord Inchiquin's letter. Harriet Palmer and I (both a sort
of believers, she almost quite, I a *demi-semi* kind of convert)
are going to copy the horoscope; and I (don't tell) have prevailed on Clarke—as great an adept in judicial astrology as
John Dryden himself—to cast my nativity, and am going to
send to our friend, the fat woman ·of Seven Dials, to get me
an ephemeris (White's London Almanac) for the year 1788,
on the 16th of December, in which year, at a quarter before
ten at night, I had the honor to be born. You shall hear the
result. Harriet wanted hers to be done, but Clarke refused
point blank, and is only tempted into doing mine ·by the
knowledge that my life has been one of vicissitudes, and will
bring his science to the test.

Would Lady Sunderland, do you think, like a plant of the
variegated jessamine, and some seed (if I can get any this
wet season) of the new snapdragon? If so, I will get her
certainly 'the one, and if possible the other. And will you
come and fetch them?

Dash has nearly been killed to-day, poor fellow! He got
into a rabbit-burrow so far that he could neither move backward nor forward; and my father, two men, and a boy, were
all busy digging for upward of two hours, in a heavy rain, to
get him out. They had to penetrate through a high bank,
with nothing to guide them but the poor dog's moans. You
never saw any one so full of gratitude, or so sensible of what
his master has done for him, as he is. He is quite recovered,
and has been sitting all the evening with his head leaning
against my father's knee, looking up in his face with eyes full
of such expression! My father was wet to the skin; but I
am sure he would have dug till this time rather than any
living creature, much less his own favorite dog, should have
perished so miserably. I really wish you could have seen

Dash's manner of expressing his gratitude. He is an animal of great sagacity at all times, and also of great sensibility.

Adieu, my own very dear friend. Pray come and see us again. Ever your affectionate, M. R. MITFORD.

To MISS JEPHSON, *Binfield Park.*

Three-mile Cross, Oct. 16, 1829.

Ten minutes after you were gone, I recollected, dearest, that it was Peele's poems you were to take home, for the sake of the "Old Wife's Tale"—the original of "Comus." I'll bring them on Tuesday, with another book edited by the same friend, Mr. Dyce, and which contains a poem that I wish you to see, by a Lady Winchilsea of a hundred years ago. I hope I shan't forget this.

I have been dining to-day at Calcot Park, where I met Dr. Routh, the President of Maudlin. He has a spaniel of King Charles's breed, who, losing his mamma by accident when a pup, was brought up by a cat. (N.B.—The identical cat belongs to the park and was present at the dinner to-day, *assisting* at the ceremony, according to both idioms, French and English.) Well; he and his brother (for there were two pups, orphans of three days old, and they are called Romulus and Remus) were nursed by this cat; and Romulus belongs to the Doctor, who has no children, and makes a great pet of it. But what I mentioned him to you for, is, to tell you the curious account which the Doctor (a man of perfect veracity) gives of his habits. He is as afraid of rain as his foster-mother; will never, if possible to avoid it, set his paw in a wet place; licks his feet two or three times a day, for the purpose of washing his face, which operation he performs in the true cattish position, sitting up on his tail; will watch a mouse-hole for hours together; and has, in short, all the ways, manners, habits, and disposition of his wet-nurse the cat.

Is not this very singular? Put it into more connected English, and tell it to Lady Sunderland. I thought it would amuse her when I heard it. But it's puzzling as well as amusing, and opens a new and strange view into that very mysterious subject, the instincts of animals. Mrs. Routh and Mrs. Blagrove (the mistress of the cat) confirmed all the facts of the case. They say that one can hardly imagine how like a cat Romulus is, unless one lived with him. Dr. Routh, by far the finest old clergyman I ever saw, knew Mr. Malone, and spoke of him very highly. Ever most faithfully and affectionately yours, M. R. MITFORD.

To MISS JEPHSON, *Hatfield, Herts.*

Three-mile Cross, Friday, Oct. 30, 1829.

Did I tell you that it is the scarlet potentilla, which sells at fifteen shillings, being manufactured (I don't know how) out of the *Potentilla Formosa* and running from the color when propagated by seed? *Our* plant, which is quite as pretty—prettier, I think—hardy and generous both in seed and root—will be an established garden-flower, like pinks and roses, and always a pet with me for your sake, dearest, and for Mr. Wordsworth's. Don't let us forget to send you some seed from the Rydal Mount plant next season.

I have had a magnificent present of greenhouse plants, chiefly geraniums—a whole cart-load—and am at present laboring under *l'embarras des richesses,* not being sure whether even the genius of Clarke will make the greenhouse hold them. *A propos* to that astrologer, I have got the ephemeris. Marianna finding even Mrs. Scott fail, took heart at last and applied to Captain Kater; who, being himself a demi-semi believer, has lent us the identical thing for our purpose, in the shape of an almanac published by order of the Board of Longitude. Between ourselves, I believe it's the identical Board of Longitude copy from which, he says, a horoscope can be framed with the most perfect nicety and exactness. I have not seen Clarke since I obtained this treasure, but am expecting him every day.

Now, my dearest, I am going to tell you of an exploit of mine which I longed for you extremely to share. Last Saturday I dined out, and was reproached by a young fox-hunter with never having seen the hounds throw off. I said I should like the sight. The lady of the house said she would drive me some day. The conversation dropped, and I never expected to hear more of it. The next day, however, Sir John Cope (the master of the hounds) calling on my friend, the thing was mentioned and settled; and the young man who originally suggested the matter rode over to let me know that at half-past nine the next day our friend would call for me. At half-past nine, accordingly, she came in a lit-

VOL. II.—E

tle limber pony-carriage drawn by a high-blooded little mare, whom she herself (the daughter and sister of a whole race of fox-hunters) had been accustomed to hunt in Wiltshire, and attended by her husband's hunting-groom excellently mounted.

The day was splendid and off we set. It was the first day of the season. The hounds were to meet in Bramshill Park, Sir John Cope's old place; and it was expected to be the greatest field and most remarkable day of many seasons; Mr. Warde, the celebrated fox-hunter—the very Nestor of the field, who, after keeping fox-hounds for fifty-seven years has just, at seventy-nine, found himself growing old and given them up—was on a visit at the house, and all the hunt were likely to assemble to see this delightful person; certainly the pleasantest old man that it ever has been my fortune to foregather with—more beautiful than my father, and in the same style.

Well, off we set—got to Bramshill just as breakfast was over—saw the hounds brought out in front of the house—drove to cover—saw the fox found, and the first grand burst at his going off—followed him to another covert, and the scent being bad and the field so numerous, that he was constantly headed back, both he, who finally ran to earth, and another fox found subsequently, kept dodging about from wood to wood in that magnificent demesne—the very perfection of park scenery, hill and dale, and wood and water—and for about four hours, we with our spirited pony, kept up with the chase, driving about over road and no road, across ditches and through gaps, often run away with, sometimes almost tossed out, but with a degree of delight and enjoyment such as I never felt before, and never, I verily believe, shall feel again. The field (above a hundred horseman, most of them the friends of my fair companion) were delighted with our sportsmanship, which in me was unexpected; they showed us the kindest attention—brought me the brush—and when, at three o'clock, we and Mr. Warde and one or two others went into luncheon, whilst the hounds went on to Eversley, I really do not believe that there was a gentleman present ungratified by our gratification. Unless you have seen such a scene you can hardly imagine its animation or its beauty. The horses are most beautiful, and the dogs, although not pretty separately, are so when collected and in their own scenery; which is also exactly the case with the fox-hunters' scarlet coats.

I had seen nothing of the park before, beyond the cricket-ground, and never could have had such a guide to its inmost recesses—the very heart of its sylvan solitudes—as the fox. The house—a superb structure of Elizabeth's day, in proud repair—is placed on so commanding an eminence that it seemed meeting us in every direction, and harmonized completely with the old English feeling of the park and the sport. You must see Bramshill. It is like nothing hereabout, but reminds me of the grand Gothic castles in the north of England—Chillingham, Alnwick, etc. It was the residence of Prince Henry, James the First's eldest son, and is worthy his memory. It has a haunted room, shut up and full of armor; a chest where they say a bride hid herself on her wedding-day, and the spring-lock closing, was lost and perished, and never found until years and years had passed (this story, by the way, is common to old houses; it was told me of the great house at Malsanger); swarms with family pictures; has a hall with the dais; much fine tapestry; and, in short, is wanting in no point of antique dignity. The Duke of Wellington went to look at it as adjoining his own estate and suiting his station; but he, unwilling, I believe, to lose the interest of so much capital, made the characteristic reply that Strathfieldsaye was good enough for the duchess, and that he saw nothing to admire at Bramshill except Sir John's pretty housekeeper. I am sure Sir John is much fitter for the master of Bramshill, with his love of cricket, his hospitality, and his fox-hounds, than the duke with all his fame.

God bless you! Tell me when you come, and how long you stay. Ever yours, in galloping fox-hunter's haste,

M. R. M.

To Miss Jephson, *Binfield Park.*

Three-mile Cross, Dec. 11, 1829.

My dearest Emily,—My horoscope turns out singularly true—one part curiously true. I have been very much entertained and interested by it, and so will you be, when our astrologer explains it to you in May in the greenhouse, for it is not easy to tell in writing, or rather it would be puzzled

and long. The misfortune to my greenhouse had not occurred when you were here: the snow got into the tube or
chimney, and generated a vapor intolerably thick and nau-
seous. We have cured the evil by a larger cap to the chimney,
but the plants are greatly injured, and that is vexatious, for,
till that misadventure, they continued to look as well as
when you saw them. However, May will repair all evils,
month of delight as it is !

Many thanks for the charming story of Napoleon, so charmingly told. I have heard a great many delightful traits of
him lately, a friend of ours having purchased the château of
Madame la Maréchale de le Febvre, Duchesse de Dantzig,
near Paris. She lived there twenty-seven years, and is quite
a chronicle of the imperial court and camp—talks of war as
if she fought by her husband's side in all his campaigns—
and is a woman of remarkable courage and vigor of mind
and body. Her late husband's room is fitted up as an ar-
mory, full of curious weapons, and contains an urn with the
heart of her son, who was killed in Russia.

By the way, my astrologer showed me the other day a horoscope of the young Napoleon. He says there is no promise
of success as a warrior, but much triumphing over ladies'
hearts. The father, I believe, was a great conqueror in both
ways.

Did I ever show you some lines which I wrote on my
picture ? Probably not. They were printed in the "Friendship's Offering " (one of the annuals for this year), and have
been transcribed into half the newspapers in the kingdom,
and will, I hope, be, as I intended, of service to the young
artist ; but why I mention them is because I should like you
—whose praise of me always pleases—to see what is said of
them in "Blackwood's Magazine" for this month. It is in an
article called "Monologue on the Annuals." In general, I
care very little for praise ; but this pleased me and touched
me, and so it will you. The lines were written under very
genuine feelings of their truth, and were occasioned by Mr.
Lucas having asked a mutual friend for a scrap of my writing, which I gave him in that form. There are two or three
mistakes in " Blackwood's " copy, which looks as if it were
transcribed from memory. The date also is wrong, and they
have said the " Forget-me-not," instead of the " Friendship's

Offering." But you'll forgive the mistakes, and also my vanity in directing you to it, when you read the article.

Ever affectionately yours, M. R. M.

To B. R. HAYDON, ESQ., *Burwood Place.*

Three-mile Cross, Friday, Dec. 12, 1829.

MY DEAR FRIEND,—Your very kind letter has given me much pleasure and some pain — pleasure, the greatest and the sincerest, to hear that you are going on so prosperously. What an exhibition it will be! how varied in talent, and how high in either scale!—the "Eucles" and the "Punch"— Rubens and Hogarth! Be quite assured that my sympathy with you and with art is as strong as ever, albeit the demonstration have lost its youthfulness and its enthusiasm, just as I myself have done. The fact is that I am much changed, much saddened—am older in mind than in years— have entirely lost that greatest gift of nature, animal spirits, and am become as nervous and good-for-nothing a person as you can imagine. Conversation excites me sometimes, but only, I think, to fall back with a deader weight. Whether there be any physical cause for this, I can not tell. I hope so, for then perhaps it may pass away ; but I rather fear that it is the overburden, the sense that more is expected of me than I can perform, which weighs me down and prevents my doing any thing. I am ashamed to say that a play bespoken last year at Drury Lane, and wanted by them beyond measure, is not yet nearly finished. I do not even know whether it will be completed in time to be produced this season. I try to write it, and cry over my lamentable inability, but I do not get on. Women were not meant to earn the bread of a family—I am sure of that—there is a want of strength. I shall, however, have a volume of "Country Stories" out in the spring, and I trust to get on with my tragedy, and bring it out still before Easter.

God bless you and yours! My best love to them all. God bless you, and farewell! Do not judge of the sincerity of an old friendship, or the warmth of an old friend, by the unfrequency or dullness of her letters. When I have any thing pleasant to tell, you shall be the first to hear. Ever yours, M. R. MITFORD.

To DOUGLAS JERROLD, ESQ., 4 *Augustus Square, Regent's Park.*

Three-mile Cross, near Reading, Dec. 14, 1829. ⎫
Saturday evening.   ⎬

MY DEAR SIR,—I have just received from Mr. Willey your very kind and gratifying note. The plays which you have been so good as to send me* are not yet arrived; but, fearing from Mr. Willey's letter that it may be some days before I receive them, I do not delay writing to acknowledge your polite attention. I have as yet read neither of them, but I *know* them, and shall be greatly delighted by the merits which I shall find in both; in the first, by that truth of the touch which has commanded a popularity quite unrivalled in our day; in the second, by the higher and prouder qualities of the tragic poet. The subject of "Thomas à Becket" interests me particularly, as I had at one time a design to write a tragedy called "Henry the Second," in which his saintship would have played a principal part. My scheme was full of license and anachronism, embracing the apochryphal story of Rosamond and Eleanor, the rebellious sons—not the hackneyed John and Richard, but the best and worst of the four, Henry and Geoffrey; linking the scenes together as best I might, and ending with the really dramatic catastrophe of Prince Henry. I do not at all know how the public would have tolerated a play so full of faults, and it is well replaced by your more classical and regular drama. I was greatly interested by the account of the enthusiastic reception given by the audiences of "Black-eyed Susan" to a successor rather above their sphere. It was hearty, genial, English—much like the cheering which an election mob might have bestowed on some speech of Pitt, or Burke, or Sheridan, which they were sure was fine, although they hardly understood it.

If I had a single copy of "Rienzi" at hand this should not go unaccompanied. I have written to ask Mr. Willey to procure me some, and I hope soon to have the pleasure of requesting your acceptance of one. In the mean time I pray you to pardon this interlined and blotted note, so very untidy and unladylike, but which I never can help, and to excuse the wafer. Very sincerely yours,

M. R. MITFORD.

* "Black-eyed Susan" and "Thomas à Becket."

CHAPTER VI. •

LETTERS FOR 1830.

To the REV. WILLIAM HARNESS, *Heathcote Street, London.*

Friday, Jan. 2, 1830.

MY DEAR FRIEND,—You will have heard from Mr. Talfourd, whom I begged to inform you of it, of my blessed
mother's seizure on Saturday morning. Her exemplary life
is now at an end; she passed away easily and quietly at
nine this morning. It is a consolation that she revived for
a few hours on Sunday, knew us, and blessed us; but the
great comfort is in the recollection of her virtues, and the
certainty of her present happiness. You knew her, and you
know that never lived a more admirable woman. God grant
that I might tread in her steps!

We are as well as can be expected under this great affliction; and surrounded by kindness and sympathy. But
what a beginning of the new year! God bless you, my dear
Mary! Ever yours,   M. R. MITFORD.

My blessed Mother's last illness. *

(Written Jan. 10, 1830.)

On Christmas Day, 1829, the dear creature was quite well
and cheerful—particularly so—ate a hearty dinner of roast
beef. She had eaten a mince-pie for luncheon, and drank
our healths and Mr. Talfourd's in a glass of port wine. She
read a sermon (one of the fifth volume of Blair's) in the
evening, and went to bed quite well and comfortable. The
next morning she was quite well and cheerful whilst she and
my father were getting up. He went down, and she said
she would soon follow. She did not, and, on going to see
for her, she was found lying across the steps between her
own inner and outer room in our little cottage at Three-
mile Cross. She spoke with her usual sweetness and pa-

* We print this paper in *extenso*, as there is a homely particularity and
perfect truthfulness in its details, which to us appears very affecting.

tience, but with an altered voice—deeper, hoarser, more in-
ward—said that she felt giddy, but in no pain. She was
carried to bed, dressed, as she had got up, in her gray cloth
gown and a cap lined with blue. When there, she ate a
hearty breakfast, drank two cups of tea and ate six slices of
bread and butter, and said she was quite easy and comfortable. When I returned to her she was getting her dear right
hand rubbed by Anne, whom she presently sent down to
breakfast, saying "she had nothing to do, and would rub
her hand herself—it would employ her"—quite vivacious,
dear angel, though her left hand and all her left side were
paralyzed. My father went into Reading for medical advice. We continued with her, and the dear saint continued
talking and cheerful. I told her of a letter I had received
from Mr. Willey, with an American play-bill of "Rienzi,"
which I took to her. I then remarked that she did not open
her eyes; her mouth was drawn a little toward the right
side; but she smiled, and spoke quite cheerfully. I read her
a note from Lady Madalina Palmer, which she was much
pleased with, and reverted to ten minutes or a quarter of an
hour after, saying, "so Madalina says all her ideas are frozen,
and every thing but her regard for her friends!" (the identical words of the note). Also she said, when I told her the
commotion Molly* had made in the bed by getting out
at the bottom, "Poor thing! so she must have made a
great fuss;" and seemed amused. She planned to have
some minced beef for her own dinner, inquiring "whether
there was any of the beef left to make it—not the roast,
which had been dressed the day before—but some boiled,
which we had had earlier in the week" (this was Saturday);
and on my telling her that my father meant to get some
chickens for chicken broth, she said "that would do nicely, for it would warm up two or three times," and seemed
to like the notion of having some gingerbread cakes of Perry's for luncheon. Her dear right hand was kept rubbed by
us: it twitched convulsively, but had some power of volun-
tary motion. Her left hand, which was under the clothes,
was terribly bruised, but that she did not know or feel. The
right hand was held up out of bed. Mr. Harris came, and the
dear saint answered his questions. He asked if she felt any

* Miss Mitford's spaniel.

pain in her head; she answered "No, she was quite easy—quite comfortable." Whilst I went down with Mr. Harris, and whilst he was telling me that it was an attack of serous apoplexy, and that nothing could be done, she had another attack, and Harriet came for us. She was then sick, her dear eyes were closed, and she was speechless. Anne Brent* had come before Mr. Harris. She did not notice my father when he returned. We gave her some water and sal volatile, which she swallowed, and then, some time after, some chicken broth, which she took well, and swallowed as well as she could for the phlegm, which sadly tormented her, and constantly wiped her mouth with her dear right hand, the only thing which had any power, and which she was constantly moving. She pushed off her cap from her forehead, so we took it off and replaced it by her night-cap, and the next morning she was undressed and put into bed altogether. The weather was bitterly cold, with snow on the ground all the time, but there was a good fire in the room constantly, and we were able to keep her warm. She untied her night-cap and strings so constantly that we were sometimes obliged to hold her dear hand to prevent her letting in the cold. She certainly knew my hand and my father's, for she would hold them herself, and sometimes press them; and once, when I had been kissing her dear hand, she suddenly brought mine to her dear lips. God bless her, sweet angel! Oh! what a grief it is to have no longer that dear feeling of my mother's warm hand! the only way she had left to show her affection! She evidently knew her silk handkerchief from the sheets and bed-clothes by the feel, and a dry and clean from a stiff and wet one; and she knew my father's voice when he spoke to her, and mine. No one else gave her any thing except my father and myself, and we very seldom left her. He and Harriet went to bed for a few hours in the first part of the night, and at four, five, or six o'clock Anne Brent and I, who sat up, woke them; then, whilst they watched, we went to bed for a few hours.

On Sunday we sent Ned after Mr. Sherwood, at Aldermaston, who would not come. Ned having staid till past dark (having gone to see his own friends at Bucklebury), the delay, and then the refusal, were hard to bear in our great

* A woman of the village, engaged as nurse.

E 2

grief. When my father and I were kneeling alone by her bedside, whilst they were at tea (Sunday evening, the night after her attack), she tried to speak to us. She said, I think, in answer to his fond calls upon her, " dear husband;" and " dear child " in answer to mine. Then I begged her blessing, and as well as she could she gave it: " Bless you, my own dear child." Then my father begged her blessing, and she blessed " her own dear husband," wiping her eyes with her dear right hand, and crying as we did. Then I begged her to pardon my many faults against her. She said, " Yes, my dear," and pressed my hand and my father's, and at last went to sleep with her hand in his.

After he was gone to bed that same night, as I was giving her some broth I thought she again seemed sensible, and asked her if she liked it: " Is it nice, dear mamma?" "Very good," she replied, quite articulately. "Do you like it, dear mamma?" "Very much," she said, as plainly as I could speak. I went on: " You are better, dear mamma ?" " Yes," the dear saint said; " I have had a good sleep." Then she seemed to drop asleep again. A little while after, as Harriet and I were at the bottom of the bed, she said, " I want some caudle." At first I thought it was her pocket-handkerchief, and gave her that; but that was not it: she said, " No, no." Then Harriet thought it was coffee, but she repeated quite distinctly, " I want some caudle," and I said, " Caudle with nutmeg and wine ?" She said, " Yes," and I said it should be made directly; and then she spoke inarticulately something we could not make out, and those were the dear saint's last words. She never complained or struggled, or did any thing but what was sweet, and gentle, and patient, and feminine; and the motions of her dear right hand were most affecting. After her last words her dear mind seemed wandering, for she put her fingers up my sleeve and tried to feel my pulse, and this I believe she did to my father afterward; but many times I think she knew us when we spoke to her, and pressed our hands when we put them in hers. Once she did this (on Tuesday morning, I think) in presence of Mr. Harris.

On Monday morning my father went into Reading for further advice: he met Dr. Smith, who returned with him. Dr. Smith advised leeches and a blister. In the evening we put on the leeches on her left temple, but no amendment took place. We now gave her caudle, with a glass of wine and nutmeg and sugar in it, and she seemed to like and relish it. We also gave her currant-jelly water to prevent the poor tongue and throat getting dry, when she breathed (as she often did) through her throat with the mouth open.

Next day (Tuesday) Dr. Smith called, and gave but little hope, if any. Mr. Harris came afterward and gave none, advising us to use no remedies, saying they would only torment her. Accordingly, we did *not* put on the blister, but gave her nourishment—as much as she would take—amounting to nearly two basins of gruel that day.

Next day (Wednesday) Dr. Smith came again, and advised leeches, though without giving hope. We did not put them on, she being in a great perspiration, and then falling asleep. Mr. Harris, who came the next day, found her much weaker, and said that if we had put on the leeches she would have died under them. Dr. Smith said that it was only to prevent suffering—that there was no chance of life—and advised support. We gave her wine with her gruel, but she got weaker and weaker—breathed fast and loud; her dear hand trembled as she lifted the handkerchief; then she could not lift it at all, she was so weak.

This was Thursday night. She grew cold, and we thought she was going, but the warmth came again, and then about twelve o'clock we heard the rattle in the throat. Before this she had great difficulty in swallowing, then we wetted her dear lips and tongue with a feather; then she took, with great difficulty, a little more gruel; then the perspiration came again, and the fast, difficult breathing; then the pulse and the breathing sank, and about nine o'clock on the morning of Friday (New Year's Day, 1830) the dear angel, after gradually sinking and catching an interrupted breath, expired without a sigh: there was a slight foam on her lips, and she was gone. I had kissed her dear hand and her dear face just before. She looked sweet, and calm, and peaceful: there was even a smile on her dear face. I thought my heart would have broken, and my dear father's too.

On Saturday I did not see her; I tried, but on opening the door I found her covered by a sheet, and had not courage to take it down. On Sunday I saw her both out of her coffin and in it; still sweet, and calm, and placid, looking like one happy. On Thursday I saw her for the last time, in the coffin, with her dear face covered, and gathered for her all the flowers I could get—chrysanthemums (now a hallowed flower), white, yellow, and purple—laurustinus, one early common primrose, a white Chinese primrose, bay and myrtle from a tree she liked, verbena, and lemon-grass also. I put some of these in the coffin with rosemary, and my dear father put some.

We kissed her cold hand, and then we followed her to her grave in Shenfield Church, near the door, very deep and in a fine soil, with room above it for her own dear husband and her own dear child. God grant we may tread in her steps! Mr. Feilde performed the service, and many persons were there, all silent and respectful—the Feildes, Mrs. T——, Harriet Palmer, and Ellen Gorton. All had been very kind, especially Harriet. So had the Walters, Moncks, Hodgkinsons—in short, every body; the respect felt for her was universal. She was in the eightieth year of her age: a small, delicately-framed woman, with a sensible countenance, a very fine head and forehead, a very beautiful and delicate hand and arm, still very upright and active, and her voice pleasant and articulate. Of her mental qualities I shall speak hereafter, and of her angelic perfection of character. No human being was ever so devoted to her duties—so just, so pious, so charitable, so true, so feminine, so industrious, so generous, so disinterested, so ladylike—never thinking of herself, always of others—the best mother, the most devoted wife, and the most faithful friend. Heaven bless her, for she is there! Her coffin (a handsome one) was made by Wheatley. The bearers were Farmer Smith, Farmer Bridgewater, Farmer Love, Bromley, Brown, and Wheatley—all persons she liked—and Hetherington was the undertaker. We had a hearse and a mourning coach, none going except ourselves. Anne Brent laid her out, as she had desired. The servants in the house at the time were Harriet and little Anne, both very attentive, and old Hathaway.

During the dear angel's illness her breath, on three different days while sleeping, seemed to speak words—to continue, as it were, in one chime. On the first day (Tuesday, I think, or perhaps Monday) it seemed to say, " Why that knell? why that knell?" and so on for many minutes. It struck on me like *words*. On Wednesday night, when not thinking of it, it again seemed to say, "Where are you going? where are you going? where are you going?" On Thursday (whilst still not thinking of it) again it struck me even more vividly: "It is home! it is home! it is home!"

And so it was—to heaven, her real home. On the Tuesday or Wednesday night preceding her death there was a large winding-sheet in the candle pointing to her bed—the candle that stood on the washing-stand near the chimney. We all saw it, but none of us cared to mention it, until at last my father took it off, that I might not see it. There was one in the maid's room, which Anne Brent saw, the same evening. Nothing could equal the dear angel's patience and gentleness. We hope she did not suffer much; but certainly she was conscious at times, from the constant attention she paid to keep her dear face nice—(there never was the slightest drivelling, or any thing unpleasant, from her opening her mouth to take in the spoon. No one ever gave her any thing except my father and myself); and from her seeming conscious of our voices and pressing our hands. Oh, that I could but again feel the living touch of that dear hand! God forgive me my many faults to her, blessed angel, and grant that I may humbly follow in her track! Nothing could be so affecting as the motion of that dear hand, from the time when its pressure was warm and comparatively strong until it became faint, and damp, and feeble.

God bless her, sainted angel! Oh, that I might live like her! She was fond of Molly. She used to say "she liked poor Molly, because she was old and faithful;" and of Dash, whom she called "her dog;" and *we* like them the better for her dear sake. God bless her! She is a saint in heaven! She told Harriet Palmer (of whom she was fond) that she meant to get a guinea, and have her father's old Bible—the little black Bible which she read every day—beautifully bound, with her initials on it, and give it to me. She told me, when "Otto" should be performed, she wanted a guinea —but not why—and would not take it before. It shall be done, blessed saint!

To the Rev. William Harness, *Heathcote Street.*

Three-mile Cross, Friday, Jan. 9, 1830.

My dear Friend,—You know how much I always feel your kindness, and may imagine that on this occasion your sympathy was most grateful to my feelings. You knew my blessed mother; knew how full she was of the highest virtues—pious, generous, disinterested, true, and just; how devoted in her attachments; what a wife, what a mother, what a friend; how feminine and ladylike in every act and thought; and, knowing all this, you may imagine how much we must grieve. These virtues are, however, at the same time a consolation—the greatest that we can ever experience. For my own part I never deserved her; but I trust to follow her example better than I have done, and to make up, as well as I can, to my dear father (the only natural tie that I have left in the world) for this grievous deprivation. He was a most excellent husband, and is a most sincere mourner. We followed her dear remains to the grave yesterday; and, I think, he is better to-day.

We have every comfort from the kindness and sympathy of our friends and neighbors, the respect held for her being universal, and this is an alleviation of our sorrow. I shall try to get my father out as soon as I can—to the sessions next week, if possible—for I am sure that nothing will do him so much good as resuming his accustomed habits and avocations. For my own part I have plenty that must be done; much connected painfully with my terrible grief; much that is calculated to force me into exertion, by the necessity of getting money to meet the inevitable expenses. Whether it were inability or inertness I can not tell, but "Otto" is still but little advanced. I lament this of all things *now;* I grieve over it as a fault as well as a misfortune.

The funeral was, of course, quite private—only ourselves, in a mourning coach—but handsome and respectful. She lies in the best part of the church, with room for us in the same grave; and, besides the stone that covers her, I wish to have a tablet. I know that you will enter into these feelings, and forgive the trouble that I cause you. Ever, my dear friend, most sincerely yours,   M. R. Mitford.

To the REV. WILLIAM HARNESS, *Heathcote Street.*

Three-mile Cross, Jan. 24, 1830.

MY DEAR FRIEND,—My father thought that, as Whittaker had published the previous volumes, this should be offered to him, and he has agreed to give a hundred and fifty pounds for it, which I think a fair price, and, as he has now two moneyed partners, I suppose the cash is safe. With regard to the American affair, the man (a deaf and most disagreeable scarecrow) has been here. He makes a great point of secrecy. So I tell you *in strict confidence* what our agreement is. He is to give me in the notes of his publisher (whom he expects to be Colburn) two hundred pounds for two selections from the lighter American literature; I mean, he is to give me that sum for my putting in the title-page, " selected and edited by Mary Russell Mitford " (the first title-page is to run thus:—" Stories of American Life by American writers; selected and edited," etc., etc.), and for two short prefaces which I am to write. They have been, of course, really selected by me from an immense mass of material; and the first work, especially, will be really very good—characteristic, national, various, and healthy—as different from the "Sketch-book " (which, in my mind, is a pack of maudlin trash) as any thing you can imagine. Mr. Talfourd earnestly advised my doing this. He says that the thing will not in the slightest degree interfere with my own works, and that it was an easy way of getting money, though I never worked harder in my life than in wading through the mass of MSS. and letter-press to make the selection.

My dear father is much better in spirits. I am tired to death with bawling to this man and reading so much MS., but greatly relieved at the prospect of getting the money. As to myself, my irreparable loss, the moment I am alone, comes over me more and more. Kindest love to dear Mary Ever, my kind friend, most faithfully yours,

M. R. MITFORD.

To MISS JEPHSON, *Bath.*

Three-mile Cross, Thursday, Feb., 1830.

MY DEAR LOVE,—My continued silence has been occasioned by excessive occupation, and also by indisposition, having had, and still having, a cough, which nothing silences but opium—a remedy which, whilst it pacifies the nights, stupefies the days. I am still terribly busy with my own volume. I had overrated the quantity of material ready, and tied myself to time, so that I am worked to death to get the original matter by the period fixed. Moreover, I am greatly worried by the American affair, the man who employed me having quarreled with his publisher, and the whole affair is afloat. We do not know who will purchase the works, or when; and instead of a large sum of money—a certainty—I find myself, after an immense deal of most irksome labor, in the midst of risks and chances and anxiety—my constant destiny, and one which no constitution can stand long.

[The remainder is wanting.]

To Miss Jephson, *Bath.*

Three-mile Cross, Thursday, Feb. 25, 1830.

My very Dear,—In the first place my cough is much better; I am sure you will be glad to hear that. These three fine days have done it incalculable good. In the next place, I am getting on rapidly with my new volume, and, altogether, am in far better heart than when I wrote last, at which time I had really a feeling of depression which no words could describe. I have still plenty to worry and torment me.

All your Italian news is very interesting, and quite new to me. Goldoni is the most insipid writer I ever read; Alfieri is a very fine one, but unactable. A friend of mine (the Rev. Maurice James) translated his "Filippo," and Charles Kemble used to want me to work on that, and make a new "Don Carlos" out of Schiller's and Alfieri's tragedies. To these I should have added the two scenes from the "Hippolitus" of Euripides, which Racine took for the famous scene in the "Phèdre," the *c'est toi qui l'as nommé* scene, which is very inferior to the original Greek. All this, perhaps, I may do some day or other, for certainly it would make a fine play. "Werner" is Lord Byron's most dramatic tragedy, and undramatic enough too. Miss Lee made a play on the subject, which was played three or four nights at Covent Garden, under the name of "The Three Strangers." But by far the most striking drama on that striking story was one which I found above twenty years ago in a table-drawer at Kirkley Hall, in Northumberland, a seat belonging to the late Nathaniel Ogle, the eldest brother of Mrs. Sheridan. I was staying there with my father, and looking for some cards in a Pembroke table in the drawing-room found the manuscript. Mr. Ogle said that Sheridan had been staying there the year before, and he supposed that he had brought it to read, and had left it in his careless way. He wrote to his sister, but she knew nothing of it, and said that her husband denied all knowledge of the subject. So then Mr. Ogle gave it to me. Lady Charles Aynesley, a cousin of my father's, to whom I went afterward, begged me to lend it to her, and I never got it back again, and never knew who wrote it. It was a most striking and interesting play, written in powerful prose, and could not have failed of eminent success. What a new combination of incidents that story contains! And how very rare a *new* story is!

How ignorant people are about their own places! Sir John Cope does not know whether Inigo Jones built his house of Bramshill, and I am obliged to send to the Duke of Bedford's and Lord Spencer's libraries for Birch's "Life of the Prince of Wales," to ascertain the fact.

God bless you, my dearest! Your letters are always grateful to me. Ever most affectionately yours, M. R. M.

To Sir William Elford, *The Priory, Totnes.*

May 22, 1830.

My dear Friend,—I have just received your very welcome letter, and I hasten to tell you that, though not likely, I fear, to see *you* at present (I have just refused a pressing invitation into Devonshire to myself and my father from Mr. Heathcote, the member for Tiverton), yet I shall see that which you will agree is next best to yourself, namely, your picture. I am going to town to witness the representation of "Ion," and after a triumphal course of parties (dinners, of course, for I never go to odious blue-stocking *soirées*) I shall, if possible, return in about a week. N.B.—I have already engagements for more than double that time, but I must break off at some point, or I might stay the whole season; and I have my father, my garden, and my yet hardly half-finished novel to draw me homeward.

I go to Mr. Sergeant Talfourd's house, 56 Russell Square, so that I shall be in the midst of his " agony of glory," and sharing it with the fullest sympathy ; and between him and Wordsworth (who is in town just now, and half living at my friend's) and my own acquaintance, I shall see all the high literary people of London in the pleasantest manner possible ; that is to say, the most undressed and familiar.   I shall also see most of the eminent Whigs in the Lords and Commons in the same way ; but I don't expect to be much thrown amongst the Tories, although Sir Robert Peel is, of course, a man of too much general taste to confine himself to one party in the intercourse of society.   I know that he applied to the author for a copy of "Ion," and I presume that they are acquainted.

It seems great presumption in me to talk in this way ; but such is the passion for persons of literary reputation nowadays that, if combined with respectability of character, it evens the professor with princes and ministers ; and I myself am so seldom in London, and have always kept so aloof from the common race of blue-stocking people, that I pass for far more than I am, and am made a fuss about, such as would really seem incredible to those who are not aware of the London passion for novelty in every thing.   It pleases my dear father, however ; and certainly I can only be gratified by the attention and kindness of so many cultivated persons. Moreover, it gives an *entrée* to pictures, etc., which is exceedingly pleasant ; and for the short time that I can stand the fatigue and the expense (for the dress is ruinous) nothing can be more agreeable.   I love the beautiful city, if it were nothing else ; most assuredly there's no such picturesque assemblage of buildings in the world.

My Dash I really believe understood your message, and looked up with his beautiful eyes, and made the pretty gentle sound which we all understand, and by which (by the way) he conveys distinctly " Yes " and " No," and three or four other phrases, and shook his head as he listened.   The inside of his ear is injured ; the outside is not at all disfigured, but in the interior there is a succession of gatherings which I fear will continue.   He goes coursing, nevertheless, and likes it as well as ever.   About three weeks ago, when a terrible operation had been performed on him in Reading,

I, not knowing it was to happen, had gone to a copse prim-
rosing, and was not returned when he came home. Poor
Dash not finding me to comfort him, slipped out after my
father, who followed me with the phaeton, and came up to
me, in the middle of the coppice, covered with blood, and
with half the inside of his ear just cut away. I sat down to
pet him, and then made my way out of the bushes as fast as
I could to get my poor dog home, when a hare crossed us,
and Dash followed it, questing all through the copse, across
half a dozen fields, along a dozen thick hedgerows, then back
to the coppice, every inch of which he beat, although it has
not been cut for six years, and is (except in the paths) the
thickest covert in the neighborhood. It was a full hour before we could get him back to put him into the phaeton to
carry him home. He never seemed to think of his poor ear,
although there was a fresh wound, as big as the palm of my
hand, cut away that very morning, and which must have
been scratched by the bushes every instant. My father
says that it was the greatest triumph of high blood and spirit that he ever saw or heard of. But he is a most extraordinary dog. Yours most affectionately.   M. R. M.

To Miss Jephson, *Bath.*

Tuesday, July 26, 1830.
I seize the opportunity of writing to you, my dear love,
before the extinction of franks, which I presume to be approaching. I hope and trust that your friend is better.

I am dreading the spread of liberal opinions. The French
Revolution is most happily over; never was any thing
French so reasonably conducted. *Our* king is ultra-popu-
lar. Have you heard Lord Alvanley's *bon mot* respecting
him? He was standing at the window at White's, when
the king, with a thousand of his loving subjects at his heels,
was walking up St. James's Street. A friend said to him,
"What are you staring at, Alvanley?" "I'm waiting to see
his Majesty's pocket picked," was the reply. And, really,
one wonders that the accident has not happened.

Did I tell you that I had had a great fright about a fortnight ago? My father was thrown out of the gig, returning from a dinner-party, and the horse and chaise came
home empty. Of course we all set off, and found him stun-

ned by the side of the road, just on this side of the vicarage
—a full mile off.   Only think what an agony of suspense it
was !   Thank Heaven, however, he escaped uninjured, except being stiff from the jar ; and I am recovering my nervousness better than I could have expected.   I find that my
book is selling so well that they talk of reprinting the whole
set in two pocket volumes, with vignette title-pages, like
the Waverley Novels.   This is a great practical compliment, for unless they sell five thousand copies they will lose
by the edition ; but I suppose they may be trusted to know
what they are about.   I don't imagine it will come out just
yet.   It is really a great circulation, for I believe that not
less than eight editions of the first volume have been printed already, and the others in proportion.

I have read Sir Walter's plays.   What a shocking conclusion that tragedy has !   The other is very pretty in an odd
way ; but both are essentially undramatic.   God bless you,
my own dear Emily !   Ever most faithfully and affectionately yours,   M. R. MITFORD.

To MISS SEDGWICK [*the American authoress*].

Three-mile Cross, Reading, Berks, Sept. 6, 1830.

MY DEAR MISS SEDGWICK,—Few things can be more gratifying to the feelings of an author than to hear of the dif-
fusion and approval of her works in such a country as America, and from such a person as you.   I should have written
instantly to thank you for your most kind and flattering
letter, had I not waited for " Clarence," the valuable present
which you announced to me.   It has not yet arrived, but I
will no longer delay expressing my strong feelings of obligation to the writer, since, having read "Redwood " and the
" New England Tale," I know how much of pleasure I shall
derive from the later production, which is no doubt waiting
at some London bookseller's till they shall send a parcel to
Reading.   I have even seen the highest possible character
of it in one of the best of our own magazines, the " Monthly
Review."   I rejoice to find that it is not merely reprinted
but published in England, and will contribute, together with
the splendid novels of Mr. Cooper, to make the literature
and manners of a country so nearly connected with us in language and ways of thinking, known and valued here.

I think that every day contributes to that great end. Cooper is certainly, next to Scott, the most popular novel-writer of the age. Washington Irving enjoys a high and fast reputation ; the eloquence of Dr. Channing, if less wide-ly, is perhaps more deeply felt; and a lady, whom I need not name, takes her place amongst these great men, as Miss Edgeworth does among our Scotts and Chalmerses. I have contributed, or, rather, am about to contribute, my mite to this most desirable interchange of mind with mind, having selected and edited three volumes of tales, taken from the great mass of your periodical literature, and called " Stories of American Life by American Authors." They are not yet published, but have been printed some time ; and I shall de-sire Mr. Colburn to send you a copy, to which, indeed, you have every way a right, since I owe to you some of the best stories in the collection. It was a Mr. Jones who put the an-nuals and magazines from which I have made this selection into my hands. He is himself an able writer and an intelli-gent man, and I owe to him, probably, the great pleasure of being known to you.

The indices of my private story in the books which have been so kindly received by the public, are for the most part strictly true. I am a woman of now past forty, and was born and reared in affluence, being the only child of very rich parents. About fifteen years ago a most expensive chancery suit and other misfortunes too long to detail, re-duced my dear father from opulence to poverty; and we are now living in the small cottage, which you will find de-scribed, in the same village with the mansion which once be-longed to us. There was, however, no loss of character amongst our other losses ; and it is to the credit of human nature to say, that our change of circumstances has been at-tended with no other change amongst our neighbors and friends than that of increased attention and kindness. In-deed, I can never be sufficiently thankful for the very great goodness which I have experienced all through life, from al-most every one with whom I have been connected. My dear mother I had the misfortune to lose last winter. She died in a good old age, universally beloved and respected. My dear father still lives, under similar advantages, a beautiful and cheerful old man, whom I should of all things like you to know; and if ever you do come to our little England you must come and see us. We should never forgive you if you did not.

I have given you this outline of my story because you expressed so kind an interest in my concerns, that I thought you would like to know all about me. Our family losses made me an authoress; for although I had, when a very young girl, published two or three very rapidly written volumes of poetry, which had much more success than they deserved, and some of which ("Poems on the Female Character," "Blanche," and the "Rival Sisters") had the honor of being reprinted in America; yet I am confident that, having repented those sins of my youth, I should have abstained from all literary offenses for the future, had not poverty driven me against my will to writing tragic verse and comic prose; thrice happy to have been able, by so doing, to be of some use to my dear family.

Once again, my dear Miss Sedgwick, accept my truest thanks for your kindness, and my sincerest good wishes for your health and happiness, and that of all belonging to you. Your dear little niece must have a postscript to herself; I am charmed with her delightfully natural letter. I remain, dearest madam, your obliged friend and servant,

M. R. MITFORD.

To MISS C. M. SEDGWICK, JUN.

MY DEAR YOUNG FRIEND,—I am very much obliged to you for your kind inquiries respecting the people in my book. It is much to be asked about by a little lady on the other side of the Atlantic, and we are very proud of it accordingly. "May" was a real greyhound, and every thing told of her was literally true; but, alas! she is no more; she died in the hard frost of last winter. "Lizzy" was also true, and is also dead. "Harriet" and "Joel" are not married yet; you shall have the very latest intelligence of her: I am expecting two or three friends to dinner, and she is making an apple-tart and custards—which I wish, with all my heart, that you and your dear aunt were coming to partake of. The rest of the people are doing well in their several ways, and I am always, my dear little girl, most sincerely yours,

M. R. MITFORD.

To Miss Jephson, *Bath.*

Three-mile Cross, Friday, Dec. 19, 1830.

Never imagine for an instant that I shall put your purse or my own in jeopardy by our book. The letters transscribed by your dear father and the later ones of Horace Walpole, combined with those of Mr. Jephson about the statue, form a most entertaining portrait of his frank, wayward, imprudent, but most delightful character. Horace Walpole also is excellently shown in his own last letter, with his gout, and his self-importance, and his courtly way of showing his anger. But I fear we still want more material.

I have the sweet-scented cyclamen and the Italian narcissus (the double Italian narcissus, sweeter far than the double jonquil) blooming in pots and glasses in the parlor window, whilst my autumn flowers, chrysanthemums, roses, Michaelmas daisies (the large new late one), and salvias, blue and red, are still in full bloom. I like this junction of the seasons, this forestalling of spring and prolonging of autumn —don't you? The parlor window would be the best place for the white evening primrose. Warmth will do it no harm, so that it has light and plenty of water, and a little air on mild days.

Did I tell you that I have six volumes of American children's books in the press? three for under, and three for over, ten years of age. The little ones are plain, practical, religious, and moral—I like them; the others varied and amusing. "A Journey through the United States to Canada" forms the chief part of one volume—children, of course, being the principal travelers; "A Sea Voyage to England" of the second; and "Evenings in a Merchant's Family at Boston," the third. This is new, at all events, and to me seems likely to take. The booksellers (Messrs. Whittaker & Co.) think so also, I imagine, for they are printing 3500 copies.

My play is, I find, coming out with the following cast, the best, I think, that they can make in that theatre :— Pedro, C. Kemble; Alphonso, Warde; Manuel, Bennett; Inez, Miss Fanny; and Constance, either Miss Ellen Tree* or Mrs. Chatterley. Mr. Talfourd, who brought me this news, and has

* Afterward Mrs. Kean.

been spending the day here, says that Fanny Kemble's Callista (odious as the part is) displays far higher talent than any thing she has hitherto done, and that, at a distance from the stage, he could almost have imagined her a smaller and younger Mrs. Siddons. This is very comfortable. He told Mr. Kemble how much he was pleased with her in that part; and Kemble said that he liked her in it best himself, and had put her into it to accustom the town to seeing her in a higher range of characters, wishing her to occupy the place of Mrs. Siddons. I have never seen Fanny Kemble act; but I am well acquainted with her off the stage, and know her to be a girl of great ability. The difference of age makes it singular that she in Paris and I in London, should have been educated by the same lady. What I hear of her acting pleases me, and I hope that my play and she will do well together. Of course I always know that *no* play is absolutely safe, and hope fearingly; but the female character is splendid, and the tragedy itself, though less powerful, far more interesting than "Rienzi."* God bless you! Ever affectionately yours,   M. R. MITFORD.

To Miss JEPHSON, *Bath.*

Three-mile Cross, Thursday night, Dec., 1830.

Oh, that you could see my chrysanthemums! I have one out now unlike any I ever saw. It is the shape and size of a large honeysuckle,† and the inside filled up with tubes. Each of the petals or florets (which are they?) is, on the outside, of a deep violet color, getting, however, paler as it approaches the end, and the inside shows itself much like the inside of a honeysuckle tube, of a shining silver white, just, in some particular lights, tinged with purple. I never saw so elegant a flower of any sort; and my jar of four kinds, golden, lemon, yellow, purple, lilac, crimson, and pink, exceeds in brilliancy any display that I ever witnessed. The brightest pot of dahlias is nothing to it. My father, who has been twice in London lately (about my American "Children's

---

* Which, after its success at Drury Lane, was acted for several weeks in succession at the Pavilion Theatre, at this time, under the name of "The Last of the Romans," to evade prosecution by the great theatres.

† This, by the way, is the shape and size of the tassel white, only that that flower is still more curved and curled, and all of one color.

Books " and your friend " Inez ") says that they have nothing approaching it in splendor in the new conservatories at Covent Garden. I am prodigiously vain of my chrysanthemums, and so is Clarke.

Mr. Macready once told me that he sat up all night in a room opposite the Old Bailey (I think) to witness the execution of Thistlewood, etc., by way, I suppose, of taking hints from their deaths. He said that there he was disappointed; that even the masked headman and the holding of the head of a traitor, was, in theatrical phrase, ineffective; but that the most tremendous thing he ever saw was the congregation of human faces, especially of human eyes, in that dense and extensive crowd, all pointed to the same object with an intensity so fixed and so absorbing. He never before, he said, knew the power of that mighty thing, the gaze of a multitude.

I never saw Mr. Denman; only he has the goodness to take a very strong and partial interest in my books and plays, and to let me know that he does so. Neither did I ever see Mr. Brougham out of a court of justice; but I know a great many of his friends and a great deal about *him*, and admire him more than I can tell. Oh, how could he stoop to be a lord! He sleeps nine, ten, eleven hours, except, of course, on great debate nights; spends some time at table; and allows himself far more relaxation in society than most lawyers; and what enables him to do this, whilst performing the work of ten busy men, is the wonderful power which he has over his attention. He says himself (talking confidentially to a clever man, his intimate friend) that he owes all his success to the habit of concentrating his mind on the particular subject needful, whatever it be; and then, the moment that is over, directing his powers to another object and never thinking of the first again, unless the course of his business leads him to it. Concentration and instantaneous transition—these are the spells by which he works. Something of this power he owes, of course, to his legal habits; but no lawyer possesses it as he does, and very few have ever embraced such a variety of objects. The same versatility belongs in part to his character. He enters with the warmest sympathy into the feelings of those with whom he converses; but though at the moment the interest be

VOL. II.—F

most unfeigned and genuine, there is great danger that it
shall vanish with the object. He is a delightful companion,
gay, simple, and frank, and so good-natured that the humblest
barrister might ask Mr. Brougham for a cast in his carriage,
and the lowest clerk in the House of Commons make sure of
a frank. I suppose the old title tempted him to be lorded;
an old title in a family *is* a temptation.

I have been reading Head's "Bruce," which pleases me
much less, because I am an adorer of Bruce's own book at
full length, and hate abridgments of a favorite author; besides, I don't think it well done, though it is so odd, that it
makes one laugh against one's will. (Before I forget, Mr.
Brougham has a remarkable trick, or rather peculiarity of
countenance; when he is beginning to be in a passion his
nostrils and his whole nose twitch in the most extraordinary
manner. They say that in debate his antagonists while
speaking know the dressing they are going to have when
they finish, by observing this indication. I have seen it myself in the Court of King's Bench, when the judge was charg-
ing against him.) Ever most faithfully and affectionately
yours,   M. R. MITFORD.

CHAPTER VII.

LETTERS FOR 1831.

To MISS JEPHSON, *Bath.*

Three-mile Cross, Thursday, Jan. 14, 1831.

You like to hear about Lord Brougham. Inquiring as to
his daughter from an intimate friend of his the other day, I
heard that she was a *blue* child—that children of that complexion never live past twelve or fourteen (I have heard this
before)—but that he dotes upon her and educates her himself. It is singular that some years ago, when not seven
years old, she prophesied that her father would be Lord
Chancellor: "Papa will be Chancellor—you'll see that!"
"Will he?" was the reply; "and what will your friend, Mr.
Denman, be?" "Oh! Master of the Rolls, perhaps—I'm not
sure about him—but you'll see that papa will be Lord Chancellor." He tells this with great glee; and I should not

wonder if it had influenced him in accepting the situation. It certainly shows a wonderful *professional* knowledge in so young a girl. What a man he is! All last summer he was up at six every morning studying chemistry; and only yes-terday I received a letter from my friend Archdeacon Wrang-ham (a man celebrated for his scholarship at Cambridge), saying that he had just received a letter from the Chancellor, whom he calls "a miracle of a man," on the subject of the Greek metres, showing a degree of learning that would do honor to any scholar of the age. This is perhaps the most astonishing thing that I have heard, even of that astonishing person.

I have not myself seen the second volume of the "Life of Byron," but doubtless the letters are to William Harness. There are several addressed to him in the first volume; and it is an honorable distinction, that of all Lord Byron's inti-mate friends William seems to be the only one whom he re-spected to the point of never addressing to him one line that might not have been sent to a delicate woman. He intend-ed, if you remember, to have dedicated to him his "Childe Harold," and refrained only lest it should injure him in the church. William still speaks of him with much affection.

My father joins in most affectionate love, and I am ever, most faithfully yours,   M. R. M.

To the DUKE OF DEVONSHIRE, *Devonshire House, London.*

Three-mile Cross, near Reading, March 15, 1831.

MY LORD DUKE,—The spirit of liberality and justice to dramatic authors by which your Grace's exercise of the func-tions of Lord High Chamberlain has been distinguished, forms the only excuse for the liberty taken in sending my tragedy of "Charles the First" direct to yourself, instead of transmitting it, in the usual mode, from the theatre to Mr. Colman. To send it to that gentleman, indeed, would be worse than useless; the play having been written at the time of the Duke of Montrose, and a license having been re-fused to it on account of the title and the subject, which Mr. Colman declared to be inadmissible on the stage. That this is not the general opinion may be inferred from the subject's having been repeatedly pointed out by different critics as one of the most dramatic points of English history, and especially recommended to me both by managers and actors. That such could not always have been the feeling of those in power is proved by the fact, that there is actually a tragedy on the very same subject, and bearing the very same title, written some sixty or seventy years since by Havard, the player, in which John Kemble, at one time, performed the principal character, and which might be represented any night, at any other theatre, without the necessity of a license or the possibility of an objection. It is the existence of this piece which makes the prohibition of mine seem doubly hard, and emboldens me to appeal to your Grace's kindness against the rigorous decree of your predecessor.

Of my own play it hardly becomes me to speak. It is an attempt to embody and present great historical events and remarkable historical characters with as much vividness and fidelity as my poor abilities will permit. The manuscript has been seen by many eminent literary persons, who have considered it as the least imperfect of my dramatic efforts, and have uniformly declared that it appeared to them quite unexceptionable as an acting play. From any thing like political allusion it is undoubtedly free. I am not aware that there is in the whole piece one line which could be construed into bearing the remotest analogy to present circumstances; or that could cause scandal or offense to the most loyal. If I had been foolish or wicked enough to have written such things, the reign of William the Fourth and the administration of Earl Grey would hardly be the time to produce them.

I have the honor to be, my Lord Duke, your Grace's most obedient servant,   MARY RUSSELL MITFORD.

To MISS JEPHSON, *Binfield Park.*

[*A Fragment.*]

Three-mile Cross, March, 1831.

You will see that literature and every body, above all his friends, have had a great loss in Thomas Hope. He had been very ill, and was getting better, but went out in an open carriage in one of these fogs, caught cold, and sank under the remedies which an inflammation on the chest rendered necessary. Of all the persons I ever knew I think he was the most delightful. There was a quick glancing delicate wit in his conversation such as I never heard before — it came sparkling in, checkering his graver sense like the sunbeam in a forest; he had also (what all people of any value have) great truth and exactness of observation, and said the wisest things in the simplest manner; above all, there was about him a little tinge of shyness—a modesty, a real and genuine diffidence, most singular and most charming in a man of his station, his fortune, and his fame. Every body knows the noble things he used to do, but he was as careful not to give pain as he was earnest to confer happiness, and perhaps this humble and easier virtue is the rarer of the two.

People called him proud, and a detestable French artist painted him and his wife, as I dare say you have heard, as " *La Belle et la Bête.*" To me he seemed almost handsome; he was very much underhung, which gave a lion-like look to the lower part of his face, but he had a grand Shakspearian pile of forehead, an expression of benevolence and intellect, and the air and bearing of a man of the highest distinction. He was not, I find, so rich as has been thought, in spite of his magnificent house in Duchess Street—the very temple of art, where Mrs. Hope's parties united all that was distinguished in rank, talent, and literature—and of his still more beautiful villa of Deepdene, where princes of all nations used to take their abode for weeks together, all was accomplished by the most admirable system of order, a large and liberal economy. He knew to a fraction the expense of every day, and even the amount of meat consumed. Nothing ever approached the exactness of his establishment; perhaps the Dutch blood may have had some influence.

To the Rev. William Harness, *Heathcote Street.*

Three-mile Cross, March 31, 1831.

My dear Friend,—You will probably have heard by this time, from your friend Mr. Collier, that the Duke of Devonshire could not—consistently with his established rule not to reverse the decisions of the Duke of Montrose—license the " Charles." Nothing could exceed the kindness and gentlemanlike feeling of his letter (for he wrote himself), and I beg you to convey my best thanks to Mr. Collier for his goodness in the affair. Never was a refusal so amiable as the Duke of Devonshire's.

I send, for your acceptance, my American Tales, and a

smaller set for a smaller—but, my father says, very delightful little—personage, your niece. The children's stories are very plain and homely, but I have been much gratified by the approbation of several sensible mothers, who say that their children are very fond of them, and that they consider them sound and practical. There was a good deal of cant in them, which I swept away, leaving, I think, as much religious feeling as children of that age can enter into. I wish you would run over half a volume, and give me your opinion on this point. If I utterly fail in the drama, and should also fail in a novel, why then children's books would be something to fall back upon. Mine would not be at all like these; but I think that I could write English stories which children would like, and which would do them no harm at least, if not much good.

So you are against the Reform Bill! Well, I should not care much for it myself, if I were not persuaded that it is the only preservative against a much worse state of things. If we have not reform we shall have revolution, and I can not help thinking but a House of Commons, chosen according to the new plan, will be a much better thing than the mob.

I hope you will contrive to come to see us this summer. Mr. Talfourd will tell you that my greenhouse is a pleasant room to live in, and that some of our Berkshire friends are nice people. We should be so proud of making you known to them. Pray do come. Mrs. W—— said the other day—what worried me at the moment, for fear you should believe it—that M—— had told you that I had looked you out a wife. Now M——, with a thousand fine qualities—good-nature, generosity, absence of selfishness, and an overflowing and faithful attachment to her friends—has one peculiarity, which has a thousand times threatened to alienate me from her, kind as she is to me. It is one which I dislike so much, and which comes so directly in opposition to my own peculiarities—I mean her habit of considering and talking of every man and every woman as if he and she were born for no other purpose than that of marrying and falling in love. She even used to joke *me*, at my age, with my person, and with my resolute old-maidishness and hatred of the subject, about every man that came near me. I think it is not possible to give a stronger instance of her determination to pursue the subject than her choosing to consider the marriage of such a one as I to come within the verge of *possibility.* It happens, however, that I hate match-making in the first place; that I should never dream of taking such a liberty as to lay schemes for you in the second; and, in the third, that the young lady whom I believe her to mean is, although a good and clever girl, one entirely unworthy of you in person, family, fortune, connections, and manners — things that, in my mind, come next to goodness, and before talents. You may come here in perfect safety. Adieu, my dear friend. Ever most gratefully and affectionately yours, M. R. MITFORD.

To MISS JEPHSON, *Binfield Park.*

May 20, 1831.

COPY OF SOME VERSES ADDRESSED TO MY FRIEND MISS JAMES, WRITTEN DURING HER STAY AT THE SWAN INN, THRÉE-MILE CROSS, JANUARY, 1829.

The village inn! The wood fire burning bright!
The solitary taper's flickering light!
The lowly couch! the casement swinging free!
My noblest friend, was this a place for thee?
Yet in that humble room, from all apart,
We poured forth mind for mind and heart for heart;
Ranging from idlest words and tales of mirth
To the deep mysteries of heaven and earth;
Yet there thine own sweet voice in accents low
First breath'd Iphigenia's tale of woe,*—
The glorious tale, by Goethe fitly told,
And cast as finely in an English mould
By Taylor's kindred spirit, high and bold.
'Twas no fit place for thee! yet that blest hour
Fell on my soul like dewdrops on a flower,—
Freshening and nourishing and making bright
The plant decaying less from time than blight,—
Flinging Hope's sunshine o'er each feeble aim,
Thy praise my motive, thine applause my fame.
No fitting place! yet (inconsistent strain
And selfish!) come, I prythee! come again!

Are not these lines (except the wood fire and the "Iphigenia") very *à propos*—quite "germane to the matter?"

* Mr. Taylor's translation of Goethe's "Iphigenia in Taurus," which is in some parts only a free imitation of Euripides—one of the finest translations in our language, and now out of print long since. Did Emily ever see it? I have a copy, but have lent it at present to Mr. Milman, who is in London.

especially the last words, the "come again, come again," which I can but reiterate with heart and soul. You can not imagine how delighted I was to hear of the Kingfisher (for it was the first word Anne told me when she came to me), and how pleased I was to see it. You must come again, although it be no fitting place, and I do really think that you will. The little girls there are honest, for they have found and have brought me your signet-ring, which I keep for you safely.

I have been but indifferent for a long while until now. Mr. Merry has been with me for two hours to-day, lamenting over his own bad singing, and hoping to see you again that he might do better. I told him I hoped he would see you again, but that *we* were quite satisfied with his doings.

I have just had a visit from Mrs. Dickenson. She was one of the poor Duchess of Wellington's most intimate friends! and she says it is certainly true that the duke is a changed man since her death—has scarcely left his room, or had courage to ring for a servant. I have been driving to Arborfield, and have heard terrible news of every body's gardens and greenhouses; all the dahlias and geraniums of the county seem to have been killed, and Mrs. Blagrove, on the other side, has lost a great part of her matchless collection. I am so sorry for her, she loved them so. God bless you, my dear love! Ever yours,   M. R. M.

To MISS JEPHSON, *Bath.*

Tuesday night, Oct. 20, 1831.

Last night I was at a phrenological lecture given by a Mr. Dowton, a traveling lecturer, in Reading, and very much pleased and interested I was. I am a sort of a demi-semi believer (are you?), and have heard Dr. Spurzheim and Mr. Deville frequently, but I prefer Mr. Dowton. Amongst the novelties, the most striking was a cast of the skull of Raphael—the veritable skull dug up at Rome. There is no doubt of the authenticity, and it displays more intellect and finer imagination (ideality is the technical word) than any skull ever before met with; finer even than Edmund Burke's. You would have liked the whole lecture. I wished for you. The worst objection to the science is, that it approaches too closely to the doctrine of election.

You will like to hear what he says of my head, which he examined so far as regards the intellectual qualities, not the moral propensities, in which I have less faith, and which it is awkward enough to have doled out to one.   First of all he was most urgent with me to have it cast, meaning, I believe, to do it himself.   He said that it was, in the size of the cranium, the greatest illustration he had ever met with of the science.   Generally speaking, the female head is much smaller than the male—almost always—and mine, he says, is larger than the average male head; and all power, all force, all reality of intellect depends upon the actual, not the relative size of the organs.

Now I half wish I had undergone the operation, for I believe they take four casts, giving you three, and you would like to have had one, for it is more a real part of one's self than a print, or even a painting—more completely the true face and head.   He remarked on the indentation of the middle of the forehead as indicating a want of the power of remembering small things, such as names of streets and numbers of houses, and names of dates generally.   Now, this is so true! And he enlarged much on the extraordinary development of imitation, the principal organ of Scott, and the one which produces dramatic, or rather creative power.   It is situated on each side of benevolence (which rather, I believe, means kindness), and when they are both large, as he says they are in me, give the peculiar roundness to the top of the head which, with the great development of the other reflective and perceptive organs, gives the remarkable shape to the forehead which all painters have observed in mine.   He says that both ideality and constructiveness are large, but that it is the striking development of imitation (by which phrenologists mean imitation of nature) which gives the power of conceiving and executing dramatic situation and character; that it was the principal characteristic of Sheridan's head, and of Shakspeare's as it appears in the monument which Ben Jonson called so like him.

This is curious, and I tell it you, in spite of the apparent vanity, because it will be sure to interest you.   He certainly did not do it to flatter me, for at first I did not like the word imitation.   It seemed to me fitter for an actor than a dramatic writer, and I dwelt on the constructiveness and ideality which painters had told me I had so large; but he stuck to his text, and convinced me, by his own head, how much larger, proportionately, my imitation was than his, though his is large. He says that Mr. Cathcart's head, though that shy and sensitive person would not let him touch it, is magnificent. And he felt Dash, and made a great hit, for he said that he was the only spaniel in whom he had ever found so large a combativeness; and he fights every dog he comes near, and is king of the street, having conquered, after twenty pitched battles, two bull-dogs, a Dane and a Newfoundland, his neighbors. He said the distance between the eyes showed an immense portion of good-humor, and the space and roundness of the top of the skull great sagacity.

Is the top of Miss Edgeworth's forehead round? and is her head large? Mr. Dowton asked me these questions, and I could not answer him. Pray are you a great educator of the poor? I am not, and I am going to give you a case against it. I took, about three days ago, a girl from a school at Reading as an under-maid. Well, I left a proof-sheet in my desk, corrected and folded, and ready for the post. I took a ride out, and on my return found that the young lady had ransacked my desk, and opened my proof. Not being able to refold it *secundum artem*, she was obliged to leave it open, and so was found out. This is a fine specimen of the march of intellect. Of course she is going. These things are exceedingly vexatious, especially to one who hates strange faces.

Have you met with the "Book of the Seasons," by William and Mary Howitt? It is very pretty indeed. Let me hear soon and often. I am quite glad you are with Mr. Smith, for whom, on your report, I have great respect, esteem, and liking. Ever, my dearest Emily, your faithful and affectionate   M. R. MITFORD.

To MISS JEPHSON, *Castle Martyr, Ireland.*

Three-mile Cross, Nov. 11, 1831.

MARY QUEEN OF SCOTS' FAREWELL TO FRANCE.

"Oh! pleasant land of France, farewell!
My country dear,
Where many a year
In peace and bliss I hope to dwell.
Oh! pleasant land of France, farewell!"

So sang the Scottish queen what time she stood
On her proud galley's prow, and saw the shores
Of France receding—the beloved shores
That she should never see again. Big tears
Dropt from her eyes, and from her lips the words
Broke in fond repetition—" Pleasant land,
Farewell! farewell!" Then silently she stood,
The lovely one, silent and motionless,
Amidst the weeping train; her lofty head
Thrown back, her fair cheek colorless, her eyes
Fixed on the cloudy heaven. There was a passion
Of grief in that fine form might have beseemed
Andromache, a captive—or the Maid
Of Thebes, Antigone, when doomed to die.
But this was a young queen—the fairest queen—
The fairest lady of the earth—whose name
Was as a spell for men to work by—Mary,
The peerless Queen of Scots, returning home
To reign. Yet there she stood all motionless,
Striving with fondest thoughts and deepest fears—
Thoughts true and tender of her tender youth,
And fears that took a tone of prophecy:
There stood she silent, till again the words
Burst from her lips:

     "Oh! pleasant land, farewell!
 Farewell to pageants glittering bright,
 The joust by day, the dance by night.
  Proud realm of chivalry, farewell!
 Farewell! in this sad hour more dear
 To loving friends and kinsmen near—
  Oh! land of loyal hearts, farewell!
 From thy fair hills and orange bowers,
 I go where dreary winter lours:
 From courteous knights, quick, ardent, bold,
 I go to bigots stern and cold:
 From Hope's gay dream forever hurled,
 I go to breast the stormy world:
  Oh! pleasant land of France, farewell!
 Thy sunny shores no more I see,
 Yet still my heart abides with thee.
 Home of my happy infancy,
 A long, a last farewell!"

I begin with this, dearest, although perhaps I may have shown it to you before, because from these few lines I derive my hope of that enduring fame which poets call immortality —not from their own merit, but from their being " married to immortal " music. About three years ago Charles Parker

asked me for a *scena* in English verse—something composed
of recitative, air and chorus, analogous to the Italian *scena*.
I happened to have begun this subject for one of the annuals,
and finding, on mentioning it to him, that it was exactly what
he wanted, he has just completed the composition, and it is
said by some of the best judges in town to be as fine as any
thing in English music. It is not published yet, but all the
great people have heard it. I invited Mr. Merry and Emma
Vines (another exquisite musician) to hear him sing it here.
They were charmed with it; and yet we heard it to a dis-
advantage, for it makes fifty pages of music, and requires the
united bands of Drury Lane and the Royal Musical Academy and above fifty chorus-women. The first five lines (an
almost literal translation of Mary's own verses,

"Adieu! plaisant pays de France!")

are the air—then the blank verse in exquisite recitative—
then a magnificent chorus—then the song again—and then
a chorus fading into the distance. No woman in England
except Mrs. Wood (Miss Paton) can sing it; so that whether it will be performed in public at present is doubtful; but
it is something to have furnished the thread on which such
pearls are strung. Charles Parker is a musical wonder, like
Mozart—a native of Reading, who *was* a pupil, and *is* a master of the Royal Musical Academy in London — not yet
twenty-one. He is a most sweet and charming lad in mind
and temper, and making a friend of every one who sees him.

It is not because Mr. Talfourd is eminent at the bar that
he beats Mr. Merry in conversation. Eloquence in conversation is quite a different thing from forensic talent. Barristers are seldom pleasant. They are coarse and loud and
noisy; and pun and vent jokes. I have known almost all
the most eminent; and, except Romilly and Lord Erskine,
can hardly name one to whom this character does not apply.
I believe that your Irish barristers are better. Of them I
only knew Mr. Curran; and he, in his latter days when I
used to see him, was certainly very coarse and disagreeable.

Are not these fires frightful? They began hereabouts;
but I hope that the example of Bristol will frighten ministers into some discretion, and force them to discourage political meetings of all sorts. The cholera will certainly do

great good in enforcing cleanliness where it never otherwise would have found its way; and, if it do take hold of some of our over-crowded cities, it will be a blessed dispensation. I am sick of the wickedness of this dense population. God bless you, my dear love! I wish you could see my chrysanthemums. My father's best love. Ever most faithfully yours, M. R. M.

To Miss Jephson, *Castle Martyr, Ireland.*

No date. Middle of November, 1831?

I write to acknowledge your dear letter just received. There is another letter of mine on the road to you—or rather probably received by you before now—but I send this chiefly to inclose some anemone seed, which we are sowing to-day. I have a great love of those gay winter flowers, which give colors so like the lost colors in old stained glass and I shall like you to sow some of my seed in your garden. How curiously the seed expands, opening and turning back like a frieze jacket: franks are nice conveyers of seed. Have you the great white Œnothera—almost as big as a saucer—which opens at night and is so like a cup of alabaster? If you have not, I must send you seed of that when it ripens, for it is one of my pet flowers. I'll also send some seed of a certain blue pea (Lord Anson's pea), which is just the color of Aqua Marina—the most beautiful blue of any flower; have you that? It has a small pink mark in the centre, which adds to the beauty greatly. It is small and scentless and very rare—and very rare it always will be, because it is very shy of seed. I inclose one of the petals. No — we don't use salt. Of course our geraniums won the prizes; and one seedling especially (which I have called the "Ion," after Mr. Sergeant Talfourd's play) is said to be the finest that has been produced for many years. I inclose the leaves of one flower of that also. We have at present twelve seedlings, each of which would win a prize anywhere, and one hundred and fifty more to blow. One effect of raising seedlings is, that one ceases to care for other plants—a very vain and dangerous feeling. My friend, Mr. Foster, has it to such a degree that he does not suffer any plant not raised by himself or his brother in his greenhouse; but even he condescended to ask for a cutting of "Ion," and I shall (if possible) rear one for you. By "if possible" I mean, if I can rear three—one for Mr. Sergeant Talfourd, one for Mr. Foster, and the third for your dear self.

Did I tell you, when talking of the Gores, that they are friends of Colonel Wildman, who lent them Newstead Abbey for their honeymoon abode, and that there they spent the first four or five months after marriage about a dozen years ago? They confirm the legend of the White Lady, and all the facts both of Washington Irving's book and the still more interesting accounts both of Newstead and of Annesley, published last year in the "Athenæum," and written by my friend William Howitt. My father, thank Heaven! is well. So is Dash. Is it not strange—just before the coursing season began, he began to dream of going out and *quested* in his sleep? So he did last year. Is not this very remarkable? By what indications could he know that the time of year was coming? He knows Saturday, when he accompanies his master to the Bench, as well as I do, and, on that day only, refrains from coming up to my room the moment I am awake, lest he should be left behind. When my father did go out two days ago, he was so enchanted with the strong boots and the gaiters that he kissed them both. He only kisses *me* when he has been ill and I have nursed him; or when I am very ill or very low-spirited; then he looks at me with such a look! and licks my hand, and lays his head against me. Can any body wonder that one loves that dog? Have you a pet dog now? They are a great source of happiness, in my mind. Yours ever affectionately,   M. R. M.

To Miss Jephson, *Castle Martyr, Ireland.*

Three-mile Cross, Dec. 14, 1831.

Your account of Miss Edgeworth is charming. High animal spirits are amongst the best of God's gifts. I had them once; but anxiety and loneliness have tamed them down. The highest I have ever known are Lady Croft's. They have borne her through all sorts of calamities—her husband's sad death—the death of her favorite son—comparative poverty—the marriage of her only daughter to a Frenchman living in France—every sort of trial; and still she is the gayest and most charming old lady in the world—as active in mind and body at nearly eighty as most girls of eighteen.

It is always bad criticism to say there is no more to be done. Beside Sir Walter's novels, the American are a new class (I mean Cooper's and Bird's—especially the Mexican stories of Dr. Bird), and so are the naval novels, for " Roderick Random" can hardly be said to have done more than opened the vein. Oh! it is false philosophy to limit the faculties and the productions of man! As well prophesy that there should be no new flowers! If T ——'s money were coming to me, I should have avaricious views of accumulating geraniums, although I have already more than I can keep; and piling chrysanthemum upon chrysanthemum, although as it is I have beaten the whole county. Don't you love that delicious flower which prolongs the season of bloom until the Roman narcissus blows, and keeps the world blossoming all the year round? My salvias have been superb this year. I planted them in the ground about the middle or toward the end of July, and took them up in October—so that we got all the growth of common ground and open air, and brought them full of bud to blow in the greenhouse. Two of them nearly reached the top of the house.

At present I am altogether immersed in music. I am writing an opera for and with Charles Parker; and you would really be diverted to find how learned I am become on the subject of choruses and double choruses and trios and septets. Very fine music carries me away more than any thing—but then it must be *very* fine. Our opera will be most splendid—a real opera—all singing and recitative—blank verse of course, and rhyme for the airs, with plenty of magic—an Eastern fairy tale.

God bless you, my dearest love! My father joins in most affectionate remembrances, and I am ever most faithfully yours, M. R. Mitford.

CHAPTER VIII.

LETTERS FOR 1832.

To MISS JEPHSON, *Castle Martyr.*

Three-mile Cross, Feb. 22, 1832.

I THINK you like Mr. Bennett's things that I have sent you; and in that case you will be glad to hear that an American visitor of mine is reprinting them in Boston. It is quite wonderful how, when our brethren across the water like an English writer, they buy editions of his works by the score. You will pardon the apparent vanity of my telling you, according to the information of the same friend, that my poor doings, prose and tragedies, have been printed and reprinted in almost every town in the Union. He sent me himself a very beautiful edition printed last year at Philadelphia; but it is the cheaper and commoner ones which are the real compliment. I am going to-morrow to hear Elihu Burritt, the American blacksmith. He is to give a lecture on Peace and Progress at our news-rooms. One of his plans is to establish a penny postage between England and America.

I have a fifth and last series of "Our Village" in the press, and having sent up too little copy, as it is technically called, I am now literally running a race with the printer. You can not conceive the miserable drudgery it is, to pass one's day in writing gay prose whilst in such bad spirits! You must therefore pardon this wretched scrawl. As to public affairs, they seem to me in a most deplorable way. But I never read newspapers and know little about them. Ever most affectionately yours,   M. R. MITFORD.

To DR. MITFORD, *Sussex Hotel, Bouverie Street, Fleet Street.*

Three-mile Cross, Tuesday, Sept. 26, 1832.

I am rather in a taking about this notice of objection to your vote, not on account of the vote, but for fear it should bring on that abominable question of the qualification for the magistracy. Ask our dear Mr. Talfourd whether the two fields, forty shilling freehold, will be enough, without bringing out the other affair. In short, it worries me exceedingly; and if there were any danger in it one way or other it would be best to keep out of the way and lose the vote, rather than do any thing that could implicate the other and far more important matter.

I send up to-day the rest of the "Tambourine" article, the best I ever wrote in my life. Pray call there and get the money—I mean in Lancaster Place. Shall we be able to go on, if the opera is delayed till February? This makes eighteen guineas there; and I have two more articles on the stocks, which will be ready by Friday, making twelve guineas more; and ten from Alaric Watts—and ten from Elder and Smith—and five from Ackermann: that will be all, except the money, which I fear you will not get, from .Westley (try for it, though). Will this and the dividend last us past Christmas, if the opera do not come out? If not, you had better get an advance from George Robins.

To-day is so beautiful, that, as the boys have had the strawberry mare up for the hay, I shall get Ben to put her into the chaise and drive up to the Merrys and round by the Fieldes. My mare is pretty well; but I shall not take her out to-day. Poor Dash is stiff, but better than I expected, and the jay quite well.

God bless you, my own dear darling! I long to see you. Ever your own,   M. R. MITFORD.

To the REV. WILLIAM HARNESS, *Heathcote Street.*

Three-mile Cross, Oct. 17, 1832.
MY DEAR FRIEND,—This last volume,* only published a month ago, is now at press for the third time—the first edition was sold the second day.

At present I am exceedingly unwell. My complaint is one which is brought on by anxiety, or fatigue, or worry, or any thing. Mr. Brodie has cured a friend of mine of the same disorder, and perhaps (though I doubt it) may cure me. But as I have promised Mr. Laporte a tragedy in January I must finish it; and as I well know that the first prescription of Mr. Brodie would be not to write, it is of no use putting myself under his care till I can follow his orders implicitly.

* The fifth of "Our Village."

I must complete the work if I can; and then try and obtain some relief for this very painful and harassing complaint, the depressing effect of which upon the spirits no one that has not experienced it can imagine. It has been coming on for some years. I should be better if I were less worried by invitations—of which, at my gayest, I never accepted one in twenty, and which I now decline altogether—and by visitors. Every idle person who comes within twenty miles gets a letter of introduction, or an introduction in the shape of an acquaintance, and comes to see my geraniums or myself—Heaven knows which! I have had seven carriages at once at the door of our little cottage; and this sort of levée —bad enough in health—is terrible when one is not well. Mr. Milman, who has established for himself a character for inaccessibility, is a wise person. I wish I could do the same: and I would have done so had I ever thought it possible that the mere fact of being a writer of books would have brought such a torment in its train.

This country is thickly inhabited, with few established rides or show-houses or lounges of any sort; and the local connection of the place and myself must, I suppose, be the cause of this kind of popularity — if popularity it be. I should certainly go to London to be *quiet;* if it were not that we have many valuable friends in the neighborhood, and that my father would lose much of happiness in relinquishing his country habits; and he must always be my first object. And, if I can but get well again, so as to be able to write with less effort, we shall get on very comfortably. I have much to be thankful for—above all, for friends.

God bless you, my dear friend! I began this letter in such bad spirits that I may perhaps have unintentionally conveyed to you a notion of my health being worse than it is. The attacks are only occasional, and my father says not dangerous. Kindest love to dear Mary. Ever yours,

M. R. MITFORD.

To the REV. WILLIAM HARNESS, *Heathcote Street.*

Three-mile Cross, Monday, Oct. 21, 1832.

MY DEAR FRIEND,—I write by the earliest post to prevent Mr. Dyce's taking any more trouble about the book which you were so kind as to mention to him, having been so lucky as to procure it unexpectedly in Reading—I mean the translation of the " Alf Von Dealman," for such, I find, is the gentleman's English name.

How pleased I was with the story you told me so kindly and so prettily—and how more than pleased was my father.* Another instance, nearly similar, came to my knowledge from the patient herself, a Miss Russell. She, when sinking under hypochondriasis, met with the book accidentally, and wrote to me that she believed the turn so given to her thoughts saved her intellect, if not her life. She still writes to me occasionally, and appears to be a woman of a fine and ardent mind, but over-stimulated—over-educated— as your rich heiresses so frequently are nowadays. She is since married to a Mr. Price. After all, this is *your* cure. Any healthy and cheerful book would have answered the purpose; but it is very pleasant to be the writer prescribed by such a physician; and it has done *me* good as well as your other patient.

Did I tell you that I had received a pressing offer from our good old relation, Mrs. Raggett,† to give up authorship altogether and live with her and her husband—who, nearly blind, requires some one to read the paper to him and write his letters; and still more, to serve as a friend and companion in their old age? The offer had great temptation, since she said with perfect sincerity that what she wanted in me was not a dependent but a daughter; and I have no doubt but we should have been happy together. It was, however, clear that my father's comfort would have been destroyed by such an arrangement. To have left him *here* would have been impossible; and if Mr. Raggett had (as I believe he would have done) given him a home at Odiam, the sacrifice of his old habits—his old friends—the blameless self-importance which results from his station as Chairman of the Reading Bench—and his really influential position in this county, where we are much respected in spite of our poverty, would have been far too much to ask or to permit. Besides, *he* would have felt himself dependent though I should

---

* The story was of a young man in a nervous fever, whose mind had been calmed and soothed by having the tales of Miss Mitford read to him.

† Mrs. Raggett was a cousin of Miss Mitford. They were people of considerable property.

not. I refused it therefore at once; and, as they will certainly engage some one of the many persons who are applying for the situation of companion, I have no expectation of any pecuniary result from their kindness. If I had gone to reside with them, of course some moderate provision would have been made by will; but as it is I have no claim, and can only think of it very thankfully with reference to the affectionate feelings and the great delicacy with which the proposal was made. They are a very fine old couple—still clear of intellect and vigorous in body, and with minds and tempers softened and mellowed by age. Kindest love to Mary. Ever most faithfully and affectionately yours,

M. R. M.

To Sir William Elford, *The Priory, Totnes.*

Three-mile Cross, Nov. 4, 1832.

The most delightful part of Miss Elford's delightful letter was her account of you, to which your own brilliant postscript bears ample testimony.* I can give an equally good report of my father, who sends his very kindest regards to his old friend; and my father's daughter, though still as poor and as busy as ever, is, you will be glad to hear, better in health and much better in spirits than when she wrote last. I have been talking to Miss Elford of the cholera. Have you happened to observe that the swallows desert the places where it appears? thus corroborating Shakspeare's observation (in the beautiful dialogue in " Macbeth," on which Sir Joshua Reynolds wrote so tasteful a note) that " where they breed the air is delicate."

Are you not grieved for Scott? And is it not most grievous that these national testimonials, which are so proper, should not have been bestowed when they might have relieved and saved him? Have you met with or heard of Miss Martineau's " Illustrations of Political Economy?" I am told that she has made above one thousand pounds by those little eighteen-penny books. I like the first, " Life in the Wilds," best: it is very interesting and Robinson Crusoeish; but I am afraid that they are rather too wise for me. I have an old aversion to do-me-good books in general, and

* Sir W. Elford was at this time nearly ninety.

to political economy in particular—perhaps because I don't understand it.

God bless you, my dear friend! Believe me ever most faithfully and affectionately yours,   M. R. MITFORD.

What a pleasant, gossiping book Moore's " Life of Byron " is! so totally free from the finery and gaudiness of the " Life of Sheridan"—leaving the hero so comfortably where it found him, except in the article of personal vanity, which seems to have been more excessive than any thing ever heard of before, *even in a man;* for you'll grant, I suppose, my good friend, that men, when they are vain, beat the women hollow in that good gift, as in others—and never tempting one to skip any thing but the criticism!

To DR. MITFORD, *Post-office, Wantage.*

> Three-mile Cross, —— night—no, Thursday
> —Nov. 15, 1832, my own dear darling's
> birthday.

Many and many happy returns of the day to you, my own dear father! I have been longing to *say* so to you, and to kiss you, and wish you joy in person, and I have drunk the toast in wine. I hope you told our dear friends of the anniversary, that they might do the same. How very good it was of you, since you could not be here, to write to me. I hope I shall get another letter to-morrow morning, for I miss you sadly. Never since the world began were people happier than ours have been this evening, especially Ben. You might almost have heard him laughing at Ilsley; and he has been singing, without music, and dancing to John's fiddle, and talking incessantly — poor urchin! The first thing he said to me was, "I wonder how we shall get on to-night," and I should imagine the question has been most satisfactorily answered. I bestowed about twenty brandy cherries upon them (the fruit, not the liquor) in addition to their beer, and you never saw people so enchanted! Also all the pets—Dashy, Selina, the fishes, the jay, the dogs, and the horses—have been taken especial care of. I fed Selina myself.

God bless you, my dear darling! Ever most fondly your own,   M. R. MITFORD.

To Sir William Elford, *The Priory, Totnes.*

Three-mile Cross, Sunday, Dec. 8, 1832.

My dear Friend,—I send the inclosed as you seem to wish, and earnestly hope you will succeed in your undertaking.*

I must be obliged to get out another book this spring, although how I shall be able to write it God only knows. I am glad you like my last volume; I myself hate all my own doings, and consider the being forced to this drudgery as the greatest misery that life can afford. But it is my wretched fate, and must be undergone—so long, at least, as my father is spared to me. If I should have the misfortune to lose him, I shall go quietly to the workhouse, and never write another line—a far preferable destiny.

God bless you, my very dear friend! Say all that is kindest to your family. Ever most faithfully yours,

M. R. Mitford.

[*Inclosure to the foregoing.*]

Three-mile Cross, Dec. 8, 1832.

My dear Friend,—I write in great haste just to say that I heartily approve of your plan for a cheap and general subscription for the purchase of Abbotsford; a feeling in which I should hope that every admirer of the great writer, whom we have unhappily lost, will most cordially join. Be so good as to advance the small sum necessary for me. Ever most affectionately yours,   M. R. Mitford.

To Sir W. Elford, Bart.

CHAPTER IX.

Letters for 1833.

To Miss Jephson, *Castle Martyr, Ireland.*

Three-mile Cross, April 8, 1833.

My dearest,—I shall certainly be a convert to your countrymen. I am turned O'Connellite, partly from love of his speeches. I have received a most curious letter, signed " A

* A subscription for the purchase of Abbotsford.

Munster Man," containing a real story, which he wants me to put into a tale; and I really think I shall try it, it is so characteristic, and curious and pleasant into the bargain.

It is, I think, one of the pleasantest signs of the times, to see how beautifully flowers are *painted* now, by the aid of the needle, on all sorts of material :—" printed in lawn," by one fair damsel, like Bellario—embroidered in silk and threads of gold and silver by another, as Clarissa was wont—cross-stitched with the fashionable *tapis d'amitié* in German wool —worked even in beads or mother-of-pearl: everywhere *flowers*, and really most beautifully imitated they are. Some of the carpet-work is quite astonishing. Lady Madalina Palmer is working one, which emulates the paintings of Van Huysum; and a most graceful amusement it is. She got her patterns and materials last year at Heidelberg; and the only objection is, that, when finished, it will cost about £500, and be too delicate for the sole of any slipper short of Cinderella's. But some of the less ambitious and less expensive things are charming, without any drawback. I saw a wreath of fuchsias the other day (by the way we have the new *Fuchsia longiflora*, six inches long, in beautiful blossom) worked in floss silk upon black net, to be worn over black satin, that was really most elegant; and I have two bags—one of forget-me-nots in beads, the other of white chrysanthemums in mother-of-pearl and floss silks—that are each of them exquisite. They even work groups of figures in tent-stitch for screens; and you can hardly conceive the fashion, or passion, for embroidering at this moment.

God bless you, my dear love! I am better, but not well. My father, thank Heaven! is brilliantly well. I am sorely afraid of a novel; and yet, I suppose, I must at least undertake some longer tales. Yours most affectionately,

M. R. M.

To Sir William Elford, *Totnes.*

Three-mile Cross, Sept. 4, 1833.

My dear Friend,—All that you say of art is most pleasant. But were you not struck with London? The town itself? *That*, in its stupendous improvements—Regent Street, the Regent's Park, and the new world all about Pall Mall, and again at Belgrave Square and Pimlico—always seems to me more beautiful and more wonderful than any thing that it contains, fine and great as the collections are. You must have missed Sir Thomas Lawrence much. Did you see Mr. Jones? I hope you have not suffered from over-exertion; for I know, by experience, that nothing is more fatiguing than to sleep out of London, and yet mix in its bustle and gayeties. But I, at forty-five, am a much older person than you are, or than my own father is, for he went yesterday forty miles to fetch me a geranium, and returned with his prize in the highest glee possible.

Pray how are you off for archery meetings in Devonshire? The people here are all turned into Robin Hoods and Maid Marians; and my nearest neighbor and most intimate friend (Mrs. Merry), being secretary to the club, and the meetings being held at Mr. Palmer's fine old place of Luckley (a beautiful Elizabethan structure, standing amongst the finest oaks in the country), I hear a great deal of it. I suppose I must go some time or other, for they have made me an honorary member;—but I have no great fancy for the thing. It is a very troublesome way of making a hole in a piece of canvas, for that seems to me to be the sole result. The intended result is, of course, the promotion of matrimony, but our girls are so ugly that I have no hopes of that sort. There really is not a pretty young woman in the county.

Dear Lady Madalina is wonderfully well; she often asks for you. I am quite of your mind about Miss Martineau, and quite in your condition. I knew nothing of Political Economy before reading some of her little books, and now I know less—so I mean to read no more of them. Very faithfully and affectionately yours, M. R. MITFORD.

If you ever look at the "Court Magazine," edited by Mrs. Norton, and published by Mr. Bull, you may find in the number for August a story of mine (which is false, of course), which contains a very exact description of Luckley, and of the frightful uniform which it has pleased our secretary to inflict upon such of the ladies as are silly enough to wear it.

To the Rev. WILLIAM HARNESS.

Three-mile Cross, Oct. 22, 1833.

MY DEAR FRIEND,—The little book of "The Rhymed Plea," first arrived to me with a short and simple inscription in the title-page, expressive of pleasure derived from my "tolerant and humanizing pen," but no note or word of any other sort from the author. I wrote back a short note expressive of my admiration of the work, and received a very long and circumstantial answer, telling me (and authorizing me to tell others) that his name was John Kenyon; that he lived during the winter at 39 Devonshire Place, with a single brother and sister of his wife's (this letter was dated "Twickenham"); that he had been for fifteen years the friend and correspondent of Wordsworth; but had only once seen Charles Lamb, and had not the pleasure of being acquainted, otherwise that by his high reputation, with Mr. Sergeant Talfourd; that he had been at Cambridge; had "stuck his prong in no profession;" had a brother who had just taken my books to Vienna, by way of counterbalance to the Police Reports in the "Times"—which brother was rather a profound and somewhat stern thinker, than an imaginative reader; and finally, that my praise had given as much pleasure to his wife, as his could have done to my father. The letter was charming; it conveyed a strong desire of acquaintance; and the frankness, coming after a little mystery—the kindness and the flattery—were altogether irresistible. In my reply, I could not help asking him if he knew you, and telling him how much I wished you to read his book; because you were in prose what he was in verse—and so you are; and this accounts for his sending you the poem. And then I told him —which is also the literal truth—that his kindness had given me the more pleasure because it had arrived at a time when the conduct of a near neighbor had given me great vexation.

Did you never read a French book called "La Théorie des Compensations?" I believe in it firmly. By the way, the obdurate person in this case is Mr. Merry. He behaved ill to Mr. Talfourd, then my guest. You know my idolatry for that dear and honored friend. I resented the thing, certainly with too much violence, at Mr. Walter's—Mrs. Walter having, with the kindest meaning, but very injudiciously, brought us together in the very moment of anger and without warning. Now, never having had a quarrel before with any body (except the one, of which you know so much, with Mr. Macready), it has vexed me more than it should; for, after all, I lose nothing in losing the Merrys except

Vol. II.—G

their friendship—or rather *his*, for I am quite sure that his good and gentle wife loves me as well as ever; and the friend who rejects an immediate and ample apology, and perseveres for six weeks in the bitterest enmity, is not worth any deep regret. If you should hear of this from Mr. Milman (for Mr. Merry has made a great story of it, and I have said nothing), be so good, my dear friend, as to give me as decent a character as you can. I should not like to incur his ill opinion. My Mr. Kenyon never can be *your* Mr. Kenyon, with the padded chest, and the dyed mustache, and the running away at Waterloo; but do let me know. The clergyman at Silchester, whom Mr. Kenyon mentions as having seen, remembers a very intelligent gentleman having asked many questions about that time, but can't recollect (the simpleton) any thing about his appearance. If a woman had seen him I should have had a full description, but men never do take notice; and, what is beyond measure provoking, the " *opposite neighbors* " to 39 Devonshire Place, to whom Mrs. Dupuy wrote for information on the subject, could tell nothing about the matter. Do let me hear any thing that comes to your knowledge on the subject. You would be still more pleased with the letters than the book.

God bless you, my dear friend! Ever yours,

M. R. MITFORD.

To MR. MERRY.

I can not suffer you to leave our neighborhood for weeks, perhaps for months, without making one more effort to soften a displeasure too justly excited—without once more acknowledging my fault, and entreating your forgiveness. Do not again repulse me—pray do not! Life is too short, and too full of calamity, for an alienation indefinitely prolonged —a pardon so long suspended. I know you better, perhaps, than you know yourself, and am sure that, were I at this moment suffering under any great affliction, you would be the first—ay, the very first—to soothe and to succor me. If my father (which may God in his mercy avert!) were dead; if I myself were on a sick bed, or in prison, or in a workhouse (and you well know that this is the destiny to which I always look forward), then you would come to me —I am sure of it. You would be as ready to fly to my as-

sistance then as the angel of peace and mercy at your side.
But do not wait for that moment; do not, for an error which
has been sincerely and severely repented, deprive a melancholy and a most anxious existence of one of its few consola-
tions. Lonely and desolate as I am—with no one belonging
to me in the world except my dear father—poor in every
sense, earning with pain and difficulty a livelihood which
every day makes more precarious, I can not afford the loss
of your sympathy. I say this without fear of misconstruc-
tion. You will understand that what I regret is the friendship and intimacy, the every-day intercourse of mind and of
heart, on which even you yourself—so much more happily
placed—did yet set some value. You did like me once; try
me again. You will find me—at least I hope so—all the
better for the rigorous discipline which my mind has lately
undergone; the salutary and unwonted course of self examination and self-abasement.

At all events, do not go without a few words of peace and
of kindness. I send you the last flowers of my garden.
Your flower seems to have continued in blossom on purpose
to assist in the work of reconciliation. Do not scorn its
sweet breath, or resist its mute pleadings, but give me in exchange one bunch of the laurustinus for which I used to ask
you last winter, and let it be a token of the full and perfect
reconciliation for which I am a suppliant; and then I shall
cherish it—oh, I can not tell you how much !

Once again, forgive me—and farewell.

M. R. MITFORD.

Three-mile Cross, Nov. 18, 1833.

To MRS. MERRY.

Nov. 20, 1833.

I do not lose a post, my very dear Mrs. Merry, in assuring
you with how much pleasure I look forward to a renewal of
our intercourse. Having said so much, I will not add a word
in palliation of the offense which I shall always be the first
to acknowledge and to deplore. The spirit of self-justifica-
tion is an evil spirit, and the sooner this unhappy affair can
be consigned to a merciful oblivion the better I am sure for
me, and I should think for all. " The strong hours conquer
us." Why should we struggle against them ?

Thank Mr. Merry for the relief which his letter has afforded me, and assure him that it is my earnest hope never by word or deed to recall to his recollection a moment which I must ever lament.

Adieu, my dear Mrs. Merry! Be so good as to present our kindest regards and good wishes to your family circle, and believe me most affectionately yours,

M. R. MITFORD.

To the Rev. WILLIAM HARNESS, *Heathcote Street.*

Christmas Eve [1833].

MY DEAR FRIEND,—I write in great haste, just to caution you, in case you should receive any authority, or pretended authority, from any quarter, to sell out our money in the funds, not to do so without communicating with me. I have no doubt of my father's integrity, but I think him likely to be imposed upon.

The post is at the door. With every good wish of this season and of all seasons, yours ever,

M. R. MITFORD.

Answer from the REV. WILLIAM HARNESS.

Dec. 26, 1833.

MY DEAR MISS MITFORD,—Depend upon it the money shall *never* be touched with my consent. It was consideration for your future welfare which prevented my father's consenting to its being sold out some years ago, when you had been persuaded, and wished to persuade him, to your own utter ruin. That £3000 I consider as the sheet-anchor of your independence, if age should ever render literature irksome to you, or infirmity incapacitate you for exertion; and, while your father lives, it shall never stir from its present post in the funds. After he has ceased (as all fathers must cease) to live, my first object will be to consult with you and my most intelligent money-managing friends, and discover the mode of making the stock most profitable to your comfort, either by annuity or any other mode that may be thought most advisable. Till then—from whatever quarter the proposition may come—I have but one black, blank, unqualified *No* for my answer. I do not doubt Dr. Mitford's integrity, but I have not the slightest confidence in his prudence; and I am fully satisfied that, if these three thousand and odd hundreds of pounds were placed at his disposal *to-day*, they would fly the way so many other thousands have gone before them, *to-morrow*. Excuse me saying this; but I can not help it. Yours most sincerely ever,

W. HARNESS.

CHAPTER X.

LETTERS FOR 1834.

To the REV. WILLIAM HARNESS.

Three-mile Cross, Thursday night, May 2, 1834.

MY DEAR FRIEND,—Mr. Milman gave my father in court to-day your sermon, for which I thank you most sincerely. It is a very able and a conciliatory plea for the church. My opinion (if an insignificant woman may presume to give one) is, that certain reforms ought to be; that very gross cases of pluralities should be abolished (it is too sweeping, I think, to say *all* pluralities); that some few of the clergy are too rich, and that a great many are too poor: but (although not holding all her doctrines) I heartily agree with you, that, as an establishment, the Church ought to remain; for to say nothing of the frightful precedent of sweeping away property, a precedent which would not stop there; the country would be overrun with fanatics, and, in the rural districts especially, a clergyman (provided he be not a magistrate) is generally, in *worldly* as well as spiritual matters, a great comfort to the poor. But our wise legislators never think of the rural districts—*never*. They legislate against gin-shops, which are the evil of great towns, and encourage beer-shops, which are the pest of the country; the cause of half the poverty and three-fourths of the demoralization. But the Church must be (as many of her members *are*) wisely tolerant: bishops must not wage war with theatres, nor rectors with a Sunday evening game of cricket. If they take up the arms of the Puritans, the Puritans will beat them. Generally speaking, moreover, I think that the Church of England is *tolerant*—incomparably more so than the sects that assail her—and, therefore, if for no other cause, ought to be protected. Do you know Professor Sedgwick, of Cambridge? We have had a young American namesake of his here for this last week—a charming person. Yours ever,

M. R. M.

[Under a more than ordinary pressure from want of money, Dr. Mitford went to London early in May, either to procure the representation, or to sell the copyright, of " Charles the First." Through the introduction of Mr. Serle, he was made acquainted with Mr. Abbott, who had quitted Covent Garden and become manager of the Victoria Theatre. To him the play was offered; and, as the theatre was on the Surrey side of the Thames, and beyond the jurisdiction of the Lord Chamberlain, there was no licenser to be consulted. The piece was immediately accepted. The terms offered were very liberal—two hundred pounds to be paid immediately, and a fourth share of the profits for a certain number of nights. But, though this was the first proposal, there was much delay in the negotiation; and it was not till the end of June that Dr. Mitford returned to Three-mile Cross, after the completion of his literary mission, and that Miss Mitford went to town to be present at the rehearsals, and witness the production of her tragedy.]

To DR. MITFORD, 8 *King Street, Cheapside.*

Three-mile Cross, May 13, 1834.

I thank you most heartily, my dearest father, for your great kindness about Mr. Bentley.*

Ben desires me to tell you to get the Wallace and the light whip for Miss Mitford; *I,* for my part, forbid you buying any thing unless you sell the play or the copyright. Ben could only get a dozen cuttings of heart's-ease yesterday, Ratten having sold all the plants. I have had the creepers planted and the dahlias, and we have two beautiful geraniums come out, and your seedling is really superb; but I am sorry to say that the cats are more mischievous than ever. They got into the greenhouse last night—broke one of our best geraniums to pieces—tore a good deal of a night-scented stock—dragged my sofa-cover all over the floor, and danced all over the looking-glass. They have also scratch-

* The publisher.

ed up our new border of red and blue flowers under the jessamine, and are really past bearing—particularly the white one, for I don't think the tabby would be so bad if alone. All the pets are well. The mare and Ben rolled the field yesterday, and Ben desires me to say that it looks very well.

Love to both the Williams and Mr. Sergeant. Ever most affectionately yours, M. R. M.

To Dr: Mitford, *King Street, Cheapside.*

May 15, 1834.

John and Ben are gone to the flower-show, and have taken some of our blooms to compare with those shown, and mean to bring home the names of the owners of any new geraniums, that we may try to get cuttings. So we shall know as much as if I went; I am so worried and out of sorts, that I should have had no sort of pleasure there. I have no doubt but you will do for the best. I should be content with £200 —£150—£100—any thing rather than risk; though I have a source of confidence in the play* that no one else has; for my reliance on Mr. Cathcart's acting increases rather than diminishes, which—fearful and doubtful as I am of every thing else—is a great comfort. But I would gladly take £100 for the tragedy nevertheless. Unless you get some money, my dear love, my going to town to spend money is absolutely out of the question. I would rather have £50 down than the chance of £500, for I know I shall be cheated, notwithstanding Mr. Serle's kindness.

My garden really looks divine; I never saw any thing so beautiful. God bless you! Ever your own, M. R. M.

To Dr. Mitford, 9 *Norfolk Street, London.*

Three-mile Cross, July 7, 1834.

We have had a most delightful evening at the Barnes's. They regretted your absence much; and so did I, because I think you would have enjoyed the party. There was Mr. McCulloch, the great political economist, whom I was glad to see; and a Mr. Walker, and a Dr. Elliotson; but the persons whom I was most delighted with were Mr. Dilke and his wife. He is the editor of the "Athenæum" (always so kind to me), and I assure you I never in my life liked any

* Charles the First.

one better.   He is quite as cordial and enthusiastic as Allan Cunningham, and one of the most perfect and accomplished gentlemen that I ever knew: you would be delighted with him.   Barnes said to me, of his own accord, that he saw from the other papers that their reporter must have made a great mistake about Mr. Cathcart, and that he would send some one else and set it to rights.   This was very pleasant; and Mr. Dilke promised also to say what was proper.   I have neither seen nor heard of Mr. Serle,* nor of Mr. Abbott, who ought to have called to-day.

God bless you, my darling !   I long for to-morrow, to hear all about you, and poor Dash, and my flowers; and when I have heard I will finish this.   So good-night.

Monday morning.

I copy, my dear father, the charming note which I have just received from the Duke of Devonshire:

"Brighton, July 6, 1834.

"MADAM,—I left London for this place on Friday, and could not till to-day reply to your letter, and thank you for the copy of 'Charles the First.'

"I am happy and proud to accept the dedication of your work, and have the honor to be, madam, your faithful, humble servant,   DEVONSHIRE."

To MISS JEPHSON, Bath.

35 Norfolk Street, Strand, July 8th, 1834.

MY DEAREST EMILY,—This is the very first moment in which I have been able to answer your very kind letter. The papers will of course have told you that both I and my actor have been completely successful—though to have succeeded under the disadvantages of bringing out such a tragedy in a minor theatre is very extraordinary.   However, we have *taught* the queen, so that she plays very finely; and the thing is admirably got up, and the theatre beautiful, and Cathcart's acting refined, intellectual, powerful, and command-

---

* Mr. Serle was a gentleman of very superior abilities, who had left the bar for the stage.   As an actor he was eminently correct and judicious, but never popular.   He was also the author of "The London Merchant" and one other play, which were beautifully written, and preserved much of the spirit and character of the old dramatists.

ing beyond any thing I ever witnessed. Mr. Serle wrote and spoke the prologue, which is just like one of Ben Jonson's, and the profound respect with which the whole thing has been treated is highly gratifying. They make a real queen of me, and would certainly demolish my humility, if I were happy enough to be humble; though I feel that over-praise, over-estimation, is a far more humbling thing—a thing that sends you back on your own mind to ask, "Have I deserved this?" —than any thing else that can be. For the first ten days I spent on an average from four to six hours every morning in the Victoria Theatre, at hard scolding, for the play has been entirely got up by me; then I dined out amongst twenty or thirty eminent strangers every evening. Since that, I have been to operas and pictures, and held a sort of drawing-room every morning; so that I am so worn out, as to have, for three days out of the last four, fainted dead away between four and five o'clock, a fine-lady trick which I never played before, and which teaches me that I must return, as soon as I can, into the country, to write another play, and run again the same round of fatigue, excitement, and pleasure. After all, my primary object is, and has been, to establish Mr. Cathcart. We have done very, very much; and if we had *two* great theatres he would certainly be engaged at one of them.

Write to me, as usual, *at home* (for I must go back or die here), and believe me ever most faithfully yours,

M. R. M.

To Sir William Elford, *The Priory, Totnes.*

Three-mile Cross, August 8, 1834.

My dear Sir William,—I never heard Lady Morley's novel mentioned; but I have no time for novel-reading, and (except Victor Hugo's matchless "Notre Dame de Paris") have not opened one since "Eugene Aram." And I don't think, from the turn conversation seemed to take in London, that novels were much read there. They are too long. The books I heard spoken of were Crabbe's Life, Mrs. Siddons's Memoirs, Sir Egerton Brydges's Autobiography, the "Bubbles from the Brunnens," and "Philip van Artevelde;" and of these, except the first and last, none will be heard of three months hence. All travels fast in London, and the book of the day is over in a week.

G 2

How splendidly beautiful London is! I had been there two or three times lately in the winter, but not for some years in the height of the season—when the bright sun throws those magnificent streets into strong light and shadow, and when there are brilliant crowds of gay carriages and well-dressed people to animate the scene.

And now, my dear Sir William, God bless you all for some months! Do not, any of you, write to me, for I am overwhelmed with business, and it interrupts me and makes me wish to reply, when I ought to be otherwise engaged.

God bless you all! As soon as I am disengaged I will let you know. In the meanwhile rest assured of my most affectionate good wishes. Ever most faithfully yours,

M. R. MITFORD.

To MISS JEPHSON, *Castle Martyr, Ireland.*

Three-mile Cross, August 30, 1834.

A thousand thanks, dearest Emily, for your most welcome letter. I am going to answer it very inadequately, being very much tired to-night, and yet not sleepy enough to go to bed. So I sit down to talk to you purely and simply to refresh me and do me good—as the very thought of you always does. My fatigue springs from two causes—one pleasant, the other very much the reverse. I have had a levée to-day, as is very common with me in the summer season—people from London, or people from America, or people from Germany, or people from France ; all clever, and almost all pleasant; and I became excited, and was quite done up, when we found out that some valuable geraniums, which had been stolen from our pits and advertised yesterday, had been carried away by a man only three doors off, whom we had employed for years, and done all for that our means would allow. He stole them and sold them to a neighbor, and then, finding that they were advertised, and that he should be detected, stole them again last night from the lady to whom he had sold them. Now this is grievous. He might have had eight plants for asking, as freely as you might. This does one harm, does it not? My father is quite unhappy, but I think that I was too vain and fond of my plants, and that it is a punishment. Well, I will talk of it no more.

Did I tell you that I had called my best seedling after Mr.

Sergeant's play?* Yes, I did. And did I tell you that I had an autograph of Mr. O'Connell's—most characteristic? Here it is:

> "Still shalt thou be my waking theme,
> Thy glories still my midnight dream;
> And every thought and wish of mine,
> Unconquered Erin!, shall be thine!
>
> "DANIEL O'CONNELL.

"*August* 4, 1834."

I was afraid that it was a regular circular autograph, but I heard of one different the other day, and have found out that this was written for me expressly, which rejoices me much. I have just been writing a sermon on Tolerance, the virtue most wanted in Ireland, on both sides, I think; you and yours, and Daniel O'Connell himself, seeming to me the only tolerant persons of your country, Protestant or Catholic.

I know your beautiful rose; it is French. I am to have that, and others, from Mr. Anderdon, whose collection of roses is as choice as his collection of pictures. Do you know the Devonshire brier? It is covered with semi-double flowers, and sweeter than any flower I ever smelt—sweeter than the magnolia, the double jonquil, the tuberose—any thing. There are three thousand roses with names!!! chiefly French. T'other day I found a golden beetle in a York and Lancaster rose, and counted above thirty glowworms in a lovely lane between our house and Mr. Palmer's. Five were close together—a constellation on the grass—earthly stars, really lighting the place. This, with the bee-bird, makes out more of summer than ought to belong to this cold weather. I heard a pretty story of a bird the other day. A friend of mine at Dover left a rare Indian bird hanging in a cage by an open window. Her house on the esplanade faces the sea. On her return she found another bird of the same species perched on the top of the cage, quite tame and gentle. All inquiries after its owner failed, and they suppose that it had escaped from some vessel, having been brought over for the purpose of traffic, and had been guided by some strange instinct to the captive of its own land.

God bless you! Ever most faithfully yours,

M. R. MITFORD.

* Sergeant Talfourd's "Ion."

To Miss Jephson, *Castle Martyr, Ireland.*

Three-mile Cross, Dec. 24, 1834.

My dear Emily,—Did you ever read Victor Hugo's
" Notre Dame ?" *That* is, in my mind, the most extraordinary work of this age, with all its painfulness ; and Victor
Hugo and Daniel O'Connell are the only two persons (not
friends) whom I would cross the threshold to meet. My
passion for Daniel is extraordinary—fed and fostered, certainly, by some delightful Irish people who have bought our old
house, Captain Edward Gore, R.N., son of the late and brother of the present Earl of Arran. The Liberator does seem
to me a most wonderful person, full of power of every sort,
and, I should think, very kind and genial. I certainly, the
next time I go to London, will manage to get acquainted
with him.

Mr. Sergeant Talfourd is growing in fame and in income.
They say that he makes £5000 or £6000 a year now, and he
has refused requisitions to stand from Derby and Bridgnorth,
and another offer to be brought into Parliament at no expense from a quarter which would be to him more tempting
than all—his native town of Reading. But he declines at
present, for fear of putting Mr. Palmer to expense or endan-
gering his seat.

My chrysanthemums have been, and many of them still
are, very splendid ; one especially, a small, but most rich and
regular flower, called the button-white, is, I really think, as
beautiful a plant as blows. It is of the purest white, whiter
even than the larger and looser flower called the paper-white ;
whiter than a lily, and of singular compactness and beauty
of form. Do you know it ? I have six kinds of white chrysanthemums, and about seventeen varieties in all. I wonder
if I could send you any slips or cuttings, or bits with roots
to them, in the spring. My finest flowers have been on cuttings not taken from the plant till late in June, or early in
July. Indeed, I believe that none are taken till the latter month. This is quick work, is it not ? My geraniums
look very promising, and I do heartily wish that you could
see my garden. It has been so much altered this year, that
Emma would not know it again.

God bless you, my very dear love ! Tell Mr. Smith, with

my kindest compliments, how very much I value his good opinion; all the more because I owe it to the kind representations of one of the friends whom I love best in the world.

I am ever, my own dear Emily, most faithfully yours,

M. R. MITFORD.

CHAPTER XI.

LETTERS FOR 1835.

To DR. MITFORD, *King Street, Cheapside.*

Three-mile Cross, Feb. 1, 1835.

I WRITE one line, my dear father, just to tell you that I have to-day an unexpected visitor, in the shape of an artist, sent by George Whittaker, to take views for an edition of "Our Village" with eighteen plates. I tell you this because it may be good to know in your negotiation with Bentley. God bless you! Ever yours,   M. R. MITFORD.

To Dr. MITFORD, *King Street, Cheapside.*

Three-mile Cross, Feb. 3, 1835.

You would be very much astonished, my dearest father, at my hasty note yesterday, but not more than I was to receive a letter from George Whittaker, begging to introduce the bearer, Mr. Baxter, as a gentleman whom he had employed to illustrate a new edition of "Our Village," and requesting me to point out the subjects. Finding that the illustrations were to consist of eighteen splendidly finished woodcuts (for I never saw engravings on copper more beautifully finished), we consulted, and agreed to sally forth immediately in quest of the most desirable scenes. Accordingly I took him to Serle's mill, which, by Mr. Terry's help and mine, he has contrived to sketch *just as it was*, and a beautiful design it makes; then to old Hodge's, he wanting to do a bit of the parsonage for a background to a scene in "The Vicar's Maid;" then to George Dawson's fishing-house, from the water, which will be most beautiful. I went in at Hodge's and called at the Smiths, who asked me and the artist to dinner to meet the Walters. However, of course, I declined; but after making these three drawings we came home in the dark, and I gave him your bed for the night, chiefly to save time in the morning, he being (as artists generally are) a very respectable, nice man. To-day Martha made him an early breakfast; and he has taken sketches of the village from both ends; a sketch of the garden from the greenhouse, of the church, of a scene on the common for a snow-storm, of an old house (the Gores'), of the bridge by Smith's for "Jessy Lucas," and, lastly and chiefly, an incomparable likeness of dear Dash, who is to be represented, on a larger scale than the other things, with the two magpies. We have also agreed on the other subjects; and I got him an early dinner, and have sent him off into Reading to get somehow or other to Windsor to-night. He wanted to take a view of the Castle to-morrow, for another work on which he is engaged. I gave him a bottle of Mr. Goodlake's claret, instead of port, and took all the care of him I could. He is very civil indeed, and has promised me some India proofs of the cuts. By-the-by, they are not to be great pictures, filling the page, but beautifully finished vignettes, printed on the same page either with the title or the beginnings of the articles. This, he says, is the present fashion for illustrating books. He is the man so much talked of in the "Athenæum," as the inventor of the new art of printing in colors, imitating oil paintings by engravings on wood. He has promised to send me a specimen; and we have had some talk of bringing out a Book of Flowers in that way, if Whittaker will agree for it. It would be beautiful; but of course that is Mr. Whittaker's affair. Ever yours,   M. R. MITFORD.

[A letter to Mr. Henry Phillips, dated April 10th, 1835, refers to Miss Mitford's opera of "Sadak and Kalascade," which had been accepted by Mr. Arnold for the Lyceum Theatre. It was produced on the 20th of April in this year.]

To Miss JEPHSON, *Castle Martyr, Ireland.*

Three-mile Cross, May 18, 1835.

I write immediately, my ever dearest Emily, to say that we shall avail ourselves of the knowledge that plants can reach you safely, to send three or four pots with little geraniums (last year's cuttings), and the white chrysanthemum which you have not, and which the gardeners hereabout call the button-white. I hope that it will blow well. It is to other white chrysanthemums what the little Banksia rose is to other roses—only that the color is as pure as milk, as lilies, as snow. I have not yet quite settled what geraniums to send; of course my best, but I am not quite sure which are my best. At present I meditate sending a "Miss Mitford," or rather one of the "Miss Mitfords," for there are several so called; it being a pretty proof of the way in which gardeners estimate my love of flowers, that they are constantly calling plants after me, and sending me one of the first cuttings as presents. There is a dahlia now selling at ten guineas a root under my name; I have not seen the flower, but have just had one sent me (a cutting), which will of course blow in the autumn.

I have your book of "Irishmen and Irishwomen," dearest; but I fear it would be dangerous to send that with the flowers. You must come and fetch it yourself. Yes, I know the beautiful tree-peony, the lovely Indian-looking flower, so gorgeously oriental, and like the old rich Chinese paper which one sees in houses fitted up eighty years ago. What a size yours must have been! The camellias nowadays, and the rhododendrons and azaleas, and the hybrids between the rhododendrons and azaleas, are really wonderful; I have seen plants that have been sold for twenty guineas, and which to rich people are fairly worth the money. The most beautiful of either tribe that I ever saw is a large buff azalea of matchless elegance, still very rare. But, after all, I like geraniums better than any thing; and it is lucky that I do, since they are comparatively easy to rear and manage, and do not lay one under any tremendous obligation to receive, for I never buy any. All my varieties (amounting to at least three hundred different sorts) have been either presents, or exchanges, or my own seedlings—chiefly exchanges; for when once one has a good collection, that becomes an easy mode of enlarging it; and it is one pleasant to all parties, for it is a very great pleasure to have a flower in a friend's garden. You, my own Emily, gave me my first plants of the potentilla, and very often as I look at them I think of you. You must send me some little seed in a letter, as a return for these plants, seeds of your own gathering and from your own garden ; and it shall go hard but I will make them grow : any seed that you think pretty.

Well, now we will talk of " Belford Regis." I presume that it has succeeded, since all my London correspondents speak of it as a *great* success; and the papers, so far as I have seen, prefer it to " Our Village," finding no other fault than that the picture of life which it exhibits is too bright and sunny—a fault which you will not quarrel with. In my opinion it is overloaded with civil notes, and too full of carelessnesses and trifling repetitions, which results, I suppose, from its having been sent up at different times ; having been first intended to appear in one volume, then in two, and now turning out three volumes. Nevertheless, I myself prefer it to my other prose works, both as bolder and more various and deeper in sentiment, and as containing one character (a sort of embodiment of the strong sense and right feeling which I believe to be common in the middling classes, emphatically *the people*) which appears and reappears in several of the stories, giving comfortable proof of the power to carry on a strongly distinguished character through three volumes, which, if I do comply (as I suppose I must) with Mr. Bentley's desire for a novel, will be very valuable. This person-age, who is neither more or less than Stephen Law, the butcher, is the chief favorite of the Duke of Devonshire ; for it is remarkable that the very great nobility, the real leaders of fashion, always delight in the simple and the true, and leave the trash called fashionable novels to their would-be imitators. As a single story, I prefer "Hester." Tell me your real and frank opinion of the book, and Mr. Smith's, and point out faults with the freedom of a friend.

Mr. Whittaker is about to bring out a new edition (the fourteenth of the *first* volume) of the whole five volumes of " Our Village," a very beautiful edition, ornamented with woodcuts of admirable softness and beauty ; amongst them a portrait of Dash, who is quite well, thank you, and as beautiful as ever. My dear father is also well. I am tolerably well after being shut up all the winter, and, at first getting about, but a severe bilious attack.

Mr. Talfourd has taken a violent fancy to Mr. O'Connell. I must tell you what he says of him in a letter to me : " In the meanwhile I quite love O'Connell. He has been most

kind and attentive to me, and most expressive of gratitude
for my attempt to show my interest for his country. He has
all the fascination which is attributed to Napoleon, with the
advantage, to us mere thinkers, which genius has when it appeals to passion rather than to action. That he is a great
man nobody can pretend to doubt; and I am equally persuaded that he is a good one. If he be not, then God and
nature do not write truly." Are not these strong expressions? I myself have taken a violent fancy to the Liberator, the more perhaps since I have seen many Irish papers
from our friends the Gores—a charming Irish family, between Whigs and Radicals and thorough O'Connellites; and
they say, and I believe, that the best chance for the payment
of the income of the Irish clergy is to have justice done to
the Irish people. You can not think how strongly they have
excited my interest for Ireland, and for O'Connell. If it were
not for leaving my father (who would never do to travel,
some interests are necessary to him, justicing, gardening, and
so forth)—if it were not for that strong and precious tie, I
would go to see you and make a pilgrimage to Derrynane,
and write a pretty book about the Emerald Isle.

Write to me soon, and long, and often, and tell me any
thing that comes in your way about Mr. O'Connell. Ever
most faithfully yours, M. R. MITFORD.

To SIR WILLIAM ELFORD, *Totnes.*

Three-mile Cross, June 1, 1835.

I thank you very much, my ever dear and kind friend, for
your kind letter, and I rejoice that you like my book. It
has been most favorably received, and is, I find, reckoned
my best; although, when one considers that "Our Village"
has passed through fourteen large editions in England, and
nearly as many in America, one can hardly expect an increase of popularity, and has only to hope for an equal success for any future production. My chief advantage in
novel-writing will be, that I shall be able to go higher and
lower than Miss Austen, and to embrace all ranks of English
life, as Scott did of Scottish. Not, of course, meaning to
compare my works with those of either of the great novelists of our time. What the present race is like I really do
not know; not having read a novel (except Victor Hugo's

magnificent "Notre Dame de Paris ") for these last three or four years.

I am in better health, and therefore in better spirits; but it is a weight under which all women sink—to support a family. Mrs. Hofland is very ill; Miss Landon is very ill; Mrs. Hall is very ill; Mrs. Hemans is dead; and such a catastrophe you will one day hear of your poor correspondent. What you suggest, my dear Sir William, would be most acceptable, and my father, whose mind and body are in full vigor, and who does at this moment nearly all the business of the county, would be most fit for the work, and would like it; but he is too old for the look of the thing, being now half way between seventy-four and seventy-five; and I believe there is a rule not to appoint any one who has not been called to the bar. So I must trust in Providence to have sufficient strength of mind and body to support us by my own efforts.

We have lost our neighbor, Mr. Milman, who has got a London living. It is quite right that he should be promoted; but I would rather have lost a hundred stupid acquaintances than one friend so entirely after my own fashion; although we are fortunate in our neighbors, having many very kind ones. God bless you, my dear Sir William! Kindest regards to all. Ever very faithfully and affectionately yours,

M. R. MITFORD.

To MISS JEPHSON, *Castle Martyr, Ireland.*

Three-mile Cross, June 13, 1835.

Since you are so kindly interested in my book, my dear Emily, perhaps you will like to hear that the story of the " Old Emigré " (I mean the poor abbé's murder) is true up to the point of discovery. The bagman was apprehended, and my father, who, as chairman of the Reading bench, gave much time and attention to the task of searching out the criminal, always thought, from the gown wound round the hilt of the sword, and other indications, that he was guilty; but the fact could not be brought home to him. I saw him when in prison. He was perhaps the handsomest and finest-made man I ever beheld—like Charles Kemble at thirty. The whole of the story belonging to the Duvals is fictitious; but I took the description of Louis, as a boy, from the son of a distant relation of my own, which relation, by-the-by (except in the fact of being an heiress) is the actual heroine of the story of "The Dissenting Minister." It is almost literally true. Perhaps you will like to hear a bit of praise which gratified me much. Mary Howitt, the Quaker poetess, says that the account of the development of intellect in the heroine of "The Dissenting Minister" might pass for the history of her own mind, and that I must have lived much amongst rigid Dissenters to give so exact a picture of the goings on in the interior of their families. Now, I don't remember ever to have been in such a house in my life. My cousin, a rigid Independent, did in that way captivate and fall in love with a *naval* (not a military) officer, on his parole, in a small town in Hampshire. He was exchanged, but at the peace he came to fetch her, and she is now living with him at Bayonne, he holding the post of captain of the port. I often talk of going to see her, only I never go anywhere. She is a most superior woman, and when in England two years ago she brought with her the most elegant and graceful boy I ever beheld, the prototype of Louis Duval. I used to call him the queen's page. "The Sailor's Wedding" is also literally true, except the description at the end—for he married his wife knowing her to be an heiress—and his early history is exactly narrated. I have not made this confession to any body else; because, if one owns to one piece of truth as to pleasant characters, people forthwith find originals for those who are less so. Poor Jack and Stephen Law are not portraits, but an embodiment of my notion of an English sailor and of a sturdy honest tradesman, who has made his own fortune by strong sense and good principle.

What a delightful work you have sent me! I read it to our excellent Irish neighbors and friends, Captain and Mrs. Gore, and they were delighted. I must give you a trait of Captain Gore, who is a very handsome man of thirty-eight or forty; very clever; very well acquainted with the world, having belonged (and still, indeed, belonging) to the household of the Duke of Sussex, and kept the best company amongst the Whig leaders; but who is the simplest-hearted, best-natured, happiest, merriest, kindest husband, and father, and friend that ever trod this earth. His sweet wife, also a woman of extraordinary ability and cultivation, has

taken to us just as he has done. So that they are such
neighbors as the dear Crowthers were; although, being poor
for their rank, they avoid the dinner-parties of the neighborhood. Well, Captain Gore is, amongst his other excellences,
a great mechanic and a capital working carpenter. One
Sunday lately—last Sunday week—they were sitting in
my greenhouse and contemplating the splendid pyramid of
two hundred geraniums before the door, withering, poor
dears, in the sun, and afraid of a thunder-shower; and we
all began lamenting for the hundredth time that we could
not devise a canvas awning to shelter them. "Can't it be
done in wood?" said Captain Gore; " any thing may be done
in wood. We must stop a week and build a roof to let up
and down by blocks, sailor fashion. I'll come to-morrow,
and see what we can devise—to-morrow or Tuesday." "Not
Tuesday, dear Captain Gore," said I, "for I am going out
as early as twelve o'clock; come to-morrow." To-morrow
arrived, and no news of Captain Gore; and we took for
granted that the thing had been thought over and found
impracticable; but on Tuesday, when I returned from my
round of visits, I found the captain and six men erecting the
machine, which is really the most serviceable and beautiful
canopy ever devised. A child can let it down and pull it
up. It completely covers the two hundred plants, and is
highly ornamental. There he sat in his glory upon the mast-
head, adjusting the blocks and ropes; having devised the
whole, and having actually made the greater part with his
own hands. Now, don't you love Captain Gore? just as I
love your dear uncle, and the bishop, and Mrs. Brinkley, and
your brothers and sisters, for your dear sake. You could
not be more in my heart than you always were; but you
are certainly more and more in my head, because I am always now thinking and talking of Ireland.

God bless you, my dearest! What a letter! Always
yours,   M. R. M.

To MISS JEPHSON, *Castle Martyr*.

Three-mile Cross, Sept. 3, 1835.

I send you, my dearest Emily, the four white œnotheras,
the blue pea, the *Salpiglossis picta*, the white Clarkia, a new
lupine, the most beautiful that I have ever seen, similar to

the *Lupinus mutabilis* in kind and fragrance, but a clear
lilac and clear white, and of far larger spikes of flowers (I inclose a flower); a new annual chrysanthemum (Cape mari-
gold) with yellow outer leaves; and two little packets of seeds
from Madeira, sent me by a gentleman whom I have never
either seen or even heard of till now, but who, having been
ordered there for his health, took my books with him, and
found them of so much amusement to him that he sent me
some seeds on his arrival by way of return, and we are likely to become great friends.   Did I tell you that I had met
at an Irish neighbor's (Mr. Fitzgerald's) an Honorable Mr.
Robert Talbot, brother to Mrs. Fitzgerald and husband to
my cousin Arabella Ogle (sister to Lady Dacre and first
cousin to the last Mr. Sheridan)—the nearest relative I have
in the world, except my dear father, and one whom I had
never seen before?   I can not tell you how pleased I was,
and so was she.   "Blood is warmer than water," especially
amongst north-country bodies; and her husband being one
of the ·thirteen translators of "Faust"—and by very far the
best—and having also printed for private distribution a very
fine translation of Schiller's "William Tell," we were friends
of course.   I tell you this because I know you like to know
any thing that pleases me.   Have you read her niece, Mrs.
Sullivan's, "Tales of the Peerage and the Peasantry," edited
by her mother, Lady Dacre?   She, too, is my cousin (we are
all authors and authoresses).   I think the tales true, and
pretty, and good—not like the common run of fashionable
nonsense.   I am very busy, having engaged to write for
"Chambers's Edinburgh Journal."   It is one of the signs of
the times, that a periodical selling for three halfpence should
engage so high-priced a writer as myself; but they have a
circulation of 200,000 or 300,000!   Do you know it!   It is
excellent.

Give my kindest respects to Mr. Smith, and to the Bells,
whom I feel to be my friends.   Heaven bless you, my dearest!   Ever faithfully yours,   M. R. MITFORD.

To MISS JEPHSON, *Castle Martyr, Ireland.*

Three-mile Cross—no date.   Autumn of 1835.

MY DEAREST EMILY,—An American of the highest class,
and the highest talent (Mr. Ticknor, of Boston, who visited

me the other day in his way from London to Dublin), assured
me that in London, even at such houses as Lord Lansdowne's
and Lord Grey's, they think no more about Ireland than they
do of St. Kitts, or any other trifling colony. The acute American added that in his country the fate of the one island was
considered to depend altogether upon the good government,
the settlement, the complete pacification of the other.   I
wish you might see the Ticknors, who were to visit Miss
Edgeworth.   They are most charming persons — intimate
friends of the two great Americans, Mr. Webster, the orator,
and Dr. Channing, the Unitarian preacher—perhaps (with
the single exception of your great countryman) the most
eloquent men now living.

Do you ever see the London weekly literary journal called the "Athenæum?"   It is the fashionable paper now, having superseded the "Literary Gazette."   It has such a circulation that, although published at the small price of four-
pence, the income derived from it by the proprietor is said
to be more than £4000 per annum.   Well, in the number of
the Saturday before last, there is an account of a "Visit to
Our Village," by William Howitt, the Quaker Poet (it is only
signed "H.," but I know by circumstances that it must be
his), which (except in the overpraise, which you will pardon)
is at once so pretty and so kind, and, to a certain point, so
true, that I should really like you to see it.   The praise does
not describe me as I am, because I fall far short of the picture; but it is just how I should wish to be—and how very
seldom does that happen! In general, people compliment
you upon possessing qualities that you do not wish to possess; but both Mary Howitt and her husband are remarkable people.   Surely you have read their "Book of the Seasons."

[*The rest of this letter is wanting.*]

To Miss Jephson, *Castle Martyr.*

Three-mile Cross, Sept. 20, 1835.

I take the chance, my own dear Emily, of your not having
the inclosed seed. The *Polyphillus lupine* is beautiful, but
not fragrant. It blows in May, bearing spikes of flowers as
thick together as possible—the one sort of a bright rich purple, the other of a very pure white. We had one plant last

spring, of which the spikes were above forty in number, and many of them from three quarters of a yard to a yard long. It was new ground, and a southern aspect : but it is almost always a magnificent plant, with its palm-like leaves, in the middle of which (the last stalk from which they spread) a drop of rain will stand and shine like a diamond. It is often raised by parting the roots, but we always propagate it by seed. It blows the second year constantly, and often the first; and we think it prospers better than from the root. The little blue lobelia is beautiful in masses ; we have a border of it under the white jessamine at the end of the greenhouse, where it is mixed with tufts of scarlet verbena—or rather the tufts of scarlet verbena are set amongst the lobelia, and they have been for three months covered with innumerable bright flowers, and will remain so till the frost. The seeds must be sown in a pot in the hot-bed early in the spring, and set out while still very small, and really their delicate strength is wonderful. The dark nasturtium is a fine color, and very luxuriant; and the new Marvel of Peru has a long white tube, which is sweet in the open air and pretty.

I dare say you have these flowers, but I send them upon the chance. So, too, I dare say you have the white petunia (which grows better from seed than from cuttings; the purple petunia I am afraid does not seed); the Virginia flax, a pretty perennial (is not sending flax to Ireland something like sending coals to Newcastle ?) ; and the *Hybiscus Africanus*, which is, by the way, one of my pet flowers. I know nothing more beautiful than the dark eye contrasted with the mellow, yellowish white of the sect of the petals. The moth mullein—for that is its true name—is full of seed, but it is not yet ripe ; I shall certainly send you the first that is ready. It is pretty, and I love it all the better because my father is so fond of it. I wish I knew whether I have any thing else you would like. I have about seventy sorts of seed done up in little packets in one of the baskets that foreign-dried fruits come in, and they look so tidy and old-maidish that I can't help laughing when I look at them. Would you like seed of the scarlet geranium ? By the way, our tuberoses this year were superb; I never saw any so large, or half so large—just like flowers carved out of marble. I suppose the hot, dry weather suited them. I am to have some Madeira lily roots from Mr. Blewitt. Do you know the Madeira lily? It is a species of the Belladonna, a bright pink.

We grieve over the rejection of the Irish Church Bills last year and this. *Here* it is almost universally said (by at least nine cultivated people out of ten) that the clergy are ruined by their pretended friends the Tories in the House of Lords; that Government and O'Connell meant them most fairly; and that to pacify the country, by establishing the principle of political equality to all forms of religion, at the least possible loss to the Protestant Church, was their settled intention. In England it is said that the Irish incumbents would probably have been very glad to have accepted the terms offered last year, had they not been swayed by the Irish bishops.

I have just had a letter from Miss Sedgwick (the American lady novelist), and her last book, "The Linwoods," is on its way to me. The motto is from my "Rienzi." I like Miss Sedgwick's letters. This is full of Miss Martineau, to whom I gave a letter to Miss Sedgwick, and who seems to have delighted them much during two long visits which she has paid to them. She (Miss Martineau) is coming to me on her return from America. How I do wish you could meet her! But we shall meet, I am sure of that, some day or other; ardent wishes realize themselves. Some day or other you and I shall meet again. Mrs. Trollope is in Italy, meaning to write her travels there next year. Her new novel is said to be clever, but not agreeable; I have not read it. Read, if you can, the "Life of Sir James Mackintosh:" it is very, very interesting. I knew him, and a most delightful man he was.

God bless you, my dear love! My father's affectionate remembrances, and my respectful ones to Mr. Smith. I hope you are quite well. Ever yours,   M. R. M.

To the REV. WILLIAM HARNESS, *Heathcote Street.*

Three-mile Cross, Oct. 19, 1835.

I have seen Mr. Talfourd to-day and delivered Mr. Wordsworth's message, with which he was much gratified. It was singular that I had also heard this very day, from a friend traveling in Switzerland, how anxious Sismondi was to see the whole of his fine play; and that a similar message arrived by the same post from Lord Holland, etc. All this is intensely gratifying.

Never was man more mistaken than you are, as to his feeling toward yourself. He always speaks of you with enthusiasm—admires, respects, esteems, and loves you. I am sure of this. But I can quite understand that there is something in his manner which makes you doubt it. I sometimes doubt myself whether he likes me, until I find him not only persevering in all manner of kindness, but coming to me and clinging to my society in a way that no one does who does not love one. It is manner. His *abord*, though soft and gentle, is at once too smooth and too cold. He does not know how to shake hands (shall I offer to teach him?), and has a way of stopping serious talk by some out-of-season jest —some mere play upon words, which, to me who love above all things good faith and simplicity in conversation, is more provoking than I have words to tell. Are not these the things that have made you doubt his regard? Unless you have stronger reasons do not give him up.

Mr. Haydon dined with us on Saturday, and was most kind to young Edmund Havell, who dined here to meet him— instructing him to finish the portrait of a boy as if he had been his own son. We had great talk of his fresco, which I saw when I was in town. It resists any wet, like china; being done upon *wet* mortar and drying in. Only peculiar colors (earths) can be used. It seems to me very extraordinary that the first English artist who has made the attempt should have succeeded on his first trial. No depth can be given—no shadow. Still there are a certain class of subjects, chiefly from the Greek mythology, where only light and air are required for the background, which will be beautiful—an Assembly of the Gods, for instance, the Deification of Psyche, Aurora and the Hours, the Car of Venus, the Chariot of the Sun. It can not be retouched; so that only a man as certain of his drawing as Mr. Haydon could succeed.

The subject of his present sketch is Uriel; and it is exquisitely bright, light, and ethereal—a presence. I should like you to see it. In these days of railways and steam-engines, a restored art, a new medium of beauty is worth look-

VoL. II.—H

ing at. Haydon himself is a very brilliant person, full of talent and fire and conversational power. His lectures are splendid things.

In this year's " Keepsake " is a very fine poem, " Upper Austria," by my friend Mr. Kenyon, composed because, from feelings of giddiness, he feared his head was attacked. He composed these verses (not writing them until the poem of four hundred or five hundred lines was complete) as a test. It turned out that the stomach was deranged, and he was set to rights in no time. God bless you, my ever dear and kind friend ! Most faithfully and affectionately yours,

M. R. MITFORD. .

To SIR WILLIAM ELFORD, The Priory, Totnes.

Three-mile Cross, Oct. 20, 1835.

MY DEAR FRIEND,—One change Lady Adams* must expect in sending her eldest hope to a public school—that he who went a boy will return a man ; for any thing so precocious as the young gentlemen who emerge from Eton, Harrow, and Westminster (I know less of William of Wykeham's disciples) one shall seldom see on a summer's day. Nevertheless, although the change be at first a little startling, I believe that it wears away, and that the lads turn out no worse than their shy, bashful, awkward predecessors of thirty years ago.

Yes, the rose beetle is of a burnished golden green. It comes in hot summers, and only in hot summers, in company with tribes of glowworms and flights of small blue butterflies, and death's-head moths and large green dragon-flies, and the thrice-beautiful *Sphinx ligustri*, or, as the common people prettily call it, the bee-bird. Another characteristic of this hot, dry summer has been the manner in which the large humble-bees (vulgarly dumbledoms) have forced open, torn apart, the buds of my geraniums ; an operation I never saw them perform before. Another novelty of this season has been, that the splendid new annual, the *Salpiglossis picta*, has, after the first crop of blossoms, produced perfect seed without flower petals, a proof (if any were needed) that the petals which constitute the beauty of a flower are not necessary to its propagation.

* Sir William Elford's daughter.

I am again suffering from nervous rheumatism in the face. It came on with the change of the weather first, as it did last year; and I suppose that nothing but a continued residence in a hot climate (which is out of the question with me) would remove it. My father, I thank Heaven, is well, and joins me in kindest regards to all near Totnes. Ever, my dear friend, very faithfully yours, M. R. MITFORD.

CHAPTER XII.

LETTERS FOR 1836.

To the REV. WILLIAM HARNESS, *London.*

Three-mile Cross, Feb. 4, 1836.

MY DEAR FRIEND,—We rejoice to find you so much recovered. My father was in town last week to dispose of a novel (I mean, to make an agreement for one, for it is not yet nearly written), and called at your house, where he saw the two Maries, but missed you. He has agreed with Saunders & Otley for £700 (seven hundred), a liberal price as times go. It is to be printed by September. I shall try my very best.

Mr. H. F. Chorley is doing a life—literary life and correspondence—of poor Mrs. Hemans, partly for the benefit of her boys. I know him only by correspondence, and by the introduction of my admirable friend Mary Howitt; but she speaks so highly of him, and his own letters so completely confirm the impression, that I feel assured that I have not done amiss in referring him either to you or Mr. Milman for the account of "The Vespers of Palermo." I never in my life saw any letters so thoroughly full of good feeling, right-minded and high-minded, as those of this very clever young man. If you can help him to any letters of Mrs. Hemans, I am sure you will.

How are the Milmans? and dear Mr. Kenyon, how is he? If you hear of the Queen Adelaide let me know; and believe me ever most faithfully yours, M. R. MITFORD.

To Miss Jephson, *Castle Martyr, Ireland.*

Three-mile Cross, April 29, 1836.

Yes, my dear love, the anemones are doubtless mine, for mine of the same seed sown at the same time are in full bloom. They are hardly red enough to please me, for I like them to be of the brightest colors, and most of mine are pale, of very pretty shades, pink and lilac and white, and some red and crimson, and many purple; but not the blaze of scarlet that I like in anemones. I want them to look like an old window of stained glass, or like my own geraniums in their summer glow, for there is nothing so bright as they are—except in the garden of Aladdin, where the blossoms were of rubies and amethysts—and so you would say if you saw them in June.

By the way, there is a most beautiful poem on the blue anemone in poor Mrs. Hemans's posthumous volume, which I have just received from her sister, Mrs. Hughes (the composer of the "Captive Knight," and other songs of hers), together with a very interesting letter. On her dying bed Mrs. Hemans used to recur to my descriptions of natural scenery, and meant if she had lived to have inscribed to me a volume of prose recollections, which she intended to have published. This would have been a very high honor; but perhaps there is a quiet, sad, serene, gratification in the private consciousness of such an intention, even more gratifying than the public distinction, and certainly more pure. She was a charming woman; and so is my friend Mary Howitt. By the way, I had a most gratifying letter from her the other day, with an account of Mr. O'Connell's visit to Nottingham. She speaks of Mrs. O'Connell with enthusiasm, as exactly fit for the wife of such a man. I always thought highly of her, because we heard so little about her. You will know what I mean. Ever, my dear love, most faithfully yours,   M. R. M.

P.S.—I am going to town (56 Russell Square) the 20th of next month, and shall stay a week or ten days.

To Dr. Mitford, *Three-mile Cross.*

Wednesday night. 56 Russell Square,
May 25, 1836.

My very dearest Father,—On arriving here, I found every thing very comfortable, and every body seemingly delighted to see me, although much disappointed not to see you, whom it seems they had expected. At dinner we had Mr. Stanfield, the painter, who is charming, and talks of coming to take *my* country; Mr. Chorley, who is also charming; Mr. Sergeant Goulbourn, stupid enough; some other lawyers (names unknown), ditto, ditto; Mr. Crosse (or some such name), a very nice young man of *your* sessions, an old scholar of Dr. Valpy's (do you know whom I mean?); William Harness and his sisters; some sisters, nieces, and cousins of Mrs. Talfourd, and last and best, Erskine Perry, who is charming. And, indeed, Stanfield and Mr. Chorley were equally charming. Oh, dear me! what a pleasant thing it is to have five or six such men talking to one all the evening. How different from the country! Dear William Harness is getting quite strong upon his feet; he is, of course, as delightful and affectionate as ever. He does not go to see " Ion " to-morrow, but joins us at supper, where, by the way, there will not be above sixty people. Mr. Wordsworth and Mr. Landor dine with us, and Milman, Proctor, Rogers, etc. All the poets and leading *literati* in town sup here. I found a note from Lady Meux, informing me that her cousin, Marianne Skerrett, is still in Naples, and inviting me to go and see her ladyship either in town or at Theobalds, where she now is for this week of recess. She is a near connection and friend of the Broughams, you know.

Thursday morning.

Mrs. Trollope and her son have been here—she looking exceedingly well; and Mr. Blewitt, a little delicate person; and Mr. Kenyon (God bless him!), who is coming for me to-morrow to show me the giraffes, etc., and who is more charming than ever. I am expecting, amongst other persons, Miss Jane Porter and the Countess Montalembert, who was Miss Forbes; and I close this letter for fear of a tribe of people coming. We are quite well; I trust that you are so. Ever most affectionately yours, M. R. MITFORD.

To DR. MITFORD, *Three-mile Cross.*

56 Russell Square, May 26, 1836.

Mr. Wordsworth, Mr. Landor, and Mr. White dined here. I like Mr. Wordsworth of all things; he is a most venerable-looking old man, delightfully mild and placid, and most kind to me. Mr. Landor is a very striking-looking person, and exceedingly clever. Also we had a Mr. Browning, a young poet (author of "Paracelsus"), and Mr. Proctor, and Mr. Chorley, and quantities more of poets, etc. Stanfield and Lucas were also there, and young Brown, Lord Jeffrey's nephew, who says that he misses you beyond description. Archdeacon Wrangham is not in London. Mr. Willis has sailed for America. Mr. Moore and Miss Edgeworth are not in town.

Mr. Crabb Robinson is to come and have a gossip with me to-morrow. We *had* a pretty good gossip to-night. We meet Henry Hope and Mr. Dyce, amongst others, to-morrow, at William Harness's. Henry Hope, they say here, has £80,000 per annum—a pretty little income !—and is just as unaffected as he was when we saw him there. You can not think how much I like Ellen Tree and Stanfield; so would you.

There was a curious affair to-night : all the sergeants went to the play* in a body, and sat in one box, except Mr. Sergeant Wilde, who had a box for himself and family. Lord Grey and his family were in a private box just opposite to us; and the house was filled with people of that class in the boxes, and the pit crammed with gentlemen. Very, very gratifying, was it not ?

God bless, you, my own dearest dear ! I am tired to death, and must go to bed.

I have just had your dear letter, and rejoice to find that you are so well. I will write to-morrow, and tell you all the news of the day.

Mr. Sergeant has forgotten to bring me a frank, and I am full of bustle.

Heaven bless you, my dearest ! Love to dear, dear Dash.

    Ever faithfully yours,   M. R. MITFORD.

To Dr. MITFORD, *Three-mile Cross.*

        Russell Square, May 27, 1836.

I told you, my dearest father, that Mr. Kenyon was to take me to the giraffes and the Diorama, with both of which I was delighted. A sweet young woman, whom we called for in Gloucester Place, went with us—a Miss Barrett—who reads Greek as I do French, and has published some transla-

*To see Sergeant Talfourd's "Ion."

tions from Æschylus, and some most striking poems. She is a delightful young creature; shy and timid and modest. Nothing but her desire to see me got her out at all, but now she is coming to us to-morrow night also.

We just missed poor Mrs. Hofland, but I hope to call upon her to-morrow, having commissioned William Harness to get me a fly, that I may go and see Mrs. Callcott (from whom I have a most charming note) and Miss Joy (from whom I have also heard), and the Dilkes, Allan Cunningham, Erskine Perry, Chantry, and Westmacott to see Mr. Perry's monument. A fly, they say, is cheaper than a glass coach, and quite as respectable, and I could not otherwise manage the matter.

Monday and Tuesday, William and Mr. Chorley are to take me to exhibitions. We had at William Harness's Wordsworth, Mr. Hope, Mr. Dyce, Mr. Chorley, Miss Sotherby (you knew her father, a friend of the Ogles—she is to meet me at Lady Dacre's), and a heap more of ladies and gentlemen; amongst the rest Mr. Knight, a very clever artist, who wants to take my portrait, in order to rescue his brother artists from the disgrace of the caricatures which have been taken of me. William says that the reason of his falling in love with me is, that I am so well dressed, and you will be glad to hear that our pains have not been thrown away, for I am just dressed like the fashionable people at the other end of the town, and really it is pleasant that it should be so. We had a delightful dinner, only dimmed by poor Mr. Chorley's distress. He has had another affliction, for Mary Howitt's book turns out to be a dead failure. He is a charming young man. We had loads of other visitors, both before and after my departure to the Zoological Gardens. Every body is more kind to me than you can imagine. All the naughty ladies were at our play, Lady B——, Mrs. N——, etc., etc. I wish you had been there. Am I not very good in writing? If you knew the immense concourse of people who are thronging here, you would think so. Heaven bless you! Love to Dash and all friends. Ever most fondly your own,   M. R. MITFORD.

To Dr. Mitford, *Three-mile Cross.*

Russell Square, May 28 and 29, 1836.

My dearest Father,—Our dinner at Mr. Kenyon's (to which I went with the Harnesses) was magnificent. Mr. Wordsworth, whom I *love*—he is an adorable old man—Mr. Landor—who is as splendid a person as Mr. Kenyon, but not so full of sweetness and sympathy—the charming Miss Barrett, Mr. Courtenay, and three or four more, came to dinner; one of the most magnificent dinners I ever saw; a much finer house and finer style than while Mrs. Kenyon lived.

Miss Barrett has translated the most difficult of the Greek plays (the "Prometheus Bound"), and written most exquisite poems in almost every style. She is so sweet and gentle, and so pretty, that one looks at her as if she were some bright flower; and she says it is like a dream that she should be talking to me, whose works she knows by heart. You can not imagine how very, very, very kindly Mr. Wordsworth speaks of my poor works. You who know what I think of him, can imagine how much I am gratified by his praise. I find that half the literary world is invited to meet me at Lady Dacre's.

To Dr. Mitford, *Three-mile Cross.*

Russell Square, May 30, 1836.

My darling will have found from my letters how we go on. Jerrold was here last night, and White, Crabb Robinson, Mr. Landor, Mr. Kenyon, Mr. Shepherd, Mr. Maule, and a thousand besides; and to-day first came Mrs. Lewis, and then, precisely at one, the Duke of Devonshire. He brought me a splendid nosegay of lilies of the valley (a thousand flowers without leaves—I hope I shall find mine in their prime) and moss roses, and staid above two hours. You would hardly believe that Mrs. Talfourd came and sprawled and bawled, but could not make him hear. I *did*, most comfortably; and he must have been pleased, for he begged me never to come to London again without giving him the opportunity of enjoying a similar pleasure. Gave me an order to see Chiswick (containing, as he said, *that* most interesting to me—pictures and flowers), and regretted that he could not show it to me himself at present, which some day or other, he said, he hoped to do.

Then came Mr. Otley, then Lady Mary Shepherd, and some more people, whom you don't know; and then I went out to Mr. Barrett's, and to William Harness's, and to call upon Dora Smith, whom I took with me to call upon the Barneses. I just missed him, but found her most cordial, making a great point of my fixing a day to dine there; which I positively declined, though very civilly. I have refused at least thirty invitations to dinner. Then I came home (still with Dora), and found that Mrs. Talfourd *had* dined, and meant me to have some tea! This, however, would not do, so I asked for a devil and a salad, and dressed and ate together, Dora helping. Then William Harness came to settle about our going to Lady Dacre's to-morrow, and to tell me that a servant (he believed Lord Lansdowne's) had been at his house to ask where I was to be found. (I had heard yesterday—I hardly know from whom—that Lord Lansdowne was inquiring about me.) Then came Mrs. Dupuy and William Ogbourn, to go with me to see Malibran. There was an immense house, and a still more immense enthusiasm. And, really, on comparing the matter, I had been deceived about the enthusiasm for "Ion," for that of to-night was incomparably greater, and the house as full. Malibran is a lovely creature, and an incomparable actress. *She* would be the only person for "Inez;" and really I should like to write an opera for her.

By the way, this new fiddler, Ole Bull, who is beating Paganini, has taken one of the airs from *our* opera as the theme of one of his variations in the concert which he gives once a week at the King's Theatre. All the artists say that the plans for the Houses of Lords and Commons are mere waste of time; indeed, no one talks of any of them, except Barry's, which we have in the "Athenæum." By the way, that "Athenæum" article is liked, for Talfourd thinks no praise half enough; talks still of acting the part himself at a small theatre; and would be capable of buying tickets to fill the house for a week provided he could in that way keep it going for that time at Covent Garden. You have no notion of our poor friend's tremendous inflation. It is specimen enough to say that he actually expressed to me great wonder that Lord Lansdowne did not put off a dinner which

H 2

he is to have next Wednesday, and for which tickets have been out these six weeks, because "Ion" is to be played a second time that night! Of me he is furiously jealous; so he is of Wordsworth; but more of me, because people come to his own house to see me, and walk up to me and crowd about me whilst he is in the room; and most of all is he jealous of Mr. Kenyon, who (Mrs. Callcott told me) is the most admired and courted man in town; and only see how kind he is to me!! I shall ask him to meet me at Chiswick, and take Wordsworth and Landor.

You can't imagine how well the duke and I got on. He is a first-rate talker—he *must* be—for I am living in the midst now of all that is best of London conversation, and I have not met with any one who exceeds him: and there was not a moment's pause. I don't think I ever spoke more to my own satisfaction, which is a comfort. He spoke of Captain and Mrs. Gore as very amiable and agreeable. He asked if I knew any Derbyshire persons, which introduced the subject. I told him of Mrs. Forster's geraniums, and he means to go and see them. What a charming person he is! How I do long to see you and Dash. Mrs. Gore says you have had a party. This was very foolish, because I am certain I should have managed it much better than you, and I can't imagine what sort of cooking or dinner you would give them. Also I am dying for my Dash and my flowers. I hope the plastering and whitewashing is done; if not, get it done before I come. I shall certainly come on Friday. Good-bye, my dearest, as I never dare trust any one to put my letters into the post except Martha; they are so often forgotten here. Ever most faithfully yours,

M. R. Mitford.

To Dr. Mitford, *Three-mile Cross.*

Russell Square, May 31, 1836. Tuesday night.

My dearest Father,—At seven William came to take me to Lord Dacre's. It is a small house, with a round table that only holds eight. The company was William, Mrs. Joanna, Mrs. Sullivan (Lady Dacre's daughter, the authoress), Lord and Lady Dacre, a famous talker called Bobus Smith (otherwise the great Bobus), and my old friend Mr. Young, the actor, who was delighted to see me, and very attentive and kind indeed. But how kind they were all! Lady Dacre is still very handsome, and most charming, but is growing a little deaf. Their kindness no words can tell

In the evening we had about fifty people; amongst others, Edwin Landseer, who invited himself to come and paint Dash. He is a charming person; recollected me instantly, and talked to me for two whole hours—that is to say, all the evening, for he took a post behind my chair, and never left it a moment. You may imagine that I was very gracious to the best dog-painter that ever lived, who asked my leave to paint Dash. Pray tell Dash. Edwin Landseer says that it is the most beautiful and rarest race of dogs in existence—the dogs who have most intellect and most *countenance*. Stanfield had talked to him of his intention to paint my country, and then Edwin Landseer resolved to paint my dog. It is very odd that Mr. Knight should want to paint *me ;* and Mr. Lucas will make the most charming picture of all—*of you.* Of course you will understand that I have not sat to Mr. Knight, nor do I mean it; but it is a remarkable combination of compliments from four of the crack artists of the exhibition, is it not? Altogether it was a delightful evening.

Talfourd is so devoured by jealousy at my reception that he does not even speak to me, and *to my certain knowledge* concealed from Lord Holland (Miss Fox told me so) that I am in town, and from Lord Lansdowne where I am.

William Harness says that the Lansdownes have been sending all about to find me out—of course to ask me to dinner to-morrow, when they have a party. William will *then* tell them where I am, but then it will be too late. Mr. Sergeant would not go to Lady Dacre's to-night, because it was a party made for me. He is really so inflated with vanity, and so bitter with envy, that you would not know him. He told me (when I said that the papers had been very far more favorable to him than to my plays) that I forgot *the difference !* And if you had seen the scorn with which he said it ! He said worse to Jerrold.

Every body says (so Mr. Kenyon tells me) that his head is completely turned with vanity. He won't go to the Shepherds, because Lady Mary came to secure me, and to make me fix the day. We have had no quarrel—no coolness, even, on *my* part. I behaved, at first, with the warmest and truest sympathy, until it was chilled by his bitter scorn; and since, thank Heaven! I have never lost my self-command—never ceased to behave to him with the most perfect politeness. But Mr. Kenyon observed the thing, and so did William; and he must change very much indeed before the old feeling will come back to me. You know that in our poor cottage he was a god. William Harness says he never saw any one received with such a mixture of enthusiasm and respect as I have been—not even Madame de Staël. Wordsworth, dear old man! aids it by his warm and approving kindness; and, only that it hurts and grieves me in my own feeling, Talfourd can injure nobody but himself by his unprecedented conduct.

To-morrow I go to Mr. Lucas's, the British Gallery, and dine at the Dilkes's; Thursday to Chiswick; and Edwin Landseer desires me to drive round by the Duke of Bedford's, Camden Hill—which I shall—and afterward I dine with Lady Mary. God bless you, my very dearest father! Ever most affectionately yours,   M. R. MITFORD.

How glad I shall be to see you once more, and my own home, and my own Dash!

To MISS JEPHSON, *Cheltenham.*

Three-mile Cross, June 19, 1836.

I was thinking of writing to you, my dear love, and am very glad to get your address, and to welcome you back to England, which seems a step toward myself. How I wish you were here at this moment! my garden is so exquisite; your recollection of it can convey nothing like the present beauty or the exquisite color. It is so changed as to be almost a new thing as to beauty, and yet retaining the old character of close and stage-like scenery, like a back scene " at a play."

I spent ten days in London—ten days crowded with gratification. Wordsworth was there; I sat next him at dinner three following days, and had the pleasure of finding my old idolatry of the poet turned into a warm affection for the kind, simple, gracious man. We met also, almost every morning; and I saw, on terms of the most agreeable intimacy, Lady Dacre, Lady Morgan, Lady Mary Shepherd, Mrs. Trollope,

Mrs. Marcet, Mrs. Callcott, Jane Porter, Joanna Baillie, and I know not how many other females of eminence, to say nothing of all the artists, poets, prosers, talkers, and actors of the day. With the artists I have particular reason to be pleased. Mr. Lucas, whose talent has ripened, and whose portraits this year are among the finest in the exhibition, is coming here to paint my father. I am now come home to work hard, if the people will let me; for the swarms of visitors and the countless packets of notes and letters which I receive surpass belief. A very clever young artist, Edmund Havell, whose talent in painting animals is really extraordinary, has been (and is) taking a likeness of Dash as large as life. Dash understands the affair, and makes an excellent sitter—very grave and dignified, and a little conscious—peeping stealthily at the portrait, as if afraid of being thought vain if he looked at it too long.

Edwin Landseer has a fine Newfoundland dog, whom he has often painted, and who is content to maintain his posture as long as his master keeps his palette in his hand, however long that may be; but the moment the palette is laid down, off darts Neptune, and will sit no more that day. Tell Mrs. Price this, if you see her—I mean about Dash's portrait—with my kind love, and that I can not write yet awhile, being so busy.

You must let me know your whereabouts, and when I am likely to see you. God bless you! My father's love. Ever yours,
M. R. MITFORD.

To Miss BARRETT, 74 *Gloucester Place.*

Three-mile Cross, June —, 1836.

MY DEAR YOUNG FRIEND,—I sit down to write to you after a day of excitement and fatigue, which (it being now four o'clock in the morning) ought to send me to bed; but my friend Mr. Chorley, who is, I am very sorry to say, going away to-morrow, will be the bearer of my letter and of a few flowers, and if he have the good luck to be let in, as I hope he may, will tell you all about our doings. He is worthy of the pleasure of seeing you, not merely in right of admiration of your poems, but because he is one of the most perfectly right-minded and high-minded persons that I have ever known.

To be sure I will come and see you when next I visit London, and I shall feel to know you better when I have had the pleasure of being introduced to Mr. Barrett; to be better authorized to love you and to take a pride in your successes— things which, at present, I take the liberty of doing without authority.

[Here follows an illegible paragraph of advice on the necessity of clearness of style.]

This is a terrible liberty from me to you, but I have seen so much high poetical faculty lost and buried from the one fault of obscurity, that I would impress upon every young writer the paramount necessity of clearness.

Use your interest with Mr. Kenyon in my favor, that he may come and see me, and stay more than one day. Ever, my dear young friend, most faithfully yours,

M. R. MITFORD.

To the REV. WILLIAM HARNESS.

Three-mile Cross, July —, 1836.

I think, after all, that you will come round to us in the matter of Miss Barrett. To say nothing of the sweetness and feeling of some of her former poems (the "Stanzas to a Poet's Child," for instance, and those called "The Sea Mew," in Miss Courtenay's Album), as well as their wonderful clearness and transparency of diction, there is a force, a vigor, and a tension, about the preface to the "Prometheus," which seems to be unmatched in modern prose. Depend upon it that, putting the learning out of the question, she is a most remarkable young woman. I have her "Essay on Mind" (written before she was seventeen, and published two years after), which, and the notes to it, contain allusions to books, as if known by every body, which Henry Cary declared to me no young man of his day at Oxford had ever looked into. Then she is such a sweet creature! You must make her acquaintance next winter. Mary and she will delight in each other; and it is the way to please one who loves to please us all—Mr. Kenyon.

I have been reading Charles and Alfred Tennyson's Poems. Have you read them? If not, do. You will like them, to use Mr. Chorley's phrase, "in spite of themselves." Also, I have just had a present of a most exquisite poem, which old

Mr. Cary (the translator of Dante and Pindar) thinks more highly of than any poem of the present day—"Sylvia; or, the May Queen," published in '27 by George Darley. Did you ever hear of it? I never did until the other day. Mrs. Cary has given it to me. It is exquisite—something between the "Faithful Shepherdess" and the "Midsummer Night's Dream." Would you like to see it? The author is the son of a rich alderman of Dublin, who disinherited him because he would write poetry; and now he supports himself by writing in the magazines.

If "Conti the Discontented" comes in your way, read it. The author is a most admirable young man, a friend of Mrs. Hemans, and about to publish her correspondence and literary life. I had a tremendous job in finding her letters to me—such is the state of my papers. Yours most sincerely,

M. R. M.

To Miss Barrett, *Glóucester Place.*

Three-mile Cross, August 16, 1836.

My dear Friend,—Did Henry Chorley call himself? He told me that his heart had failed him. The nosegay was a very shabby one—I was myself in all the grief of parting from this same Henry Chorley, one of the most affable companions I have ever known, and I was besides *befraddled* by the eternal visitors, morning and evening visitors, who make this cottage during the summer and autumn months a sort of tea-garden, or rural Beulah Spa—then, John, the lad who manages my geraniums, was, on his part, in the joyful agony of preparing for the Reading Horticultural Show. For my own part, my vanity goes rather to the beauty of the flowers in a mass, or in that great nosegay my garden, than to the mere points of growth, and bloom, and sorts, by which the judges at flower-shows decide their merit. Nevertheless, as John loves to get prizes, and I have no objection, why we take the thing in very good part; only it certainly (joined with my grief at losing a pet visitor) spoilt your posy; at least made that shabby which ought to have been splendid.

You should take my venturing to criticise your verses as a proof of the perfect truth of my praise. I do not think there can be a better test of the sincerity of applause than the venturing to blame. It is also the fault, the one single

fault, found by persons more accustomed to judge of poetry
than myself; by Mr. Dilke, for instance (the proprietor of
the "Athenæum"), and Mr. Chorley (one of its principal
writers). Charles Kemble once said to me, with regard to
the drama: "Think of the stupidest person of your acquaintance, and, when you have made your play so clear that you
are sure that he would comprehend it, then you may venture
to hope that it will be understood by your audience." And
really I think the rule would hold good with regard to poetry
in general, as well as tragedies. My Dash sends his respects
to your doves; faithful and gentle they are both. Ever, my
dear friend, most affectionately yours,   M. R. M.

To Miss Jephson, *Cheltenham.*

Three-mile Cross, Sept. 20, 1836.

My own dear Emily,—I am rejoiced that Mr. Smith is so
pleased with the *Lupinus Crookshankii* (for that is its name).
I think it one of our most beautiful flowers. I am going to
send great parcels of dahlia roots and flower seeds and ivy to
America, in March, to my late visitors, the Sedgwicks. Did I
not tell you the brother and nephew of Miss Sedgwick (brother-in-law and nephew of the President, General Jackson) were
with us for a long time. They are gone now, to the great
benefit of my book, but to my own personal sorrow. Theodore was a most charming person, and to be parted three
thousand miles from a dear friend is no small grief; it seems
like a separation for three thousand years.

I am expecting Henry Chorley; he is a first-rate young
man. He was, you know, the friend of poor Mrs. Hemans,
and his book about her (do try and get it at the library,
"Memorials of Mrs. Hemans," in two volumes) is more to
my taste than any biography that I have lately read, except
Southey's "Lives," and the exquisite memoir of Crabbe, by
his son. Do read it. Her love for me touched me deeply.
It seemed as if truly, as I had always loved and honored her,
I had never prized and valued her enough. One feels so at
the death-bed of a dear friend; and this book gave me such
feelings.

Yes, I have a notion that Cheltenham is "a fine vulgar
place;" but your friends are never of that stamp. I love
Ireland; it is odd, but I do; and I always feel as if, some

time or other, I was destined to see that fine country. Will
this vision ever come to pass? The Duke of Devonshire is
so good as to wish me to go to Chatsworth some time or
other; and I have a scheme (Heaven knows when it will happen) to go through England, beginning in Hertfordshire, at
the Hoo (Lord Dacre's), visiting all the way by Derbyshire,
and the Lakes to Northumberland; then *viâ* Abbotsford to
Edinburgh; then to the Scottish lakes; then to the north of
Ireland; then to you, and Killarney, and—and—and—(don't
be shocked), to Derrynane, and so home again. This would
make a nice book: but how I could stand the fatigue; and
whether my father would go or would stay; and whether I
could leave him: these are the puzzling questions. Else every
body says that it would do me good, and Martha would like
it, and the book would more than pay the charge—but my
father! and Dash! Oh, it will never be! It is a pretty dream
nevertheless.

Don't, dear, write to me about science; I never can understand what scientific people mean; and I used to pose poor
dear Captain Kater, and to shock scientific ladies by asking
what good it did; for really I never could make out. So, as
to the Bristol affair, it seems to me to be exquisite nonsense.
I had rather see that old house at Swindon, with the children
and the magpie (*we* have a magpie of our own who follows
my father about like a dog), and have one hour's chat with
you, than hear all the science that ever was talked, or see all
the philosophers that ever trod the earth. And I am right,
am I not? That old house must be exquisite. Did I tell
you that George Dawson is about to build an Elizabethan
house in *our* old grounds at Arborfield? That will be pretty,
will it not?

Lady Sidmouth has given six acres of most valuable land
for our hospital. Yours most affectionately,   M. R. M.

To Miss Barrett, *Gloucester Place.*

Three-mile Cross, Oct. 13, 1836.

Dearest Miss Barrett,—I have just read your delightful
ballad. My earliest book was "Percy's Reliques," the delight of my childhood; and after them came Scott's "Min-
strelsy of the Borders," the favorite of my youth; so that I
am prepared to love ballads, although perhaps a little biased

in favor of great directness and simplicity, by the earnest plainness of my old pet. Do read Tennyson's "Ladye of Shalot." You will be charmed with its spirit and picturesqueness. Are you a great reader of the old English drama? I am—preferring it to every other sort of reading; of course admitting, and regretting, the grossness of the age; but that, from habit, one skips, without a thought, just as I should over so much Greek or Hebrew which I knew that I could not comprehend. Have you read Victor Hugo's Plays? (he also is one of my naughty pets), and his " Notre Dame?" I admit the bad taste of these, the excess; but the power and the pathos are to me indescribably great. And then he has broken through the conventional phrases, and made the French a new language. He has accomplished this partly by going back to the old fountains, Froissart, etc. Again, these old Chronicles are great books of mine.

Heaven bless you, my dear young friend! Ever your faithful and affectionate   M. R. M.

To Miss Jephson, *Cheltenham.*

Three-mile Cross, Oct. —, 1836.

My dear Emily,—I have been longing for you all day to-day. I told you, I believe, that upon my young friend Mr. Lucas asking me to let him repaint my head (which he had painted six years ago, and which, from his youth and want of practice, had been a failure), I had said laughingly, " No! No!" upon which he rejoined to me: " Well; if you won't sit to me yourself, perhaps you will let me paint your father?"—an offer which I had not been able to refuse. Nothing was ever so pretty; for he is now the fashionable portrait-painter. He painted the Princess Lieven, the Duchess de Dino, Lady Cowper, Lady Sandwich, Lady Clanricarde, Lady Mahon, all the Court beauties, Prince George of Cambridge, and a longer list of grandees than I can count. Well, liking his model and having completely his own way, and my father turning out unexpectedly the best sitter ever seen, he has produced such a picture, both for painting and likeness, as I am certain has not been produced in England since Sir Joshua's time. . It is as like as the looking-glass; beautiful old man that he is! and is the pleasantest likeness, the finest combination of power, and beauty, and sweetness, and spirit, that ever you saw. Such a piece of color, too! He used all his carmine the first day, and was forced to go into Reading for a fresh supply. He says that my father's complexion is exactly like the sunny side of a peach, and so is his picture. Imagine how grateful I am! He has come all the way from London to paint this picture as a gift to me. These are amongst the compensations of literature! But yet, to have him for a week in the house, to go with him to the painting, which was done at our old home (Captain Gore's) a mile off, every day, then take him a drive till dinner, then either dine out or have company at home (with our small establishment), and I to do every thing, and talk all day, and receive eight or ten sets of visitors, and answer ten or twelve notes every day; is so exhausting that it has really brought on a bilious attack. I must shut myself up, or the novel will never be finished.

My father is awfully lame. Coursing a fortnight ago, he brought on a recurrence of an old injury to the tendon under the left knee; but to-day he is better, and our very clever surgeon promises to cure him.

I liked Lady Sidmouth very much; she returned my visit the next day and staid two hours. God bless you, my sweetest! Edwin Landseer has had an accident, so that I suppose poor Dash's portrait won't be done this year. You would be affected to see the interest which this picture of my father creates amongst the poor people round. It was quite affecting to see my dear father's manly modesty about that picture! He would hardly look at it until finished, and then said, over and over again, how much too handsome it was. I have just had a magnificent present of geraniums from the Duke of Devonshire. Poor Malibran! Believe me ever most faithfully yours, M. R. MITFORD.

To MISS BARRETT, *Wimpole Street.*

Three-mile Cross, Oct. 17, 1836.

I prefer the man of action to the man of letters—the *mere* man of letters. But, certainly, the cultivation and faculty enhances and embellishes the sterner stuff. But I am made for mere country pleasures, rather than for those of literature. I was this afternoon for an hour on Heckfield Heath: a common dotted with cottages and a large piece of water backed

by woody hills; the nearer portion of ground a forest of oak
and birch, and hawthorn and holly, and fern, intersected by
grassy glades; a road winding through; and behind us the
tall trees of Strathfieldsaye Park. On an open space, just
large enough for the purpose, a cricket match was going on—
the older people sitting by on benches; the younger ones
lying about under the trees; and a party of boys just seen
glancing backward and forward in a sunny glade, where they
were engaged in an equally merry and far more noisy game.
Well, there we stood, Ben and I and Flush, watching and enjoying the enjoyment we witnessed. And I thought if I had
no pecuniary anxiety, if my dear father were stronger and
our dear friend well, I should be the happiest creature in the
world, so strong was the influence of that happy scene.

Let me say, my sweetest, that the "Romaunt of the Page"
(which is a tragedy of the very deepest and highest order)
always seems to me by far the finest thing that you have
ever written; and I do entreat and conjure you to write more
ballads or tragedies—call them what you will—like that;
that is to say, poems of human feelings and human actions.
They will be finer, because truer, than any "Psyche" can be.

I inclose a note to Mr. Haydon. Miss Arabel will like
his vivacity and good spirits. Those high animal spirits are
a gift from heaven, and frequently pass for genius; or rather
make talent pass for genius—silver-gilded. Mr. Lucas is of
a far higher and purer stamp. There is no gilding there; it
is the true metal and without alloy, as far, I think, as can be
said of any mortal.

Did I tell you his story? His father was a clerk in the War
Office, an inferior clerk; and he, showing very strongly a genius for design when a boy, was apprenticed to Reynolds the
mezzotint engraver. At Mr. Reynolds's he worked six days
in every week from six o'clock in the morning till eight
o'clock at night, and he did work so honestly toward his
master and himself that he could *now* earn from £1200 to
£2000 a year as an engraver; but his aim was higher. His
master being of so much eminence as to have such pictures
as the "Chapeau de Paille," etc., to engrave, he rose at four
in the morning, abstracted from his breakfast and dinner hours
every moment not absolutely required for the support of life,
and devoted every stolen minute to the study of oil-painting

in those great pictures, and that with such success that the
moment he was out of his time he was ready and able to earn
his bread as a portrait painter—not only to earn his own
bread, but to support (as he has done ever since) a widowed
mother.   One of his early patrons was Mr. Milton, Mrs. Trollope's brother, and at his request, he thinking that any one
whose name was at all known would be of service to the
young artist, I sat to him for my portrait.   Of course it was
a failure.   A plain, middle-aged woman could hardly be otherwise.   We paid for it the too modest sum that he required,
and never demanded it after it returned from the exhibition,
where, in spite of its ugliness, it had a good place.   He did
not like the picture and did not send it back.   We had, however, been charmed with *him ;* had heard with delight of his
rapidly increasing reputation ; and had perhaps been of some
little use to him in the early part of his career, by recommending him to different friends.   This, however, was nothing;
his own great talent, astonishing industry, and exemplary
character were his best patrons.   However, when we met in
town, I said to him, "You used to like our poor cottage.
Come and see us again ; will you not ?" and he answered, "I
have been hoping that you would say this, because that head
of you is upon my conscience, and I want to paint it over
again." *I replied, of course, "No; I asked you to come and
see us for recreation, not for work.   I sha'n't sit to you, I assure you."   "Well," said he, "if you won't let me paint you,
you'll let me paint your father?"   And I could not resist;
and he did come ; and the portrait of my father is one of the
very finest ever painted, and only less precious to me than
the original.   Think of the difference of his prices now and
then ; think of his coming to my father as he would to Prince
Albert, and you will feel the full value of his unostentatious
and generous piece of kindness.

I love John Lucas.   He is less talked of than many who
have not half his real reputation ; but next to Sir Thomas
Lawrence, no man has painted half so many of the highest
nobility.   The Duke of Wellington (an excellent judge) will
sit to nobody else.   The Duchesse de Dino, Princess Lieven,
and all the great foreigners preferred him to any portrait
painter at home or abroad.   I must inclose you a letter
about him, from a dear friend, received to-day, and a note

to him for Miss Arabel. He has now more pictures bespoken than he can paint for two years. Oh! if I had but a head of you by him! What a head of you he would make! I should like Mr. Barrett to see his portraits, and to know him. He is modest almost to shyness; but it is such a mind, so well worth a little trouble to get at. I love John Lucas. His wife I have never seen.

The tamarind-water has been my father's best friend; it has given great relief. Love to all.

Yours most faithfully,   M. R. MITFORD.

CHAPTER XIII.

LETTERS FOR 1837.

To DR. MITFORD, 8 *King Street, Cheapside.*

Three-mile Cross, Feb. 1, 1837.

THIS afternoon, being so fine, I went to see Mrs. Gore, and found Lady Oranmore in a great fidget because she had not been able to get any body to show her the way to me; poor Miss Swift being in bed, I suppose with influenza. Lord Arran has made a very proper will; he has left the Irish estates to Philip Gore, charged, however, with so many legacies and annuities as will make him for the present a poor earl; but then the annuities, etc., are proper: £600 a year to his mother, the same to Colonel Charles Gore, the brother of our friends, as to them, and so on. We had a very pleasant chat indeed, Lady Oranmore being a very pleasant woman. I had to-day two most affectionate notes; one from Mrs. Walter, communicating the sad news of poor Mr. Bowles's death after a very short illness.

Your telling me that you had been to the play did my heart good, it was such a proof of your being well. Ever yours,   M. R. MITFORD.

To MISS BARRETT, *Gloucester Place.*

Three-mile Cross, Feb. 22, 1837.

MY DEAR FRIEND,—My father is, I thank Heaven, well. He is charmed with your story of the doves, being a complete bird fancier. He told me a story, when talking of your doves, of having, when a boy of eight years old at school at Hexham, been made free of a strolling company, in consequence of lending them a tame bullfinch to act in "The Padlock," the first play he ever saw. It would be well for me if I had never seen any; and you are wise for keeping out of the atmosphere. Before I forget it, the work you see advertised is a little volume of " Country Stories." The novel will come out in the autumn—late in the autumn, I suppose —and I must complete a third work in the winter to make up for this year's loss of income in " Otto :" so that I have no chance of seeing you, or indeed any other prospect in this life than that of incessant labor, anxiety, and disappointment. God grant me strength to bear it so long as my father lives!

To be sure Amorah *is* the " Faithful Shepherdess." If you look farther into the plays, you will find that the undramatic character of that charming poem results from its pastoral and poetical qualities. Generally, Fletcher (for Beaumont had little to say in the matter) is highly dramatic, although his plots are wild and improbable and impossible, and deal in the most provoking incongruities. He is a great poet, and certainly next to Shakspeare as a dramatist, whether in tragedy or comedy.

Adieu, my dear Miss Barrett, and believe me, ever most faithfully yours,   M. R. MITFORD.

Henry Chorley wishes me to go to town to sit for the " Portrait Annual ;" Miss Edgeworth, Mrs. Hemans, Lady Blessington, and myself being the ladies chosen for this first volume.

To the Rev. WILLIAM HARNESS, *London.*

Three-mile Cross, April 4, 1837.

MY DEAR WILLIAM,—I have only one moment, in which to proffer a petition to you. I have a little trumpery volume called " Country Stories," about to be published by Saunders & Otley. Will you permit me to give these tales some little value in my own eyes by inscribing them (of course in a few true and simple words) to you, my very old and most kind friend ? I would not dedicate a play to you, for fear of causing you injury in your profession ; but I do not think that this slight testimony of a very sincere affection could do you harm in that way, for even those who do not allow novels in their house sanction my little books. Love to both the Maries. Ever affectionately yours,   M. R. MITFORD.

How sad was poor Mr. Bowles's death!

To Miss BARRETT, *Gloucester Place.*

Three-mile Cross, May 4, 1837.

A thousand thanks, my dear friend, for your kind inquiries after Dash. He is quite well again, better and younger than he has been for months, or even years. Yesterday he ran at least twenty miles, having accompanied my father and myself in a flowering expedition to Penge Wood for the delicate wood-sorrel and other wood flowers, and to the Kennett Meadows for the white and speckled fritillary and other meadow blossoms. By the way, is it not an extraordinary thing that the blackthorn (sloe blossom) is just coming into bloom in the hedges and the fritillary is in bloom in the meadows; the one being a blossom (as you well know) of March, early March; the other seldom out until the middle of May, along with its cousins the tulips? Well, we went on this expedition in a pony phaeton, leaving it at the wood and the meadows, and walking about there and gathering flowers, so that of some ten miles we contrived to make a four hours' ride, and Dash ran away four several times, beguiled by hares and so forth, and had a *démêlé*, which I should like you to have seen and heard, with a huge hedgehog, whose passive resistance was too much for my poor pet, but which we brought home in a basket, and put into the kitchen garden, where there is a hedge and water, and from which if he should choose to run away he can. I think he won't, for he was very sociable in coming home, and as we put milk in his way, and shall continue to do so, I expect him to remain in that state of semi-tameness, which, in the country, is what I like best to see in birds or wild animals, protected but not confined. My love to your doves. How I wish the eggs would be good! It would be such a delight to you to help the parent birds to bring up their young. I told the story of the bird's nest-making to my young artist Edmund Havell, and he said, "What a picture!" If he painted faces as well as he paints animals, I am sure that he would try.

So far as I can find, the people who call themselves scientific never chance upon useful inventions, and the objects that they pursue are as devoid of use as they are of beauty. Moreover, they are themselves, for the most part, so scornful and conceited, that we are at perfect liberty to "scorn the scorner." Only think, for instance, of botanists, who know no more of the cultivation of a plant than the desk I am writing on, despising florists and horticulturists, who bring the lovely flowers and the goodly thing, fruit, to such perfection! And they can't even agree about their own jargon! We had the other day a pitched battle in my garden between a set of Linnæans and a set of Jussieuans. Oh! if you had heard the clatter! I was fain to bring forth my own list of new annuals (I have sixty, most of which have never blown in England), and had the glory of out-long-wording both parties, to the shame of floriculture, who ought to speak plain. I wish you had been present; it was a curious scene. The best stroke at science which I have met with for a long time is in the last "Pickwick." I hope you love humor; I, for my part, delight in it, and hold Mr. Dickens to be the next great benefactor of the age to Sir Walter Scott. There is about him, too, an anti-cant and anti-humbug spirit which is worth any thing.

My book is called "Country Stories." It is passing slowly through the press, and will not, I suppose, be advertised till nearly ready. I speak the real truth in saying that I do not like it. If ever I did like any of my prose works it was "Belford Regis," and this is more in the way of "Our Village." Mr. Browning seems studiously to have thrown poetry aside in his tragedy, as Shelley did; though I doubt if his subject can be so dramatic as the horribly powerful story of the "Cenci."

And now, my ever-dear love, Heaven bless you! We are going flowering again, to a copse full of primroses and ground ivy, and wood anemones. I wish you were with us! Ever yours, M. R. M.

To the Rev. WILLIAM HARNESS, *Heathcote Street.*

Three-mile Cross, Sunday, May 15, 1837.

MY DEAR FRIEND,—I have taken your advice and have written at once to Lord Melbourne. I have not the honor of knowing him, but my letter is brief and plain, saying that

VOL. II.—I

my poor earnings are the support of my family; that I had this year, from the state of the drama, been compelled to withdraw a tragedy,* for which I had hoped to have been paid in ready money; that this blow was followed by a failure of health and spirits, which had nearly deprived me of the power of literary exertion; and that the pension granted to Lady Morgan had caused a friend of mine to press upon me the present application. Of course my letter is better put together, but *that* is the material. I added that I had no interest, that my life had been one of struggle and of labor, almost as much withdrawn from the literary as the fashionable world; and that I was emboldened to take a step which seemed so presumptuous, by the sight of my father's white hairs, and the certainty that such another winter as the last would take from me all power of literary exertion, and send those white hairs in sorrow to the grave.

Now, this is strictly true. Have I done right? I have also written to the Duke of Devonshire, telling him what I have done, and saying, that I dare not ask him to intercede for me—but if he will—. Also I have written to Miss Fox, who is very kind to me, and I have inclosed my letter to her in one to Lady Dacre; and I shall inclose *this* in one to Mr. Sergeant Talfourd, who wrote to me very kindly the other day, to tell me of Mr. Forrest's leaving Drury Lane, he supposed because he did not draw the expenses of the house.

Is all this right? It may not succeed, but it can do no harm. If it do succeed, I shall owe all to you, who have spirited me up to the exertion. No woman's constitution can stand the wear and tear of all this anxiety. It killed poor Mrs. Hemans, and will, if not averted, kill me. Ever faithfully and gratefully yours,   M. R. MITFORD.

To the REV. WILLIAM HARNESS, *London.*

Three-mile Cross, May 20, 1837.

MY DEAR FRIEND,—I have just received the following letter from Miss Fox. How adorably kind Lady Dacre is!

"MY DEAR MADAM,—Lady Dacre brought me your letter on Monday; and certainly, however much it may overstate the probability of my being of any use in this business, it can not express more strongly than I feel, a wish to be so.

* "Otto."

I sent your letter to my brother immediately; and this is the copy of his answer:

" 'Lady Holland' (so I at last find it runs) 'has long felt a great interest about Miss Mitford; and, when we know how the pension question stands, and what are Melbourne's views about it, we may judge if any and what use may be made of the letter you have sent me. Miss Mitford, both as a woman and as an author, is certainly a very deserving person and a fit object for such favors. I heartily hope she may succeed, and I will do my best to support her wishes.' "

Then follow most kind expressions from Miss Fox, and so forth. Now, I thought it right to send you this letter, the only one that I have received to-day, because it seems to me that, turn out how it may, Lord Holland has given a great sanction to our application. You can not think how much it has comforted me, because, in spite of my entire reliance on your judgment, I could not help having certain misgivings, and fearing that you had been misled by the feelings of an old friendship to overrate my claims,* and that I might be accused of presumption and impertinence in making the application, although certainly the terms in which my letters were couched would not be liable to that objection.

Not hearing either from Lord Melbourne or the duke seems to me to prove, at least, that the one will not refuse his kind word and that the other does not consider it a thing to be rejected without a little consideration. I am very glad Lady Holland favors our suit; because, having both Miss Fox and her ladyship, we shall have Lord H. strongly with us.

How I torment you, but I could not help sending you this letter. Ever yours, M. R. M.

To Miss Jephson, *Castle Martyr, Ireland.*

Three-mile Cross, Sunday night, May 31, 1837.

I can not suffer one four-and-twenty hours to pass, my own dearest Emily, without telling you, what I am sure will give you so much pleasure, that I have had to-day an announcement from Lord Melbourne of a pension of £100 a year. The sum is small, but that can not be considered as deroga-

---

* " Claims " is a wrong word, for I make no such pretension. I mean rather " literary standing," as the Americans would say.

tory which was the amount given by Sir Robert Peel to Mrs.
Hemans and Mrs. Somerville; and it is a great comfort to
have something to look forward to as a certainty, however
small, in sickness or old age, unlikely as it is that I should
ever live to be old.   But the real gratificàtion of this trans-
action has been the kindness, the warmth of heart, the cordiality, and the delicacy of every human being connected
with the circumstances.   It originated with dear William
Harness, and that most kind and zealous friend, Lady Dacre;
and the manner in which it was taken up by the Duke of
Devonshire, Lord and Lady Holland, Lord and Lady Radnor, Lord Palmerston, and many others—some of whom I
have never even seen, whose talents, and character, as well
as their rank and station, render their notice and approbation a distinction as well as an advantage—has been such as
to make this one of the most pleasurable events of my life.
Even your partiality would be astonished at the mass of
letters which I have received, their genuine sympathy and
their profound respect.

Is not this very honorable to the kind feelings of our aris-
tocracy? I always knew that I had, as a writer, a strong
hold in that quarter; that they turned with disgust from the
trash called fashionable novels to the common life of Miss
Austen, the Irish Tales of Miss Edgeworth, and my humble
Village Stories; but I did not suspect the strong personal
interest which these stories had excited, and I am intensely
grateful for it.

Dash has been at the point of death, but is quite well
again. You know that the dog, Dash, and the maid, Martha, are my home comforts, next to my dear father.   Heaven
bless you! Ever yours,   M. R. MITFORD.

To the REV. WILLIAM HARNESS, *Heathcote Street.*

Three-mile Cross, May 31, 1837.

MY DEAR FRIEND,—I have this morning the most positive
assurances from Mr. Heathcote (who has been one powerful
and efficient ally in this matter) that he consented to accept
the sum only as an *installment*, and that he has the most decided promise that as soon as ministers have the power, the
pension shall be enlarged. The Act of Parliament is this:
Every pension that falls in is reduced by one-half, and the

other half granted to some fresh applicant. A pension of £200 fell in yesterday week, and Mr. Heathcote and Lord Palmerston accepted the £100 under condition that it should be augmented within the twelvemonth. I find, too, from a neighbor that heard it in town, but most discreetly kept the secret, that another most powerful person (he will not tell me the name, but some one of whom neither you nor I have heard in the business) has declared that he will not be satisfied unless it be £300. I am *most sincerely and unfeignedly thankful* for what has been done, and shall be quite content if here it rests, although if there be that feeling among the persons named it would, of course, be foolish not to take advantage of it, should opportunity offer. I am most thankful, and I love to own so much to you, my earliest and truest friend.

God bless you! Ever most gratefully yours,

M. R. MITFORD.

To MISS BARRETT, *Gloucester Place.*

Three-mile Cross, June 28, 1837.

MY SWEET LOVE,—I want you to write me a poem in illustration of a very charming group of Hindoo girls floating their lamps upon the Ganges—launching them, I should say. You know that pretty superstition. I want a poem in stanzas. It must be long enough for two large pages and may be as much longer as you choose. It is for " Finden's Tableaux," of which I have undertaken the editorship; and I must entreat it within a fortnight or three weeks if possible, because I am limited to time, and have only till the end of next month to send up the whole copy cut and dry. I do entreat you, my sweet young friend, not to refuse me this favor. I could not think of going to press without your assistance, and have chosen for you the very prettiest subject and, I think, the prettiest plate of the whole twelve. I am quite sure that, if you favor me with a poem, it will be the gem of the collection.

Now to less pretty considerations. My proprietor, Mr. Tilt, has put into my hands £30; that is to say, £5 each for my six poets (I am to do all the prose and dramatic scenes myself); and with this £5, which is, I believe, the usual price, I shall have the honor of sending a copy of the work, which will be all the prettier and more valuable for your assistance. *I will not contemplate a refusal, and have only to request that I may receive one line to tell me that you consent, as speedily as may be. If you like I will send you the engraving, or rather an unfinished proof of it in my possession. Heaven bless you! Ever yours,

M. R. MITFORD.

If you can give me time and thought enough to write one of those ballad-stories, it would give an inexpressible grace and value to my volume. Depend upon it that the time will come when those verses of yours will have a money value.

To Miss JEPHSON, *Castle Martyr, Ireland.*

Three-mile Cross, June 30, 1837.

So you never heard of the "Pickwick Papers!" Well! They publish a number once a month, and print 25,000. The bookseller has made about £10,000 by the speculation. It is fun—London life—but without any thing unpleasant: a lady might read it all *aloud;* and it is so graphic, so individual, and so true, that you could courtesy to all the people as you met them in the streets. I did not think there had been a place where English was spoken to which "Boz" had not penetrated. All the boys and girls talk his fun—the boys in the streets; and yet they who are of the highest taste like it the most. Sir Benjamin Brodie takes it to read in his carriage between patient and patient; and Lord Denman studies "Pickwick" on the bench whilst the jury are deliberating. Do take some means to borrow the "Pickwick Papers." It seems like not having heard of Hogarth, whom he resembles greatly, except that he takes a far more cheerful view, a Shakspearian view, of humanity. It is rather fragmentary, except the trial (No. 11 or 12), which is as complete and perfect as any bit of comic writing in the English language. You must read the "Pickwick Papers."

My geraniums are splendid this year—magnificent. We have the whole world to see them. I wish you were amongst them at this moment; but we are parching with drought. Have you read Harriet Martineau's "America?" It is a splendid book—ardent, eloquent, earnest, sincere, full of pictures, full of heart. I do not agree in her theories, but that is another matter. She is a great honor to her sex and country.

Another book, which is much the fashion, is Mr. Sergeant Talfourd's "Life of Charles Lamb." It consists almost wholly
of his letters, which are entertaining, although not elegant
enough to give me much pleasure. It is very odd that I
should not mind the perfectly low-life of the "Pickwick Papers," because the closest copies of things that are, and yet
dislike the want of elegance in Charles Lamb's letters, which
are merely his own fancies; but I think you will understand
the feeling. If I had time and room I could tell you fifty
pretty stories of our young queen. Ever most affectionately
yours, M. R. MITFORD.

To MISS BARRETT, *Torquay*.

Three-mile Cross, July —, 1837.
MY BELOVED FRIEND,—I am in great anxiety again. My
dearest father has had in the past week two several attacks
of English cholera. They have reduced him exceedingly,
more than you can fancy, and I am now sitting on the ground
outside his door, with my paper on my knee, watching to
hear whether he sleeps. Oh my dearest love, at how high a
price do we buy the joy of one great undivided affection,
such as binds us heart to heart! For the last two years I
have not had a week without anxiety and alarm, so that fear
seems now to be a part of my very self; and I love him so
much the more tenderly for this clinging fear, and for his entire reliance upon me! You, with so many to love, and so
many to love you, can hardly imagine what it is to be so totally the whole world to each other as we are. And oh!
when sickness comes, when one attack of a different kind follows another, so that the insecurity of our treasure is pressed
upon our attention every hour—oh! how tremblingly, throb-
bingly sensible do we become to the consciousness of that
insecurity! I hardly now dare leave him for half an hour.
I have not left him for a drive, or to drink tea with a friend,
for years. But I must not worry you with my depression.
Heaven bless you! Ever yours, M. R. M.

To the REV. WILLIAM HARNESS, *Heathcote Street*.

Three-mile Cross, Oct. 1, 1838.
MY DEAR FRIEND,—I have been very unwell during the
greater part of this summer, for two months never past the

outer door, and now that I am pretty well again we are in great trouble. Our landlady, who is a most singular compound of miser and shrew, refuses to put this poor cottage, where we have lived for seventeen years without having one shilling laid out by the owner, into the decent repair without which a great part of it will fall upon our heads, so that we are compelled to move.

Luckily, a comfortable roomy farmhouse, about half a mile off, is vacant, the farmer who rents the land living at another farm; and we may have this at thirty pounds a year, he, the farmer, paying the rates, taxes, etc., and we having a meadow of three acres into the bargain. But the garden is a potato-ground, and I am heart-broken at leaving my flowers, and frightened to death at the expense of moving and making a garden; for we having the materials, my father insists upon transporting them to our new abode; and certainly it will be less expensive to make the garden there than to do all that must be done to this poor cabin, which I love dearly in spite of all its deficiencies and faults. Still it will be a great expense, and I shall never like the new house as I do the old.

I must tell you a pretty thing that has happened close by. The journeyman of our neighbor the shoemaker has caught my love of flowers, and having borrowed of his brother the blacksmith a little bit of waste ground by the forge, behind some poplars which draw all the nourishment from the earth, so that they could not raise cabbages there, planted it with seedling dahlias (about two hundred), which he used to water night and morning all the summer with a *can*, which he carried backward and forward from the pond at the top of the street. Well, he has got the best seedling of the year, the very best. It happened to be in bloom in time for the last Reading show; gained, of course, the cottagers' prize, and he will get something between £5 and £10 for the root, besides the honor. I never, I think, saw such a happy face in my life as his at the flower-show. He never stirred from his flower. All the gardeners far and near (for it was a grand dahlia-show open to all England, and we had twelve prizes for strangers, and they came from beyond London) clustered about him; and John Brown and his dahlia were the lions of the day. I think I enjoyed it as much as he did; his love of flowers was so genuine, and his success so entirely deserved.

A dear friend of mine, who is appointed superintendent of the queen's dressers, gives a very interesting account of her. She says she is a girl of great power, sedate and serious far beyond her years, and fully equal to all that she will be required to do. Of the queen of the Belgians she speaks with enthusiasm. She says that in any rank of life she would be one of the kindest, gayest, most obliging, and easily-pleased persons that ever lived, one for whom it would he a privilege and a happiness to do any thing. She also speaks most favorably of her husband. He told the housekeeper at Windsor that he never went to Claremont without a recurrence of the same feelings as when he first returned there after his irreparable loss. Ever most faithfully yours,

M. R. MITFORD.

To MISS BARRETT, *Gloucester Place.*

Three-mile Cross, Dec. 2, 1837.

MY DEAR LOVE,—My book has been hindered by my ill health, by my many visitors, and lately by workmen. You can hardly imagine the demands upon my time: my father, eight or ten letters to read and answer in a day, almost as many notes, often more sets of visitors, the care of my small household, the necessity of seeing every thing done, and generally of doing that which my dear father (who, if he take a key in hand, leaves it in the door or in the drawer) is sure to leave undone.

All this, and care, and fear, and anxiety beyond measure; responsibility without power; make it wonderful that I should in a twelvemonth (being, besides, slow and barren without conception) have written " Otto," " Country Stories," the " Tableaux," and a story (longer than all the " Tableaux ") *lost* in the road to Edinburgh, or at Edinburgh—at all events lost; a loss, first and last, of above seventy pounds. All this makes it more wonderful that I should have done so much, than that I should have not done more. Even if I have not the nausea, the other fearful suffering is sure to come on every morning, sometimes at four or five o'clock, and last till noon. Think how that incapacitates! and think what it is to feel that more ought to be done, and yet that I can not do it!

I 2

To feel incapacity as a sin! Latterly, the din and the bustle of workmen have wholly hindered all composition. I have had to move, or to see moved, all our goods (as the country people say) from one room to another, and back again, and again away; and this is likely to last for some weeks. We shall gain great comfort, and at comparatively small expense, though still far more than we can afford. But that expense was inevitable, for the house was falling in, and the cost will be less than that of moving would have been; but still far, far more than we can afford or ought to spend; and this frets and worries me past expression. I believe there is not a laborer's wife in the parish who thinks so much of spending a shilling as I do.

By the accidental delay of a letter sent to be franked by the brother of my correspondent, the offer of a large roomy house in Wales, completely furnished, with two gardens and a large rich meadow, at a rent merely nominal, did not arrive till all was settled about this place. To this offer was added that of cows, ponies, a rick of old hay, key of cellar and storeroom, and every thoughtful attention that you can devise, and the assurance (I believe a most sincere one) that the acceptance of this proposal would make my kind friend a happy one; that it would turn a dissatisfied and melancholy life into one of cheerfulness and comfort. It would have been difficult to have resisted this offer, coming from a person in affluence and without children, to whom I felt that our society would have been an equivalent, and for whom I have myself the affection which renders obligations light; but my father—it would have been a great risk for him. Seventy-seven is too old for transplanting. I could not have moved him from his old friends and amusements without feeling that it was risking his happiness, and if any thing had happened to him, and I had even fancied that the change of place had had to do with it, I should have been miserable. As to myself, I should most certainly have gone; the beautiful country, the fine climate, the getting rid of a horde of idle acquaintances, and the cheapness, above all, would certainly have carried me away. As it is, I have only the gratification (a very true one) produced by the having been the object of so much kindness. She, too, is one of my gains by literature; her husband and herself came to Reading this spring to make my acquaintance, returned again for some weeks, after a short visit to London, and now it is certainly a friendship for life.

By the way, we have just had Mr. Lucas here, who painted that fine portrait of my father. He has been painting the queen dowager and her sister, and has given so much satisfaction that they have ordered two copies of each picture. The portrait of Queen Adelaide is, he says, very interesting, in her weeds. He speaks highly of her, and says that her portraits have never done her justice—that her forehead is fine—and that there is in her eyes an intensity of expression which has never been caught by any one. Her handwriting (which he showed me) is admirable—bold, and firm, and free. Ever yours, M. R. M.

CHAPTER XIV.

LETTERS FOR 1838.

To MISS BARRETT, *Gloucester Place.*

Three-mile Cross, Feb. 1, 1838.

MY DEAR LOVE,—I have got to think your obscurity of style, my love, merely the far-reaching and far-seeing of a spirit more elevated than ours, and look at the passages till I see light breaking through, as we see the sun shining upon some bright point (Oxford, for instance) in some noble landscape. I have just been reading Racine's "Letters," and Boileau's. How much one should like both, if it were not for their slavish, servile devotion to the king (and I think it was real), and to that odious woman Madame de Maintenon. Also Racine was a bigot, but sincere. My liking for Madame de Sevigné, is, I suppose, owing to my very ignoble love of gossip, which, if it be but honest and natural, I always like, whether on paper or *de vive voix.* And French, being the very language of chit-chat and prittle-prattle, is one reason why I like so much the *mémoires* and letters of that gossiping nation. Certainly Molière is their greatest man. Do you know Foote's farces? They have more of Molière than any other English writer, to say nothing of a neatness of dialogue the most perfect imaginable—as perfect as the dialogue part of the "Critic," which I take to be the most finished bit of Sheridan. I think you will like Mr. Townsend's smaller pieces. Lady Dacre you will love. Heaven bless you! Love to all. Ever most faithfully yours,   M. R. MITFORD.

To the REV. WILLIAM HARNESS, *Heathcote Street.*

Three-mile Cross, Monday evening, Feb. 5, 1838.

MY DEAR FRIEND,—I am going to ask you a very great favor, which, as it depends entirely upon yourself, and as there are many reasons for granting it, and none against it, I can not doubt your complying with. It is that you will sell out our money, the funds being now so high; let me have £600, and buy an annuity on my life and my father's with the rest. This will bring us in more in income than we now have; will relieve my mind from an insupportable weight; and will make me from a most anxious and miserable, a comfortable woman. My father has nothing to do with the matter. If I had written the novel as agreed upon, it would not have been wanted; but ever since the affair of "Otto" I have been a martyr to a most painful complaint, which, not confining me (except occasionally, in very violent attacks), has yet kept me in a state of constant suffering during many hours, either of the night or day.

This winter, luckily, it came on with a violence so dangerous, that my father was forced to send, at midnight, for a very clever Reading surgeon, and he has put me in such a train, that, though I can hardly expect a cure, the incapacitating pain is much abated, and even the exceeding inconvenience lessened. So that the £200 a year which will be in future all that we shall need to go on as we are going on, can be gained without inconvenience, if it please God to continue to me health and faculty. Even so ill as I have been this last year, I have gained that and more; but before the publication of "Country Stories," in short, as soon as, in consequence of "Otto," I had failed in my agreement with Saunders & Otley, they wrote to me to say that the state of literature was so much changed that they could only give £400 down for a novel, adding £150, if a certain number were sold, and the same sum after another stipulated sale. Now I know, and so, I take for granted, do you, that these sort of payments never are made ; so that it was a diminution of nearly one half. Colburn would possibly give more (some years ago he offered £1000) ; but still he might not. And under every circumstance the plan which I have proposed is the best.

I have no one to leave the money to—no one, I mean, who has upon me any claim of nature or adoption; my father's life is much the better of the two ; the getting quit of these debts (which to my certain knowledge it will completely do) is a question of more than life—of health, happiness, comfort, independence, respectability—of all that makes life not merely valuable but endurable; so it is to my dear father, who did not propose this scheme, but who is now certainly anxious (although not so anxious as I am) that it should be accomplished. If it be not, I shall sell my plants, my only pleasure; shall write under a miserable anxiety which will make all I write worthless; and shall very likely (a free and easy mind being the first thing prescribed for my complaint, which any worry brings on immediately) get quite as ill as I was before. This is the very truth.

God bless you, my dear friend ; Write and say " Yes."
Ever most faithfully yours,   M. R. MITFORD.

[The request made in the foregoing letter was conceded, the debts paid, and the residue placed out on mortgage.]

To the REV. WILLIAM HARNESS, *Heathcote Street.*

Three-mile Cross, March 6, 1838.
MY DEAR FRIEND,—If we go on with the " Annual " I shall certainly hope for a dramatic scene from you. People are quite crazy about your play. I threaten to have it chained to the wall, as used to be the fate of bigger books, for they put it into pockets and reticules, and keep one in a constant fume for fear of losing the treasure. Mr. Joy, your brother-trustee, has fallen in love with the extracts in the " Quarterly," and I have been obliged to write his good old aunt a full and particular account of you and your belongings. I know nothing more delightful than these sort of vindications by the public of one's own peculiar feelings of appreciation. Ever yours,   M. R. MITFORD.

To Miss Jephson, *Bath.*

Three-mile Cross, July 4, 1838.

Did I tell you that we have a very pretty little brown spaniel? He was Ben's. A year ago a savage boy broke his poor little leg. We nursed him and cured him, and he staid about the place, and now he has crept in by degrees, and is a most loving and amusing little creature, with the most beautiful short shiny curly coat that can be. My father is very fond of him indeed. I have been offered dogs of all sorts, but we could not be better off than with poor little Flush (that is his name, Flush) unless we could get such another as my lamented and noble Dash. It is one of Flush's recommendations that he was very, very fond of dear, dear Dash, and that our noble and gracious pet liked him. Indeed, I don't believe that my father would now change Flush for any dog.

My present passion is for indigenous orchises. I had a good collection last year, but they were trampled under foot during the winter, when I was too ill to attend to them. I have now one or two specimens only of the bee orchis, and several of the butterfly, which is the most exquisitely fragrant of the night-scented plants. If I could get about amongst the Oxfordshire woods I could enlarge my collection, but, as it is, I am obliged to trust to the kindness of friends, having only been able to make one excursion to get the butterfly orchises. Your convolvulus major is in great beauty, so are my geraniums, and a certain exquisite carmine pea; also a delicate white pea, freaked in blue and pink, a most unusual union of color, quite like old china. You will be glad to hear that the bay tree is coming up strong from the roots at one part, better than if from several, and we shall be magnificent in dahlias, having one hundred and eight of the very finest known. Oh, if you could but come to see us! My father would delight in seeing you. The Merrys asked for you to-day most kindly. Make my affectionate regards to the dear Crowthers. Ever, my very dear friend, yours most faithfully,　　M. R. Mitford.

To Miss Jephson, *Bath.*

Three-mile Cross, August 20, 1838.

I assure you, my dearest, that I, like yourself, have had applications *for money*, even since it has been generally known that for twenty years my dear parents have been mainly supported by my poor labors; supported, not in the parish-allowance sense of the word, but kept in comfort, and in every way genteelly and respectably, except as regards this poor cottage, where, to say a truth which I tell to few, I stay principally, because it is only the fewness and smallness of our closets here which could restrain my dear, dear father from the exercise of that too large and liberal hospitality, which, added to other causes, drove him through *three* good fortunes. Even since that has been known (a fact which I was forced to make public, from the hope of restraining such applications), I have been requested to lend hundreds, approaching the fourth figure, to become security for *thousands*, to ask for livings, for demyships or scholarships at college, for writerships and cadetships in India (all this for persons many of whom I had never heard of), to correct plays, to write them up, and *then* get them acted, to write a volume or half a volume for one, to give my name to volumes which I never saw for another, to subscribe and to get subscriptions without end.

I am perfectly sure that no week passes without some such application. If I answer, "I myself write for bread," the reply is, "I know this; but being yourself popular and well paid, of course your first pleasure is to assist obscure merit," and so forth. And in many instances, where the absolute want of money forces me to continue obdurate, pleading that I have myself nothing to give, and have long been compelled to make a general rule not to torment my friends by begging for subscriptions, I have been assailed by letters of the coarsest abuse. I am perfectly certain that £200 a year would not cover the amount of *claims* urged upon me in this manner, nor £500 of petitions to get subscriptions or donations from my friends: sometimes by name, as Lady Sidmouth, Lady Dacre, the Duke of Devonshire, etc; sometimes—generally—fixing £50 or £60 as the sum depended upon from me, that is to say, to be raised amongst my friends by my importunity.

Some of these applicants I have never heard of, most of them I have never seen; some have introduced themselves by a visit *here,* arising (according to their assertion) from a real or pretended enthusiasm, and followed up, after the stay of a day or two, accompanied by all the attention that we could pay them, by such demands, repeated upon every occasion. One, in particular, took advantage of having dined with us here and in town, to introduce himself as a friend of ours to my father's old wine-merchant, whom he favored with a large order; and happening, in a morning call, to meet with another friend deeply engaged in the coal trade, would also have given *him* the advantage of his custom, had not the shrewdness of the last-mentioned person saved him from the infliction. Then, when they have gained all that you are able to give, they quarrel with you and abuse you, and do all that they can to injure you in the reviews and papers with which they may happen to be connected. And these are poets ! !

Of one man, a poet in the annuals, who, because I only sent him a guinea to assist a sick mother, followed me with the grossest denunciations, I took the trouble to ascertain all that I could of the history. He had sent a letter, representing himself as starving and naked, to my excellent old friend Mrs. Hofland, who, setting out instantly to his lodgings on a cold winter's night, found his story apparently true, an old lady lying in a ragged bed in a most comfortless room, and he sitting wretchedly clad writing at a table. She sent them that very night food, firing, clothes; got, using her own name, an advertisement the very next morning into the "Times," collected £50, and introduced him to a merchant, who took him into his counting-house at £80 a year. Six months afterward, being in exactly the same condition, he had the effrontery to apply again to the same benevolent person, and, upon her asking why he had left his situation, replied, "How could a man of genius be fettered to a desk ?" Well, these are the men; the women are, I think, very much worse.

I am so glad that you like the plan of my new book: "The Miscellany," it might be called. The letters *are* gossiping. My father is gone up to sell it. I hope that he may not be disappointed in the sum. He is at once generous and sanguine; and it having pleased God, somehow or other, to enable me hitherto to provide what was absolutely wanted, he now, I think, relies upon it, just as if it were money in the funds—his only fault, God bless him! But if he could tell how debt presses upon the mind—upon the heart, as if it were a sin, and sometimes, I do believe, makes me ill, when otherwise I should be well—he would be more careful. But men do not change at eighty; and I do think that while he wants me, and for what he wants me, I shall be spared. Finden has not yet paid me.

I am not exceedingly worse, only there is more and more fatigue and severe pain. Yours most affectionately,

M. R. MITFORD.

To MISS BARRETT, *Torquay.*

Three-mile Cross, Sept. 20, 1838.

Ten thousand thanks, my dear young friend, for the clouted cream, that pastoral luxury, which is so welcome to me, because my father is so fond of it. I am not myself suffered to partake of the delicacy, but what my father enjoys is more than enjoyment to me, and it is mere selfishness that makes it so. I love to feed Flush even, and to see my tame pigeons feed at the window, and the saucy hen tap the glass, if the casement be shut. She likes to come in and to sit on the innermost ledge of the window-sill, and listen and turn her pretty top-knotted head to this side and that while I talk to her. This pleasure I owe to you, having taken to the homely pigeons as a rustic imitation of your doves, and they blend well with my flowery garden.

In spite of his physical debility, Mr. Thatcher is in no common degree *manly;* and when I say this, and add that he is also mild and gentle, I say more for him than can be said for most of the " pen and ink " people, who are by very far the most effeminate class in existence. If it take nine tailors to make a man, according to my calculation it would take nine authors to make a tailor.

I hope favorably for Miss Landon's marriage. Dr. Buckland had seen (he told me) her husband, a little boyish-looking fair-haired Scotchman, but really thirty-six. He spoke well of him; and a story, which I will tell you, looks liberal and gentlemanly: Mr. Maclean was showing some rings of

negro workmanship at a party, where he accidentally met
Dr. Buckland, and offered him a large and heavy one.
"Not that," said Dr. Buckland, unwilling to accept so valuable a present; "give me one of the small and slight ones,
for my wife or daughter." Upon which Mr. Maclean forced
three rings upon him, the original and two of the slighter
fabric. This looked well. The rings I saw, and they were
beautiful. The things that go under Lady Stepney's *title**
were all written over by Miss Landon, or the grammar and
spelling would have disgraced a lady's maid. This is a want
of self-respect which one can not pardon; and, coupled with
other facts of a similar nature, they explain my distaste toward her as a sister authoress.

Did I tell you that I have had accounts of Joanna Baillie,
who was seventy-six on the 11th of this month? She is losing her memory, and conscious of her loss. Heaven bless
you, my ever dearest! Let me hear soon, soon. Ever yours,

M. R. MITFORD.

CHAPTER XV.

LETTERS FOR 1839 AND 1840.

To MISS JEPHSON, *Castle Martyr, Ireland.*

Three-mile Cross, March 1, 1839.

MY DEAREST EMILY,—Poor dear Lady Dacre has written
me the most affecting letter I ever read. Mrs. Sullivan was
all that is good, and Lady Dacre's love for her was like that
of Madame de Sevigné for Madame de Grignan. Poor Mrs.
Dupuy, too, is in equal distress for the loss of Mrs. Blagrave.
Lady Sidmouth, Lady Morton tells me, is worse instead of
better since her sojourn in town, where she has put herself
under the care of Dr. Chambers and Sir Benjamin Brodie.
I fear that my sweet Miss Barrett is no better at Torquay.
The Milmans have lost their favorite child, a girl, whose little hand was always in her father's. Mrs. Milman's mother
is also dead. In short, Death is busy around us. I am
doubly thankful to have had my beloved father spared to
me. If I could but give my whole life to him, reading to

* In the Annual.

him, driving out with him, playing cribbage with him, never five minutes away from him, except when he is asleep (for this is what makes him happy), it would be the breath of life to me; for the complete and child-like dependence which he has upon my love to supply to him food and rest and amusement is the most endearing of all ties. I love him a million times better than ever, and can quite understand that love of a mother for her first-born, which this so fond dependence produces in the one so looked to.

How entirely I sympathize in all the troubles of that tremendous storm. To me the fall of an oak always seems like death. Flush is his master's darling, and certainly the prettiest and merriest and most affectionate little creature that ever lived. We thought he would have died of grief during my father's illness; he would not eat, and passed his whole life at the chamber door.

My father's love to you. He is so well! Ever yours,

M. R. MITFORD.

To MISS BARRETT, *Torquay.*

Three-mile Cross, May 28, 1839.

MY DEAR FRIEND,—I should always doubt any preference of mine when opposed to yours, always, even if my ignorance of languages did not make my writing about foreign poetry a very great presumption. French I read just like English, and always shall, and I have a tendency toward the comedies and memoirs, that makes me open a French book with real gusto. And little as I know of Italian, I like the gem-like bits of Ariosto. But after all to be English, with our boundless vistas in verse and in prose, is a privilege and a glory; and *you* are born among those who make it such, be sure of that. I do not believe, my sweetest, that the very highest poetry does sell at once. Look at Wordsworth! The hour will arrive, and all the sooner if to poetry unmatched in truth and beauty and feeling you condescend to add story and a happy ending, that being among the conditions of recurrence to every book with the mass even of cultivated readers—I do not mean the few.

I once remember puzzling an epicure by adding to an apple tart, in the making, the remains of a pot of preserved pine, syrup and all, a most unexpected luxury in our cot-

tage; such would a bit of your writing be in a book of mine
—flavor, sweetness, perfume, and unexpectedness.... Yes,
for one year, from eight and a half to nine and a half—I
lived—*we* lived, at Lyme Regis. Our abode was a fine old
house in the middle of the chief street; a porch and great
gables with spread-eagles distinguish it. It was built round
a quadrangle, and the back looked into a garden, which de-
scended by terraces to a small stream, a descent so abrupt
that a grotto with its basin and spring formed a natural shelter under the hilly bank, planted with strawberries. Arbu-
tus, passion-flowers, myrtles, and moss-roses abounded in that
lovely garden and covered the front of the house; and the
drawing-room chimney-piece was a copy of the monument
to Shakspeare in Westminster Abbey. How I loved that
house! There is an account of a visit to Lyme in Miss Austen's exquisite "Persuasion." Some of the scenery in the
back of the Isle of Wight resembles Pinny, but it is inferior.

I shall tell dear Lady Dacre of your sympathy. Heaven
bless you, my own sweet love. Ever yours,

M. R. MITFORD.

To MISS JEPHSON, *Castle Martyr.*

Three-mile Cross, May 30, 1839.

Have you heard that there has been a report—false of
course—that Miss Clarke (Lady Morgan's niece) was to be
married to Rogers the poet? He is seventy-seven at least.
All London believed it for some time; but it is not so.

If you have a single anemone seed to spare, send me some
inclosed to Mr. Sergeant Talfourd, M.P. Ever most affectionately yours,   M. R. MITFORD.

We have an exquisite lithograph of Lucas's portrait of my
father.

To DOUGLAS JERROLD, ESQ.

About July, 1839.

Your graceful and gracious method of asking for contributions, my dear Mr. Jerrold, could not have been answered
by a denial, even if the name of the editor, the striking individuality of the illustrations, and the general power and popularity of the work, had not been such as to insure my read-
iest compliance. Will you have the goodness to tell the pro-

prietor, with my compliments, that I accept his terms of five guineas for an article not exceeding eight pages, and will endeavor to approach that length as closely as my usual blundering with regard to the respective quantities of MS. and letter-press will permit. But I shall not be able to send any contributions just yet. It has pleased Messrs. Finden at the eleventh hour to apply to me to edit a fourth volume of their splendid "Tableaux," and to desire that two-thirds at least of the book be written by myself, and until that be fairly out of hand, I can not turn to any other work. Even after that I have another short engagement, which ought to precede yours; but that may perhaps wait until I have furnished you with one article. Has Mr. Hammond really taken Drury Lane? And would he, do you think, like a ghost-story, which upon a large stage would be effective, for an afterpiece? If so, I have one by me. Ever faithfully yours,

M. R. MITFORD.

To the REV. WILLIAM HARNESS, London.

Three-mile Cross, August 2, 1839.

MY DEAR FRIEND,—Of all the persons I have ever seen, Daniel Webster most completely answers my notion of a truly great man—good as well as great—with the gentleness and repose of power in his words and in his smile. It really does one good to think that such a man has arisen from among the tillers of the earth, to take his place as a legislator and ruler of nations. Of all Mr. Kenyon's kindnesses, I value none so much as his having brought him and his family here. My father was as much charmed with him as I was. The Sedgwicks are very likable, and there is a freedom from cant about the authoress, which, considering the do-me-good nature of her books, I could not have anticipated. Certainly the Pickwick countenance, as given in the prints, *is* like our dear friend, and I presume that consciousness has made him throw off his spectacles; but he is, with all his kindness, a great deal too shrewd and clever for that very benevolent and rather simple personage.

The Websters spoke of you with real affection: it was nothing less; and I have a letter from that warm-hearted person, Mrs. Opie, so delighted with Mary! Our best love to you all. Ever, my dear friend, most faithfully yours,

M. R. MITFORD.

The book is finished, somehow. At the last I was incapable of correcting the proofs, literally fainting on the ground.

To Miss Jephson, *Bath.*

Three-mile Cross, Sept. 21, 1839.

[The beginning of this letter is irreparably defaced.]

—on the contrary, it is one of the qualities with which I have the most sympathy: and my admiration for, and interest in Daniel Webster, is a case in point.

Did I tell you his story? I think not; and if not, I must do so now. It happens oddly enough that Mr. Ticknor, who is his intimate friend and fellow-townsman, and from whom, oddly enough, I heard it five or six years ago, found nobody, except myself, who knew any thing about Webster, and I had actually told it, long before I dreamt of his coming to England, to John Kenyon, William Harness, and many of his own now most intimate London friends. The knowledge of this, of course, threw almost a feeling of old acquaintanceship over our intercourse; and I think that when you read the story you will say that it is one of the most noble that ever occurred. His father was the son of a New-England farmer, and took (as is common with them) an axe in one hand and a wife in the other, to " fix " in the backwoods as what is called a " squatter;" for *then* land might be had in those wild forests for the clearing. When Daniel was fifteen —till then he had been " a hewer of wood and a drawer of water "—he said to his father: " Father, give me a few dollars and let me go to the old States for some education; you have my eldest brother, who is your right hand, and plenty of younger boys; the clearing is large and the house comfortable; you can spare me, and I want to get a little education; give me what you can and let me go." The father did give him a few dollars, and very few. "Take these, boy; they are all I can spare, and make them last as long as you can; for when they are gone you must take care of yourself."

Well, Daniel set off to the next village, fifty miles off, where he found a school—better than our national schools, something, I suppose, like the Scotch schools—and by the time he was through that, he traveled on to the next town, where there was a college, not like Oxford or Cambridge, certainly, but much like Rugby school, a very excellent mixture of classical, scientific, and general literature. There he entered himself, and maintained himself, until he was the head youth there, by copying deeds for a lawyer at night. When he was, as I have said, first in every class, the lawyer said to him (for he was still in one of the new States), "If you wish to go to New England, I can give you a letter to a relation which will I am sure lead to a most excellent engagement now, and open the door to permanent fortune and distinction." Of course the offer was thankfully accepted, and the young man went home to his family to take leave of them and inform them of his prospects. On his arrival, he found the elder brother, whom I have mentioned, hungering and thirsting, as he had done, after education; he returned with him to his old master, the lawyer, re-engaged himself in his service, saw his brother through school and college, and only when he was, like himself, the head boy in all the classes, went eastward to pursue his own course of prosperity and honor. Now this postponement of all his own hopes and aspirations—this total self-sacrifice and self-oblivion, does seem to me the very finest thing I ever heard in my life. Is it not noble in the highest degree? I asked if the brother had turned out well. The answer was that he had lived to justify the exertion—to prove that, if spared, he would have been the first lawyer in Massachusetts, and then had died.

Daniel Webster is himself not more than fifty-five now—the first lawyer, orator, and statesman of America, certainly, and the next, or next but one, President. He is the noblest-looking man I ever saw, both in face and person. The portrait prefixed to his "Speeches" does him great injustice, for his countenance is delightfully gracious—such a smile! and he is a broad, muscular, splendid figure. His manner, too, is all that one can imagine of calm, and sweet, and gracious—as charming as the Duke of Devonshire; as courteous even as that prince of courtesy, and equally free from condescension—whilst amidst the perfect simplicity and gentleness there is great conversational power. His wife and daughters seem to adore his very footsteps; and he has conquered for himself a degree of real consideration and respect in London never before shown to any Transatlantic personage; least of all to a lion. My father adores him. I think he liked him even better than I did; and he says that he promised him to come again, and that he is sure he will keep his word.

I should like you to see Daniel Webster! When I tell you that expecting from him what I did, and hearing from twenty people, accustomed to see in perfect intimacy all distinguished people, that he alone gave them the idea of a truly great man—when I say that he exceeded our expectations by very far; you may imagine what he is. I am to send them all my flower-seeds, and they are to send me all theirs. I chose the Murder Speech (is it not wonderfully fine? like Sheil, without the tawdriness, I think) to read to my father, because *that* is free from the alloy, to an English ear, of allusions intelligible across the water, but not to us. Two very clever friends of ours went to Oxford to hear him speak, and they say that they would walk there again, and back, to hear him only speak the same speech over again! Is not that praise?

God bless you, my beloved friend! We have had six days' and nights' incessant rain, and, if succeeded by frost, we shall have no seed ripen of any thing. Ever yours,

M. R. MITFORD.

To JOHN LUCAS, ESQ., *Newman Street, London.*

Sunday, Oct. 27, 1839.

MY DEAR FRIEND,—I can't help writing one line, although you will find a letter of mine in town which has not yet reached you, to tell you, from the bottom of my heart, how much I rejoice at what you tell me of the Duke of Wellington— God bless him! The great captain is an equally good judge of pictures and of men; and, having once adopted you as his painter, will never change. So that you will go down to posterity together, an honor to both; for even his great name will derive a fresh lustre from his choice of an artist so certain to justify his choice. I don't know when any thing has given so much gratification to my father and myself.

Poor Haydon! What you will be, he, with prudence, steadiness, good sense, and modesty (for conceit has been his worst enemy), might have been. He had power, and with the cultivation of higher and better intellectual and moral qualities, he might have had taste—for taste *is* a moral quality. But he surrounds himself with flatterers, he becomes

hopelessly involved, and how can he paint then? That is
the secret of his failure. And yet, remembering what he
was, and what he might have been, one still says, Poor Haydon! I am glad that you have seen him, and that he thinks
of me kindly.

My father's kindest love. Ever, my dear friend, most faithfully yours,   M. R. MITFORD.

To the REV. WILLIAM HARNESS, *London.*

Three-mile Cross, Tuesday night, Oct. 29, 1839.

MY DEAR FRIEND,—I expect this letter to be franked by
Mr. Sergeant Talfourd, who has been at Reading this week
past, and from whom I have received an exceedingly affectionate and cordial note, although we have not met yet. It
is a note that breathes more of the old spirit of intimacy and
sympathy than any which I have received from him for years.
He says that he knows nothing more than the newspapers
tell him, " of any design to make him that awful thing a judge,
or that perilous (perhaps ruinous) one, a solicitor-general."
These are his words. Where is Mr. Kenyon? Does Mr.
Webster return to England? Have I any chance of seeing
any of you? Ever, my dear friend, most faithfully yours,
M. R. MITFORD.

To MISS BARRETT, *Torquay.*

Three-mile Cross, Jan. 3, 1840.

MY BELOVED FRIEND,—My father and I sat to-night looking at the fire in silence and in sadness, the wind rising and
sighing with its most mournful rather than its more threat-
ening sound through the branches, from which the snow was
falling silently—contradicting by sight and feeling (for the
cold was intense) the evidence of another sense, as the double
Roman narcissus and the white and purple hyacinths shed
their delicious fragrance from the window—my father and
myself sat pensively over the wood fire, until he said suddenly, " You are thinking of dear Miss Barrett; so was I. God
bless her! How long is it since you have heard from her?"
Every night at that time I had thought of you, my sweetest,
sitting over the glowing embers, and at last I determined to
write to you before I slept. I have told you of my little
girl, Agnes Niven, just twelve years old. Her mother and I
VOL. II.—K

sometimes call her our pet lamb. She sent me this week a
pair of delicate mittens, knit of the finest wool and silk, with
the following stanza:

> "A tuft of flax to a Grecian bride
>   Was ancient Hymen's offer;
> A tuft of wool is England's pride:
>   What more can a pet-lamb offer?"

Are not these lines, with their combination of point and grace-
fulness, their Mr. Kenyon-like terseness and turn, very re-
markable.in a girl of that age?

I have been reading "Jack Sheppard," and have been struck
by the great danger, in these times, of representing authority so constantly and fearfully in the wrong, so tyrannous, so
devilish, as the author has been pleased to portray it in
" Jack Sheppard;" for he does not seem so much a man, or
even an incarnate fiend, as a representation of power—government or law, call it as you may—the ruling power. Of
course Mr. Ainsworth had no such design, but such is the effect; and as the millions who see it represented at the minor
theatres will not distinguish between now and a hundred
years back, all the Chartists in the land are less dangerous
than this nightmare of a book, and I, Radical as I am, lament
any additional temptations to outbreak, with all its train of
horrors. Seriously, what things these are—the Jack Shep-
pards, and Squeers's, and Oliver Twists, and Michael Arm-
strongs—all the worse for the power which, except the last,
the others contain! Grievously the worse!

My friend Mr. Hughes speaks well of Mr. Ainsworth. His
father was a collector of these old robber stories, and used to
repeat the local ballads upon Turpin, etc., to his son as he sat
upon his knee; and this has perhaps been at the bottom of
the matter. A good antiquarian I believe him to be, but what
a use to make of the picturesque old knowledge! Well, one
comfort is that it will wear itself out; and then it will be
cast aside like an old fashion. Ever most faithfully yours,

M. R. M.

To Miss Jephson, *Castle Martyr.*

Three-mile Cross, Feb. 19, 1840.

My dear Emily,—I must tell you of a suggestion which
has been made to me, and which, upon mentioning it to Hen-

ry Chorley, he has taken up enthusiastically. Thirty years ago, when I was a young woman, Sir William Elford, an old friend of my father's (they were great whist-players, and used to meet at Graham's Club, in St. James's Street), took a fancy to me as a girl of promising talents, and being himself even then elderly (he died four or five years ago at the age of ninety),* and an excellent letter-writer (there was something of Horace Walpole's mixture of humor and courtliness about his style), he coaxed me into a correspondence, which although it languished latterly, he living out of the world, and I having too much writing on my hands already, had yet been of no small use to me, as giving me a command of my pen, and the habit of arranging and expressing my thoughts. He always said that none of my writings were so pleasant as those letters; and Miss Elford, upon looking them over this winter, urged me to print them. I named the thing to Mr. Kenyon, and he advises it beyond all measure. Do you? I thought at first of appearing as editor only, calling it "Letters from the Valley" (you remember Mrs. Grant's "Letters from the Mountains," and what a run they had), or "Letters from a Young Lady to an Elderly Gentleman."

Ever most faithfully yours,   M. R. M.

To Miss Barrett, *Torquay.*

Three-mile Cross, March 3, 1840.

I had a kind message from Captain Marryat once, when somebody whom he knew was coming here, but have never seen him. Without being one of his indiscriminate admirers, I like parts of his books (some of which I have read to my father), and have been told that they have done good in the profession—suggestions thrown out in them having been taken up and acted upon by the Lords of the Admiralty; and, although a Tory, he takes part with the common sailors. Did I tell you that, the day I wrote in the midst of a quantity of people, a niece of the late Mr. Trollope called, and a nephew of Mrs. Trollope's—both twins, she having a twin sister and he a twin brother. Odd, is it not?

Did you know Dr. Parry? I did; and it is really sad how every lion, who behaves as if he thought himself a lion, shrinks into a very tame menagerie wild beast when one

* He died in 1837.

comes before him face to face. I suspect that Sir Walter was about the only one that thoroughly stood the test, and poor Mrs. Hemans, because both were honest lovers of society, with no exclusive veneration for their own books, and therefore came within the exceptive clause in my first sentence.

Heaven bless you, my dearest! I am better, but have had two or three returns of sickness. These winds! Yours ever,

M. R. M.

To Miss Jephson, *Castle Martyr, Ireland.*

Three-mile Cross, July 25, 1840.

—The land comprising our garden is to be sold, and will probably be purchased by some sordid person upon the speculation of making us pay an inordinate rent for the luxury. To me individually it would be a great release to be quit of the trouble and expense of the garden; but how to supply its place, both as an amusement and exercise to my dear father, I can not tell. However, it is to be sold, and will probably be purchased and taken from us, for it is out of the question to think of our paying any increase of rent. The lot, about an acre, is to be sold on the first of next month, so that this cause of alarm will soon be settled one way or another.

We had an interesting person here yesterday, Mary Duff, one of the Maries to whom Lord Byron was so devotedly attached. She is still a most lovely woman, not very tall, and full enough to prevent the haggard look which comes upon women who grow thin at fifty; of a bright clear complexion, with dark hair, eyebrows, and eyelashes, and hazel eyes, beautiful features, a most sweet and intelligent expression—with such a smile both of the eyes and the lips—an accent slightly Scottish, and a manner full of grace and charm.

My father being better, we made last week an excursion to Windsor. I had not been out before for ten months, nor had I even drunk tea from home, so completely have I been absorbed by the care of my father. Blessed be God, he bore the journey well! We found the private garden and terrace open at Windsor, and I walked all over that beautiful scene, not going into the apartments, which, in all their splendors, are less interesting to me than that magnificent mixture of matchless architecture and unrivaled situation. Nothing can exceed the blending of those great walls with tree and flower, as seen in the castle and the slopes. The day was exquisite, and the very air heavy with the rich perfume of the seringas and acacias. How I should have liked you to have been at my side! My father enjoyed it too; and I could not have believed that mere external circumstances could have given me so much gratification.

I am almost a prisoner in our little home and three miles round, and owe, doubtless, to that circumscription the great pleasure which that rare thing, an excursion, gives me; so even-handed is fortune in dispensing her favors! They who eat pine-apple every day lose all consciousness of the flavor; we who taste it but once a year feel the fragrance of the aroma, the delicious sweetness and pungency of the fruit.

I have taken a great fancy to Mr. James's writings, and to Mr. James himself. I never saw him, and have only heard of him through Lady Madalina Palmer and Lady Sidmouth. When I have time (not, I fear, just yet) I will tell you about him. Heaven bless you, my very dear friend! Write to me. Ever yours,   M. R. M.

[A friend of the Mitfords bought the garden above mentioned for their benefit, and added to it a small farm-yard.]

To Miss Jephson, *Castle Martyr, Ireland.*

Three-mile Cross, Sept. 2, 1840.

You will be glad to hear, my ever-dear love, that my father is better, and that consequently we, K.,* Flush and myself, are also upon the mend; for most certainly it was his illness that overset all three. My present distress—and it is a most serious one—arises from the difficulty of uniting the two duties of giving to him the time which he needs for attendance and amusement, and of managing also to complete the book for Colburn, which is necessary for our subsistence. Nobody can conceive how much my dear father misses me, if only an hour absent. He could read, I think; but, somehow, to read to himself seems to give him no pleasure; and if any one else is so kind as to offer to read to him, *that* does not do. They don't know what he likes, and where to skip, and how to lighten heavy parts without losing the thread of

* The abreviation by which she designated her maid Kerenhappuck.

the story. By practice I can contrive to do this, even with books that I have never seen before. There's an instinct in it, I think. So that I have been obliged to resume my old habits, and to read to him and play cribbage with him during more hours of each day (every day except Sundays) than you could well believe. Ever yours, M. R. M.

CHAPTER XVI.

LETTERS FOR 1841.

To MISS BARRETT, *Torquay.*

Three-mile Cross, Jan. 14, 1841.

I WRITE, my beloved friend, by my dear father's bedside; for he is again very ill. Last Tuesday was the Quarter Sessions, and he *would* go, and he seemed so well that Mr. May thought it best to indulge him. Accordingly he went at nine A.M. to open the Court, sat all day next the chairman in Court, and afterward at dinner, returning at two o'clock, A.M., in the highest spirits—not tired at all, and setting forth the next day for a similar eighteen hours of business and pleasure. Again he came home delighted and unwearied. He had seen many old and dear friends, and had received (to use his own words) the attentions which do an old man's heart good; and *these*, joined to his original vigor of constitution and his high animal spirits, had enabled him to do that which to those who saw him at home infirm and feeble, requiring three persons to help him from his chair, and many minutes before he could even move—would seem as impossible as a fall of snow between the tropics, or the ripening pine-apples in Nova Zembla.

All this he had done, but not with impunity. He has caught a severe cold; and having on Saturday taken nearly the same liberties at Reading, and not suffering me to send for Mr. May, until rendered bold by fear I did send last night—he is now seriously ill. I am watching by his bedside in deep anxiety; but as silence is my part to-night, and I have prayed (for when those we love—*so love*—are in danger, thought is prayer), I write to you, my beloved friend, as my best solace. Mr. May is hopeful; but the season, his age, my great and still increasing love, and the habit of anxiety which has grown from long tending, fill me with a fear that I can hardly describe. He is so restless too—so very, very restless—and every thing depends upon quiet, upon sleep, and upon perspiration; and yet, for the last twelve hours I am sure that he has not been two minutes in the same posture, and not twelve minutes without his getting out of bed, or up in bed, or something as bad. God grant that he may drop asleep! I read to him until I found that reading only increased the irritability. Well, I do hope and trust that he is rather quieter now; and I am quite sure that I shall myself be quieter in mind, if I can but fix my thoughts upon you. Heaven be with you all! Ever yours,

M. R. M.

To MISS BARRETT, *Torquay.*

Three-mile Cross, April 20, 1841.

How startling coincidences are! Sometimes how painful! Just as I had sent to you the little jar of honey from Hymettus, brought from thence by Sir Robert Inglis, and sent to me by a dear old friend, Lady Sidmouth, two letters arrived from her at the same time, of which, that which bore the latest date, anticipated with delightful cheerfulness our speedy meeting; and, not five minutes after dispatching that trifling token of honor to the muse, I found, in reading the paper to my father, that poor Lady Sidmouth was dead! Imagine the shock! She was, you know, daughter of Lord Stowell, niece of Lord Eldon, and wife of Lord Sidmouth, all remarkable men in themselves, and connected with the most memorable personages of the last half-century. And fully worthy was she of such association.

I have seldom known any one more thoroughly awake and alive to all that was best worth knowing. She had an enlightened curiosity, a love of natural history, of antiquities, of literature, of art; was herself full of talent, intelligence, and gayety, and had a quick and peculiar humor; the more surprising as her physical sufferings were great and constant. For many years she had suffered under a spine complaint—suffered to such an extent that, for very many years, instead of being (as she used to be) dragged between two strong supporters round my garden, she had been carried in the arms of an old servant into the greenhouse, and there deposited until her visit was over. In the fine season she used to pass many hours of every day in her carriage or in a garden chair; but frequently her sufferings were so severe that the perspiration would pour down her face from pain, and for days and weeks together she remained unable to see her favorite friends. She had submitted to that tremendous operation, the actual cutting down either side of the spinal column (I forget the technical phrase), but without any benefit; and had tried Dr. Jephson's system equally without success. Still, such was her sweetness, that Lord Sidmouth told me that some sculptor (I think Behnes) earnestly wished to be allowed to model her face for the expression, which, as he said, was more full of lively sweetness than any he ever saw. She was twenty-seven years younger than the husband who now has to mourn her loss.

The first thing she did when coming into her father's large fortune was to portion her two step-daughters, each of whom had been for many years engaged to a man too poor to marry a poor lord's daughter. All her dealings about money were munificent in themselves and most graceful in the manner. She gave to the Berkshire Hospital six acres of land (valued at a thousand pounds an acre for building leases), standing on the finest situation of the outskirts of Reading, and told every body that it was Lord Sidmouth's gift? And in the same way she built a new market cross in his name in the town of Devizes, of which he is high steward.

I have lost a most kind and affectionate friend, one of the very many of whom the last two or three years have deprived me. Lord Sidmouth retains his unmarried daughter, who officiated as his private secretary when he was prime minister, and is a very cultivated and excellent person; but not to me what Lady S. was. We, indeed, had many mutual ties. Her father, like mine, was of Northumberland; and we had connections and friends near Newcastle—her cousins married to cousins of mine. The most amiable of these—a young and lovely girl of remarkable talent—died last autumn.

Every body that loves me does die! Oh! take care of yourself, my very dearest! Did I tell you that her father, Lord Stowell (the Sir William Scott of Dr. Johnson's time), died at a very advanced age in a state worse than idiotcy? The old servants have told me that his expressions were awful. That must have been a great grief. Her only brother, too, killed himself by drinking. At the same time that Lord Stowell was wearing out the dregs of life so painfully four miles on one side of us, Sir Henry Russell, the only other survivor of the "Literary Club," was lingering in equal imbecility four miles on the other; a remarkable and humbling fact to the pride of intellect.

At Stowell (poor Lady Sidmouth's estate) is a hazel coppice of such extent that all the fairs of the south of England are supplied from it with cob-nuts—the favorite present of a country lad to his sweetheart. Gypsies and other wanderers pitch their tents around it in the nutting season; and for three weeks the coppice is as populous as a vineyard or a hop-garden in their gathering-time. Poor dear Lady Sidmouth! how fond she was of distributing little bags of her own nuts, purchased from the licensed plunderers! You would have liked Lady Sidmouth.

[*The continuation of this letter is wanting.*]

To Miss Jephson, *Clifton.*

Three-mile Cross, May 1, 1841.

MY DEAREST EMILY,—I rejoice to hear such good news of your health. For the last week it has been finer than any we had during the whole of last summer, but without wind or scorching dryness—the hedges all bursting into foliage, and lilacs and horse-chestnuts in full bloom—in short (I am writing on May-day) the very May of the old poets. Heaven grant it last! I am better, but my father is out of spirits and very feeble. Ben, too, has been very ill indeed.

What a sad, sad tragedy that life of Sir Walter is! How much, in its splendor and its melancholy close, does it resemble the course of Napoleon. And surely the same ambition ran through both, only taking a different direction. I love his works. Strange that no one stretched out a hand to save him! But all literary people die overwrought; it is the destiny of the class. Poor Southey! his fate is equally or even more deplorable—and excellent men they were both.

Can you suggest to me a story for a tragedy? The hero must be a young man? Mrs. Kean wants me to write one

K 2

for her son Charles. I want, chiefly, some very interesting story as a groundwork for the play. Think of this, my dearest. I know nobody so likely to hit upon a good plot. The hero must be young and interesting—must have *to do*, and not merely suffer. Heaven bless you! Ever faithfully yours, M. R. MITFORD.

To MISS BARRETT, *Torquay.*

Three-mile Cross, June 20, 1841.

I have not written to you, my beloved friend, because until to-day I could have given you no pleasure. I have been very ill, but I am now getting well. Did I tell you that just before I took to my bed I drove out with K—— for a few miles?—very ill *then*. About four miles from home one of the traces came undone. The horse (an old Irish thoroughbred) feeling the trace beat against his side, began kicking; and, the splashing-board of our little chaise being very high, so that he could do no harm, galloped off at a speed such as few horses could have exceeded. He trod upon the trace and broke it—a fresh jerk and an additional fright. We met men, ten or twelve; we passed a turnpike-gate, but the men flew from us as we passed; the gate was flung open (wisely, or the horse, an excellent leaper, would have taken it), and for a mile and a half we had as close a view of death as has happened to many people. K—— behaved bravely. She gave me the whip, or rather I took it from her, and wound the reins round her arms to increase her power. At last, the remaining trace brought the collar into such a position as to half choke the horse; and a boy driving a donkey across the road, we stopped—I so frightened that I could not stand. We were forced to be tied up with string and led home. If I had not been ill I should have stood it better; as it was, I kept it from my father till next day, when it became necessary to tell him for fear he should hear it from another. And since then I have been very ill, or rather, I was very ill, and now I am getting better. But I have not sent for Mr. May. I very seldom do; it frightens my father.

After all, a wretched life is mine. Health is gone; but if I can but last while my dear father requires me; if the little money we have can but last; then it would matter little how soon I, too, were released. We live alone in the world, and I feel that neither will long outlast the other. My life is only valuable as being useful to *him*. I have lived for him and him only; and it seems to me, God, in his infinite mercy, does release those who have so lived, nearly at the same time. The spring is broken and the watch goes down. Have you not seen it so?

I have been reading Mr. Blanchard's life of poor L. E. L. When looking into the chronology you will be struck with the closeness of the two events—the acceptance of Mr. McLean and the other affair of the rejection. There was another, too, about the same time, Mr. C—— tells me. Then Mr. Blanchard alludes to the scandals of different persons (I don't remember the words, but they implied scandals regarding more than one); and the very manner in which our very slight intercourse is mentioned proves that there was a dearth of female friends. She had written to ask me to write something for somebody, and apologized for addressing me as "My dear Miss Mitford." I, of course, replied, as you will see.

Poor thing! The book is to me deeply affecting. She was a fine creature thrown away; and just when that mysterious event occurred there seemed to me more hope and chance of happiness, and more development of power, and (which is more important than either) a greater chance for goodness and usefulness than there had ever been before. Poor thing! Nothing seems to me so melancholy as the lives of authors— Sir Walter Scott, Mrs. Hemans, this of Miss Landon. I hardly know an exception. And these are the successful! Heaven bless you! Ever yours, M. R. MITFORD.

To MISS BARRETT, *Torquay.*

Three-mile Cross, June 28, 1841.

First, my beloved friend, let me answer your most kind inquiries. I am greatly better. It has been a most remarkable escape; but a real escape. I can not yet turn in my bed; but when up I get about astonishingly well. To say truth, I am, and always have been, a very active person— country-born and country-bred—with great fearlessness and safety of foot and limb. Even *since* this misfortune, Ben having said that half the parish had mounted on a hay-rick close by to look at the garden, which lies beneath it (an acre of flowers rich in color as a painter's palette), I could not resist the sight of the ladder, and one evening when all the men were away, climbed up to take myself a view of my flowery domain. I wish you could see it! Masses of the Siberian larkspur, and sweet-williams, mostly double, the still brighter new larkspur (*Delphinium Chinensis*), rich as an oriental butterfly—such a size and such a blue! amongst roses in millions, with the blue and white Canterbury bells (also double), and the white foxglove, and the variegated monkshood, the carmine pea, in its stalwart beauty, the nemophila, like the sky above its head, the new erysimum, with its gay orange tufts, hundreds of lesser annuals, and fuchsias, zinnias, salvias, geraniums past compt; so bright are the flowers that the green really does not predominate amongst them!

Yes! I knew you would like those old houses! Orkwells surpasses in beauty and in preservation any thing I ever saw. Our ancestors were rare architects. Their painted glass and their carved oak are unequaled. Heaven be with you, my dearest! Ever yours,   ·   M. R. MITFORD.

To the REV. WILLIAM HARNESS, *Heathcote Street.*

Three-mile Cross, July 22, 1841.

MY DEAR FRIEND,—I have to entreat of you that you will suffer so much money as may be necessary to pay our debts to be taken from that in Mr. Blandy's hands—say the two hundred pounds lately paid in. The necessity for this has arisen, partly from the infamous conduct of Messrs. Finden, but chiefly from my dear father's state of health and spirits, which has made me little better than a nurse; and, lastly, from my own want of strength, which has prevented my exerting myself, as I ought to have done, to remedy these disappointments. Nobody, to see me, would believe the wretched state of my health. Could you know all I have to undergo and suffer, you would rather wonder that I am alive, than that (joined to all I have to do with my dear father, reading to him, waiting upon him, playing at cribbage with him, and bearing, *alone*, the depression of a man once so strong and so active, and now so feeble)—you would rather wonder that I have lived through this winter than that I have failed to provide the means of support for our little household.

I am, however, rather better now, and feel that, if relieved from this debt, which weighs me down, I shall (as I
have told my dear father that I must) rather seem to neglect
him in the minor points of reading to him, etc., than again
fail in working at my desk.   Be assured that, if you enable
me to go to my writing with a clear mind, I shall not again
be found wanting.   It has been all my fault now, and if that
fault be visited upon my father's white head, and he be sent
to jail for my omissions, I should certainly not long remain
to grieve over my sin, for such it is.   It is a great trial, for
my father has never, for the last four years, been two months
without some attack of immediate danger, and the nursing
and attending him are in themselves almost more than can
be done by a person whose own state of health involves constant attention and leaves her well-nigh exhausted and un-
nerved in mind and body.   But I see now that a portion of
the more fatiguing part of this attendance (say the reading
aloud) must be relinquished, and, however grievous, it *shall*
be so for the more stringent duty of earning our daily bread.
I will do this, and you, I am sure, will enable me to go with
a free mind to my task; I am sure that you will do so.   It
would be a most false and mistaken friendship for me, which
should induce you to hesitate, for my very heart would be
broken if aught should befall his gray hairs.

In sanctioning the appropriation of the two hundred pounds
now in Mr. Blandy's hands, you will relieve my dear father's
mind and mine, and enable me to work with a free and willing spirit.   If you refuse, *he* may be sent to jail, which he
would not survive; or if he survived, it would be with a
spirit so broken that he would never leave his arm-chair,
which (to say nothing of the misery) would totally disable
me from working in any way.   Or there is a third probability, worse than either; that such a catastrophe would bring
on seizure and not death, and that, for months and years, he
might linger a living corpse, alive only to suffering.   I say
this, because I know that you, from the kindest of motives,
would think more of my future interest than of immediate
relief; and I do assure you that your refusal would very,
very probably prevent there being any future to provide
for; since I am quite sure that, if I saw my dear, dear father
hurried in this way from the world, driven to death or to

mortal sickness through my fault, I could never for an instant know happiness again, and should probably, most probably, fill the same grave.

My dear father has, years ago, been improvident; he still is irritable and difficult to live with; but he is a person of a thousand virtues—honest, faithful, just, and true, and kind. There are very, very few half so good in this mixed world. It is my fault that this money is needed—entirely my fault; and, if it be withheld, I am well assured of the consequences to both: law proceedings will be commenced; my dear father will be overthrown mind and body; and I shall never know another happy hour. I feel after this that you will not refuse me the kindness that I ask. Let me have a letter (authorizing the appropriation of this money) to Mr. Blandy; whose kindness is, and has been, constant and undeviating. I can not believe that you will refuse this great favor; it will be a most mistaken kindness if you do.*

Love to the Maries, and all happiness to you all! Ever most faithfully yours,   M. R. MITFORD.

This has been a summer of extraordinary escapes. Six weeks back I was dragged by a friend, who was handing me over the rafters in an unfloored room, across the joists, a depth of four feet and a half—a terrible jar upon the spine, which I have only just recovered; and two nights ago I was writing with a low candle by the side of the desk when the frill of my nightcap (the edging of the border) took fire. I saw and felt the flames. Every body was in bed and asleep. My hands trembled so that I could not undo the strings of the cap, and I flung myself upon the ground and extinguished it with the hearth-rug; frightening nobody except poor dear little Flush, who was asleep on my father's chair, but (roused I suppose by the smell of fire) sat up, with his beautiful eyes dilated to three times their usual size fixed upon me, shaking as if in an ague, and whining with distress. He nearly devoured me with caresses when I went to him. My head was a good deal scorched (it was a very startling sensation to see and feel the flames), but the immediate application of Goulard prevented any mischief; and I am so thankful not to have alarmed my father or indeed any one.

* The money, of course, was conceded; but it was a sad diminution of the little that remained of her mother's once large fortune.

To Miss Jephson, *Clifton.*

Three-mile Cross, August 16, 1841.

Flush is quite well again, and likely to prove one of the best sporting dogs in the country. My father has received a hundred applications for him; amongst them is one from Mr. Pusey, one of the Members for Berkshire, and elder brother of the Dr. Pusey who is associated with Mr. Newman in the "Oxford Tracts," and the promulgation of the tenets which pass by his name. Mr. Newman is, besides his power as a preacher, a man of extensive acquirement and much elegant accomplishment. My friends the Carys (son and daughter-in-law of the translator of Dante) are very intimate with Mr. Newman and very fond of him. His power in Oxford is extraordinary. You can't go into any of the halls on a fast-day of the Church without seeing four or five young men dining upon bread and water. It is a perfect resuscitation of Archbishop Laud—for they cling to their own peculiar notions, which are a sort of English Papistry, and yet abjure the real old Popish doctrine with great zeal. That Mr. Newman is a man of remarkable power and perfect sincerity, I have no doubt. I have some of the "Oxford Tracts," and shall borrow his sermons the first time I see Mrs. Cary. Adieu! Yours most affectionately,

M. R. M.

I can quite enter into your delight at the hanging up of an old family portrait. We have one, of my grandfather Russell, which carries one back to the age of Pope, whom, indeed, he remembered.

To Miss Jephson, *Castle Martyr, Ireland.*

Three-mile Cross, Nov. —, 1841.

The Websters have again written to me — so kindly! There is a chance, Mr. Kenyon says, of his coming here as American minister, inasmuch as General Harrison will certainly supersede Mr. Van Buren, who was expected at one time to be re-elected. The reason is curious: some partisan of Van Buren's, speaking most scornfully of Harrison, said, "Here is a President, forsooth! a man who lives in a log hut and drinks hard cider!" Now 100,000 electors do live in log huts, and 200,000 drink hard cider; so all their party papers are now printed with a portrait of General Harrison on one side and a barrel of cider on the other; and this unlucky taunt of Van Buren's friend will bring Harrison in!

Another piece of American news is very sad; three or four years ago, two Theodore Sedgwicks, father and son, were staying with us for ten days. The younger, an only son, was a young man of great talent. He returned to America and succeeded to his uncle's business as a lawyer in New York. The father, who lived three hundred miles off on the borders of New England, went to hear him plead (they unite there the advocate and attorney as in our provinces), and was so affected that he dropped down dead in court. He was not old, and a tall, spare man, very unlikely to die a sudden death; but the pleasure and the excitement acting on his strong paternal feeling were too much for him. Is not this melancholy?

You have heard, I suppose, of the sad state of poor Southey; the mind gone—dark depression and utter failure of intellect—overworn. It is very, very sad. Mr. Kenyon, who has been traveling with Mr. Bezzi, tells me a most interesting story of the manner in which his friend has caused a portrait of Dante to be discovered which had been lost for two centuries. There was a tradition that, under the whitewash of a painting in one of the prisons in Florence, a fresco containing such a portrait existed. Mr. Bezzi went to the authorities and said that he and some English gentlemen were prepared to undertake the process (a tedious and somewhat expensive one) of clearing the picture; but that he, though a naturalized Englishman, was born an Italian, and could not bear that any foreigners should gain the credit, or the Florentines incur the odium attending such a proceeding. The result was that the authorities did undertake it, and that a magnificent fresco has been disclosed, containing by far the most striking portrait of the great poet now in existence. Mr. Bezzi, as I think I must have told you, was an exile on account of his connection with the Silvio Pellico plot. By-the-by, Silvio himself is now a monk and a celebrated preacher, such a change was probable, I think, from his book.

My father is so anxious for a cow, that I can not object, else the buying the cow, the fitting-up the dairy and cow-house, and the purchasing the different utensils will come, I suppose, to thirty pounds. And, if Finden heard of my having incurred the expense, I would not wonder if he laid hold of it as an excuse for not merely delaying what he owes me, but for not paying me at all! However, I must hope as long as I can, and work as hard.

What a letter this is! Heaven be with you! Ever faithfully yours,   M. R. MITFORD.

To MISS BARRETT, *Wimpole Street.*

Three-mile Cross, Dec. 30, 1841.

—Mr. Hughes, too, told me the other day of a dream of a friend of his father's, a country gentleman of fortune and character. He thought that his gardener was digging a pit in a certain part of his garden; he watched him, wondering what it could be, until it assumed the form of a grave. Then the gardener went away and fetched the body of a young woman, in whom he recognized his own dairymaid, and deposited the corpse in the ground, and shoveled the earth over it. Then he awoke. He awakened his wife and told her his dream. "Nonsense," said she; "go to sleep again; it is the nightmare." Again he went to sleep, and the dream returned. He again awakened his wife, and she, although a little startled, persuaded him that it had arisen from some talk which they had had respecting the dairymaid's appearance; and at last he composed himself to sleep once more. For the third time the dream returned, and then, arming himself with his pistols, he walked down into the garden. At the very spot indicated he saw the gardener just finishing the operation of digging the grave, and rushing upon him suddenly, the man in his panic confessed that the dairymaid was pregnant by him; that she had threatened to appeal to her mistress; that he had appointed to meet her in a retired part of the grounds at that very hour; and that, in short, if not prevented by his master, before the sun rose the poor young woman would have lain murdered in the pit before them. *This* is a certain fact.

K——, a young woman of remarkable intelligence and presence of mind, has told me frequently of an appearance that she saw, about five years back, when living with a respectable grocer in Buckinghamshire—not as servant but as shopwoman. Her bedroom opened into an anteroom common to two or three chambers belonging to the family. In this room a rushlight was burnt, and she had the habit of leaving her door open, and, after laying her head down upon the pillow, of half rising to look if the rushlight were safe. Two of her brothers and a favorite cousin were at sea in different merchant vessels, and she had that evening expressed to the grocer's daughter her strong impression that she should never see her cousin again. On raising herself up, as usual, to look at the light, she saw just before her, standing in the doorway, ·the figure of a young sailor. She felt that *it* was no living man: the head drooped on the bosom, and the straw hat fell over the face, which she could not discern. The dress was the usual jacket and trowsers, the open shirt, and loosely-tied neckerchief of a seaman. It might have been, from height and appearance, either her elder brother or her cousin. She believed it to be the latter, and spoke to it by his name. It made no answer—but remained during two or three minutes, and then slowly and gradually melted into air. She was as strongly convinced of the reality of the appearance as of her own existence, and is so still.

Both her cousin and her brother returned to London, but the former had had a fall from some part of the rigging of the vessel on that very day (the day of his apparition), and died on shore without her seeing him. Nor has she again seen her elder brother, who, shortly after his return, sailed on another voyage, and must have been lost at sea, since, although four years have elapsed since he was expected, neither he nor the vessel has ever been heard of; indeed the underwriters have paid the insurance-money. K—— was not alarmed, she said; the only painful sensation was the immediate fear that something had occurred to one or other of these dear relatives, and she shall always, she says, be sure that *it* was her cousin who appeared to her. I believe that these are her very words, and I have no doubt whatever that she did see what she describes; nor would you if you could hear the truthful simplicity, the graphic minuteness, and the invariable consistency with which she relates both the apparition and her own feelings on the occasion. The story, as she tells it, is exceedingly impressive, from the absence of exaggeration and of those circumstances which are usually thrown in for the sake of effect. The door opening upon the staircase

was fastened, bolted within; no man slept in the house except the master of the shop, a grave elderly man who officiated as a Wesleyan minister, and whom no money would have
bribed into attempting a trick upon such a subject; and the
females, besides a general coincidence of character with their
husband and father, were all considerably shorter, and in
every respect different from the figure in question. K——
has never used the word ghost or spirit or apparition, in speaking to me; she generally says "*it*," and certainly thinks of
the appearance with great awe.

I agree partly with you that there are glimpses of another
world. It seems impossible to refer all these well-attested
stories to imposition or credulity.

Another story I remember well. Old Mr. Knyvett, the
king's organist (George the Third's—one of whose favorite
pleasures it was to hear this splendid musician play and sing
the "Hallelujah Chorus" upon a grand pianoforte thrown
open—I have heard it often; a wonderful feat it was, accomplished by a perfect knowledge of the score, wonderful dex-
terity of hand, and a matchless power and compass of voice)
—this old man, a wit and a jester, one whose sin was levity
—lightness not of conduct but of speech—the very reverse
of superstition—this wag lived at a pretty village near Reading, called Sonning, a river-side village reached by a deep
winding lane, now shaded by tall close hedgerows, now by
the high irregular paling of Holme Park. Over the latter at
one particular point, regularly as the clock struck twelve (and
it was within hearing both of the church clock and of that
belonging to the park) a woman was seen to emerge from
the shady lane and disappear *over* the paling—rising gradually and sinking slowly—always the same figure, dressed in
the costume of the middle of the last century, and with the
self-same disposition and fluctuation of drapery—not a hair's
breadth more or less. There was no background to form a
phantasmagoria deception, since the part plainest to be seen
was the figure as it rose and sank above the paling. When
the moonlight was strong the apparition appeared semi-trans-
parent. I have heard Mr. Knyvett speak in answer to a
skeptical friend of his and mine, upon this subject—in answer
only, for voluntarily he never approached the topic; and the
manner in which this thorough man of the world trembled

and quivered—cheek and lip blanching as the topic was approached—the doubtful half-glance around and behind him, and the low tremulous voice I shall never forget. It would have been a study for a tragedian in "Hamlet," for it was real. I do not disbelieve in the possibility of such appearances, though I heartily agree with Stilling in the sinfulness and danger of seeking them. By danger, I mean the peril lest such presumption should be punished by madness, or such tremor as is one form of that awful infliction; or by fits or other physical infirmities brought on by mortal fear.

I wonder, my sweetest, how you will get through this sadly tedious scrawl. My father has a grievous cough: it is while in and out of his room that I have written, partly on a low stool at the foot of the bed, using a chair as my table.

Once, again, Heaven be with you! Ever yours,

M. R. MITFORD.

CHAPTER XVII.

LETTERS FOR 1842.

To MISS JEPHSON, *Castle Martyr.*

Three-mile Cross, Jan. 10, 1842.

MY DEAR EMILY,—I passed one evening in town with dear Mr. Lucas. He is painting Prince Albert just now, and speaks very highly of him, and of his knowledge and love of art especially. He says that he could not speak with more taste of painting if he had studied under Raphael. At Mr. Lucas's I met Mr. Brown, the young artist who, under the name of "Phiz," has so much aided Mr. Dickens's reputation. He has just returned from Brussels, where he had been spending three weeks with Mr. Lever ("Harry Lorrequer," etc.). Of him he speaks enthusiastically, as the pleasantest man in the world, his store of anecdote never flagging for a moment. I like Mr. Brown himself exceedingly.

I long to be able to earn money. On myself I spend none. That's all I can do. I have not bought a bonnet, a cloak, a gown, hardly a pair of gloves, for four years; but I dare not touch my father's comforts, and therefore have gone on as usual with all that concerns him, in hopes that my little property may last while he needs it. For me it's of very little consequence. I feel that my vocation is to attend him, and that, when that is over, my poor life will go down like a watch when the owner no longer winds it up, or out like a lamp, when the oil is spent. However on the whole we are both better.

Mrs. Cox and Sir Richard and Lady Keane went to Buckingham Palace the other day, where Prince Albert showed them the little boy; a very lovely baby Mrs. Cox says he is. Mr. Wood told me that when the princess was born, Prince Albert was reading English law with a friend of his. He did not attend him for a week or two after; and when sent for, the prince desired him to come with him and see the little girl. "But stop," said he, "you are cold, warm yourself well before we go up, or it may hurt the child." This amused me greatly! it was such a pretty piece of young fathership.

Adelaide Kemble is making four hundred pounds a month. It is a singular instance of hereditary talent. My precious Miss Barrett continues better. Is Daniel O'Connell going to be married to a girl of nineteen? The papers say so. Heaven bless you, my dearest Emily! Ever most faithfully and affectionately yours, M. R. M.

To Miss Barrett, 50 *Wimpole Street.*

Three-mile Cross, Jan. 13, 1842.

My beloved Friend,—Mr. James, who might do better, has made a complete mistake (a wonder) about hanging in chains. At Mortimer Common, a beautiful tract of wild country, now for the most part planted, near us, there is an inclosure of one hundred or two hundred acres, chiefly covered with heath and gorse, and called " The Gallows Piece;" because a murderer had been hanged in chains there, on a bit of broken ground, the scene of his crime. I remember the relics of the gibbet, and finding a hare just under it, which poor May, after killing, brought to me in her mouth full half a mile, and laid down at my feet. We had an old keeper with us who took the opportunity of telling me the story of the murder and of the execution, at which he had been present (having known both the murderer and his victim), and which he described most graphically. The man

was hanged with *a rope* till he was dead, cut down at the
expiration of an hour, and then, instead of being placed in a
shell; the body was fastened by irons to the gibbet; indeed,
some of the rusty "gibbet arms" were still swinging and
clanking overhead.   My father confirmed this to-night, remembering the circumstance well, and having seen other
criminals suspended in the same manner, and often shudder-
ed at the peculiar creaking of the chains.   This critique is
rather too elaborate for the occasion; but an author like Mr.
James ought to take care to be right.   Scott did always.
It is a part of *truth*, which in art, as in every thing, is a grace
above all graces.

I hope that one day or other you will know Mrs. Niven.
She is a very extraordinary person, the client in a very 'remarkable cause (she was a Miss Vordill) which, at the end
of twenty-one years, she has just won; or rather it was decided in the House of Lords, after two or three adjournments,
at the end of last session.   The story is too long to tell to-
night; but shortly, the question was, whether a Scotch marriage could pass an English estate?   And such à marriage!
So extreme a case!   I must tell it.   Her uncle—an old de-
bauchee, living on his fine old place in the scenery which
Scott copied in Ellangowan—finding that an old relation, a
lady of title, was coming to his house to sleep on a journey,
ejaculated: "Eh! my leddy's coming and we maun hae
a gude wife to receive her!   Off wi' ye, loons, to Meg, and
Jean, and Katie, and Beenie, and Bakie, and Beckie, and say
that she that wins first to the house shall take possession
and hae me into the bargain."   Off set his myrmidons to all
quarters to summon the usual seraglio, and the first that arrived was introduced to the "leddy," to her great horror;
and as she happened to have a bare-legged boy of some
twelve years old, this coarse frolic passed to that urchin
eight thousand a year of Scottish estates, and cost more suits
than I can well reckon; for it was litigated in every stage,
until it arrived at the House of Peers, and argued there in
three different sessions (chiefly on account of the obstinacy of Lord Brougham), in order to secure the English property to the real descendant, no drop of the true blood being in the veins of the boy, who came in so curious a way
into the Scottish property; at least the probability is ex-

ceedingly against it, the mother being as bad as bad could be.

Heaven bless you! The books shall come back in a day or two, with some flowers. Ever most faithfully yours,

M. R. MITFORD.

To MISS BARRETT.

Three-mile Cross, Jan. 21, 1842.

I could not, my beloved, honestly suffer my contract to go on without telling C—— what had happened; and he will assuredly make use of it to beat me down in the price. Oh! my dear, dear love, long, very long, may you be preserved in the blessed ignorance of pecuniary care! Never may you have to feel what it is to fear that the little you possess may not last while the one you love best on earth requires it! Never to feel that you can not supply to him that which habit has made indispensable! *I* feel these things pressing upon me like so many crimes. It seems to me that any one with more firmness and more exertion, would put aside all else and work for him. I am sensible that one of stronger resolution would do more. God aid me! I only pray for strength and power to help that dear, dear father. Except for him my existence has no value to any earthly creature. But when I think of not being able to administer to his comforts, my very heart sickens within me.

Oh! my dear love, you can not feel what that dreadful feeling is of one leaning upon you whilst you have no power to bear him up—of letting him fall through your own helpless weakness! Forgive my paining you in this way with a useless sympathy. But the expression is repressed to him, and sometimes it will have way. Forgive me, I implore you!

Heaven bless you! Your own,   M. R. M.

To the REV. WILLIAM HARNESS, *Heathcote Street.*

Three-mile Cross, Feb. —, 1842.

I sit down with inexpressible reluctance to write to you, my ever dear and kind friend, because I well know that you will blame me for the occasion; but it must be said, and I can only entreat your indulgence and your sympathy. My poor father has passed this winter in a miserable state of health and spirits. His eyesight fails him now so completely that he can not even read the leading articles in the newspaper. Accordingly, I have not only every day gone through the daily paper, debates and all, which forms a sort of necessity to one who has so long taken an interest in every thing that passes, but, after that, I have read to him from dark till bedtime, and then have often (generally) sat at his bedside almost till morning, sometimes reading, sometimes answering letters as he slept, expecting the terrible attacks of cramp, three or four of a night, during which he gets out of bed to walk the room, unable to get in again without my assistance. I have been left no time for composition—neither time nor heart—so that we have spent money without earning any.

What I have to ask of you, then, is to authorize Mr. Blandy to withdraw sufficient money to set us clear with the world, with a few pounds to start with, and then I *must* prefer the greater duty to the less—I must so far neglect my dear father as to gain time for writing what may support us. The season is coming on when he will be able to sit in the garden, and perhaps to see a few friends of an afternoon, and then this incessant reading will be less necessary to him. At all events the thing must be done, and shall. It was a great weakness in me, a self-indulgence, not to do so before, for the fault is entirely mine. I believe, when these debts are paid, his own spirits will lose that terrible depression, broken only by excessive irritability, which has rendered this winter such a scene of misery to himself and such a trial to me.

Do not fancy, my dear friend, that I cast the slightest blame on my dear father. The dejection and the violence belong to disease fully as much as any other symptom. If any body be to blame, *I* am the person, for not having taken care that he should have no anxiety—nothing but age and infirmity—to bear. God forgive me for my want of energy! for suffering myself to be wholly engrossed by the easier duty of reading to him! I will not do so again. Once a week he goes into Reading to the bench, and *then* he rallies; and nobody seeing him then could imagine what the trial is at home; and, with nobody but myself, it has been some excuse for getting through the day and the night as best I could, but it shall be so no longer.

Heaven bless you! Do not refuse me this most urgent prayer, and do not think worse of me than you can help! If you knew all that I have gone through this winter—alone, day after day, week after week—you would wonder that I am still left to cumber the earth. Nothing could bear up under it but the love that is mercifully given to the object of anxiety—such love as the mother bears to her sickly babe. Once again may Heaven bless you, my ever kind friend! Love to the Maries. Ever gratefully yours,

M. R. MITFORD.

To MISS BARRETT, *Wimpole Street.*

Three-mile Cross, March 2, 1842.

Since writing to you yesterday, my beloved friend, I have read in H. F. C——'s "Music and Manners" the account of a visit which he made to Madame d'Abrantes, I think in '39. He speaks of the thing among Parisian contrasts. He went to see her, he says, in her two small rooms, humbly furnished; describes her as clumsy of figure, with dim eyes, a hoarse voice, and feverish spirits, and adds that the three last evils were caused by the excess of opiates in which she indulged. He says that the room rung with anecdote and repartee; that she took her full part of the noise; and that, in particular, she cajoled two or three black-bearded men, who wore "Journalist" imprinted in visible letters on every hair of their mustaches. He adds that a few months afterward she died in a hospital; that almost at the last, a party of visitors going through the wards, one of the nurses pointed her out to their notice, on which the dying woman exclaimed, "Are you making a show of me?" Think of the ambassadress, the governess of Paris, the vice-queen of Portugal, laboring as a bookseller's drudge; fancy the wife of Napoleon's first aide-de-camp and friend, the companion of Josephine, of Hortense, of Duroc, of Madame Mère, forced to court such creatures as Balzac has painted in the "Journalists of Paris!"

Is poor King Louis still alive? Hortense is dead, I know. And is the captive of Ham the single or the married brother? One of the two remaining sons of Louis died, I think; but, of these two, one was the husband of a daughter of his uncle Joseph, so that *he* would unite hereafter every right to

VOL. II.—L

the Crown that the settlement under the Empire could give. This, I suppose, is Louis Philippe's excuse.

Now, good-night! It has just occurred to me that when a young girl, some eleven years old or less, I went with my father to the pit of one of the theatres—Drury Lane, I believe; yes, Drury Lane—to see a tragedy from "The Monk."* Kemble played the hero, and Mrs. Siddons the heroine. *She* had to go into a dungeon where a frail nun had produced an infant, or rather she had to come out of a small door on to the stage, with the supposed baby in her arms. The door was what is technically called "practicable," that is to say, a *real* door, frame and all, made to open in the scene, and to sustain the illusion of a dungeon, as well as in that huge stage such an illusion can be sustained—for, paradoxical as it sounds, so many are the discrepancies in the present ambitious state of scenery, that I am quite convinced that in the days of Shakspeare, when all was trusted to the imagination of the spectator, the fitting state of willing illusion was much more frequently obtained than now—however, to make the scene as dungeon-like as possible, the door was deeply arched, hollow and low; and Mrs. Siddons, miscalculating the width, knocked the head of the huge wax doll she carried so violently against the wooden framework that the unlucky figure broke its neck with the force of the blow, and the waxen head came rolling along the front of the stage. Lear could not have survived such a *contretemps*. The theatre echoed and re-echoed with shouts of laughter, and the tragedy being comfortably full of bombast, not only that act, but the whole piece, finished amidst peals of merriment unrivaled since the production of "Tom Thumb." I remember it as if it were yesterday. Ever most affectionately yours,   M. R. M.

To Miss Barrett, *Wimpole Street.*

Three-mile Cross, March 24, 1842.

Thanks upon thanks, my beloved friend, for the kindness which humors even my fancies. I am delighted to have the reading of Anna Seward's letters. Perhaps we both of us like those works which show us men and women as they are —faults, frailties, and all. I confess that I do love all that identifies and individualizes character—the warts upon Crom-

* Sotheby's "Julia and Agnes." 1800.

well's face, which, like a great man as he was, he would not
allow the artist to omit when painting his portrait. Therefore I like Hayley, and therefore was I a goose of the first
magnitude, when, for a passing moment, just by way of gaining for the poor bard a portion of *your* good graces (for I did
not want to gain for him the applause of the public—he had
it, and lost it), I wished his editor to have un-Hayley'd him
by wiping away some of the affectations—the warts—no—
the rouge, upon his face.

My love and my ambition for you often seems to be more
like that of a mother for a son, or a father for a daughter
(the two fondest of natural emotions), than the common
bonds of even a close friendship between two women of different ages and similar pursuits. I sit and think of you, and
of the poems that you will write, and of that strange, brief
rainbow crown called Fame, until the vision is before me as
vividly as ever a mother's heart hailed the eloquence of a
patriot son. Do you understand this? and do you pardon
it? You must, my precious, for there is no chance that I
should unbuild *that* house of clouds; and the position that
I long to see you fill is higher, firmer, prouder than ever
has been filled by woman. It is a strange feeling, but one
of indescribable pleasure. My pride and my hopes seem
altogether merged in you. Well, I will not talk more of
this; but at my time of life, and with so few to love, and
with a tendency to body forth images of gladness and of
glory, you can not think what joy it is to anticipate the
time. How kind you are to pardon my gossiping, and to
like it.

God bless you, my sweetest, for the dear love which finds
something to like in these jottings! It is the instinct of the
bee, that sucks honey from the hedge-flower.

I made my father happy in reading what you say of Sir
Robert: his eyes brightened like diamonds at the sound.
For my part, I incline to think with one of Miss Edgeworth's
heroines, that " he can not be so very artful as is said, because every body does say so." The perfection of cunning
is to conceal its own quality. Mortally dull are those debates. I rather have a fancy for Mr. Roebuck, who is as can-
tankerous and humorous (in the old Shakspearian sense) as
Cassius himself. I would know him at any time by half a line

—so perfectly in keeping are his speeches—which is more than I can say for any of the rest.

Certainly, in point of wearisome insipidity Sir Robert and Lord John are well matched one against the other. Did it ever occur to you to hear the debates read aloud for a whole session? The impression upon me is the exceeding want of power, the flat mediocrity, the total absence of any thing like eloquence. I remember a few years ago reading speeches by O'Connell in one of the Irish papers, which, with the faults of Irish oratory, had yet life and power. Now, so far as we have hitherto gone, I really have not met with a single speech that might not have been delivered by any tolerably-taught schoolboy. After all, these men are no such marvels.

Did you ever read Holcroft's Memoirs? If not, I think you would like them. I did *exceedingly*. He was a poor boy, who carried Staffordshire ware about the country; then he exercised the horses at Newmarket. Do read it; I know nothing more graphic or more true. Do you know his comedy, "The Road to Ruin?" The serious scenes of that play, between the father and son, are amongst the most touching in the language.

Dear Mr. Kenyon! How true in him the feeling always is! How few wits are like him—so bright, so playful, and yet so exquisitely kind! Heaven bless you, my beloved! Ever yours,   M. R. MITFORD.

To MISS BARRETT, *Wimpole Street.*

Three-mile Cross, March —, 1842.

I have only read the first volume of Madame D'Arblay's "Diary." Dr. Johnson appears to the greatest possible advantage—gentle, tender, kind and true; and Mrs. Thrale—oh, that warm heart! that lively sweetness! My old governess* knew her as Mrs. Piozzi, in Wales. She was there as a governess—neglected, uncared for, as governesses too often are; and that sweetest person sought her out, brought her forward, talked to her, wrote to her, gave her heart and hope and happiness. There have been few women who have used riches, and the station that riches give, so wisely as Mrs. Piozzi. I used to ask, "Was she happy?" and the answer was, "I hope so; but her animal spirits were so buoyant—she

* Miss Rowdin, afterward Mrs. St. Quintin.

was so entirely one of those who become themselves cheered
by the effort to cheer another—that the question is more difficult to answer than if it concerned one of a temper less elas-
tic." As to the little Burney, I don't like her at all, and
that's the truth. A girl of the world—a woman of the world,
for she was twenty-seven or thereabout—thought clearly and
evidently of nothing on this earth but herself and "Eve-
lina." Ever most faithfully yours, M. R. M.

To Miss Barrett, *Wimpole Street.*

Three-mile Cross, April 4, 1842.

I am an inconsistent politician, I confess it, with my aris-
tocratic prejudices and my radical opinions. By-and-by, perhaps, when education is more diffused, these prejudices may
lose their ground; at present there is certainly a great difference between the well-born, well-bred, simple, frank, and
gentle people who had grandfathers, and the fine, fussy pre-
tenders who have never known such progenitors. All the
Whigs seem to me, in all their measures, afraid of the people
—afraid to make any popular concession. Moore said once,
in my hearing, that he " liked the Whigs when they were out
of power." And certainly they are better then. But even
then they seem as if always guarding against whole measures
—devoted to bit-by-bit legislation. If they had flung themselves upon the people heartily and honestly, they might
have set the Tories at defiance. Free trade—that seems to
me the one great want now; and I can not but believe that
we shall live to see the principles advocated by Grote and
Warburton (neither of them now in Parliament), in the
ascendant. O'Connell is versatile in his words and ways,
and the Repeal seems to me incomprehensible; nevertheless,
as an Irishman (for doubtless he looks upon us as the English enemy), I can not but think him a great patriot. And
if you had but to read all those dull speeches you would feel
the relief of coming across his eloquence. Ever your own,
M. R. M.

To Miss Barrett, *Wimpole Street.*

Three-mile Cross, April 9, 1842.

It will help you to understand how impossible it is for me
to earn money as I ought to do, when I tell you that this

very day I received your dear letter, and sixteen others;
that then my dear father brought into my room the newspaper to hear the ten or twelve columns of news from India;
then I dined and breakfasted in one, then I got up. By that
time there were three parties of people in the garden; eight
others arrived soon after—some friends, some acquaintances,
and some strangers; the two first classes went away, and I
was forced to leave two sets of the last, being engaged to
call upon Lady Madalina Palmer, who has an old friend of
both on a visit at her house. She took me some six miles
(on foot) in Mr. Palmer's beautiful plantations in search of
that exquisite wild flower the buck-bean (do you know it
—most beautiful of flowers? wild, or as K—— puts it,
" tame ?"). After long search we found the *plant* not yet in
bloom. Then I hurried home, threw my own cocoa down my
throat, and read to my father Mrs. Cowley's comedy, " Which
is the Man ?" and here I am (after answering, as briefly as I
can, many very kind letters), talking to you.

My father sees me greatly fatigued—much worn—losing
my voice even in common conversation; and he lays it all
to the last drive or walk—the only thing that keeps me alive
—and tells every body he sees that am I killing myself by
walking or driving; and he hopes that I shall at last take
some little care of myself and not stir beyond the garden.
Is not this the perfection of self-deception? And yet I
would not awaken him from this dream—no, not for all the
world—so strong a hold sometimes does a light word take
of his memory and his heart—he broods over it—cries over
it! No, my beloved friend, we must for the present submit.
There may be some happy change. He may himself wish me
to go to town, and then— In the mean while my heart is
with you. Ever yours,   M. R. M.

                   To Miss BARRETT, *Wimpole Street.*
                                  Three-mile Cross, April 27, 1842.

No! my dear love, I am not now about to write on the
subject of the South Seas. The first volume of any size that
I printed was on the story—which came to me from a friend
of the American captain who visited them—of Christian's
Colony on Pitcairn's Island. A large edition was sold.
Then I published a second edition of a volume of miscella-

neous poems; then another volume of narrative poems called
"Blanche and the Rival Sisters." All sold well, and might
have been reprinted; but I had (of this proof of tolerable
taste I am rather proud) the sense to see that they were
good for nothing, so that I left off writing for twelve or fifteen years, and should never have committed any more pen-
and-ink sins, had not our circumstances become such as to
render the very humblest exertions right. My dear mother's health was then almost what my father's is now; only
then we were three, so that, except by staying at home, I
was not so absolutely chained as I am now.

Well, perhaps if I could be all the time I covet, among the
sweet flowers and the fresh grass, I should not enjoy as I do
the brief intervals into which I do contrive to concentrate so
much childish felicity. Who it is that talks of "the cowslip
vales of England?" is it you, my beloved? The words are
most true and most dear. Oh! how I love those meadows,
yellow with cowslips and primroses; those winding brooks,
or rather *that* winding brook, golden with the water ranun-
culus; those Silchester coppices, clothed with wood-sorrel,
wood-anemone, wild hyacinth, and primroses in clusters as
large as the table at which I write! I do not love musk—
almost the only odor called sweet that I do not love; yet
coming this evening on the night-scented odora with its
beautiful green cups, I almost loved the scent for the form
on which it grew. But the cowslips, the wild hyacinths,
the primroses, the violet—oh, what scent may match with
theirs? I try to like the garden, but my heart is in the
fields and woods. I have been in the meadows to-night—I
ran away, leaving my father asleep — I could not help it.
And oh! what a three hours of enjoyment we had, Flush, and
the puppies, and I! I myself, I verily believe, the youngest-
hearted of all. Then I have been to Silchester too. My father went there; and I got out and ran round the walls and
coppices one way, as he drove the other. How grateful I am
to that great gracious Providence who makes the most intense enjoyment the cheapest and the commonest! I do love
the woods and fields! Oh! surely all the stars under the
sun, even if they were brighter than those earthly stars ever
seem to me, could not compare with the green grass and the
sweet flowers of this delicious season!

I mistrust the feeling of poetry of all those who consent to pass the spring amongst brick walls, when they might come and saunter amongst lanes and coppices. To live in the country is, in my mind, to bring the poetry of Nature home to the eyes and heart. And how can those who do love the country talk of autumn as rivalling the beauty of spring? Only look at the texture of the young leaves; see the sap mounting into the transparent twigs as you stand under an oak; feel the delicious buds; inhale the fragrance of bough and herb, of leaf and flower; listen to the birds and the happy insects; feel the fresh balmy air. This is a rhapsody; but I have no one to whom to talk, for if I mention it to my father, he talks of "my killing myself," as if that which is balm and renovation were poison and suicide.

Heaven bless you, my most precious! My father's love. Ever most faithfully your own, M. R. MITFORD.

To MISS BARRETT, *Wimpole Street.*

Three-mile Cross, May 4, 1842.

Charlotte Smith's works, with all their faults, have yet a love of external nature, and a power of describing it, which I never take a spring walk without feeling. Only yesterday I strolled round the park-like paddock of an old place in our neighborhood—an old neglected ride, overgrown with moss, and grass, and primroses, and wild strawberries—overshadowed by horse-chestnuts, and lilacs, and huge firs, and roses, and sweet-brier, shot up to the height of forest-trees. Exquisitely beautiful was that wild, rude walk, terminating in a decayed carthouse, covered with ivy; and, oh! so like some of her descriptions of scenery! My mother knew her when her husband was sheriff of Hampshire; and she lived in a place (about four miles from the little town of Alresford, where I was born) where the scenery and the story of the "Old Manor House" may still be traced. There was a true feeling of nature about Charlotte Smith.

Of the three—Wordsworth, Southey, Coleridge—how very much the greater poet Coleridge seems to me! Poor Cowper! I never doubted his insanity, knowing as I did his kinswoman, whose melancholy tale I must have told you (Mrs. Frances Hill, sister to the Eve Hill of the letters, and his first cousin) whose madness was always said to be hereditary.

There could be no question of the taint in the blood. That the hands into which he fell were not likely to administer the best remedies, even with the best and purest motives, there can be as little doubt. So you have actually seen and known one who believed in that melancholy tenet! I always held the imputation to be untrue: it seemed to be so impossible that any one mind could at once believe *that* and the mediation. Yours ever, M. R. M.

To Miss Barrett, *Wimpole Street.*

Three-mile Cross, June 20, 1842.

My dear Love,—It is now half past one, and my father has only this very moment gone into his room to bed. He sleeps all the afternoon in the garden, and then would sit up all night to be read to. I have now several letters to answer before going to bed. At present, I write to say that on Saturday next (the very day on which you will receive this) we shall send you some flowers. Oh, how I wish we could transport you into the garden where they grow! You would like it—the "*entourage*," as Mrs. Mackie calls it, is so pretty: one side (it is nearly an acre of show flowers) a high hedge of hawthorn, with giant trees rising above it beyond the hedge, whilst all down within the garden are clumps of matchless hollyhocks and splendid dahlias; the top of the garden being shut in by the old irregular cottage, with its dark brick-work covered with vines and roses, and its picturesque chimneys mingling with the bay tree, again rising into its bright and shining cone, and two old pear-trees festooned with honeysuckle; the bottom of the garden and the remaining side consisting of lower hedgerows melting into wooded uplands, dotted with white cottages and patches of common. Nothing can well be imagined more beautiful than this little bit of ground is now. Huge masses of lupines (say fifty or sixty spiral spikes), some white, some lilac; immense clumps of the enameled Siberian larkspur, glittering like some enormous Chinese jar; the white and azure blossoms of the variegated monkshood; flags of all colors; roses of every shade, some covering the house and stables and over-topping the roofs, others mingling with tall apple-trees, others again (especially the beautiful double Scotch rose) low but broad, standing in bright relief to the

L 2

blues and purples; and the oriental poppy, like an orange lamp (for it really seems to have light within it) shining amidst the deeper greens; above all, the pyramid of geraniums, beautiful beyond all beauty, rising in front of our garden room, whilst each corner is filled with the same beautiful flower, and the whole air perfumed by the delicious honeysuckle. Nothing can be more lovely.

[*The rest is wanting.*]

To MISS BARRETT, *Wimpole Street.*

Three-mile Cross, June 25, 1842.

I wonder, my very dearest, when I shall be quiet again! Last Monday I set forth to get a flower of the buck-bean. I had set my heart upon it. Whole beds of that rare plant grow upon either side of a stream that runs amongst Mr. Tyshe Palmer's plantations, crossed by two bridges, called Kingsbridge and Queensbridge, on two roads which diverge so (, about four miles from the little town of Wokingham. Now, Wokingham is eight miles from us; but, by crossing the heath, we save about two, at the expense of walking those two miles under the firs—a delicious walk in these balmy summer evenings, when the scent is as of Arabia. Well, I had been three times to this Kingsbridge in chase of this flower—twice quite in vain; but the third time we had found the plant, its buds and leaves in profusion, so that I was determined not to give up the flower. Accordingly, Ben being busy finishing the hay, Marianne (my hysterical maid) and I set forth, with the pony and Flush for all our company. The road is exquisite—by Arborfield first, and through delicious lanes walled with honeysuckle hedges, and cradled above with beech and oak and elm—over the Lodden, with its floating water-lilies—then through the still wilder lanes and woodlands of Barkham, until we reached the heath, pink and purple with the flowers from which it takes its name—and then Mr. Tyshe Palmer's exquisite plantations of fir, and larch, and beech, and mountain ash.

The name of the road we took will tell you the extent of these plantations—"The Nine-mile Ride;" but of their beauty, diversified by little valleys with wandering brooks, and varied by the most sudden rise and fall of the ground,

by bits of wild road hollowed out of the hill-side, and overgrown by shaggy precipices, and of the exquisite odors of
the pines and the heath-flowers of a thousand sorts, I can
give you no notion. For the last two miles we had to lead
the pony, because this Nine-mile Ride may be a ride, but is
no road for a wheeled vehicle. That we did not mind. We
did, however, begin to fret when, on reaching the streamlet
where the buck-bean grew, and traversing it on either side
for above an hour, we found thousands, millions of plants,
but not one blossom—most carefully had they been cut off!
Ben says " mowed;" I rather think cut by people employed
by the London druggists, it being a celebrated remedy for
erysipelas. However that may be, gone it was, and we had
no other consolation than that of finding in profusion the
equally rare bog asphodel. Do you know *that* pretty wild
flower ? Wet high above our boots (for we had traversed
miles of bog), we prepared to set off on our way home, when
a tremendous roll of thunder over our heads gave token of
what was about to ensue. The pony curvetted ; Flush was
uneasy ; hail and rain poured down in torrents—hail such as
in my life I never saw ; in fact, it broke all the glass it came
near. In fewer minutes than I care to say we were wet to
the skin ; the bottom of the pony-chaise was as full of water
as a bucket, and the pony was so frightened, it was clear that
the best we could do was to lead it home. This we did, not
meeting a creature till we got to Arborfield, by which time
we had made up our minds to follow out the adventure. At
first we were violently angry to be so deserted, and said to
one another, rather oftener than was quite magnanimous,
" Well, if K—— had been out in this rain, we should have
sent after *her!* Thank Heaven, we never deserted any body
in such a manner !" But by the time we had passed Barkham we began to perceive by the state of the roads how
completely local the storm had been ; in fact we were, I
really believe, completely in the centre both of the lightning
and the hail and rain.

Never was such a plight as ours. It has spoiled my two
cloaks (one a fur one—a real loss), which had been hung
over the back of the chaise, and which we abandoned, as adding to the weight of water which we had to carry ; but beyond this misfortune, which I shall feel severely in the win-

ter (I must try to buy one second-hand), we escaped wonderfully. I suppose we should have been very stiff the next day if we had had time; but on Tuesday that gander feast, the Reading Whist Club, dined with us; and then, between helping to cook, and talking and waiting upon the good folks, we got the stiffness rubbed out of our bones in a wonderful manner. Ever your own, M. R. M.

To Miss Barrett, *Wimpole Street.*

Three-mile Cross, July 23, 1842.

Yes, my dearest, my mother's fortune was large, my father's good, legacies from both sides, a twenty thousand pound prize in the lottery—all have vanished. My uncle's estates, his wife's, his father's and mother's (a fine old place called Old Wall, in Westmoreland; she—my grandmother—was a Graham " of the Netherby clan ")—all have disappeared; so that I, the only child amongst six or seven good fortunes (for my mother—herself an only child—inherited an even splendid inheritance), have been, during the better part of my life, struggling with actual difficulty; and, if I should live long enough, shall probably die in a workhouse—content so to die if preserved from the far bitterer misery of seeing my dear, dear father want his accustomed comforts;—content, ay, happy, if that far deeper wretchedness be spared.

The leaving the dear old house was a grief—would have been a greater had not this cottage stood ready to receive us, so that my strong local predilections were indulged, and I soon came to love our pretty garden better than the grounds that I left. I could not, I think, so quietly have borne the change to a town. And yet I don't know; there is a blessed principle of conformity in human nature, and I should have fallen into the artist-society of London, where clever and cultivated men and intelligent women, after a day spent in their various pursuits, meet at night—or rather *did* meet at night, for I question if even that society be not spoilt by the all-pervading finery and pretension which desecrates all classes—but where they did meet at night, without fuss or ceremony, or dress or regale of any sort—calling in quietly, without preparation, at each other's houses between seven and eight o'clock, and staying till ten, or going, with equal disregard of appearance, to the theatre; for, trust me, to have seen John Kemble and his sister in "Macbeth," and Kean in "Othello," and Cooke in "Sir Pertinax," and Miss O'Neil in "Juliet," are things never to forget. Such a life might have had its enjoyments even in London, though I doubt if now I could get through the spring and summer out of reach of fields and woods. Trees and fresh air are necessities to my constitution.

Miss Martineau is a person of great singleness of mind, sincere and truthful; but I have always thought that she did not very well know her own mind. She is so one-sided that I never should be astonished to find her turn short round and change her opinions plump. And this, I suppose, must have been the case here, for really it does not seem possible that the two books* could have been written by the same person, unless upon such a theory. How much damage the two parties, high and low, are doing to the Church by these contests! In the midst of them, freedom of conscience and true religion will probably take deep root; but it is grievous to see the holiest names profaned to the uses of the basest passions.

You are right, dearest, about Dryden, quite; and about Johnson, whom I should like to have seen. I had a fancy that Parr resembled him in manner till I saw him, or rather till I heard him, and then—what a disappointment! I dined in company with him at Mr. Perry's, the then proprietor and editor of the "Morning Chronicle," who, as Porson's brother-in-law, and a man of admirable sense and wit, had a no profound veneration for the buzzwig doctor. He was a little, insignificant man, peculiar in dress, with a low insignificant voice, and a lisp that totally took away all the oracular effect of his sayings. Not one word did he say that day that any body could have cared to remember. He brought three persons with him; one, in whose house he was staying; another, in whose carriage they both came; and a third, a *protégé*, whom he wished to introduce to some great people invited to meet him: none of the three being invited or expected until they made their appearance. One of these (Basil Montague) said a very good thing. Talking of the Doctor's illegible MS., "Ay," said he, "his letters are illegi-

* "The Crofton Boys" and "Principle and Practice."

ble, except they contain a commission or an announcement that he is coming to see you, and then no man can write plainer."

There was nothing of this sort about Porson. I did not know him, but his brother-in-law and his stepdaughter, my intimate friends, spoke of him as a noble nature unhappily ·wasted—as a kind, careless, generous, open-hearted creature, to be pitied and mourned, much as one thinks of Burns. I hope to inclose Dryden's letter.

Now, good-night, my precious love! I have been interrupted by my dear father's cramp, but that seems now gone, · so I am going to bed myself. God bless you, my own dear friend! Ever yours,   M. R. M.

To Miss Barrett, *Wimpole Street.*

Three-mile Cross, July 25, 1842.

I have had two or three interesting visits lately, dearest. One, the last (to-day), from a Dr. Carter, a friend of Dr. Elliotson, and a believer in, if not a practicer of, animal magnetism. He has traveled all through America, North and South, visiting Chili and Mexico, doubling Cape Horn, rambling over Juan Fernandez, etc., etc. He says that, allowing for a little coloring, Stephens's "Central America" comes very near the truth; prefers South America to North; but declares that, after rambling over all that is fairest in Europe, Greece, Italy, the Peninsula, the lovely islands of the Pacific, all that is called finest in point of scenery, he knows nothing so beautiful, for mere beauty, as our own dear England. The Americas are on too large a scale, he says; neither the eye nor the mind can take in a whole. I can understand this. And the result of their too bright skies is a want of atmospheric illusion— of shifting shadow—of that transition which is as expression to a lovely face.

I wish you had seen Dr. Carter, you would have been pleased with him. He told me what I did not before know, that Mrs. Trollope is a thorough-going mesmerite, constantly at Dr. Elliotson's, and believing through thick and thin. Another thing which he told me gratified me greatly: being ill in Spain, home-sick and longing for some English or Englishlike book, he sent to see if such a treat could be procured, and received a Spanish translation of "Our Village!" So few

English works are published in a Spanish dress that it is a real compliment, and I tell you of it just as I told my father, because I know that it will please your dear heart.

Another visitor is Lord Brougham's thrice-charming and thrice-excellent sister. She is full of life, and spirit, and brilliancy—as clever, Marianne says, as her brother, and kind cordial, generous, frank, and full of all that is admirable and all that is charming. We have only spent one afternoon together, and I feel that we are friends for life. She says that her brother's health and spirits are better than she once feared they would be. He finds in constant employment a medicine for great grief—the loss of his mother weighing even more heavily than the loss of his daughter. Both were to be expected, but Miss Brougham said that she believed her brother had reconciled himself to the one as inevitable—had even assigned to it (through the foresight of the medical men) something very near the actual date; whilst the green old age of his mother, the absence of change or decay either of health, spirits, or faculty, had blinded him to the danger, so that the shock, the surprise, was greater in the death of the very old than of the very young.

He has lost one eye, and the other fails him, so that he dictates instead of writing. His newspaper is the "Sun." He has never had the courage to revisit Brougham since his mother's death, and Miss B. says she doubts if he ever will. His place in the south of France is his great amusement; and the giving judgments in the House of Peers. How I wished for you during Miss Brougham's visit! God bless them both! Ever your own, M. R. M.

To MISS BARRETT.

Three-mile Cross, August 18, 1842.

What you say of Milton is full of truth. But *one* truth you have, I think, not perceived, that the want of distinctive character causes much of the heaviness, of character, individuality, the power of identification, which is the salt of all literature from Horace to Scott. It is the one great merit of your own Chaucer, the glory of Shakspeare, the one grand quality by which writers worthy to live will live to all time, and without which they may indeed exist, praised, but unread, amongst moths and cobwebs. Heaven bless you, my beloved friend! Ever yours, M. R. M.

To Miss Barrett, *Wimpole Street.*

Three-mile Cross, Sept. 2, 1842.

You may imagine, my beloved friend, how very much my dear father is restored when I tell you that carrying with us, and sending on before, the four persons absolutely necessary to help him in and out of his very low open carriage, he was well enough to attend at the stone-laying ceremony yesterday* (Wednesday), and that the exertion, as Mr. May foretold, rather did him good than harm. It was really a pretty ceremony. I suppose there'll be an account of it in the Reading paper next week; if so, I'll send it. Perhaps, after reading, you will be so good as to return it, since I should like to keep the detail. If ever I am ungrateful enough to bemoan my isolated position, I ought to think over the assemblage in the morning, and at the evening tea-party and concert (where my father insisted on my appearing for an hour), in order to feel the thankfulness that thrilled through my very heart at the true and honest kindness with which I was received. It was an enthusiasm of man, woman, and child— hundreds—thousands—such as I can hardly venture to describe, and it lasted all the time I staid. Indeed, the pleasure amounted to pain, so confusing was it to hear the overpraise of which I felt myself unworthy. But it was not the praise that was so touching, it was the kindliness, the affection. My father cried, K—— cried, Dora Smith cried, I think more than all, at the true, honest, generous heartiness of the people. There is in Reading a very eloquent man, really eloquent, and it is a high and rare gift. He is a physician, young and deeply religious, very clever, very scientific, and one who interests himself greatly in the instruction of the people, giving courses of lectures every winter. He spoke the oration, a very fine one; and if the reporter have done him justice, you will see that he is a speaker of no common stamp. If the account be badly done, I sha'n't send it; but will then write again to supply the omissions of this letter; taking for granted frankly, my most dearest, that to you it will be as full of interest as such a thing happening to you would be to me. Think how full of thanksgiving were my prayers last night that my dear father had enjoyed such gratification.

* The first stone of the Reading reading-room.

I must see the "North American Review," and the condemned tragedies, chiefly the "North American." I know very well Mrs. Stirling, the mother of the poet. His father is the most trenchant and violent writer of the "Times." Mrs. Stirling is very charming — a Cornelia-like woman—stately and noble, whose pride in her son is charming. It is long since I have seen her. No, Mr. Milnes is not cold! I love his poetry.

Heaven bless you, my love! I am tired to death. Ever your own,   M. R. MITFORD.

To MISS BARRETT, *Wimpole Street.*

Three-mile Cross, Sept. 9, 1842.

I have to-day a letter from Marianne Skerrett. She says the queen's procession, nine carriages and four, Life Guards and Highlanders, winding along those woody mountains and by the side of the lakes—every nook and corner and turfy hillside covered with crowds of people—was beautiful beyond all beauty. She speaks well of the three duchesses, particularly of the Duchess of Norfolk, a woman, she says, of wonderful reading and knowledge, and great kindness. Lady Willoughby d'Eresby, chief of the Clan Drummond, through her father the Earl of Perth, is also, she says, a very charming woman. She wore at dinner, in compliment to the queen, the chieftain's bonnet with two eagle's feathers.

My nearest relation, except my dear father, *his* first cousin and my namesake, Mary Mitford—a little active, buoyant, cheerful, good-humored old maid—who is on a visit to the Duchess of Athole, told me that among the preparations to receive her majesty were thirty tents on the lawn at Dunkeld for a thousand kilted Highlanders in Murray tartan; whilst in a splendid tent for the queen and her party is to be laid out a sumptuous luncheon, which Gunter and his people were to come from London to prepare! Is not this a very amusing conjunction of names and things?—a singular union of the old times and the new?

The queen does not mean to visit the places which would interest me—those which Scott and Burns have commemorated. Heaven bless you!   M. R. M.

To Miss Barrett, *Wimpole Street.*

Three-mile Cross, Nov. 20, 1842.

No, my precious ! do not send any thing else *yet:* perhaps, by-and-by, a few oysters, but not for this week, Mrs. Cockburn having sent a brace of grouse. Did I tell you that my father took last night with Mr. Cox three glasses of claret, and afterward two glasses more ; enjoying them, not taking them, as he does the gravy, medicinally ; but feeling the pleasure, the strange pleasure, that gentlemen do feel in the scent and taste of fine wine, especially when shared with a friend. Surely this is a sign of amendment ! And he called me again " my treasure ;" always his favorite word for his poor daughter. It rejoices my heart. Of course the previous omission was accidental. I feel sure now that he was not angry; but before, I had *so* feared it: and it had *so* grieved me—grieved me to the very bottom of my heart. So that, if it had pleased God to take him *then*, I do believe that I should have died of very grief. I thought that I must have said something, or done something, or left something unsaid or undone, that had displeased him. *Now*, so far as that goes, my heart is at ease, and it is the taking off of a great load.

Love to your dear people. Ever your own,   M. R. M.

To Miss Jephson, *Castle Martyr, Ireland.*

Three-mile Cross, Nov., 1842.

My dear father continues much as when I wrote last. For two days he has been composed and collected, so as to derive much comfort from the clergyman of the parish, and from my reading to him and praying with him—as, indeed, I have done for many months—ever since he was unable to read the Bible himself. He prefers St. John's gospel ; so do I. There is more tenderness, I think, in the beloved disciple. But all are full of comfort.

Heaven bless you, my beloved friend ! I will write you a longer letter when I have more time and steadier fingers.

Ever yours,   M. R. M.

To Miss Barrett, *Wimpole Street.*

Three-mile Cross, Dec. 1, 1842.

On Saturday, my beloved, I had again the bitter, bitter fear of my dear father's immediate death. Every symptom was alarming. So it was on Sunday morning; and by Sunday evening, finding that Mr. May did not arrive, I determined to go to Reading to see our dear friend, and find from him whether I should not discontinue the medicine which seemed to affect him, and whether he could not substitute some other for it. Having waited for Mr. May at home till half past five, it was, when we started, dark and rainy. When we got to his house he was not at home, but was expected in half an hour. So I waited for him that and another half-hour; and at last, finding that the chance of his return rather diminished than increased, I took the advice of his partner, to persist in the brandy and water and discontinue the medicine, and with his promise that Mr. May should see us early on Monday set off on my return home about seven o'clock. After we left the Reading lights we found the darkness tremendous. The very hedges of the highroad were invisible; but Ben assured me that "the pony could see in the dark;" that there was no danger; and that we should be back in a quarter of an hour—his usual time for performing the journey. Well, it rained drivingly, so that I held an umbrella over the side next the outside of the gig—the side that was not Ben's; and when we had reached a hill half way between Reading and the Cross— "just on the pitch of the hill," to use Ben's phrase—two men rushed from the path by the roadside, on my side, the left, and one caught hold of the pony's rein, and the other clutched at my umbrella—failing to catch it, but driving it against me in the effort. Not a word was spoken; but we felt the jar both of the rein and of the umbrella, Ben of one and I of the other, and heard the sharp heavy sound of a bludgeon striking against the shaft, which, luckily, as we imagine, also hit the pony. He darted on like the wind; threw off the man who had caught the rein, and who, stricken either by the shaft or the step, was knocked under the wheel. The sudden shock disengaging us also from the man who was still trying to grasp the umbrella—and who had actually seized hold of the back of the chaise—we were in an instant flying along the road at full gallop, and free. The plunging of the chaise, as we passed over the footpad was tremendous; and it is wonderful that I was not thrown out by the jolt. The sensation of being, as we literally were, run away with for nearly two miles in a darkness which might almost be felt, was any thing but pleasant. Ben had no earthly power over the pony; but by the mercy of Providence, we did not meet any carriage of any sort, and the dear, dear pony slackened his pace as soon as he saw the lights of our little street, and drove quietly up to our own door.

Was not this a sad trial to nerves already so shaken? I am most thankful for my escape; but it was a great trial, and will go far to hinder me from ever walking at night. I am writing on Tuesday, and have *not* had a letter to-day. Good-bye. Ever faithfully your own,   M. R. M.

To Miss Barrett.

Three-mile Cross, Dec. 5, 1842.

It is great presumption to differ from you, my dearest; but we love one another all the better, I think, for the truth with which each tells the impression made by books and people; and for the differences as well as the similarities of our taste. Some day or other I shall certainly read these books; but I doubt if I shall be much smitten by works so extravagant. It seems to me that the real test of power is to produce great effects by seemingly small and ordinary means— by truth, not by excess. Moreover, I delight in the bright and the cheerful. Next to Molière, the French dramatist that I like best is Beaumarchais, whose *two* plays, "Le Barbier" and "Le Mariage," seem to me amongst the most delightful pieces of gayety ever dreamt by poet. Now, these new people have no notion of chiaroscuro. They are all oscuro— dark, dark shade, with as little light as may be, and that little moonlight—not the bright beams of the sun. No! there is no danger of my being ever smitten by these sorts of naughtinesses. And yet I shall most assuredly read them, as soon as I can without dishonesty; because, as you do *not* say, my dearest, there is no sending me Saunders & Otley's books. The time will come when you shall make me a list of the best. Surely the one you last mention can not be amongst them?

Do me the justice to believe that my real feeling is one of intense thankfulness, that what I have has lasted so as to furnish to my dear father all that he has wanted; that for the last twenty years he has known no want in this poor cottage. What I earned and what I had has been enough. It was before. In the terrible embarrassment of falling circumstances :—first, in the struggle after appearances, with a great establishment in a fine place; then with that long lawsuit and the up-hill striving in literature and the drama (always a series of expectations unfulfilled, and blighted hopes, and sharp, sudden, cutting disappointments); and more or less even during these last twenty years—although want, actual want, has not come, yet fear and anxiety have never been absent.

I may truly say that ever since I was a very young girl I have never, although for many years living apparently in affluence, been without pecuniary care—a care that pressed upon my thoughts the last thing at night, and woke in the morning with a dreary, heavy sense of pain and pressure of something which weighed me to the earth—which I would fain cast off, but could not. Oh, my dear friend! be sure that poverty is indeed a most real and clinging evil. Here, I think, is one reason of the difference of taste between us—I like the sunny and the bright, because my own thoughts are full of sadness, and I require the change. You know what Coleridge says of Genévieve,

> "Few sorrows had she of her own."

Now I have always had many, and therefore I love things that make me gay—therefore, amongst other reasons, I love Miss Austen. I shall be sure to read the Swedish book, and sure to like it; but Mary Howitt's English will be one take-off; and is there not some strange morbid tale woven in with it, for another? Oh! if it were indeed Miss Austen, that would be discovering a mine of diamonds.

To Miss Barrett, *Wimpole Street.*

Three-mile Cross, Dec. 11, 1842.

My dear Friend,—All is over—my dear, dear father breathed his last at six o'clock this morning, without a struggle or a sigh. He had been speechless for many hours. All that you say is right, my beloved friend; and I will try to bear up as you would have me—I will, indeed. I am not ill, except from shiverings, which come across me whether up or in bed. But they are merely nervous, Mr. May says, and will subside after a little while. It is selfish to wish him alive again, unless he could be well as he used to be. I must pray for submission. I am so sure of his happiness! So would you be if you could see him. Mr. Harrison, Mr. May's partner, has written to request permission to take a cast of his face. It is full of heavenly calm; and, if Mr. Harrison succeeds, I shall be most thankful to possess such a memorial. A friend and neighbor is coming this after-noon for a few hours, and I expect George Dawson to-mor-row. So that I am well seen to. Heaven bless you, my be-loved friend! Thank you for all your goodness. Ever yours, 　　　　　　　　　　　　　　　　　　M. R. M.

To Miss Barrett, *Wimpole Street.*

Three-mile Cross, Dec. 12, 1842.

All friends are kind and very soothing, but not half so soothing as your sweet kindness, my dearest. Oh! let me think of you as a most dear friend—almost a daughter, for such you have been to me.

I'll let you know when the French books arrive. You should not have done it, my sweetest—I would have con-trived to see them some way or other. In the mean while, even in all my affliction, Tennyson has had a power over my imagination which I could not have believed possible. You love the great and the deep—I, the bright and the beautiful, and therefore, each loving those delicious poems, we prefer the different ones, according to our several fancies. I thought so as I read them.

Every body is so kind! The principal farmers are striv-ing who shall carry the coffin. Surely this is not common—to an impoverished man—one long impoverished—one whose successor is utterly powerless! This is disinterested, if ever any thing were so, and therefore very touching, very dear. Perhaps I have shed more tears for the gratitude caused by this kindness and other kindnesses than for the great, great grief! That seems to lock up the fountain; this to unseal it. Bless you, my beloved, for all your inimitable kindness!

Oh! how he loved to bless you! He seldom spoke the dear name without the benediction—"Miss Barrett! dear Miss Barrett! Heaven bless her!" How often has he said that! I seem to love the name the better for that recollection. And now, my most beloved friend, good-night! Let me say how very, very kind every body is! I think, I am sure, that you will like to hear that.

God bless you, my precious friend! I am resigned—indeed I am. I know that it is right; and that is His will. Heaven bless you, my very dearest—my best comforter! Ever your own, M. R. M.

To Miss Barrett, *Wimpole Street.*

Three-mile Cross, Dec. 15, 1842.

My beloved Friend,—I thank you from the bottom of my heart for your dear, precious letter. You would be astonished at my composure—*I* am. I have scarcely shed a tear since Saturday. And I woo cheerful thoughts, and take all care of myself, as *he* would have wished. If ever spirit were in heaven, *there*, through the mercy of God, and the atonement of the Savior, is he—whose faith and trust were in that mercy and that atonement—whose last moments were peace—whose every thought was of kindness to man and trust in heavenly mercy through the mediation of the Redeemer. And so, feeling and knowing that to have kept him here, even if that had been possible, would have been to detain him amongst care and sorrow, in feebleness, helplessness, and suffering—it would indeed be a wicked selfishness, not to strive, with all my strength, for resignation and for cheerfulness.

It would be a base ingratitude to you, too, my beloved friend, and to the many, many kind and affectionate people who are around me. I can not tell you how good and kind every body is. It seems as if they were inspired with your spirit. Those whom he best loved will follow him. I have just strewn flowers over him (the lovely chrysanthemums that he loved so well, that he helped me to strew over my dear mother), and he looks with a heavenly composure, and almost with his own beautiful color, the exquisite vermilion for which he was so famous, on his sweet, serene countenance. I could not touch him. Mr. May desired me not. He said there was danger in renewing the chill, which has now passed away. I mean the shiverings. So that I am greatly better, my beloved friend, and when I get into the air again shall do well. Still, I am alone; that is the thought that clings to me, though when I think of you, sister of my heart, it presses less heavily.

I read Tennyson. "Locksley Hall" is very fine; but should it not have finished at

> "I myself must mix with action,
> Lest I wither by despair?"

It seems to me that all after that weakens the impression of the story, which has its appropriate finish with that line. What do we not owe to such a poet? One, who can be thought of at such a time!

I must limit my correspondence. I have written above a hundred letters; and now feel that some, who had real claims, have been forgotten. Heaven bless you, my beloved friend!

Ever faithfully yours,   M. R. M.

[Dr. Mitford died considerably in debt, and Miss Mitford, writing at this time, observes: "Every body shall be paid, if I sell the gown off my back or pledge my little pension." At the suggestion of friends a subscription was raised to meet these liabilities.]

CHAPTER XVIII.

LETTERS FOR 1843 AND 1844.

To MISS JEPHSON, *Castle Martyr, Ireland.*

Three-mile Cross, March 16, 1843.

I TAKE my chance, dearest Emily, of not having written to tell you how favorably the subscription goes on (for such is the number of letters that I have to answer every day that I really can not tell), being sure that you would rather receive two letters on this subject than none. I have not been at the bank since last Saturday, but then the money received had been near a thousand pounds, and I knew of some hundreds more, and the very next post brought news of seventy-five pounds additional. Among the subscribers are the queen, who desires her name *not* to be mentioned, as she gives from her private income, and fears being subjected to solicitation (this adds to the compliment, as it proves it is not a matter of form); the queen dowager, the Archbishop of Dublin, his brother Mr. Whately (is he a clergyman?), the Bishop of Durham, the Dukes of Bedford and Devonshire, the Duchess of Norfolk, the Marquises of Lansdowne and Northampton, Earls Fitzwilliam, Spencer, and Radnor, Viscount Sidmouth, Lord Redesdale, Lady Byron, Lady Dacre, Joanna Baillie, Maria Edgeworth, Mrs. Trollope, Mrs. Opie, Mr. Moore, Mr. Rogers, Mr. Horace Smith, Mr. Morier, and many other persons of station, talent, and character. Nothing can exceed their cordiality and delicacy, so that their benefactions are given as a compliment.

I half think that I *have* written all this to you, my dear love. If so, forgive it. I have been very poorly, but am now better, except that having walked with a view of walking the sickness off, I have rendered myself quite lame. I hope to get well soon in order to go to Bath next month, and return home *viâ* Devonshire. Heaven bless you, my dear friend!

Ever yours,   M. R. M.

To the REV. WILLIAM HARNESS, *London.*

Three-mile Cross, April 4, 1843.

MY DEAR FRIEND,—How troublesome I am to you, and how kind you are to me! We shall have time enough to think over the question of residence when we see to what my little income may amount. But it does not seem to me as if I could ever live in any town; and I doubt whether a small cottage in the country be not cheaper than lodgings. A friend of mine has such a cottage adjoining his own house at Caversham, two miles north of Reading. He built it for his wife's father, who is now dead, and has since let every year for three months. He offers it to me on the same condition, that is to say, to let it for three months in the summer, which will clear every expense; so that I shall live there for nine months in the year rent free, with the additional comfort of most kind, good, agreeable people close by, and the privilege of having letters, etc., brought by their servants, and a general feeling of protection from living almost under the same roof with a man of honor and of intelligence. You won't think

VOL. II.—M

the worse of him for being in business in Reading. You will be glad to hear that my subscription proceeds well: a thousand pounds, or very nearly so, have been received at the different banks, and I know of some hundreds more; so that the debts are, I bless God, paid in full. But still my health is so bad, and my poverty so great, that my friends hope there may be sufficient for the purchase of a small annuity— and this is what they are now trying for. I never before had an idea of my own popularity; and I have on two or three occasions shed tears of pure thankfulness at reading the letters which have been written to, or about, me—from Archbishop Whately and men of his class. I only pray to God that I may deserve half that has been said of me. So far as the truest and humblest thankfulness may merit such kindness, I am perhaps, not wholly undeserving, for praise always makes me humble. I always feel that I am overvalued; and such is, I suppose, its effect on every mind not exceedingly vain-glorious. Yours most sincerely,   M. R. M.

To MISS JEPHSON, *Castle Martyr, Ireland.*

Three-mile Cross, April —, 1843.

· This has been a very fortunate day to my heart. First came your sweet letter, with its promise to come and see me; then came a dear letter from Miss Barrett, more cheerful and healthy than any I have received for a very long time; then a packet sent by order of the Archbishop of Dublin, containing a charming story, called "Reverses," for young people, his father's essay on Shakspeare (I take it for granted it is his father's), and an edition, revised and partly re-written, of the "Tales of the Genii." I am delighted at this sort of intercourse. Of all the Church of England I know none whom I so much admire as Archbishop Whately, and *this* present from *him* has enchanted me.

What will become of me just now I can't tell. Mr. Blandy wants to get this cottage put into the best possible order and lowered in rent, and then that I should remain here. But this will be settled soon: at all events I shall, I hope, and believe, continue in my own dear village. The other house would take me from much that is interesting in association and beautiful in home scenery: the bay-tree, for instance, and the honeysuckles, and rose-trees, and lilies of the valley of

this garden, as well as the pretty garden-room.   On the whole,
taking into consideration the expense and trouble of moving,
I might really lose by it; and though Ben sometimes says
that I *may* live six or eight years, yet I feel very strongly
the uncertainty of my life.   I have suffered much this spring
from headache and sickness: all existence partakes that form,
whether painful or pleasurable.   You seem, my beloved
friend, to think of throwing your visit backward in the summer: that I should like.   The time that I should prefer would
be the season of geraniums and strawberries, when half the
county used to assemble to parties of strawberries and cream
in the greenhouse.   Perhaps we may still be able to manage
that: you would like the scene and some of the people here.

Have I told you that Wordsworth wrote an interesting letter to Mr. Crabb Robinson on the death of Southey?   He
said that, in spite of the curtain that had dropped between
him and the world, he had felt most acutely the death of the
friend of his youth.   This for Wordsworth, so cold in manner,
is much.   For men so united in pursuits and tastes, and only
twenty or thirty miles apart, they saw little of each other;
and that may perhaps be a reason for Wordsworth's feeling
the total separation the more.   Southey died of typhus fever,
having had some weeks ago an apoplectic fit, so that he suffered many forms of death before the great change.   It is the
extinction of a great light, perhaps—prose and poetry considered, and the extent and variety of his learning—the greatest
since Scott.

You are right, dearest, about not meeting me at Bath.   I
shall only stay a week, and nothing can be so uncertain as the
time when I may go.   I have not heard any particulars of the
subscription lately, but it certainly exceeds fifteen hundred
pounds.   I am most thankful for the amount, and still more
so for the kindness.   Heaven bless you!   Ever most faithfully and affectionately yours,   M. R. MITFORD.

To MISS JEPHSON, *Castle Martyr, Ireland.*

Three-mile Cross, May —, 1843.

The accompanying note, my beloved friend, has been waiting till I could send you a definitive sketch of my plans.
Now, a complete change has taken place.   Mr. Blandy has persuaded *me* to stay, and the agent (receiver) of the Court of

Chancery to lower the rent and assist in repairing, painting, and papering this cottage, so that *here* is to be my home— here in my old abode. But as Mr. May declares that paint would be to me just as fatal as prussic acid, I am going to Bath to-morrow, from thence to Devonshire, North and South, not to return till all smell is gone. Mr. May says that the journey is necessary—that I should otherwise fall into hopeless ill health; but that, with the journey and care, I should do well. At present I am very poorly, and look upon moving with such dread that, but for being driven out by the paint, I don't think I could muster courage for to-morrow's journey. Ever yours most affectionately,   M. R. M.

To Miss Jephson, *Ireland.*

Bath, May —, 1843.

First, dearest Emily, let me thank you, and beg you to thank Mrs. and Miss Edgeworth repeatedly for their great kindness. I have been at Bath for a fortnight, but have never been able to see the pictures you were so good as to offer me the sight of—never able to get to them—and but for Mr. Reade and Mr. Musgrove, should actually leave the neighborhood without seeing Mr. Beckford's house and tower. The greatest pleasure that I have enjoyed has been last Sunday and this, both of which have been spent at Prior Park. I do not know when I have been so thoroughly interested as by Bishop Baines and his secretary, Mr. Bonomi, the old priest and the young. The bishop is the very incarnation of taste, combined with an intelligence, a liberality, a gracious indulgence most rare among Protestant clergymen, who, frequently excellent, are seldom charming; while the younger one is full of sweetness and purity. My maid K—— is much afraid of my turning Catholic, and I have been really amused to-night at her fears. But one may love the good of every faith, and put the Catholic bishop by the side of the Protestant archbishop with no injury to any person, least of all to one's self. On Thursday I went to Clifton, and prefer Bristol to Bath for its color and its variety of street architecture, which, I suppose, is a great heresy. But this place, besides that it has rained more or less every day since my arrival, is too cold to please me, and seems like a city of the dead—from the absence of horsemen and horsewomen, and the little open carriages which swarm in our roads like motes in the sunbeam. There is much beauty, nevertheless, in the old town—that *one* side of Queen Square especially—and the environs are lovely; but trees are wanting—real fine trees—and water—real brimming rivers like the Lodden, the Kennett, and the Thames. Nevertheless, there is much beauty, and I have walked over a great deal of it. The man who showed me over Bristol the other day (a man from the railway) says that I walked twelve miles. K—— never stirred for two days. I took a long walk the next, but I can't sleep, and sickness and headache come as surely as heat, so that the sooner I get out of Bath the better. Clifton is lovely. I wish you were here to walk over it with me. Ever yours, dearest Emily,   M. R. M.

To Miss Jephson, *Castle Martyr, Ireland.*

Three-mile Cross, Tuesday, June —, 1843.

Here I am, dearest Emily, to the great astonishment of every body, and not a little to my own. Last Wednesday, at half past four, I went down to the Bristol station to go on to Barnstaple, but I found the traveling in Devonshire at this season so difficult for women ; the weather so bad, and myself so poorly (I had had one of my fits of sickness the night before); that I followed the example of a fly-full of women whom I met at the station—drove over the way—and, instead of embarking in the down train, took a passage in the up. This has turned out lucky for my affairs at home, for I found them dawdling over every room, never having had above one workman at a time in the house ; and a little ungrateful jade, whom I kept only till I could get her a place, having gone out every night, and being actually at the play when I came home ; so that now things will proceed better, and I shall probably (if my book be done, or likely to be done) finish my tour in August, or somewhere thereabout. I am delighted with my journey, places, and people, though Bath is a disappointment—cold, monotonous, bald, poor, and dead ; and Clifton leaves all the beauty behind at the Hot-wells. But, then, what a scene *that* is ! and what a glorious old city is Bristol! and how lovely past all loveliness is Prior Park! But Bath leaves few and faint impressions. Bristol, on the other hand, is warm, glowing, picturesque. At Bath I was forced to follow about shadows—Miss Austen, Anne Elliott,

and Catherine Morland; at Bristol I trod in the footsteps of
Coleridge, Southey, Chatterton.   One afternoon I spent with
Mr. Cottle, among his interesting letters and portraits.   Twice
I went over the Redcliffe church, twice over the mayor's
chapel, the cathedral, and the great iron ship.

If I can get my house to rights, and finish my book by
August (which I doubt), it will remain much according to
your will whether I stay here with you or go on into Devonshire.   At present I have Ben's mother's bedroom, in a
cottage at three pounds a year—a real laborer's cottage.   I
have no grate, but have to build up my fire between two
bricks, with an old poker laid across the front for a bar.   The
way to it is by a roundabout stair, as steep and dark as that
into the muniment chamber above the porch in Redcliffe
church; but it is airy, sweet, and clean.   It is such a comfort to have found dear little Flush and Ben so glad to see
us again.   Ben turned every body out of bed, rummaged
out the sheets, aired them, carried my bed down to his mother's room through the dark and rain, stuffed two pillows into
a case to make one hard one, as he knew I liked; got my
cocoa out of the trunk, boiled it; ran over the place for
brown bread, toasted that; got a kettleful of boiling water,
which he knew was wanted for something; tossed over the
carpet-bag till he came to the night things, and warmed
them : finding time, between all and every of these woman-
ish jobs, to talk all sorts of manly and womanly gossip.
God bless him, poor boy ! It is worth much to be *so* welcomed.
I had dreaded the coming back alone to a lonely home, but
Ben and Flush, and the bustle all together, and the scolding
which I found it my duty to administer, quite took the edge
off my sadness.   You must come to me, dearest Emily.   I
hope I shall be able to get the book, which at present is my
Old Man of the Sea, off my shoulders.   My cottage will be
very clean and simple, and like any other poor laborer's cottage, and the garden will be pretty.

Adieu, my very dear friend.   I send you a long exposition
of crotchets past and present.   Ever yours,

M. R. M.

To Miss Jephson, *Castle Martyr, Ireland.*

Three-mile Cross, July 7, 1843.

Thanks upon thanks, my very dear Emily, for your most
kind and welcome letter. No! Lismore will not do. I
can not *wait* in the matter of books. I have been too much
spoiled. At this moment I have eight sets of books belonging to Mr. Lovejoy. I have every periodical within a week,
and generally cut open every interesting new publication—
getting them literally the day before publication. Guess if
that would do for patient waiting, either in Ireland or Devonshire! From all that I can hear, the flowers that live in
those places flourish in Jersey. St. Heliers is a town better
than Reading; the libraries, French and English, are excellent; the houses a mile or two from the town (and I should
prefer that) not dearer than here; the country of exquisite
beauty, combining delicious wooded valleys and bold coast
scenery; and the society good. It is the combination of
these things with one other that attracts me—I mean the
opportunity of regaining French, so that I might take a look
at Paris, Rouen, etc., etc. I read it just like English, but
have so lost the habit of talking it that I should hesitate at
going abroad. Now, in Jersey I could practice in shops and
markets; and with a home, English in every respect of comfort, etc., etc., I could leave it for a few weeks in Paris, without much trouble. But I shall not decide on this till the
summer.

Absentees, or clergy without congregations, will doubtless eventually disappear from Ireland. They ought to do
so. But still there will doubtless be left an effective clergy
of the Church of England persuasion; though I confess I
should like to see churches for the Catholics also. I do not
say clergy, for a zealous and devoted priesthood they have.
There ought to be a provision for both—for all. But I suppose the Catholics would not accept a stipend now. Well,
I have a faith in all righting itself, and that fine people becoming eventually as tranquil and as prosperous as the English. What a magnificent speech Mr. Sheil's was! I hope
Daniel O'Connell will not be imprisoned. He is too old for
the punishment; and to make a martyr of him is no way to
lessen his influence. I have a strong feeling toward Ireland,

as my having thought of going there proves; though the vicinity of Lismore to Castle Martyr was one great reason for my desire. But the want of books is final: I could far better do without society, provided I had a friend near. If I were to live at Bath, I should have to get books from Reading. They are so ill supplied, and we so well.

Poor dear Bishop Baines! Never was I more affected. He had consecrated the Bristol Chapel; preached a long sermon; entertained a party to dinner at Prior Park; and was found dead in his bed the next morning, having been warned against the exertion. Five friends wrote to acquaint me of the sad event. He was a great and a good man. Have you read "Jack Hinton?" if not, do; it's charming. Also a most delightful novel called "The Old English Gentleman." Heaven bless you, dearest Emily! Ever most faithfully yours,   M. R. MITFORD.

All our annuals failed this year. If you could save me some seeds it would be a great favor.

1844.

To MISS BARRETT, *Wimpole Street.*

Three-mile Cross, Feb. 28, 1844.

[*The greater part of the following letter is missing.*]

Charles Kingsley spoke during two hours and twenty minutes, with such earnestness! such conviction! such passion! such beauty! There is nothing like real high eloquence. It is poetry living and breathing, and carrying you on like a torrent, in its magnificent course. Oh, how I longed for you! There was nothing to frighten any body. Of course the principles were large and general; but the whole address was most conciliatory. It was power in all its gentleness. He is a very great man. Ever yours,   M. R. M.

To MISS BARRETT, *Wimpole Street.*

Three-mile Cross, Nov. 27, 1844.

MY BELOVED FRIEND,—Jane has been mesmerized twice. The second time Mr. Cowderoy produced catalepsy in the right arm, and she has told me that she perceived all that passed behind her, so that we are in a train to get a *clairvoy-ante* subject if we like. But I have no such intention. . . . Mr. Cowderoy says that if Miss Martineau writes her own cure only, she will do good; but if mixed up with details of a marvelous nature she will only get wrecked upon the sharp edges of prejudice in every quarter. Just look again at her letter, and see if there be not every risk of her pro-claiming the dicta of this young ignorant girl, not as the pro-duction of a singular state brought about by this new and powerful physical agent, but as real and actual " spiritual dicta "—as things true in themselves, and to be believed, not as the mere expression of a certain sort of delirium, and valu-able only as showing the power of the agent. For certainly what is wanted of mesmerism is, not the wild notions of girls of nineteen, but the power to alleviate disease and perform operations without pain. Be quite sure that Miss Martineau will do the cause much harm if she writes about these spirit-ual dicta in the spirit of her letter.

Do you ever see the " Phrenological Journal?" In the number for September, Mr. Donovan, whom I have seen here and like much, has an article on an imputed head of Crom-well, which is admirable. If they have it at Saunders & Ot-ley's, do send for the number.

The Oxford papers say that the queen, when at Strathfield-saye, is coming here to call upon me. God forbid! No great danger. Ever your own, my dearest, M. R. M.

To Miss Barrett.

Three-mile Cross, Autumn, 1844.

What a very cheap thing childish happiness is! You will be astonished to hear what (besides a sharp feverish attack and writing to you) has occupied my last week—very much astonished. This, dearest, is the fact. I found that the queen's visit to Strathfieldsaye had strongly excited the in-terest and curiosity of the little children here, and I deter-mined they should see her and have a holiday. Every body expected that she would return by Reading (indeed the un-lucky mayor sent me word, so late as yesterday morning, that " he had no conviction of her not returning through his town,"—a very grand diplomatic message); and it was only on Wednesday afternoon that I finally ascertained that she

M 2

would go back by Wokingham, as she came. I then arranged to take all the children (two hundred and ninety) in wagons lent by the kind farmers, as far as Swallowfield Lane, the point where her Majesty turned off from the Basingstoke Road into the Cross Lanes which lead to Wokingham; that they and their schoolmasters and mistresses should meet at nine o'clock at my house, to have delivered to each of them a pretty hand-flag of pink and white, made by Jane (who has fitted up three yachts and was flag-maker-general to the Isle of Wight); that we should then march in procession to the lane, the children riding in wagons decked with laurel and large flags of the same colors: which was done accordingly, I leading the way with Mrs. Amott and her children, the clergyman's family, and some other gentry, followed by a body-guard of great boys, who seeing me walk would not ride (was not that pretty of them?), and meeting there eight or ten carriages containing all the gentlemen's families of the parish.

We had chosen our place well, for the queen was escorted to that point by her noble host, who took leave of her just in front of our wagons, which looked between the laurels and the pink and white flags like so many masses of painted-lady sweet peas. The party made exactly such a pause in parting, and afforded such a little incident as allowed to every body the fullest and pleasantest view of those they came to see. After this we all returned, I the last, this time, with Miss Lay—still walking, though I had got into Mrs. Praed's pony chaise to see the sight. We all returned—carriages, wagons, body-guard and all—to my house, where the gentlefolks had sandwiches and cake and wine; and where the children had each a bun as large as a soup-plate, made doubly nice as well as doubly large, a glass of wine, and a mug of ale. All this seems little enough; but the ecstasy of the children made it much. They had been active from four o'clock in the morning. They had been shouting and singing all day. They did sing and shout all the afternoon, for I had made it my particular request to the schoolmistresses and masters that there might be no scolding or keeping in order—flinging ourselves upon the children's own sense of right. And well did they justify the trust! Never was such harmless jollity! Not an accident! not a squabble!

not a misword! It did one's very heart good. Of course
we took care of the mistresses and masters also; and their
pleasure in the children's pleasure was very good to see—
the sympathy all through. To be sure it was a good deal
of trouble, and Jane is done up. Indeed, the night before
last we none of us went to bed. But it was quite worth it
—one of the few days of promised pleasure which in spite of
Seyed, Emperor of Ethiopia, do sometimes keep their word.
It rained, I believe; somebody said so; but nobody minded
it, the children least of all. I shall never forget their delight.

The queen looked pale and ill—simply dressed—smiling
and well-behaved; the horses going at a foot pace, and the
glasses down. Prince Albert is decidedly handsome. Our
duke went to no great expense. One strip of carpet he
bought, the rest of the additional furniture he hired in Reading for the week! The ringers at Strathfieldsaye (and the
church is so near the house that William the Fourth, when
Duke of Clarence, who had a genius for blundering, when visiting poor Lord Rivers asked if it was not the dog-kennel!)
the ringers, after being hard at work for four hours, sent a
can to the house to ask for some strong beer, and the can was
sent back empty! Also a poor band, who had been playing
till the breath was out of their bodies, begged for a little dinner, and received such a piece of bread as is laid on a napkin
for dinner, and such a piece of cheese as is sent round on a
napkin after dinner. The duke is a *just* master—as John-
stone, his gardener, said to me once when I idly asked if he
were a *kind* one—and not a very bad landlord; but he has
no open-heartedness. He is without that high sense of what
is due to his own position which made Napoleon, with all his
spirit of order, so truly magnificent. It was a fine balance
in Napoleon, which made him equally displeased at Madame
Mère's economy and Josephine's debts. The duke looked
relieved beyond all expression when he had made his last
bow to his royal visitors; his whole countenance said plainly, " Thank God it's over !" and no doubt he felt so. There
was only one most extraordinary thing in our children; Sir
Robert Peel passed us, going to town by railway, just at the
top of the village, and Jane says that they hissed him! Is
not this most remarkable? All our gentry are Conserva-
tives. Now that my dear father is dead, we have not a

Whig in the parish. But they said, "There goes Sir Bob-
by," and they hissed him!

To Miss Barrett, 50 Wimpole Street.

Three-mile Cross, Nov. 28, 1844.

My dear Love,—I should like to have known Madame
d'Abrantes, that is, if she had not been too rich and high a
lady; for my adoration of Napoleon, which increases every
day, is so borne out by the testimony of one who had such
opportunities of knowing him, that it is a most satisfactory
and comfortable thing to read all that she says on that subject. Think how he would have enjoyed Balzac! I am
sure he would—just as we do. By the way, old Mr. Robert (the excellent translator of "Notre Dame") says he does
not think Balzac would suit the taste of the English. The
fact is, that there is great peculiarity in the manner as well
as matter of Balzac; and it is necessary to learn the character of his style, fine as that style is, just as it is necessary to
master a difficult handwriting before enjoying the letters of
a correspondent. Also I doubt whether Balzac be not too
good for the taste of English novel-readers. Every now and
then I find people talking of poor Miss Pickering, as I should
talk of Miss Austen or of Scott—persons of sense and education, and high station. And the taste for Mrs. Howitt's
translations of Fredrika Bremer (always begging your pardon) seems to me an indication of the same sort.

By the way, if I were not so old and stupid and lazy, I
should like to try my own hand at translating Balzac, and
see if I could not put one of his novels into such English as
should give some faint idea of his French. This is not so
vain as it seems; for I should try, by the closest adherence
to his vivid and colored language, to produce an almost
Chinese copy of this great original; and any person tolerably familiar with prose composition might do this by taking
proper pains. Such a translation, giving to it great labor,
might, I think, succeed. I do not mean merely sell, but might
do justice to the manner of the author. This, however,
would require an experienced English writer. Dearest love,
what works of Casimir Delavigne have you read? Surely
not his plays! I have read "Louis the Eleventh," "Marino
Faliero," "Les Enfans d'Edouard," "Don Juan d'Autriche,"

"La Popularité," "La Fille du Cid," "Une Famille du temps de Luther," forming the second and third series of his "Théâtre." To me they seem full of talent; striking the just medium between the slowness and dullness of what they call the classical drama (I agree with you that is a gross misnomer) and the unnatural and exaggerated contrasts and surprises of Victor Hugo, who strives after effects until he forgets that a true effect should be something perfectly natural—happening at an unexpected moment—or brought about in a striking manner; but always something *natural* —something that we all feel to be *true*. Now, nobody can say that of Victor Hugo's later plays especially; witness "Ruy Blas." Do read Delavigne's plays, pray do. Let me have a conversion to boast of, as you have had in the case of Balzac. (N.B.—I don't mean to say that M. Delavigne is as great a man as Balzac; but of a surety he is no common dramatist, and his comedies are of the high serious comedy like "Le Misanthrope" carved in marble). I like that Alexandre Dumas! "Christina" is a clever drama; but his verse is inferior to Casimir Delavigne's, whose wife was a *protegée* of Josephine and Hortense. Heaven bless you, dearest love! Ever yours,   M. R. M.

To MISS BARRETT, *Wimpole Street.*

Three-mile Cross, Dec. 21, 1844.

Thank you, dearest, for your recommendations of books. The only work of Eugene Sue which I have read among those you ask about, is "Le Salamandre." You need not regret it. As strange a work it is as ever was written—with few indications of the power to come. The only remarkable thing is the preface, in which, by way of reason for making all his people unhappy in this world, or rather for taking them out of it by being shot and shooting themselves, he says that to represent good people as successful in this world and rogues as unsuccessful would take away the chief argument for a future life. Now I do really hold that virtue, although not always prosperous, is yet upon the whole far happier than vice. Is not it Pope who calls virtue that " beloved contemned thing?" I am quite sure that to represent systematically vice as fortunate, and goodness as wretched, tends to make selfish people vicious; and it is really wicked in Balzac to give one the pain he does in this way, In " Une Ténébreuse Affaire," for instance, I was so provoked with him for making Napoleon kill Michu and forgive those dolts of gentlemen, that I could have flung the book at his (Balzac's) head, if luckily that wonderful head had been within reach.

Oh! I see that you will not like Casimir Delavigne. It confirms an opinion which I have long entertained, that the drama, *as drama*, is a sealed book to those who have never been in the habit of seeing acted plays. He is just half way between Victor Hugo and Racine; and you may rely upon it, that upon the stage he is much more effective than Victor Hugo, because he deals in none of those violent exaggerations which must frequently come out like caricature when brought into action. Ah! dearest love, Fredrika Bremer! I did read half " The Neighbors," and really you are the only person of a high class of mind whom I have found liking her works. Mrs. Jameson said " they could not live;" and William Harness called them " that trash."

Now I think I have written quite enough of sauciness for one evening. Ah! if I were as well behaved as Mrs. Jameson!!! I am glad you have seen her. Heaven bless you, my well-beloved! Ever your own,   M. R. MITFORD.

To MISS BARRETT, *Wimpole Street.*

Three-mile Cross, Dec. 29, 1844.

MY BELOVED FRIEND,—I have read the "Chimes." I don't like it. If the story—which now passes, or does not pass in a vision, or a nightmare—had been told as a truth simply and earnestly, there might have been some meaning in it; but as the matter is, I don't like it. Mr. Dickens wants the earnest good faith in narration which makes Balzac so enchanting.

I am enchanted to find that you mean to write narrative poetry, and narrative poetry of real life. We must talk over subjects and stories. I still wonder that Napoleon does not inspire you. Oh, what a man! I would have given a limb to have been in the place of Madame Rechard or Madame de Montholon, or even of one of the Miss Balcombs—ay, or to have been concealed somewhere just to have heard him conversing and dictating, but rather conversing. After all, his prophecies are realized. He is the glory of France. Louis

Philippe would hardly have sat on the throne so long had he not called in the memory of its idol to fix him in the love of the nation. You won't be sorry, if you happen to forget it, to hear what Napoleon said of Junot—that he was the man to whom he had given more than to any other of his generals; that his extravagance was beyond all bounds; that he never saw him without some fresh demand; that he lived a life of sad debauchery, which, at last, ended in insanity; that, after behaving very strangely in Moscow, Napoleon had given him the government of the Illyrian provinces, where the malady broke out; that he wounded himself fearfully, and shortly after died. He (the Emperor) sent for Madame d'Abrantes to remonstrate with her on the necessity of restraining her husband's extravagances, as well as her own; that she behaved very ill—Napoleon's phrase is, "She treated me like a child." He also speaks quietly of her mother, as having been greatly obliged to his. In short, it is perfectly clear that, in the romance of Napoleon's love for Madame Permon (a woman ten years older than Josephine), and of his fancy for herself, Madame d'Abrantes says the thing that is not. I always felt that part of her Mémoires to be false. But they are very charming, nevertheless; and the idea of her dying in a hospital is frightful. Do read "Un Homme Sérieux" and Béranger's "Cinq de Mai."

I can't quite tell yet, dearest, when I shall come, because the weather must get a little better first. But be quite sure that it shall be *soon*. I hope the cessation of frost will be good for you. For my own part, I liked the cold weather; it was so dry. We had, and indeed have still, a family of blackbirds and redbreasts, who came to us every time we opened the door for crumbs and water, and were so tame that they all but fed out of our hands. That's the way I like to have birds. They are quite as tame with Flush; and he likes them as well as we do.

Heaven bless you, my beloved friend! Ever yours,

M. R. M.

CHAPTER XIX.

LETTERS FOR 1845.

To MISS BARRETT, *Wimpole Street.*

Three-mile Cross, Jan. 7, 1845.

I HAVE often wondered, my very dear love, how people can be so foolish, after publishing good works, as to put forth bad ones. It is true that posterity remembers only the good; but how often does it happen that the immediate public, looking at the new bad, forgets or is ignorant of the old good! Just this occurred to me in reading Lamartine's dull piece of extravagance, " La Chute d'un Ange." Nothing but your recommendation could have induced me to read another line of his writing. Now, I have gone through "Jocelyn;" and, although I dislike the story—the heroine in man's clothes, and the hero made a priest, Heaven knows how—I have yet been delighted with the general feeling and beauty of the poem, particularly with one portion full of toleration, and another about dogs. In short, if I could but have forgotten " La Femme de Quarante Ans "—that inimitable story which is as indelible as " Don Quixote," or " Gil Blas " —I should enter into " Jocelyn " with real affection. Lamartine is Wordsworthian, certainly; but his sympathies are far wider—I should say far truer. He would never have written the "Letter on Railways." Thank you, dear love, for recommending " Jocelyn." There are no inspirations, like "Le Roi s'amuse;" no exquisite thoughts, exquisitely finished, as in Béranger; still it is a tender, graceful, gracious poem—one that accounts for the feeling expressed toward the writer by his brother authors. By the way, Charles de Bernard follows up his attack by another in " Un Homme Sérieux," but so good-humoredly and so lightly touched that nobody can be offended. Still his arrows stick. There is no looking at the closed volumes of " Jocelyn " without thinking of the lover on duty, reading a portion to his mistress to solace her *migraine,* or repeating her favorite lines whilst looking at his star. Those books will live; they are so true, so

full of character, and so cheerful. A laugh has a long echo.
I agree with you as to "Un Homme Sérieux." A happy conclusion has an even infinite advantage over a tragical one.

Heaven bless you! Ever your own, M. R. MITFORD.

To MISS JEPHSON, *Castle Martyr, Ireland.*

Three-mile Cross, Winter, 1845.

Every body is talking of Miss Martineau's "Somnambule."
She writes to Miss Barrett, who forwards her letters to me.
The last intelligence is, that Lord Morpeth was on his knees
the other evening, talking Greek and Latin, and three modern languages to the poor girl; the Miss Liddells being present. When Imitation was touched, she translated what was
said; when Language, she replied to it. I can well believe
this, having seen myself things as wonderful. For my own
part, I see no good in these experiments; while they will certainly destroy the innocent contentment of the patient, thus
forced upon that miserable pinnacle called notoriety. Charlotte Elizabeth has addressed a letter to Miss Martineau, in
which she attributes the agency to Satan.

Before I forget it, let me say that a friend of mine, to
whom I was speaking of Dr. Arnold, said, "I knew him well:
he was the finest great boy in the world; and the fault of
the life is that it does not show him half young enough."
This I can well believe. Have you seen dear Miss Barrett's
poems? They are making a great impression both in England and America. The last poem in the first volume,
"Lady Geraldine's Courtship," forty-two pages, was written
in a day, and is perhaps the best in the book, almost as wonderful an exploit as any of the feats of mesmerism. Thomas
Carlyle, after throwing one MS. into the fire, has sent his
"Life of Cromwell" to the press. Poor Mr. Horne has dislocated his shoulder in skating on the Elbe.

Heaven bless you, dear friend! Believe me, ever faithfully yours, M. R. M.

To MISS JEPHSON, *Castle Martyr, Ireland.*

Three-mile Cross, Winter, 1845.

I write to you, dearest Emily, in the midst of a fall of snow,
a foot deep at least, which is bad for me, who hate dirt like
a cat, and yet shall have to wade through it for the rest of

the month; my daily walks being not only the necessity of existence to me, so far as health is concerned, but also the chief means of my social pleasures; for since I have made the grand discovery that a lantern is as good as a moon, I trot about at night with a maid, not merely to country neighbors, but to lectures and concerts in Reading, where I have a whole Mechanics' Institute as an object of interest and pleasure. It does me good to see how cultivated and civilized the young artisans are become. For instance, Reading, with its noisy, bustling, craving commerce, is struck with admiration of Elizabeth Barrett's high-toned poetry; and the League Committee have sent to request her to contribute a poem to the ladies' bazar. Whether she will do so or not I can not tell. But I am sure the poem will be written, although her father, who is only a Whig, may have influence enough to prevent his Radical daughter from complying with the request.

Have you read Dr. Arnold's " Lectures on History ?"—the Oxford lectures ? I think it the most remarkable of all his works for large and luminous views.

Have you read Lever's " O'Donoghue ?" It promises even better than his other works, and I think him one of our best living writers of fiction. But our literature seems really cold and dead by the side of the intense and palpitating writings of *La jeune France,* so full of genius, with all their faults. Ever, dearest friend, very faithfully yours,   M. R. M.

To Miss Barrett, *Wimpole Street.*

Three-mile Cross, Jan. 17, 1845.

What disenchanting things these autographs are! When I was at Clifton, my friend Mr. Johnson brought to show Miss James some American signatures, South and North, curious Spanish documents as far back as the Conquest, and all the Presidents' autographs; and those of the men who signed the Declaration of Independence. Amongst them was a correspondent of General Washington's.

Washington was a Virginian, remember, and they are all horse-jockeys, just as the Yorkshire squires of the last century were; and this series of letters from the great patriot contain as notable an endeavor to " do " an acquaintance in the sale of an English horse as ever figured in the annals of

Newmarket. I have no great fancy for the celebrated personage in question. He was much too cold and calculating for me, and I was exceedingly amused at the correspondence, the *genuineness* of which was testified in a manner that could not be disputed. Also there were certain directions about his blacks, not a little shocking to the Abolitionists of the present day. Fine words—patriotism and disinterestedness, and so forth! grand to write and to listen to! But look at the real truth, and out comes the great patriot jockeying his acquaintance (for he " dear-sir'd " the poor man all through, after a fashion which would have merited a place in " Bell's Life," and run a chance of incurring the wider celebrity of the Old Bailey. Ah! it is a fine thing, is patriotism!

Nevertheless, you may laugh at me in turn, for dear Mr. Kenyon can bear witness that I *once* asked for an autograph myself—no less than Daniel O'Connell's, the only one I ever did ask, and which (except I could add to it the signature of Napoleon) will ever remain alone in my desk, for a great man I still think him, and one whom I should gladly know. Mr. Townsend (he is, you know, a proctor of Doctors' Commons) promised me, if I came there to see him, that I should hold in my hands, at one time, *his* and Milton's, and Shakspeare's signatures to wills, of unquestioned and unquestionable authenticity. Mr. Kenyon had the goodness to help me to Mr. O'Connell's.

To Miss Barrett, *Wimpole Street.*

Three-mile Cross, March 18, 1845.

Oh, my very dear love, I grieve that, as I had feared, you are suffering from this weather. It can not last long, indeed I think that it is breaking already. I have had a present of some roses blown in a hot-house—cut flowers. Yesterday morning they were found on the drawing-room table, with their stalks in ice, instead of water. All the contents of the vase was frozen into a solid mass; and that, in a room with a fire every day, on the 17th of March! Poor pretty roses! They did not mind it at all, and looked just as fresh and smelt as sweet as in their native conservatory. It was a strange contrast, to look at the green stalks crowned with such splendid blossoms and fixed into a mass of solid ice—summer and winter in one's hand at once. But the ice melted and the roses remained; and that is an emblem of what we may hope for now. There is comfort in that thought. My poor Flush suffers much from the weather. He has had a bad cough; and now that that is gone he has had a frightful attack of cramp from the cold. I was obliged to get him carried to Mrs. Amott's, for he could not walk; and, in her warm room, in about an hour he so far recovered as to walk home. But poor love, he has been very, very poorly, and will hardly get out.

I have the first volume of Victor Hugo's "Odes et Ballades," but they are slavishly loyal to those vile old Bourbons. What could he see in them? I suppose I shall like the second volume better.

Heaven bless you, my beloved friend! Ever your own,

M. R. M.

To Miss Barrett, *Wimpole Street.*

Three-mile Cross, April 10, 1845.

Mine own Love,—I have had a wandering poetess here to-day. She and her mother are driving about the land in a pony-chaise, selling, for five shillings, books typographically worth about eightpence—poetically, good for nothing. The mamma asks one to patronize her daughter—one's "fellow-poetess"—and won't go till she has got the money. She wanted to pay *you* a visit, "having heard your name at Bear Wood." Of course I stopped that, and as they are going westward, there is no danger of any incursion. I gave both ladies some very good advice, which will very certainly not be taken; for such conceit, such ignorance, above all, such total ignorance of the state of literature at this time I never encountered. They asked me for a book to teach the art of poetry—a book of rules, as in arithmetic. For certain, the young lady wants one; she makes "reign" rhyme to "name;" "line" to "lime," and so on, and is, by very far, too vain and self-absorbed ever to do better. She has not an atom of the enthusiasm of youth, and admires nobody but herself. But think of the impudence of stopping at the door of every body whose name they ever heard, and demanding five shillings before it is possible to get quit of them! Their first step was to put their horse in the stable and demand hay and corn. Nothing but pen and ink could inspire such surpassing assurance.

Poor Dr. Baines! I have been inexpressibly affected by hearing from Mr. Bonomi that, on the very last day of his honored life, when returning from Bristol, he had said to him, "Now that we are quiet again, we will write and ask Miss Mitford to come to Prior Park for a week or ten days." I never saw any man so perfectly interesting, not merely from talent, but from simplicity and goodness. There was a mixture of playfulness and *bonhomie* most enchanting. And he liked me—one always finds out that, and was kinder than I have words to tell. You can hardly imagine, my dearest Emily, how much his death has saddened Bath to me. I had been exceedingly disappointed in the town itself—its deadness and dullness—the cold color and the monotony of the buildings. Any one accustomed to London must have that feeling; but Prior Park redeemed all. Did you go there? Mr. Bonomi is coming to me on his return from his relatives at York, and I think the establishment will continue. But the guiding spirit is gone. You would have loved Dr. Baines.

There have been, doubtless, difficulties of all sorts during the last unprecedented month of March. Even the violets have been not only late, but scarce; and yet what enjoyment I have had in getting them! Ever your own,

M. R. M.

To Miss Jephson, *Castle Martyr, Ireland.*

Three-mile Cross [about July, 1845].

It is very long since I have written to you, dearest Emily; but I have been to town, partly to see dearest Miss Barrett, partly moving about—and staying far too short a time, as may be proved by my leaving twenty-seven invitations behind me, so full is London, and so seldom do I visit it. I saw many celebrated people, among them Mrs. Gore, who, by the way, having inherited what she calls forty thousand acres of rattlesnakes in Nova Scotia, is going there and to America, and will make a piquant book about it. The Houses of Parliament are very fine. I also went to the Horticultural Fête at Chiswick—a pretty sight, but so fatiguing that I firmly resolved never to go again. Think of fifteen thousand people—fine people—and the heat and dust and crowd—all standing and walking for five hours. The fruit was guarded by twelve policemen, and the refreshments, not only served by tickets purchased at another part of the garden, but guarded by palisades, and handed out through little sliding panels, like those in the doors of our model prison; the barricades being rendered necessary by an onslaught a year or two ago, in which the ice was carried off by the company! Now, I am returned, and expecting Mrs. Davidson and Mr. Horne—not in the house, but to lodge near—and look for Mrs. Jameson, Mr. Lucas, Mr. Browne, Mr. Chorley, Mr. Wright, and others of my friends, to spend a day here. I did talk of going to France, but must give it up for want of money; and I am going to part with my geraniums and pets for the same reason.

Have you seen Hood's "Song of the Shirt?"—a most striking bit of homely pathos. I like Dickens's "Christmas Carol," too, very much—not the ghostly part, of course, which is very bad; but the scenes of the clerk's family are very fine and touching. Also Harriet Martineau's new book is striking ("Life in a Sick Room"), though rather exaggerated and overwrought.

Did I tell you that Mr. Taylor, the medical lecturer at Guy's and one of the cleverest persons I ever knew, was taking rubbings of the different brasses in the churches round this year; I was much struck by the simplicity and piety of the old inscriptions, and Mr. Taylor agreeing with me, he has had the goodness to procure an inscription for me to be executed in London, to be placed over my dear father and mother in Shenfield Church. I send you a rubbing of it, which you will perhaps, my dear friend, have the goodness to return, as I wish to show it to different friends. Mr. Taylor took it to the Camden Society, where the simplicity and novelty excited very considerable sensation. Above a hundred people have taken down the name of the engraver; and it is very probable that the old fashion will be revived. I did not think of *that*, as you may well imagine; at the same time I fully expect that such will be the consequence; for besides the beauty of the execution, and the durability (for the letters are cut full half an inch into the brass, and it would last a thousand years), the cheapness is extraordinary, this exquisitely executed plate having only cost fifty shillings. Tell me if you do not prefer this humble inscription to the pompous epitaphs one commonly sees? I do.

I went to town last week, to see Miss Barrett—going at nine o'clock, and returning the same evening at six—a great fatigue. The favorite subject in London is the *clairvoyance*, Dr. Elliotson having made over his pupils and patients to Mr. Babbage, and other scientific persons, for examination. Really the stories they tell (and they entered upon the subject with the impression that it was all a cheat) are more startling than any thing I have heard in my day, only far too long for a letter.

No! I have not seen the Chinese dogs. I should like to do so; but I only walk now, and want to find a good master or mistress for my pretty pony. He goes into Reading, to the station (four miles), in fourteen minutes, is six years old, under duty, and most beautiful. Do mention him to your correspondents. I am afraid to sell him at fairs, for fear of his falling into hands who would make bets upon him, poor little thing! He follows me round the garden, and into the house, and eats apples and carrots out of my hand. We have had here four incendiary fires! I don't know for what —mere wantonness.

Heaven bless you, my very dear love! Ever yours,
M. R. M.

To Miss Jephson, *Castle Martyr.*

Three-mile Cross, Autumn, 1845.

My dear Love,—Your dear letter found me after a three weeks' confinement from sickness every night, and the most acute pain in the lower limbs. Mr. May says that the terrible pain, which is just like tic douloureux, in the knee-joints, *is* a pressure upon some nerve; but I can not get rid of the fear that it is rheumatic, and that I may some day or other lose the use of my limbs, and go about like those poor cripples in Bath, dragged along in tall chairs, looking to me the very emblems of misery. I can't help quoting Shakspeare's "cold sciatica;" for the pain only yields to dry heat, actual washing in front of the fire, and the flesh is often as cold as marble, while the perspiration is pouring over the limb. To-day, however, I am a little better, and have crept into the

garden to look at my dahlias. One of my seedlings is so
fine that we have sold it for twenty pounds, the highest price
given for a dahlia this year. Are we not lucky to have so
good a dahlia? I don't know what the nursery-man (Mr.
Bragge, of Slough) means to call it. It is white, of the most
exquisite shape and cleanness, tipped with puce color. We
have some very fine seedlings *this* year, and our great bed is
also full of fine old dahlias—I mean those raised by other
growers; for I don't believe that we have one more than
three years old, except the old Springfield, which I insist
upon keeping for " auld lang syne." It seems to me quite
grievous to throw away our ancient favorites in flowers;
still it is what must be done, to keep pace with the collections round.

We have only twenty-four new seedling geraniums, having
given our cast-off seedlings chiefly to nursery-men for sale,
in exchange for pots and new plants of other sorts, and Mr.
Foster's and Mr. Garth's best new sorts—not one past three
years old even of theirs, and not one raised by any other
grower. This looks like great boasting, but you must come
and see next year. In the mean while, this twenty pounds,
besides the credit, will pay for glass and coals (Ben does the
glazing and carpentering and blacksmith's work all himself,
as well as the painting), and justify me to myself for my only
extravagance—my dear flowers. What should I, who have
only Flush to love me, and poor Ben and K——, and K——'s
little boy, do without flowers? Ah! dearest Emily, I often
think that of all the goodness of God, as shown to us in this
beautiful world, that little world of flowers is, in its sweetness and innocence and peace, the truest and best example
of what we ought to try to be ourselves ; opening our hearts,
as best we may, to the bright sunshine and the pure air of
heaven ; and sweetening and beautifying, to our fellow creatures, the path of life along which we dwell.

No, my dear, that iris is not the fleur-de-lis, nor any thing
like it. It is a pretty, but not rare iris; whereas the real
fleur-de-lis is very rare indeed. It is of that class popularly
called the flag iris, above six feet high and two or three times
as large—I mean the flower. I suspect the plant to be semi-
aquatic. Its having blown in two gardens after this wet
spring—in one of which it had been for twelve years, in the

other for twenty—without flowering, looks like it, does it not? These two are the only ones I know. The lower petal of the true flower is much more opaque, with a large oval golden spot, like ivory inlaid with gold and surrounded with alabaster.

Do you read "Blackwood?" If you do, you will be pleased with Mr. Eagle's account of Mr. Poole's great picture.

Make my kindest love to the dear Crowthers. Did you know my friend Lady Morton, the young widow of the old lord chamberlain? She is again a widow, and wants me to spend the autumn and winter with her in Essex. I feel that I can not; and yet I must, unless too ill for the effort.

Yours ever, M. R. M.

CHAPTER XX.

LETTERS FOR 1846-51.

To MISS JEPHSON, *Castle Martyr, Ireland.*

Three-mile Cross, Spring, 1846.

DID you hear that my beloved friend Elizabeth Barrett is married? Love really is the wizard the poets have called him; a fact which I always doubted till now. But never was such a miraculous proof of his power as her traveling across France by diligence, by railway, by Rhone boat—anyhow, in fact; and having arrived in Pisa so much improved in health that Mrs. Jameson, who traveled with them, says she is "not merely improved but transformed." I do not know Mr. Browning; but this fact is enough to make me his friend. He is a poet also; but I believe that his acquirements are more remarkable than his poetry, although that has been held to be of high promise.

. Mr. May tells me that I shall do better by-and-by—that the cold weather brought the rheumatism—and that the warm weather will carry it away. Every one has suffered from this most ungenial winter, and even now we can hardly call it spring.

If you write to any one in London, recommend their going to see a magnificent portrait of Charles the First when Prince

VOL. II.—N

Charles, taken during his romantic expedition into Spain, and supposed to be the last picture which Velasquez painted.

It is full of health and life, and although there be something in the full eyelid that gives a shade of pensiveness to the face, yet there is so much spirit and youthfulness that it is quite free from the sadness of the Vandyke and Dobson portraits. Did I tell you that I had found a mention of this very picture in the notes to Hayley's poem on painting? He (Hayley) was, you know, a great Spanish scholar. All together I think it the very finest picture I have ever seen.

Ever most faithfully yours,   M. R. M.

To Miss Jephson, *Castle Martyr, Ireland.*

Three-mile Cross, Spring, 1846.

Thank you heartily for your dear letter, dear Emily, and the pretty knitted square for the pincushion. I do not need any thing to be reminded of you, but if I did that would do it. Can you send me a bit of the plait that the queen does? I remember, thirty years ago, that I made plait for three or four nets and bonnets, and liked the work much, inasmuch as it required no attention, and I could go on even while I was reading. I hate all the Berlin wool misdoings, which require counting, and seem to me calculated to keep down the intellect while they employ the fingers; but work (like tatting, for instance) which goes on without requiring any thought is sometimes pleasant.

I am still so lame as to be obliged to get a pony chaise, under pain of not being able to put foot to the ground if I persisted in taking long walks; and K—— not only drives the pony, but feeds him and takes care of the harness, while a respectable man next door takes charge of the garden. So that I may perhaps escape the danger of being whirled to the Queen's Bench by my new equipage, although compelled to the most minute attention to economy by this new and inevitable expense. Without it I could hardly crawl to church.

I am convinced that all education should be based upon religion; but it seems to me that religious instruction is rather aided than impeded by being accompanied by other means of cultivating the intellect and the affections. Rich people do not confine all education to religious instruction;

and I don't think that poor ones should be restricted to that only. For instance, there is a school in Reading, one of the old-fashioned endowments, where children were clothed, fed, and taught, and where they used to take in turn the house-work, the cooking, the laundry; to do plain work; to make and cut out their own linen and clothes; and, in short, to be trained into excellent servants. Well! since the town has become so Puseyite that the different churches are open al-most all day for different services, these children are taken in procession to the different churches four times every day —four times—interrupting all their avocations, and entirely putting a stop to their needlework.

Does not it strike you that this must tend either to weary the children or to make them hypocrites? I think so; and a very clever clergyman with whom I was talking of it this very day at Sir John Conroy's said that there could be no doubt in his mind but that when they left the school to go out to service they would leave it less religious than in the old days, when they went twice on a Sunday to church, and on Wednesday and Friday evenings to a lecture. One thing certain is, that they have quite lost their old repute for good training as servants; and that it is difficult now to find them places, because (as the mistress herself told me) nearly all their time is passed in going to church or dressing to pre-pare for it. I believe the intention to be good; but I doubt its efficacy as I doubt all excess. Yours ever,

M. R. M.

To Miss Jephson, *Castle Martyr, Ireland.*

Three-mile Cross, July, 1846.

My dear Emily,—I am sincerely rejoiced to hear that you have not suffered so much as I feared from the hot weather. It disagreed exceedingly with me; but, nevertheless, I con-trived to walk through it, although the dust and the unmit-igated glare were most painful and trying. My roses were blighted, my annuals dried off, and my geraniums have flag-ged and fallen under the glare in a most miserable manner. The peas, too, lasted only four or five days; and, in short, all vegetation has suffered. The rhododendrons at White-knights and at Bearwood I never saw so fine, and my straw-berries have prospered; but the currants are blighted, and they say there are in this county no apples at all.

I have been shocked past expression by the death of poor Haydon. He had sent me a ticket for a private view of his pictures only a month or two back; and we had been friends and correspondents for above thirty years. Poor fellow! He was a most brilliant person, and deserved a better fate, although he never quite kept the promise of his earlier works —never, indeed, brought out any thing so really fine as the "Judgment of Solomon," which my friend Sir William Elford purchased for six hundred pounds; and which first brought him into notice. Sir Robert Peel's conduct on this occasion has been very noble.

Have you read the "Life and Letters of John Foster?" I think them even finer than Dr. Arnold's; and you know what that is saying. I always thought the "Essays" amongst the finest ever written; but the "Life and Letters" make me think the man himself even nobler than his works? Did you know him? He lived for the better part of his life near Bristol. How wonderful that a small sect like the Baptists should have, at one time and in one narrow locality, two such giants as John Foster and Robert Hall!

Miss Gladstone used to write to me occasionally; and I have heard much of her from some mutual friends now dead. She ceased to write upon her conversion; and dear Dr. Baines told me that it was of no use for me to write to her in her nunnery (she is a professed nun, is she not?), for that all communication with the world was discouraged in those institutions. He disliked them much.

Yours affectionately,   M. R. M.

1847.

Fragment of a Letter to MISS JEPHSON. [No date.]

For my part I hate conversions. There is enough for salvation in the gospels, under whatever form of Christianity we may worship; and to convert from one form to another is always to unsettle—to root up old associations—and often to loosen the larger and more vital articles of faith. Dryden has somewhere a fine thought—I forget the words—but the meaning is this: "The soul is like a bird at roost; dislodge it from its twig and it flutters from branch to branch, unable to settle once again in peace and quietness." I have known many such. A daughter of one of my dearest friends was brought up a Protestant like her two sisters—the father being Protestant, the mother (a French woman) Roman Catholic. Since the father's death the eldest daughter has joined her mother's communion, the youngest remains a bigoted Protestant, and this middle girl goes to no church and professes no faith whatsoever.

To the REV. ALEXANDER DYCE, *Gray's Inn.*

Three-mile Cross, July, 1847.

I can not thank you enough, my dear Mr. Dyce, for all your kindness to me, and to the dear little girl whose album your beautiful verses will tend so much to enrich.

"The Beggar Girl"* is so exactly in the garb in which I first read her some five-and-forty years ago in Hans Place, that I can't help thinking it must be the same copy, and anticipate the same delight from the perusal that I had in those young days. I remember that I liked it not only for the character and the liveliness, but for the abundant story —incident toppling upon incident; all sufficiently natural and probable, after a fashion which the novelists of these times seem to have lost; for nowadays they generously give us one or two great impossibilities, and fill up their outline with declamation and sentiment generally false.

Accept once again my earnest thanks for your kindness; above all, for your goodness in coming to see me with our dear friend Mr. Harness. Pray, come again. Ever, my dear Mr. Dyce, very faithfully yours,   M. R. MITFORD.

1848.

To MRS. BROWNING, *Florence, Italy.*

Taplow, July 30, 1848.

I have taken so much of your advice, my very dear love, as Mr. May thought right—that is to say, the part that regarded change of air and change of scene. He said that the sea, in my particular case, would be rather bad than good,

* A novel by Mrs. Bennett, once extremely popular, which Mr. Dyce, after some difficulty, had procured for her.

and advised a short journey, where I could have my pony chaise among interesting scenery, and not beyond reach of him. Accordingly here I am, about twenty miles from home —in a pretty house, with our rooms opening on a garden full of trees and flowers, which goes down to the Thames (we have our own private stairs and landing from the little terrace), and the beautiful old bridge just below. A prettier English scene does not exist. I have already driven to Ork-wells, the beautiful old hall of the Norreys, part of which is just as it was in the reign of Henry the Sixth—and that part the most important—the banquet-hall, with its dais and music-gallery and long range of painted windows—the open galleries, buttery hatch, porch and gables, with the exquisite carving of their fretted roof as delicate as a lady's fan. Then I have been (where I have permission to go every day) through Lord Orkney's noble woods to Cliefden Spring—a woody acclivity (of I am afraid to say what height) on one side, and the bright river on the other—the actual

"Cliefden's proud alcove,"

where Lady Shrewsbury held her lover the Duke of Bucking-ham's horse, while he fought with and killed her husband. Then to Burnham Beeches—a piece of forest scenery hardly to be matched in England, whether as regards the ground or the magnificent trees. Then to the vaults at Lady Place, where the Revolution of 1688 was hatched, and which looks just fit for such a holy conspiracy, standing, as it does now, with the old mansion taken down, in the midst of its romantic lawn. All these I have seen, and to-morrow I am going to Dropmore; and I am more improved in health and strength and spirits than I had thought possible.

One reason why I was so much better here is, that I have only one female friend (and that a very favorite one) within reach—half of my worries proceeding from a quantity of tiresome visitors. Some I have seen this summer who are not tiresome—the Miss Goldsmids, Sir Isaac Goldsmid's daughters. The eldest is a very remarkable woman, and she spoke of Mr. Browning with great interest, as having been at the London University with her brothers. Also Mr. Ruskin spoke of some vintage verses of his as singularly true to nature; and his praise is worth having. He is a most charming person, but was, when I last heard of him, laid up at Salisbury. I fear for his health, and so does his mother.

Ah! my dear love, I have nothing but fear for France. As to Lamartine, I never did expect any good from him; except "Les Girondins," I always detested his writings—so weak and wordy and full of vanity. And "Les Girondins," they say, is untrue beyond the usual untruthfulness of history—a mere party pamphlet. When he was in London a few years ago Mr. Rogers asked him, with strong interest, to give him some details about Béranger, "the greatest French poet." "Ah! Béranger," said M. de Lamartine, "he made advances to me, and, of course, wished for my acquaintance; but he is a sort of man with whom I do not choose to have any connection!" Think of that! Mr. Rogers told the story himself, with the greatest indignation, to the Ruskins, and they told it to me.

Dumas has been in England with his *Théâtre Historique*—the whole company—playing "Monte Christo" (which takes two evenings) at Drury Lane. To the great disgrace of our people, authors and actors, the French troop were hissed off. I am told that what astonished him most in our country was to find what a number of persons (turnpike commissioners, county magistrates, deputy lieutenants, etc.) exercised their offices gratuitously; but the poverty of the French would not admit of their working for nothing. It is wonderful how poor they all seem. Dumas' last works are "Les Quarante Cinq," "De Paris à Cadiz," and a book on Algiers. Sir Edward Bulwer Lytton has just brought out an historical novel called "Harold"—good as history, but dull as a story. Bentley gave fifteen hundred pounds for the copyright—an immense sum. Mr. Kingsley's play upon Elizabeth of Hungary, "The Saint's Tragedy," is really fine and striking, but miserably painful to read; the more so, as the most disgusting parts are literally true.

I shall be returning to Three-mile Cross in about ten days or a fortnight, having by that time, if it please God, laid in a stock of health for the winter. God bless you, my beloved friend! A pleasant excursion to Mr. Browning. Ever most faithfully yours,   M. R. MITFORD.

To Mrs. Browning, *Florence.*

How earnestly I rejoice, my beloved friend, in your continued health! and how very, very glad I shall be to see you and
your baby. Remember me to Wilson, and tell her that I am
quite prepared to admire him as much as will even satisfy her
appetite for praise. How beautifully you describe your beautiful country! Oh! that I were with you, to lose myself in
the chestnut forests, and gather grapes at the vintage! If I
had but Prince Houssein's carpet, I would set forth and leave
Mr. May to scold and wonder, when he comes to see me to-
morrow. He seems well disposed to shut me up for a month
or two. Besides the chestnut woods and you, your own-
selves, I should be delighted to see Mr. Lever. You know
I have always had a mannish sort of fancy for those " Charles
O'Malley " and " Jack Hinton " books, which always put me
in good spirits and good humor (I wish he wrote so now);
and I remember hearing from his illustrator, Mr. Browne,
that he was exactly the "Harry Lorrequer" he describes—
that is to say, full of life and glee, and all that is animating
and agreeable. I remember, too, most gratefully the pleasure his books gave to my father.

"The Princess" has fine things, but would certainly not
have made a reputation. It is a poem of a hundred and fifty
pages, all in blank verse—inclosed within a setting of blank
verse also—and the very songs introduced are of the same
metre. The story is very unskillfully told, with an entire
want of dramatic power, and full of the strangest words
brought in after the strangest fashion. It begins in mock-
ery, and becomes earnest as it goes on; but there are, as I
said before, fine things in it.

God bless you, my beloved friend! Say every thing for
me to Mr. Browning. Kiss baby for me, and pat Flush. I
have written out the pain. Ever yours,   M. R. M.

I have made many inquiries about Miss Martineau; but my
only answer has been from Mrs. Onory (Jane Nicholls), who
lives in her circle, and says, " All I know about her is that
she has brought a pipe from the East, and smokes it every
day. Perhaps that may be to subdue pain or deaden irrita-
tion."

1849.

To Mrs. Browning, *Florence.*

Swallowfield, March 11, 1849.

I have been miserably ill all this winter, dearest love. For above three months I do not think that I was three times out of bed at eight o'clock; and to any one who knew my late habits, *that* says enough. If I went out for a little walk (and I have been now so lame for a twelvemonth that I can only walk a very little way), or even if a friend came to see me, I became so exhausted as to be compelled to go to bed, hardly able often to get up stairs. And with this entire loss of power came total loss of spirits. Mr. May said the only remedy was air without fatigue, and ordered me to go out every day in an open carriage. In consequence, we bought a high-priced highly recommended pony—the vendor, a very rich man, and supposed to be respectable, knowing that it was for an elderly invalid lady and her maid, and answering for it as sound and right. Ben drove it ten miles and it went beautifully (we suppose it was starved for the occasion). The next day K—— and I set forth to go to Reading, and at the bottom of the hill leading to the town it kicked the carriage to pieces with me in it; and afterward kicked another carriage to atoms into which it was put, to try if two vigorous and experienced coachmen could manage it. Under Providence I owe my life entirely to the courage and fidelity of my brave and faithful little maid. She got off (we neither of us knew how) and flew to the head of the furious animal, holding on to the bit and bridle, at the peril of life and limb for many minutes, until a sufficient number of men was collected to draw me out (pretty much as a plant might be drawn out by the roots) and carry me across the road. Five or six men were afraid to hold the vicious beast that she had held. Does not this justify affection by affection—for that was her strength? Her left hand was much sprained, and her right side strained by her efforts; but I am sure that she would have held on until she was dead or I rescued. The two people (strong men, used to furious horses all their lives) who afterward got up behind the pony, both escaped from the carriage and left it to work its will. The vendor knew perfectly the beast he was selling. This accident has shaken me

N 2

much. · My health and strength seem gone altogether. In short, dearest love, I am full ten years older than before my lameness last year.

Who told you, my dear love, that William Harness praised "The Princess" in MS. ? When he was with me in August, and the poem was printing, he had not read it. His friend, Mr. Dyce, who accompanied him, had, and spoke of it sweetly and indulgently, as he speaks of all things, but on the whole very truly, as an imperfect work with very fine bits. Heaven bless you, my beloved friend ! Ever most faithfully and affectionately yours,   M. R. MITFORD.

To MRS. BROWNING, *Lucca, Italy.*

Three-mile Cross, Dec. 16, 1849.

This is my birthday (sixty-two), my beloved friend, and I can not better employ it than in answering your dear letter received two days ago. For myself, I should certainly have said that I was much better than this time last year, if it were not that I have had to day a touch of that painful neuralgia, and that I have been suffering in consequence of having the small-pox in the house. It has been most rife in the neighborhood, and very heavy. Three or four persons have died of it after vaccination.

All the world is publishing. Alfred Tennyson says that people nowadays are not merely indifferent to poetry—that they absolutely hate it. I heard this from a sweet young woman (Mary Repton, daughter of one of the prebendaries of Westminster), who is staying close by, at Mrs. Anderdon's, and has taken to me as young people sometimes do. She is intimate, very, with all the Tennysons, and speaks of them more highly than I ever heard any one; perhaps because she knows them better. She says that they are the most unworldly people she ever knew, valuing every body by the personal qualities, apart from all considerations of rank or wealth or fame or consideration. Indolence is the besetting sin of the race; but they can work if they will. For instance, she made Alfred dig up the whole garden at her father's country living near Sevenoaks; and he did it capitally.

1850.

To MRS. BROWNING, *Florence, Italy.*

Three-mile Cross, March 25, 1850.

My "Country Stories" are just coming out, to my great contentment, in the "Parlor Library," for a shilling, or perhaps ninepence—that being the price of Miss Austen's novels. I delight in this, and have no sympathy with your bemoanings over American editions. Think of the American editions of my prose. "Our Village" has been reprinted in twenty or thirty places, and "Belford Regis" in almost as many; and I like it. So do *you*, say what you may. Mr. Fields, the handsome Boston bookseller, Mr. Ticknor's partner, sent me a copy of their edition of Mr. Browning's poems, and very nicely done it is, preceded by Mr. Landor's sonnet.

After all, my dear friend, Mrs. Acton Tindal was mistaken in her account of the authorship of "Jane Eyre." It was really written by a Miss Brontë, a clergyman's daughter, diminutive almost to dwarfishness—a woman of thirty, who had hardly ever left her father's parish in Yorkshire. There is great success in mystery. I think, from a thing that I have heard lately, that Sir R. Vyvyan *is* the author of the "Vestiges."

Well; but was not that song most sweet and harmonious, and full of grace and beauty? and what would you ask for more? A song is not necessarily an ode. For my part, I delight in such bits of melody, floating about you upon the air. I wish I dared give it to Henry Phillips, to whom I have just sent a fine translation of a German song written, words and music, by one of Prince Eugene's old troopers, and picked up by a friend of mine among the soldiers at Ehrenbreitstein.

God bless you, my very dear love! K—— has been very ill, but is better. Say every thing for me to Mr. Browning, and believe me ever, faithfully and most affectionately yours,

M. R. MITFORD.

To MRS. JENNINGS.

Three-mile Cross, April 16, 1850.

Yes! dearest Mrs. Jennings, there certainly is a sympathy, I have remarked it a hundred times, and I think our writing just at one time proves it completely. I do trust that it will lead me to London before you leave it. In other words, I constantly hope that we may meet this spring; but my coming is still uncertain, and depends upon half a dozen small circumstances over which I have myself no control. First of all, my poor cottage is falling about my ears. We were compelled to move my little pony from his stable to the chaise-house, because there were in the stable three large holes big enough for me to escape through. Then came a windy night and blew the roof from the chaise-house. And truly the cottage proper, where we two-legged creatures dwell, is in little better condition; the walls seem to be mouldering from the bottom, crumbling, as it were, like an old cheese; and, whether any thing can be done with it, is doubtful. Besides which, as it belongs to chancery wards, there is a further doubt whether the master will do what may be done.

I only want a cottage with a good bedroom, a decent sitting-room, and perhaps two odd rooms, anywhere, for books; for I find, upon taking stock, that I shall have from five thousand to six thousand. All these are reasons against going far; and, indeed, there is a cottage here which, if I can take, I shall. Yours most sincerely,　　　　M. R. M.

To Mrs. Browning, *Florence, Italy.*

Three-mile Cross, July 1, 1850.

I can not enough thank you, my beloved friend, for your most welcome letter. The pleasure it gave me would have been unmingled but for its delaying the hope of seeing you. But, if you come so near as France, then we shall meet here, I hope, and there—I mean both in France and in England; for I do still hope to get as far as Paris before I die. At present I can not tell you where I am going. The cottage at Swallowfield that I want to rent, belonged to a crotchety old bachelor; he, dying, left it for her life to a sister, a rich widow, aged seventy-seven, and after her death to another relative. It is about six miles from Reading, on this same road, leading up from which is a short ascending lane, terminated by this small dwelling, with a court in front, and a garden and paddock behind. Trees overarch it like the frame of a picture, and the cottage itself, although not pretty, yet too unpretending to be vulgar, and abundantly snug and comfortable, leading by different paths to all my favorite walks, and still within distance of my most valuable neighbors. It will be provoking if this woman, who has known me for forty years, and to whom my father rendered a thousand services, should, from spite to Captain Beauchamp and his excellent father, resolve rather to let the cottage tumble to pieces than admit a tenant whom they wish to see there, or indeed any tenant at all.

You are most kind in your inquiries about my health. I can not but think myself better on the whole than when I wrote last, and you will wonder to hear that I have again taken pen in hand. It reminds me of Benedick's speech— "When I said I should die a bachelor, I never thought to live to be married;" but it is our friend Henry Chorley's fault. He has taken to "The Lady's Companion," a weekly journal, belonging to Bradbury and Evans, that was going to decay (like my dwellings, present and future) under the mismanagement of Mrs. Loudon, and came to me to help him. He wanted a novel; then, finding that out of the question, he wanted something else; and, though I have refused every applicant to right and left for these eight years, this very Mrs. Loudon included, and began, of course, by refusing him, he is such a very old friend, that I really could not persist in saying No to him. So at last it ended in my undertaking to give him a series of papers to be called " Readings of Poetry, Old and New," consisting of as much prose as he can get, and extracts from favorite poets.

[Conclusion lost.]

To Mrs. Jennings, Portland Place.

Three-mile Cross, Nov. 9, 1850.

Your two delightful letters, my very dear Mrs. Jennings, deserve a better return than they are likely to get at this moment. Nevertheless, I can not put off writing any longer. When the days get a little longer—that is to say, early in the new year—I shall do by you what I used to do by Elizabeth Barrett—take a return ticket to go up for the day to Portland Place, arriving about three o'clock, or two perhaps, and returning by the half past seven o'clock train. Then we can have a grand discussion upon a Welsh cottage. You and Mr. Jennings are the temptations; the distance,

and absence of books, the objections. But we must meet
and have a long talk. Are there dry winter walks? that is
a great point. I live entirely, I may say, on boiled sole,
boiled whiting, and fruit; fish of any other sort I could
not touch. And fruit—strawberries, for instance, currants,
grapes—must be come-at-able, in large quantities and for a
long time. We have now out-of-door grapes hung up to
last till March. This, dear friend, is a point of health with
me. I never can eat meat or butter, or milk or eggs, or
poultry. Is there good *brown* bread? All these questions
we can discuss, and I mention them now that you may ask.
But I dread the want of books; I have the habit of running
over almost every book of any note that is published; and a
book club always has seemed to me a sort of mental imprisonment—a shutting into one little room, and being kept on
water gruel. Then I have five thousand or six thousand volumes to move, as well as furniture. About neighbors I do
not care. Mr. Jennings and you, and one clever man, would
do. I rather dislike neighbors—don't you. Do you remember what Horace Walpole says of the country?—" Questions
grow there, and the Christian commodity neighbors." That
has always seemed to me among the raciest of his racy bits.
You and Mr. Jennings are the temptation. And then, this .
cottage is likely to fall about my ears; yet I cling to it—to
the green lanes—which you have not seen—to the commons,
the copses, the old trees—every bit of the old country. It
is only a person brought up in the midst of woods and fields
in one country place, who can understand that strong local
attachment. But we must talk over the matter; most assuredly nothing but illness shall prevent my having the great
pleasure of going to see you in London. You must thank
for me your pleasant friend. I am ashamed not to recollect
him; but that Manor House has had so many guests, that
one gets confounded amongst them. Was he a visitor of
Sir William Pym?

Just now, I have been much interested by a painting that
has been going on in the corner of our village street—the inside of an old wheelwright's shop—a large barn-like place,
open to the roof, full of detail, with the light admitted
through the half of hatch doors, and spreading upward. It
is a fine subject, and finely treated. The artist is one not

yet much known, of the name of Pasmore. But I judge by this he will make a name for interiors. It is capitally peopled, too—with children, picking up chips and watching an old man sharpening a saw, and peeping in through windows, stretching up to look through them. I hear it has pleased Henry Phillips, the bass singer, to make one of his pleasant musical entertainments out of my book—for the libretto is as much his as the music—and accordingly he is coming to sing and recite "Our Village," and I am going to hear him. Have you read "Alton Locke?" I have not; nor, although he is almost a neighbor, do I know Mr. Kingsley. His other work, "The Saint's Tragedy," was full of power, but painful, disagreeable, and inconclusive; and I think it likely, from all that I hear, that this is the same; although my friend Mr. Pearson, the vicar of Sonning, said to me yesterday that there was in it a startling amount of world-wide truth.

Yours ever most faithfully,   M. R. M.

[This is the last letter from Three-mile Cross. The Court of Chancery refused to repair the cottage. Terms were arranged for the house at Swallowfield, and Miss Mitford removed so late in the autumn to secure a safe shelter for the winter.]

To Mrs. Jennings, *Portland Place.*

Swallowfield, Dec. 31, 1850.

How glad I am to see your dear handwriting again, dearest Mrs. Jennings, and how much more glad should I be to see yourself! It was a great temptation that which Mrs. Dupuy put in my way, to come to town and go with her to your house on Christmas day. I do quite understand your feelings. A father (and such a father) is a loss never to be replaced; but there is comfort and satisfaction in such a recollection; and even your children will be the better, ay! much the better, for having to look back to such a grandfather, linked to them by such parents. So out of grief springs hope.

Mr. Kingsley took me quite by surprise in his extraordinary fascination. I have never seen a man of letters the least like him, for, in general, the *beau-idéal* of a young poet remains a *beau-idéal.* They are mostly middle-aged (sometimes elderly), conceited, affected, foppish, vulgar. Mr. Kingsley is not only a high-bred gentleman, but has the most charming admixture of softness and gentleness, with spirit, manliness, and frankness — a frankness quite transparent — and a cordiality and courtesy that would win any heart. He did win his own sweet wife entirely by this charm of character. She was a girl of family, fortune, fashion, and beauty; he a young curate, without distinction of any sort— without even literary distinction, for he had not then published. He loved her—she loved him; and, without any unseemly elopement, they lived down and loved down a pretty strong family opposition, and were married. Since that, Sir John Cope gave him the living of Eversley; and he has won a very high fame, and the love of all his parish and all his neighborhood. He is quite young; and though, I suppose, he does not generally intend to go fox-hunting, yet it sometimes happens that his horse carries him into the midst of the chase, when he is always in at the death, eager and delighted as a boy. I can not tell you how much I like him. Miss Bremer was at his house, just before we became acquainted, and he was much pleased with her. She staid too short a time, or we should have met. He is now engaged upon a work (in " Fraser ") treating of Alexandria in the fifth century—a sort of story like Lockhart's " Valerius " or Mr. Ware's " Palmyra "—but he is greatest as a poet. I know nothing more touching than that song in " Alton Locke."

I am charmed with my new cottage. The scenery is delightful, and the neighbors most kind and pleasant. Perhaps, when the days get long and the weather fine you will come and see me—won't you? I do hope to get to town in time to see you this year. You know that my last visit was regulated by the arrival of Mrs. Browning. Your attached and affectionate, M. R. MITFORD.

1851.

To MRS. JENNINGS, *Portland Place.*

Swallowfield, June, 1851.

Thank you most heartily, dearest Mrs. Jennings, for your most kind invitation. But, besides general weakness and debility, which would render the pleasant fatigue of London quite impossible just now, I am so lame that I could no more walk over the Exhibition than I could fly. I do hope to get better of an incapacity which is very painful, but certainly it will take time. Every body speaks in the same way of that great sight—which is so much more than a sight—and yet I regret more the missing kind and valued friends.

CHAPTER XXI.

LETTERS FOR 1852.

To MISS GOLDSMID.

Swallowfield, April 12, 1852.

THANK you most heartily, dear Miss Goldsmid, for Mr. Robertson's admirable lectures. I shall put them in the hands of my friend, Mr. Fields, of Boston, whom I am expecting every day, and who will, I am pretty sure, spread them through America. I agree generally with Mr. Robertson, differing, of course, in some particulars, as all people who think and like and admire for themselves must do and ought to do. But those lectures are the very things that ought to be heard and read; and they will be. I am not one of those who think this age without taste for poetry. Its very richness in graceful verse makes it difficult to attain a reputation—as Rogers did, for instance : but the taste exists in many unsuspected quarters. I have had proofs of this by my own book, if I may venture with you—I think I may— to be so egotistical as to mention it. Ever since it has been published I have had, day by day, letters upon letters, packets upon packets, books upon books, from all parts of the country—remote villages in Wales and Scotland and Ireland —not merely from enthusiastic girls and young poets at Oxford and Cambridge, but from people the most unexpected— grave old merchants, half ashamed—self-educated men, who toil all day and read and write half the night—and professional men in our great towns, who find relief from their mind-weariness in the soothing delights of poetry. I should be afraid to tell you how many strangers have written to me during the last three months; and I hail it, not merely as a mark of personal kindness to myself, but as a pregnant proof of the interest taken in the main subject of the work. Adieu, dear Miss Goldsmid. Ever most gratefully and affectionately yours, M. R. MITFORD.

To MRS. JENNINGS.

Swallowfield, June 1, 1852.

Do, please, send me "The Laird of Caithness," and any ballads *you* think good. I can securely trust your taste. I presume my version of "Bonnie Dundee" to be correct, since it is taken from Scott's own text, in his quite-forgotten or rather never-known play, "The Doom of Devorgoil," one of those weak dramas which it seems really incredible that such a poet and such a novelist should have written. The most incredible of all is, that, besides its absolute want of merit, this ballad is introduced as having been written thirty years; and a prior of some monastery is also introduced, as having, about the same period, been driven from his priory by the Reformation, thus making contemporaries of John Knox and Claverhouse!

Another ballad that I have been long in search of is "We'll gae nae mair a roving," by James the Fifth of Scotland, called by Scott the best comic ballad in any language. "The Gaberlunzie Man," by the same royal author, is in Percy; but the other I can nowhere find, although I have half a dozen different collections myself, and sent for Chambers's "Comic Ballads of Scotland," making sure to find it there.

The Kossuth trait is capital. I hold the man to be a mere adventurer, and one of the worst sort, blowing up strife amongst the nations. Have you any sympathy with Louis Napoleon? I have. Two or three of my friends, who have been in Paris since the autumn—Mrs. Browning for one—say that "the French people have been with him from the first to the last;" and the ability and courage of the man are worthy of his name. In another thing, too, every letter from France is unanimous—that war with England would be most popular with army and with people, whilst we are as unprepared for such a contingency as any thing well can be. Well, I hope the primroses will come first, and you with them.

Yes, I delight in Longfellow, especially "The Golden Legend," which is full of salt and savor—rich, racy, graphic,—breathing the air of the middle ages, of Gothic architecture, grand cathedrals, quaint German towns.   There is an open-air sermon upon bells that one can fancy to have been preached at Paul's Cross before the Reformation; and a scene in the Scriptorium, or rather a soliloquy of an old monk, employed on illuminating a manuscript, that one can really hear and see, it is so true.   Always faithfully and affectionately yours,   M. R. MITFORD.

To Mrs. HOARE,* *Monkstown, Ireland.*

Swallowfield, June, 1852.

DEAR MADAM,—Almost every post for the last two or three weeks has brought me two or three letters from persons hitherto unknown to me, and one or two books, many of them of considerable merit.   Very few, however, have given me so much pleasure as your amusing and characteristic little work† and your kind letter.   Poor Mrs. James Gray interested me much.   I have been hoping that my book, which has brought English reprints of Holcroft's Memoirs, and of several other works that I see announced, might have produced a collected edition of her poems; but I suppose the state of Ireland is not favorable to such an enterprise.   If you could without much trouble procure for me copies of the poems you mention I should be glad.   A few years back there was a great influx of Irish poetry, most of which I possess, but it is now scarce.   A friend of mine once ran off with a six-penny volume of " Poetry of the Nation," and has not since been able to find it, either in her husband's fine library in town or at their seat in the country; and this little book I have been unable to replace.   Have you read " The Autobiography of a Working Man ?"   It is as graphic as Defoe, and with a fine illustration of Burns's " Cotter's Saturday Night,"

* Mrs. Hoare, the lady to whom the following letters are addressed, had from childhood been an ardent admirer of Miss Mitford's writings, but was unacquainted with her till the publication of the " Recollections of a Literary Life."   That book contained a brief notice of Mrs. James Gray, of whose life and writings Mrs. Hoare knew much of which Miss Mitford was a ignorant. She therefore ventured to write to her on that subject, and the result was a correspondence which continued till within a short period of Miss Mitford's death.

† A volume of Irish stories.

in the account the author gives of the piety of his own family, belonging to the South Highlands. Ever, dear madam, very faithfully yours,   M. R. MITFORD.

Was there any thing sudden in poor Mrs. James Gray's death? I thought so from the announcement in the "Dublin University Magazine."

To MRS. HOARE, *Monkstown, Ireland.*

Swallowfield, Summer, 1852.

DEAREST MRS. HOARE,—Mr. Macaulay I have not the honor to know; but I agree with you in thinking him at the very head of English literature,—certainly our greatest prose writer (although perhaps John Ruskin may be more eloquent) —almost our greatest *poet.* He is quite as delightful a companion as he is a writer. I am, for my sins, so fidgety respecting style, that I have the bad habit of expecting a book which pretends to be written in our language to be English; therefore I can not read Miss Strickland, or the Howitts, or Thomas Carlyle, or Emerson, or the serious part of Dickens, although liking very heartily the fun of "Pickwick." Some day or other you will yourself become more fastidious; and then you will find excuses for my want of indulgence.

Their wild violets are not sweet. I suspect they call the pansy the violet, since Mr. Bryant somewhere talks of the yellow violet, a phenomenon not known with us. Have you the white wild hyacinth? It makes a charming variety amongst its blue sisters, and is amongst the purest of white flowers, all so pure. A bank close to my little field is rich in both. Have you the frittillaries? They are beautiful in our water meadows, looking like painted glass. Indeed, a young friend of mine in putting up a memorial window after his grandfather's death, suggested to the artist the use of this beautiful local flower, an idea with which he was charmed. Have you the rarer English orchises—the bee, the fly, the spider, the butterfly, the dead-leaf, the lily of the valley orchis, and the man orchis? They grow on chalky soils amongst beech woods.

As a general rule I may say that through life I have met with singular kindness and sympathy; and I firmly believe that any one pursuing a straightforward course, and not courting the notice of those who are called the upper classes, will always command their respect, and very often their regard. Adieu, dear friend. Believe me ever faithfully yours, M. R. MITFORD.

To MRS. HOARE, *Monkstown, Ireland.*

Swallowfield, Summer, 1852.

Somewhere or other, dear Mrs. Hoare, I have a letter half written to you, which I could not finish when begun, having been interrupted by a violent attack of fever, above three weeks ago, which has become intermittent. I am, I believe, slowly mending. My excellent little maid, who has every talent except the talent epistolary, is an admirable nurse, and I have a most skillful medical man. Add that this cottage stands under the shadow of superb old trees, oak and elm, upon a scrap of common which catches every breeze; and that I see the coolest of waters from my window, or rather from my bed—and, indeed, this is, they say, the coolest house in the neighborhood: you will then agree that I have much for which to be thankful. Still it is a depressing sort of illness, and has not been wanting in depressing circumstances.

And so you think a party pamphlet will make me change my mind about Louis Napoleon! Before my illness I saw from twenty to thirty people who had spent the winter at Paris, many who had been living there for years. They all laugh at the nice English prejudices against a man whose popularity in his own country is as great as ever was enjoyed by man. Look at the price of stocks; the only real fact which appears about France in the English press. During my illness I have been reading his own works, in French of course; and the deep interest inspired by the beautiful writing of those three volumes is greater than I can describe. Many of the persons whom I saw had seen much of him. One had been over the rooms just made ready for him at St. Cloud. Their taste and simplicity, the manly absence of finery, is said to be most indicative of character. Adieu! This is the longest letter I have written. M. R. M.

To MRS. HOARE, *Monkstown.*

Swallowfield, Summer, 1852.

MY DEAR MRS. HOARE,—I think you had been reading Margaret Fuller's life—a strange, wild woman, who was, they say, insupportable at Boston, but became better at New York, where she was treated only as a lion; better still at Paris, where she knew little French; still softer in England, where she was talked over by Carlyle; and really good and interesting in Italy, where the woman took completely the place of the sibyl. Some American friends who were here on Friday knew her well. They were disgusted by her conceit and arrogance and affectation; but spoke of her purity, her strong sense of duty, and her general powers. One had read in America that letter which contained her adventures when lost in Scotland; all had heard of her admirable conduct in the hospitals at Rome. A curious story was told to them of Ossoli by the sculptor himself who figures in it. Margaret went to an eminent sculptor, and said that Ossoli had much time and much taste for his art, would he admit him to his studio? "Certainly," replied the artist, and questioned Ossoli on his vocation. He said if he had any taste or talent it was for sculpture; and a foot for a model with proper clay was put into his hands. A fortnight after Ossoli brought back the model and his copy, in which the great toe was placed on the wrong side of the foot!

Can you tell me where to find the line

"A fellow-feeling makes us wondrous kind?"

All America is looking for it.   Adieu, dear Mrs. Hoare.
Ever very faithfully yours,   M. R. MITFORD.

To MRS. HOARE, Monkstown.

Swallowfield, Autumn, 1852.

Did I tell you that Mr. Fields expects to bring Mr. Hawthorne to England with him in the spring? And did I also say that the last act of my excellent friend, before leaving England, was to carry to Mr. De Quincey, in Scotland, the author's profits of the seven volumes of his collected works, which he (Mr. Fields) had collected with so much care and pains, and edited himself? This piece of generosity, unprecedented in any publisher, English or American, gave great pleasure to the "Opium-eater," whom Mr. Fields describes as the most courtly gentleman that he has seen in Europe.

Adieu, dear Mrs. Hoare. Forgive me if I be long silent. They scold me for writing. Ever yours,   M. R. M.

To Mrs. Jennings.

Swallowfield, July 30, 1852.

I heartily agree in the wisdom of your theory of education. I know now a little boy of seven (only son of a near neighbor) speaking four or five languages, far advanced in Greek, with Latin in proportion; but oh! the pale, sickly child! His mother, a very clever woman, is proud of this boy, and seems to be blind to the small chance of rearing him, in the first place; and to the great probability that this precocious intellect will be far inferior, at seven-and-twenty, to your boys, who are developing their physical powers in the hay-field and on the Welsh mountains, and who will learn healthily and rapidly when the time comes.

I have been reading Edgar Poe's Tales and Poems—very remarkable; and am just now trying to get over the painfulness of "Uncle Tom's Cabin." Have you read it? It is a negro story, and certainly there is much humor and much pathos; but the question, as regards America, must have two sides, when Daniel Webster, the wisest of her statesmen, has forfeited his presidentship, and risked his popularity, rather than join the Abolitionists, at a certainty of a disruption of the Union.

Adieu, dearest friend. Say every thing for me to Mr. Jennings. Ever faithfully yours, . M. R. Mitford.

To Miss Goldsmid.

Swallowfield, Summer, 1852.

Ah! dearest Miss Goldsmid, how can I ever thank you and dear Lady Goldsmid half enough for your exquisite kindness! and how I wish that I could by any chance profit by it? But although quite as cheerful as ever, the very good spirits which have been the support and solace of my life are now a danger, for they excite and exhaust me; and, if I be more than four or five hours in company—especially the company I like best—I never close my eyes all night, and am almost as ill as ever next day. But this dream of coming near you seems too good to happen. Mr. May dislikes my seeing any body; and I must be better than I fear is likely, to be able to realize such a hope. Nevertheless, I can not quite give it up; but if I can come I will write again.

I am so very sorry to hear of Sir Isaac's illness; he seemed so full of life, so young in mind and body, that one can not bear to think of him as an invalid and an object of anxiety to that large and happy family who spread such sunshine around them. I have never forgotten the sight of Lady Goldsmid (that impersonation of all that is womanly and motherly) in the midst of her children and grandchildren. Remember me to her, and to all who are so kind as to think of me, most gratefully. Ever, dear Miss Goldsmid, most affectionately and faithfully yours, M. R. MITFORD.

To Miss Goldsmid, *Summerhill, Tonbridge.*

Swallowfield, August, 1852.

A week before receiving your kind note, dearest Miss Goldsmid, I had myself found the line* in Garrick's Epilogue. Yet I was glad of your letter, because although Mr. Fields has no doubt about the matter, Mr. Harness seems to think it a quotation. Indeed, except Mr. Harness, I have found nobody to doubt, and his is a vague suspicion without any indication of another habitat for the flower. By the way, this most dear friend of mine has been here for ten days—came here for one—found himself a lodging—has staid ever since, and will stay ten days longer. Did you ever hear of him? He is well known as a preacher, and is one of the most charming persons that ever trod the earth, and as good as he is charming. His father gave away my mother. We were close friends in childhood, and have remained such ever since; and now he leaves the Deepdene, with all its beauty of scenery and society, to come to me, a poor sick old woman, just because I am sick and old and poor, and because we have loved each other like brother and sister all our lives. How I wish you were here, dear Mrs. Hoare, to hear him read Shakspeare—far above any acting—and to listen to conversation that leaves his reading far behind.

Poor Margaret Fuller! The deeper tragedies are the true ones; and I know no one sadder than hers. Women of genius make great mistakes in choosing husbands, and she seems to have been one. An American friend told me the other day a curious trait of Daniel Webster, which has made his fish-propensity very diverting to his countrymen. His

* "A fellow-feeling makes us wondrous kind."

passion for fish, in every way—to catch, and to cook, and to eat—is something fabulous. It is an epoch in an American's life to eat fish-chowder (a soup composed of cod and other ingredients) at Marshfield; and whatever be the rank of the guests, the great statesman leaves them, to compound the dainty with his own hands, asserting that no woman that was ever born can hit the exact proportions.

Oh! dearest Miss Goldsmid, what a pedigree for Summerhill! But how could the woman, who had been the wife of *that* Lord Essex, ever marry again? He has always been amongst my pet heroes in history. One even overlooks his flattery of that odious queen for the sake of his chivalry of character, and for a largeness and tolerance far rarer in that age than any knightly quality. What a combination of temptations to visit you!—you and Lady Goldsmid, and the house, that comes so near to the highest tragedy in Lord Essex, and the highest comedy in the " Mémoires de Grammont!" I am afraid that I care less for the associations of Penshurst, although I do care for them also. Oh! I must come next year.

Since you do not mention Sir Isaac's health, I trust that he is improving. All health and happiness to you all. Ever dearest Miss Goldsmid, most gratefully and affectionately yours, M. R. MITFORD.

To MISS GOLDSMID, *Summerhill, Tonbridge.*

Swallowfield, Sept., 1852.

DEAREST MISS GOLDSMID,—If we had met this year, I should have ventured to tell you that the copy of your translation of Dr. Solomon's Sermons never reached me. Why I name this now is, because after preaching one of his own fine sermons Friday week, Mr. Harness read me in the evening one of yours, and expressed himself so delighted with its spirit and with its English (which he said he could hardly believe a translation) as to desire of all things to possess the volume. He even, upon my telling him it was not to be purchased, requested me to beg one for him of your own dear self. I wish you had heard all he said. He went on to speak of Jewish literature—of the high and deep interest attached to the Hebrew religion—and to the want of a clear English version of the Old Testament by a Jew. He said

VOL. II.—O

that he himself possessed two, if not three, which professed to be. such; but that they were founded on the English translation—I mean the authorized Church of England translation—with variations, instead of being newly executed throughout; and that the effect was rather to produce confusion in the familiar version than to convey the exact impression entertained by the chosen people of their own sacred books. He said that a translation of the Bible, according to the Hebrew faith, executed in the manner of Dr. Solomon's sermons, would be a very precious contribution to English theology. I wish you had heard him.

I have been poorly during the last week. That low fever hangs about me, and will not go. I shall certainly read Dumas; Cuvier's fine work I have read. Adieu. Ever most affectionately yours,　　　　　　　　　　　　M. R. M.

To MRS. HOARE, *Monkstown, Ireland.*

Swallowfield, Autumn, 1852.

I have been reading your book with great attention. It has about it unmistakable truth, a quality rare among modern Irish works—I mean, the works of living Irish writers. An Englishman feels it difficult to realize the terrible trials of those famine years. We hear of starvation as of a town taken by storm—an evil remote and all but impossible. It must have been a most painful trial of fortitude to witness such misery and to be only able to alleviate it here and there. Even now, how strange is the state of Ireland! How little any one seems to know how to deal with those frightful murders of landlord and agent which prevent the introduction of capital and the stimulus to labor—to self-support and self-reliance, which seem the master-want of your people—a people who, in other lands, come out in healthy strength, and in their own country are elements of danger and of weakness.

In your graphic description of the grounds of an old house, you talk of the *pink* harebell as a wild flower. We have the harebell in heathy lands, *blue*, sometimes *white* as a cultivated flower, but *pink* I have never seen it.

Be sure, dear Mrs. Hoare, that I have no political sympathy with the poets of the "Nation;" but they were full of *verve*, and (speaking as an Englishwoman, and, therefore, perhaps, ignorantly) I should have been glad if such men as John Mitchell, and Smith O'Brien, and young Meagher, above all, had been suffered, after sentence, to expiate their crime by exile in America, rather than by being sent as convicts to a penal colony. They would have been quite forgotten there.

May every happiness be with you! Faithfully yours,

M. R. MITFORD.

To MRS. HOARE, *Monkstown, Ireland.*

Swallowfield, Autumn, 1852.

Thank you, my dearest Mrs. Hoare, for the touching French verses, and the touching English prose story. All dogs follow me too! It is strange. I have one here, a young retriever called Seal, really belonging to a son of my kind neighbor, Sir Henry Russell, but who has adopted me. I suppose when he comes to be old enough to go a-shooting that he will discover that I am no sportswoman, but at present he sticks to my skirts (he's just like a shaggy young bear) and won't go away. I like him, and he knows it. Fanchon holds him in high scorn, and he returns the compliment. Thanks for the bog-myrtle; it is still fragrant; but of all fragrance that of the night-scented orchis you mention is most exquisite. The wild hyacinth, dear Mrs. Hoare, differs much from the flower which we call the harebell in England: a small campanula, bearing two or three exquisite, thin, bell-like papery flowers (you can hear them rustle when shaken) on a very thin and fragile stalk, growing among wild thyme, and under heather, in the month of August. There is a white variety cultivated in gardens, but no pink one. I have heard both the harebell and the wild hyacinth called blue-bells. As to botany, my knowledge is very scanty; I, like you, love flowers for their beauty and their odor. Adieu, dear friend. Ever very gratefully and faithfully yours,

M. R. MITFORD.

To MRS. HOARE, *Monkstown, Ireland.*

Swallowfield, Autumn, 1852.

Your admiration of Jane Austen is so far from being a heresy, that I never met any high literary people in my life who did not prefer her to any female prose writer. The only dissent I ever heard was from one very clever man, who stood up for the "Simple Story" as still finer; but then that was only one novel, and only the first half of that.   For my own part, I delight in her, and really can not read the present race of novel-writers—although my old friend Mrs. Trollope, in spite of her terrible coarseness, has certainly done two or three marvelously clever things.   She was brought up within three miles of this house, being the daughter of a former vicar of Heckfield, and is, in spite of her works, a most elegant and agreeable woman.   I have known her these fifty years; she must be turned of seventy, and is wonderful for energy of mind and body.   Her story is very curious; put me in mind to tell it you.   She used to be such a Radical that her house in London was a perfect emporium of escaped state criminals.   I remember asking her at one of her parties how many of her guests would have been shot or guillotined if they had remained in their own country.

Yes, I ought to have liked Shelley better.   But I have a love of clearness—a perfect hatred of all that is vague and obscure—and I still think, with the grand exception of the "Cenci," and of a few of the shorter poems, that there was rather the making of a great poet, if he had been spared, than the actual accomplishment of any great work.   It was an immense promise.

I have been hearing a most curious detail of the man who perpetrated the forgery of the Shelley letters.   My friend Mr. Bennett, besides being a very pleasing poet, is an eminent jeweler and watchmaker.   Two or three years ago a person calling himself a natural son of Lord Byron presented himself at his shop, and desired to have a locket constructed for three curls, cut, he said, from his father's head at different ages (I dare say the curls were hair forgeries—cut from wigs). He gave much trouble about this locket, and called often, and at last invited Mr. Bennett to accompany him home to inspect a collection of drawings, portraits, and MSS. of various sorts, which he had been many years getting together for the purpose of a grand illustrated life of Lord Byron. Mr. Bennett says there was a whole chest full of drawings, prints, and MSS.; portraits of all his friends; engravings of all the houses, and even the Italian towns, in which Byron had lived; above all, bundles of letters—fifty at least—of different handwritings, different ages, on various papers, with various postmarks, some well preserved, some tattered and torn. They would have deceived any body, and doubtless contained amongst them those which did deceive booksellers, publishers, autograph collectors, and autograph auctioneers. Besides this collection there was a most elegant young woman, whom he introduced as his wife—of course the negotiatrix of the forgeries. It is now thought that they were not married; but she was certainly educated at a great finishing-school at Blackheath.

The conclusion of the adventure is characteristic: he ran up a bill of from thirty to forty pounds, and was heard of no more. One curious thing in this is the way in which the old designation of "bastard" is becoming a title again, as in the days of Dunois. Half a dozen people lay claim to the honor of belonging in that way to the Emperor Napoleon—Emile de Girardin being one. This man was like enough to Lord Byron to justify the claim.

Yes, I like the "Blackwood" review. I seldom see critiques on myself—never, unless somebody sends them. Adieu, dearest Mrs. Hoare. Ever faithfully yours,

M. R. M.

To Mrs. Hoare, *Monkstown, Ireland.*

Swallowfield, Autumn, 1852.

Dearest Mrs. Hoare,—Did you see Mrs. Browning? She is gone first to Paris and then on to Italy, and is sorely afraid they will not let her in at Florence, where one wing of the "Casa Guidi" is full of their furniture. For my part, I think the danger is rather that they may put her in prison and keep her there. She is suffering from a return of cough, and so is Mrs. Southey. Indeed, with us the autumn has been so unusually cold that the oldest people hardly remember so many leaves gone at this time of year—more than in December last year. An odd circumstance is that the oak-leaves this year are falling as soon as those of the elm. Nothing can exceed our verdure always. The grass of Swallowfield Park and of Strathfieldsaye is like an emerald in any season. I once lived for a twelvemonth on the exquisite coast of the south of England, on the borders of Dorset and Devonshire, and have been by the sea in Northumberland, the Isle of Wight, and other parts. I feel its grandeur, but I like inland scenery better, especially forest scenery. My passion is trees, and our lanes and woodland commons are unrivaled.

Mr. Thompson, one of the principal American artists, spent a day here last month, and has promised me a portrait of Louis Napoleon—a gift indeed! I have four memoirs of him, each with a print, and all his works. What a man he is! The only really great man now living, or who has lived (except, perhaps, Sir Robert) since the glorious Emperor. I have just parted from a young man, high Tory, who was with a Legitimist family making the tour of the south of France at the same time with the prince. They stood, in dead silence, in a garden in Montpelier to witness his entrance; but he says that the reality of his popularity can no more be questioned than the splendor of his genius. Certainly the Bordeaux speech is magnificent. I have read Victor Hugo's book. It is impossible that the odious falsehoods and the want of logic could have been surpassed.

This is half a dozen letters in one. Yours ever,

M. R. M.

TO THE AUTHORESS OF "OUR VILLAGE."

The single eye; the daughter of the light,
  Well pleased to recognize in lowliest shade
  Each glimmer of its parent ray, and made,
By daily draughts of brightness, inly bright;
The style severe, yet graceful, trained aright
  To classic depths of clearness and repaid
  By thanks and honor from the wise and staid;
By pleasant skill to blame and yet delight,
  And hold communion with the eloquent throng
  Of those who shaped and toned our speech and song;
All these are yours. The same examples here
You in rich woodland, me on breezy moor,
  With kindred aims the same sweet paths along,
To knit in loving knowledge rich and poor.

CHARLES KINGSLEY.

Eversley, Oct. 25, 1852.

To the REV. WILLIAM HARNESS, *Kensington Gore.*

Swallowfield, Nov. 10, 1852.

Thank you a thousand times, dear friend, for your most kind and tempting invitation; but although much better, I can not help feeling that a very little exertion and excitement would overset me.

I have heard often from M—— S—— lately, and I know no part of her letters that gave me greater pleasure than when, speaking of Windsor Castle, she said, " and with seven children, there is at least plenty of noise;" it sounded quite homely and hearty, for a palace.

The people are crazy about "Uncle Tom's Cabin." I read about a hundred pages, and found the book so painful, that I put it down, and certainly am not likely to take it up again. It is one-sided, exaggerated, false—with some cleverness, but of a very disagreeable kind. Nevertheless, if there had been the great literary merit they talk of I think I should have gone on. My belief is, that the *de*-merits of the book have more to do with its popularity than any sort of excellence ; the cant about slavery being a good cry—such as we English love to get up on certain subjects—against the Emperors, for instance, uncle and nephew, or against the Pope. After all, how little has this sort of immediate popularity to do with lasting reputation ! Look at the great novelists of the day, Dickens and Thackeray (although it is some injustice to Thackeray to class them together, for he can write good English when he chooses, and produce a striking and consistent character) ; but look at their books, so thoroughly false and unhealthy in different ways ; Thackeray's so world-stained and so cynical, Dickens's so meretricious in sentiment and so full of caricature. Compare them with Scott and Miss Austen, and then say if they can live. Neither of them can produce an intelligent, right - minded, straightforward woman, such as one sees every day : and a love-story from Thackeray could hardly fail to be an abomination.

Have you read Mr. Kingsley's "Phaeton ?" A dialogue in the manner of Plato—or rather a dialogue within a dialogue. There is the usual inconclusiveness; but yet one gathers much good ; warnings not to let the love of nature degenerate into an exclusive worship, to the neglect of the Creator; and injunctions to seek the faith of the Low Church, without the narrowness. Perhaps I like this pamphlet the better because I so entirely like the author. He spent one of these wet mornings with me, and is certainly one of the most charming persons in the world. You must meet. He was so sorry to have missed you! He is not a bit like an author—only a frank, charming, genial young man. Then I have had all manner of visitors spending the day here; Bayard Taylor, the American traveler, Agnes Niven and Miss Denman. By the way, Miss Denman has the ladies' college mania! The more I hear of it, the more I dislike it.—I shall do nothing for it.—I should not, even if I did not wish to help the dear Russells with the Swallowfield schools.—The college being a device for the promotion of governesses, of whom, poor things, there are already too many.

Poor Daniel Webster! Mr. Fields wrote to me whilst the mourning guns were booming over the harbor. He says that, never since Washington, has America had such a loss, and that every body is lamenting his death, as if he were a near friend. I have had quantities of papers and letters from America, where the grief for that great man seems to have been wonderfully real, and the funeral admirable in its simplicity. I don't think any of the English papers have said that he was buried in full dress, like Napoleon—a blue coat and white cravat, waistcoat, trowsers, and gloves. Everett's speech was very fine; and so are some of the poems. They have reprinted my paper on him in almost every journal in the States. Love to all. Ever faithfully yours,   M. R. M.

To Miss Goldsmid, *Regent's Park.*

Swallowfield, Dec. 1, 1852.

How good and kind you are, dearest Miss Goldsmid, to think of me so often and to write to me so kindly, in the midst of your numerous claims. Be quite sure that no one can be more grateful for such goodness, or can sympathize more sincerely in your anxiety respecting the niece, who can hardly be called motherless, when she has such an aunt as you to supply the place of her lost parent. May she reward your cares and affections! It is a charming age, just like those days of early June (the May of the old poets) when flower and foliage, light air and bright sunbeam come upon us in the loveliest union of summer and of spring. To look upon a fresh and innocent girl at that happy age is to feel one's own heart grow younger.

Have you read Haydon's Life? The family wished me to

edit it; but I felt that it would be a most difficult task; that he would write much which must be painful to others, and much about himself which no friend could wish published. Whenever he put his own portrait into one of his pictures he always so exaggerated the points he thought good, as to turn them almost into deformities; and of course he would do the same in pen and ink. So I declined it, and Mr. Tom Taylor has done it (I am told, for I have not seen the work) much better than I could have hoped to do. He was a most brilliant talker—racy, bold, original, and vigorous; and his early pictures were full of promise; but a vanity, that amounted to self-idolatry, and a terrible carelessness, unjustifiable in many matters, degraded his mind, and even impaired his talent in art. I was always certain that his suicide proceeded from a desire to provide for his family. And, thanks to Sir Robert Peel's benevolence, it succeeded; although one of his sons has thrown up a good situation in the Custom-house, and has gone to Australia.

For my own part, I am convinced that without pains there will be no really good writing. I find the most successful writers the most careful. I am still so difficult to satisfy, that I have written a long preface (it will run, I think, to thirty or forty pages) to the dramatic works three times over, many parts far more than three times; and I can foresee that there will still be much to do when the pages go through my hands.

The success of poor Haydon's Life has induced a design to publish his letters; and as I was perhaps his most constant correspondent—the one to whom he wrote most freely—I have been hunting up his letters through five boxes, trunks, and portmanteaus, two huge hampers—baskets innumerable —and half a dozen great drawers! Imagine the job! And, dear friend, think of the emotions recalled by the letters of fifty years, from so many whom I have loved and lost!

If you know any one who wants a thoroughly good and charming young woman as a companion I can most thoroughly recommend poor Miss Haydon. She is now teaching as a daily governess at eight shillings a week! She is very accomplished and intelligent, and has learned truth and goodness from her many trials. Adieu, dearest Miss Goldsmid.

Ever most affectionately yours,   M. R. MITFORD.

O 2

To Miss Goldsmid, *Summerhill, Tonbridge.*

Swallowfield [no date, 1852].

I rejoice to hear good news of you all, dearest Miss Goldsmid; and I answer at once, lest, being just now overwhelmed with double work of correcting the sheets of one book, and writing another, I should delay too long.   You will pardon a brief and unworthy letter.

I know that you would like poor Haydon's Life; and I heartily agree with you that the home test is the true test, and that his domestic affections might have redeemed him much.   If you had known him personally, his great power of conversation and constant life of mind would have carried you away.   He was a sort of Benvenuto Cellini; or rather he was like Shakspeare's description of the Dauphin's horse —"all air and fire—the duller elements of earth and water never appeared in him."   Any thing so rapid, so brilliant, so vigorous as his talk, I have never known.   His letters give some notion of that, and I suppose they will appear soon.   I sent sixty-five—some of them very long—to Messrs. Longman, the other day, without reading them, having been nearly blinded in the search through the terrible masses of my . correspondence.   He was just as loyal to the few whom he really called friends as to his family.   You remember his sending some papers to Mrs. Browning (then Miss Barrett) to be taken care of, a few days before his death.   Well, he had painted a portrait of me, far bigger than life, and with equal excess of color, but otherwise like.   My father, however, had not praised it enough to please him.   His nice taste had found that he disliked it.   So it had been kept by the artist, and he had cut out the head.   This head was amongst the things sent to Miss Barrett.   He gave it to her, he said, because he knew she would value it.   The next day he called again in Wimpole Street, to say that he could not part with that portrait, he would only lend it to her.   This was three days before his death.   You may imagine how it touched me when I heard of it.   By the way, I find this morning that this portrait, now in the possession of his and my friend Mr. Barrett, is about to be engraved for the Tragedies.

Say every thing for me to dear Lady Goldsmid.   Ever, dearest friend, very faithfully yours,   M. R. Mitford.

To the REV. WILLIAM HARNESS, *Kensington Gore.*

Swallowfield, Dec. 24, 1852.

MY DEAR FRIEND,—Lest you should hear some imperfect or exaggerated account, it seems better that I should tell you that last Monday I had a serious accident—an overturn in dear Lady Russell's park. I was thrown, with great violence, upon the hard road. No bones are broken; and the head, I thank God, is quite untouched; but the nerves of the left side, that which is called the circular nerve round the shoulder-bone, and the principal nerves of the hip and thigh are severely bruised, so that my arm is bound to my body, and I have not the slightest power of moving except when lifted. Poor K——'s situation, and the absence of all nurses or helps of any sort in this place, adds to our evil condition. However, Sam is a host in himself; and we must do as well as we can. Dear Lady Russell is all that is kind, and Mr. May all that is skillful; though, as he is tiring eight horses a day in the sickly season, I can't expect to see much of him.

Don't come down, dear friend—at least till we get a little round. There is no danger, and the untidiness, which we can not help, would drive any body accustomed to Christianlike ways, crazy—and then drive me crazy through sympathy. The chief thing to blame was an awkward gate in the park —that beyond the bridge.

Did I tell you that Bentley is most desirous of getting me to give him another series of my "Recollections?" I have been looking at Eugene Sue's "Mystères du Peuple," a weak book, but curious, as making angels of every body *behind* a barricade, and devils of those before them; treating the reds in France just as Mrs. Stowe treats the blacks in America. It would make a good paper, to review the two works from that point of view. Adieu, dear friend. Love to all. Ever yours, M. R. M.

CHAPTER XXII.

LETTERS FOR 1853.

To the REV. HUGH PEARSON,* *Sonning.*

New Year's Day, 1853.

I THANK you, dearest Mr. Pearson, for your most kind note. I know you will come and see me when you can, just as you would any other poor old woman in similar plight, or rather sooner; because you can do me more good.

So you really like "Esmond." But I can not quarrel with one of the things that I love best in you—the faculty of finding, in every thing, all that there is to like. For my part, I thought it painful, and unpleasant, and false—I mean the love-story; and which, I suppose, is still worse in a novel, tedious and long. I demur, too, to much of the criticism. Did you ever observe how much Macaulay has studied Bolingbroke? But the modern author has the great fault of constantly drawing attention to his style. We are always thinking, How brilliant! Whereas, in reading his far greater predecessor, one never stops to exclaim and admire, the medium is so pellucid that we see straight to the thought. The words and their arrangement are so exquisite, that it seems as if no other were possible. No: I can not take pleasure in modern English novels. Luckily, we have French ones, and although Balzac be gone, we have Dumas in his place. I was pleased and surprised to find him, Dumas, in the midst of such depreciation of Casimir Delavigne (according to the old quarrel of classic and romantic), quoting those charming ballads, which I have been collecting for two or three years past, and of which not one-half are published in his Poesies. Do you know them? They are worth all Lamartine and Alfred de Vigny, and almost all of Victor Hugo.

Adieu, dear friend. I am going on very well, and am quite

* The Rev. Hugh Pearson was preferred in 1841 to the Rectory of Sonning. A kindred taste for literature attracted him to Miss Mitford, and he became one of her most valued friends.

a pattern of quietness and obedience. Always affectionately yours. All happiness to you and yours.

M. R. MITFORD.

To Mrs. JENNINGS, *Portland Place.*

Swallowfield, Jan. 3, 1853.

All that love-story in "Esmond" is detestable; and, which is still worse, the book seems to me long and tedious. A clever young man, writing to me about it from Trinity College, Cambridge, said: "I took it with me into the Theological Hall, and listened to the Professor by preference." I dare say he did. Then I demur to the criticism,—holding with Hazlitt, that Steele is worth twenty Addisons. And he underrates Bolingbroke (of course I am not speaking of his infidelity, but of his style); as a prose writer he was one of the greatest of his day.

You are quite right about the "Blithedale Romance." Hawthorne is writing another, which I hope will redeem his reputation. I had the pleasure of sending him word a month ago of a Russian translation of the "House of the Seven Gables." Mrs. Stowe, from the poorest of the poor, is become quite a millionaire, having purchased a fine house and grounds with part of her book money. She, too, is at work on another tale. I never read "Uncle Tom's Cabin," having stopped short at a hundred pages. They were so painful, so unpleasant, so exaggerated, and so sure to injure their own cause, that I had no taste for the matter. That slavery is the great difficulty of a great nation, and it must not be treated by appeals to the passions. Mr. Bentley is pressing me of all things for another series. If it please God that I recover, I suppose I must try. I knew you would come round to Louis Napoleon—the only great man since his uncle. How graciously and gratefully he does every thing and says every thing. Adieu, dear friend. I am going on well. Ever affectionately yours, M. R. MITFORD.

I send you the best poem I have seen on the death of the duke. The new duke has not yet signed his title; he still writes "Douro"—rather a good sign.

To Miss Goldsmid, *Summerhill, Tonbridge.*

Swallowfield, Jan. 4, 1853.

No; I have not yet read the " Life and Letters of Thomas
Moore." Very many years ago I used to see much of him in
a house which gathered together all that was best of the
great Whig party—Mr. Perry's, the editor and proprietor of
the " Morning Chronicle ;" a man so genial and so accomplished, that, even when Erskine and Romilly and Tierney
and Moore were present, he was the most charming talker
at his own table. I saw Mr. Moore many years afterward
at Mr. Walter's of the " Times." Such a contrast ! I am
speaking of old Mr. Walter—the shyest and awkwardest of
men—who could not bear to hear the slightest allusion to
the journal from which he derived both his fortune and his
fame. The poet had arrived with Mr. Barnes, the editor, and
put his host and his introducer into an agony by talking all
through the dinner as frankly of the " Times " as he used to
do at Mr. Perry's of the " Chronicle." It was a most amusing scene; and I think when I enlightened him upon the subject he was very glad of the mistake he had made. " They
deserve it," said he to me, " for being ashamed of what, right-
ly conducted, would be an honor." Two or three months
afterward the paper had turned completely round.

I am reading Alexandre Dumas—I mean his " Mémoires."
He is a strange, outspoken man, giving things their coarsest
names, as our authors did in the Augustan age of Queen
Anne; but the book is exceedingly amusing, and full of curious revelations. There is all the history of Marie-Stella, who
pretended to be—perhaps was—changed for Louis Philippe.
She, after marrying Lord Newborough, married, after his
death, a Baron de Sternberg, and died in Paris, leaving many
children by her first and one son by her second husband.
Now this summer I have had several letters (about my own
last work) from a Baroness de Sternberg, who dates from
Belsfield, Windermere—most likely the wife, or widow, of
this son.

I continue much as when I wrote; my arm still confined,
and no power of the lower limbs; but I think I mend a little.
Heaven bless you ! Ever gratefully yours,   M. R. M.

P.S.—I had a letter to-day from an intimate friend of old

Mr. Croker, who says that he (Croker) is reading "Moore's Life" with huge delight. According to one's knowledge of the man, I should think that, in some future volume, Mr. Croker may chance to light upon something which will lessen the enchantment he now feels; unless, indeed, Lord John should pursue in literature, as in politics, the old Whiggish policy of treating his enemies better than his friends.

To the REV. WILLIAM HARNESS, *Kensington Gore.*

Swallowfield, Jan., 1853.

MY DEAR FRIEND,—I can quite conceive your tribulation amongst Christmas-trees and enthusiastic Tennysonians. Even in my youth I always detested the noise and nonsense of Christmas parties—a noise which, in my mind, whilst pretending to be gay but really killing all honest cheerfulness, makes me melancholy; and which is not improved by the dash of German sentimentality hanging, amongst other cloying tinsel, on the branches of the Christmas-tree.

As to the adorers of Alfred Tennyson, they unluckily haunt one at all seasons. I am well used to such speeches. Mrs. Browning used to say things very like it about her own poetry. I like some of Alfred Tennyson's earlier poems; but I confess that I like them much less since all these pretended enthusiasts have made such a cry of him.

I have had a magnificent packet of portraits and autographs from America—a view of the house inhabited by Professor Longfellow, formerly Washington's head-quarters. Mr. Fields makes very light of this munificent present; but I am enchanted. What is very curious is, that the portrait of David Webster (the brother) is far more like Daniel than the one which bears the name of the great statesman. Mr. Fields says that he must know you when he returns to England.

I suppose I must look about for a garden-chair upon springs, easy and strong, that Sam may draw me about. It will not be thrown away; because, if I do my book, I shall like to write out of doors in the spring and summer, and Sam could deposit me in it, in the copse or under a tree, without danger of chill. As yet I have seen nobody except Mr. May and the Russells. How Lady Russell contrives to wade through the dirt I can't imagine, and it rains every day. *We* have had no damp; but I fear that her side of Swallowfield must feel the constant inundations. One stream overflows one day and subsides another, the flood never staying. Ours is the Whitewater, theirs is the Blackwater, which rests upon the ground.

Did I tell you that Miss Goldsmid writes me word that the Jews are now pretty sure to get into Parliament! Several circumstances have combined, especially the death of the duke and the new ministry. I forget whether you are for or against. I, for my part, think that every one has a claim to the enjoyment of civil rights, were he Hindoo or Mohammedan; and I shall be very glad that poor Sir Isaac, who has been the real worker of the movement, should live to see it accomplished. The very prospect has revived him greatly.

I had a long letter to-day from John Ruskin, who is in the Highlands with two young friends, the pre-Raphaelite painter and his brother, and his own beautiful wife. They are living in a hut on the borders of Loch Achray, playing at cottagers, as rich people like to do. His new volume of the "The Stones" is most beautiful. I am expecting Hawthorne in a week or two—his first visit out of Liverpool.

Adieu, my very dear friend. Say every thing for me to your dear people, and *be sure to send back the ballads,* with the check.* Ever most affectionately yours,

M. R. MITFORD.

To the REV. WILLIAM HARNESS, *Kensington Gore.*

Swallowfield, Feb. 25, 1853.

I rejoice to hear of you, my dear friend, although the news be not so good as I could wish. I do trust that when the thaw really comes (here it has frozen again) your cough will disappear and your voice return. For my part, about a month ago I was getting on favorably—that is to say, I could just stand upon both feet for half a minute and drag one foot after the other for a yard or two by way of walking; but the moment the cold came the helplessness returned just as bad as at first, and the pain far worse.

Don't you like the Emperor's marriage? I shall transcribe for you a part of a letter which I have just received from

---

* For the pension which Mr. H. received for her.

Mrs. Browning at Florence. She says: " I wonder if the Empress pleases you as well as the Emperor! I approve altogether—and none the less, that he has offended Austria in the mode of announcement. Every cut of the whip. on the face of Austria is an especial compliment to me, or so I feel it. Let him lead the Democracy to do its duty to the world, and use, to the utmost, his great opportunities. Mr. Cobden and the Peace Society are pleasing me infinitely just now, in making head against the immorality (that's the word) of the English press. The tone taken up toward France is immoral in the highest degree, and the invasion cry would be idiotic if it were not something worse. The Empress, I heard the other day from high authority, is charming and good at heart. She was educated at a respectable school at Bristol, and is very English—which does not prevent her shooting with pistols, leaping gates, driving four-in-hand and upsetting the carriage when the frolic requires it—as brave as a lion and as true as a dog. Her complexion is like marble, white and pale and pure—her hair light, rather sandy;—they say she powders it with gold dust for effect. But her beauty is less physical and more intellectual than is generally supposed. She is a woman of very decided opinions. I like all this, don't you? And I liked her letter to the Préfet as every body must. Ah ! if the English press were sincere in its love of liberty there would be something to say for our poor trampled-down Italy—much to say, I mean. Under my eyes is a country really oppressed—really groaning its heart out ; but those things are spoken of with measure." So far Mrs. Browning. I hear from Paris that young Alexandre Dumas (a thorough *mauvais sujet*) is one of the slanderers taken up for libel, and that Lamartine is completely ruined. Mrs. George Dering saw the other day, at Mr. Huddlestone's, a portrait of the Empress on horseback. You know, I suppose, that Mr. Huddlestone was desperately in love with her in Spain—followed her to France—was called home by his father's illness, and, after that father's death, was just about to return to Paris to lay himself and his forty thousand pounds a year at her feet, when the Emperor stepped in and carried off the prize. You have probably seen the inclosed curious instance of figures turning into a word, and that word into a prophecy, but I send it upon the chance.

I am so glad you have had your charming niece with you. Say every thing for me to all your dear people. Ever most affectionately and gratefully yours,   M. R. M.

The numbers for the election of President of France in favor of Louis Napoleon were:

For.   Against.
7119791/1119.

Look through the back of this against the candle, or the fire, or any light.

To Mrs. Hoare, *Monkstown, Ireland.*

Swallowfield, Spring, 1853.

Forgive me my silence, dearest Mrs. Hoare. Ah! if I be to write another book, as every body tells me, it must be at the expense of very long silences to those whom I value most. But my late remissness in answering your letter has arisen partly from illness, which still continues—partly from one of the most fatiguing trials which an invalid can undergo, sitting for a portrait. Mr. Bentley has set his heart upon a portrait of me, as I am, to put side by side with a little miniature which was taken when I was between three and four years old. Mr. Lucas, an excellent painter of female portraits, and one of the most charming persons in the world, has had the infinite kindness to come down here and paint me. His picture is now in the engraver's hands. As a work of art it is absolutely marvelous—literal, as a likeness, in feature and complexion, but wonderful in the expression—so like, yet so idealized that I think it shows me as I never do look, but yet as, by some strange possibility, I may have looked. I am a very cheerful person; and any vulgar artist—any artist but John Lucas—would have fallen into the trap of giving an animated look to the picture, which, in an ugly old woman, would have been hideous. The present expression—*his* expression—is thoughtful, happy, tender—as if the mind were dwelling in a pleasant frame on some dear friend. I doubt if any skill can transfer that evanescent and ideal look to the steel; the likeness of form, which is as striking as a looking-glass, the engraver will of course translate. Two hideous caricatures of me (not meant as such, for they are appended to flattering memoirs) arrived, to our great amusement, whilst my friend the artist was here. One is distinguished by a mass of coal-black hair and a cocked-up nose—my hair having been light brown before it was white, and my nose slightly aquiline.

When we meet we will talk over authors—as a general rule (of course there are exceptions) the most disappointing people in the world. My old bookseller, George Whittaker, used to say that "booksellers, next to authors, were the most stupid and ignorant persons under the sun."

Mrs. Southey (she and her husband were quite exceptions, and I believe—indeed I know—that he thought of London authors just as I do)—Mrs. Southey is still living in her old neighborhood, near Lymington, in Hampshire. We are not personally acquainted, but often interchange kind messages. That marriage was most unfortunate. His disease (softening of the brain, of which Scott and Moore died, and Buckland is dying) had declared itself between the engagement and the wedding. She consulted his brother, Dr. Southey, as to the propriety of the union, and he strongly advised it. But the disease closed gloomily round him; and his family, I fear, instead of feeling the sacrifice she had made, hardly received her with kindness. After his death, nothing could equal the dissensions among them. Mrs. Southey actually lost a hundred pounds a year by the marriage, having resigned an annuity to that amount left her by a gentleman to whom she had been engaged in her youth, and retaining only her own fortune. She is said to be an interesting and amiable person —much like her works. Mrs. Trollope is as unlike her as is possible—a lively, brilliant woman of the world, with a warm heart and cordial manner.

I hear also that your countryman, Mr. Lever, is a delightful person. We have interchanged warm messages of goodwill—each being a good deal astonished at the appreciation of the other. I used to read his works to my father, who delighted in them, and whose taste was infallible. He never would listen to any thing not excellent in its way.

We have had here nine weeks of drought and east wind; hardly a flower to be seen—no verdure in the meadows, no leaves in the hedgerows. If a poor miserable violet or primrose did make its appearance it was scentless. I have not once heard my aversion, the cuckoo, whom of course—hating him—I do hear more than any body. And in this place—so eminently the rendezvous of the swallows that it takes its name from them—not a swallow has yet appeared. The only time that I have heard the nightingale I owe the pleasure to you, dearest Mrs. Hoare—for I drove, the one mild day we have had (that on which I received your last charming letter), to a wood where I used to find the wood sorrel in beds. Only two blossoms of that could be found; but a whole chorus of nightingales saluted me the moment I drove into the wood. I have not heard one since. Yesterday the wind changed, and the rain (after nine weeks without a shower) is coming gently down—to the great discomfiture of Professor Airy, who predicted to Mr. Lucas, a few days ago, five weeks more of east wind. It has lasted too long for me already. I can hardly rise from my chair; and, if I contrive to crawl down stairs, am forced to be lifted up again—I, two years ago the most active woman in Berkshire! Ah! we are smitten in our vanities! The power of walking was the only power I ever remember to have been proud of. I may get a little better—be able, perhaps, to drag myself into my low pony phaeton, instead of being placed in it: but the real power is, I fear, gone beyond recall. Well I must be thankful for what I have left—the genuine love of nature and of books, and kind and dear friends, new and old, whom my heart springs forth to meet, as if that heart were Irish. I have felt this blessing, of being able to respond to new friendships very strongly lately; for I have lost many old and valued connections during this trying spring. It is a consolation to have such persons as you, dear Mrs. Hoare, to replace those whom Providence calls to a better world. I thank God far more earnestly for such blessings, than even for my daily bread—for friendship is the bread of the heart.

How entirely I agree with you about Molière! Surely he is almost as much the greatest writer of France as Shakspeare of England. One of their writers calls him "*Le sublime Molière;*" and it is true. Ever yours, · M. R. Mitford.

To Mrs. Hoare, *Monkstown, Ireland.*

Swallowfield, Spring, 1853.

I do, indeed, adopt you, dearest Mrs. Hoare, as " a friend upon paper "—a true and dear friend! My best and most congenial habits of association and intercourse have so begun; and I do not think that I have ever lost one, who has so taken to me and to whom I have so taken. As to differences of opinion — why the first condition of social intercourse seems to me to be, to agree to differ. I am an old woman, and have always had friends of all parties; and really I hardly know which may count the greater number of gifted and excellent persons. For my own part, I am of no extreme—just midway between dear Mrs. Browning, who is a furious Radical, and dear Mrs. Jennings, who is an equally furious Tory. We have twenty subjects of dispute, at the very least, to which if conversation flags, we can resort ding-dong. But I have a notion that party disputes in Ireland are much more inveterate than in England; as, indeed, they have lasted for centuries, and have all the elements of different religions, as well as different races, to promote the discord.

Thank you for the capital sketch (your own—it is an amplification of the Castle Rackrent scenes, which Lever also paints so well), and for Callanan's poems. What a beautiful wild country that Lodge of yours is in! Ah! I know how flowers get local names. I was told the other day that the delicate campanula, which we call the *hare*bell, ought to be *hair*bell, from the little fibrous membrane which does give a hairy aspect to its dry, graceful, pendulous flowers. For my part I accept the common names of flowers, and abjure, above all things, the pedantry of being over-right. I thought you might have a *pink* variety in a soil and climate different from ours and more favorable to vegetation. Our harebell belongs to turfy, sandy commons — the lovely commons which, I am sorry to say, are fast disappearing in our country.

Did I tell you that I am just now almost crippled with rheumatism in knees and ankles, which not only lames me completely, but keeps me prisoner. I live quite alone, having no relations—almost literally none, except a few distant relations too grand to claim. Many kind friends I have—some of them persons of note in literature; but I think I prefer those who love letters without actually following the trade of authorship—the intelligent audience to the actors on the stage. Adieu, dear friend! Ever faithfully yours,

M. R. MITFORD.

ON BEING ASKED IF MISS MITFORD WERE NOT OLD.

Ye would not ask it of the sun, who shines upon us daily;
Or of the fleecy painted clouds, that float above us gayly ;
Or of the spring-returning flowers, or the dew their petals lading;
Or the heaven-besprinkling stars, when now their gold is fading ;
Or of the crested billows, when upon the shore they're casting
Their flashing sprays of diamond ; for ye know them everlasting,
Till their Ruler's might shall gather them within His wondrous holding,
For which we look half-fearfully, frail creatures of His moulding.
The beautiful is never old ; our minds are still extending,
And new emotions in the soul are with each moment blending.
And so her spirit seems to me an ever-rising mountain,
Upon whose glorious side still plays that famed Castilian fountain:
Or as an oak, whose green boughs spread and throw luxuriantly
A shelter o'er small birds of song, scarce worthy there to be ;
But verdure rests upon her leaves—they dread no frosts decaying—
Her charm upon the landscape cast will ever there be staying.
As mid her own dear village haunts my gauntlet down I'm flinging,
The very birds that flutter round are blythe, my measure singing.
She is not old! the spirit's youth will but to heaven be winging.

You will think me as vain as all the authors of London
put together for sending you these verses; but, in truth, I receive too many commendatory poems (as the old dramatists
used to call them, when printed at the head of their works)
not to know and feel how utterly worthless they are, either
as evidences of reputation or for their own sake. But these
lines struck both Mr. Lucas and myself as exceedingly beautiful. They are written by a young girl, almost self-educated, to whom I have lent books and given the best advice
I could—a very charming person.

To MRS. HOARE, *Monkstown, Ireland.*

Swallowfield, 1853.

I suspect, dearest Mrs. Hoare, that the general run of country society in Ireland is inferior to ours, and that one cause
of your authorial hero-worship is a love of books. Now here
every body has a good library and subscribes to two or three
in town or country; has people from London two or three
times a week; and talks of literature with as much readiness
as writers do. Whilst, in general, they—the country gentry,
members of Parliament, magistrates, landed proprietors, retired merchants, London bankers, baronets, lords, the upper
clergy, and the womankind belonging to these personages,

which forms the fair average of the sixty or seventy families who visit me—are agreeable, simple, unaffected and unpretending. We have no exclusive classes. Whig and Tory meet, and agree to differ—or, rather, never think about it. And, except a few Puseyite curates and·elderly young ladies, their admirers and followers, there really is no such thing as pretension or exclusiveness to be found. Being within fifty miles of London perhaps makes some difference; and, for my own especial part, I know more people, or rather receive more visitors, from the great metropolis than from my own neighborhood. But I believe that Ireland has been for so many years broken into different races, different religions, and castes of various kinds, that there is less of the fusion of the alloy, which is necessary to render even gold ductile and malleable, than in any other part of the United Kingdom. Then with us—let me say this for the higher classes of English people —where there is talent and character, without vulgar finery or vulgar pretension — above all, without tuft-hunting—I have never found, either in town or country, that the absence of wealth had any·other effect than to add to the attention and kindness shown to their visitors. A little of this may, in my case, be attributed to my going out very rarely, and never as a *lion*—no, never!—I had not time and I had not inclination. So friendships have been formed as tastes suited; sometimes with those much richer; sometimes with those much poorer ; sometimes with persons of rank ; sometimes with tradesmen ;—and I never, either in my own case or in that of others, saw the slightest distinction of caste in any one whom I liked well enough to go visit, or (as is always the case now, and has been very long most frequent with me) to invite. All this seems terribly egotistical.

Do get the volume of the " Readable Library," containing the works, or selections from the works, of Edgar Poe. The pieces most praised are "The Raven" and "The Maelstrom;" those that I prefer are "The Bells" (finer than Schiller's " Song of the Bells ") and some wonderful tales upon circumstantial evidence. God bless you, my dear friend! Ever most faithfully yours,   M. R. MITFORD.

To MISS GOLDSMID, *Summerhill, Tonbridge.*

Swallowfield, June, 1853.

I shall, indeed, rejoice to meet you at Whiteknights on Thursday, dearest Miss Goldsmid, and earnestly trust that the weather may be favorable. Here, we have gentle showers to-day—not impeding the mowers in an opposite meadow,—only enough to freshen the perfume of an exquisite, old-fashioned rose-tree, which I have been so lucky as to find in this true cottage garden, and which possesses all the fragrance that these new roses, with all their beauty, are pretty sure to want.

From many quarters I have heard of Herr Devrient—all speaking just as you do. He must be a great actor. John Kemble is the only satisfactory Hamlet I ever saw—owing much to personal grace and beauty—something to a natural melancholy, or rather pensiveness of manner—much, of course, to consummate art. But this is to talk of.

I have only one floating engagement, which I trust will not fall in the way of a meeting, from which I derive so much pleasure even in anticipation. That engagement is in itself interesting. Do you remember, dear Miss Goldsmid, in Gibbon's posthumous works, edited by Lord Sheffield, a very striking letter written by his daughter, Maria Holroyd, to the great historian, with an account of the massacre of the Carmelites, and dated 1792? Well, the writer of that letter (now Lady Stanley, of Alderley, and still as vigorous in mind and body as she was sixty years ago) is coming to see me on some speedy day not yet fixed, and one can hardly postpone or alter the time named by a lady of eighty-two, who comes twenty-four miles for an interview of two hours. But the stars will be propitious, and the two pleasures will not jostle.

Poor Dr. Mainzer! or rather his poor wife! For one so generous and unselfish must be gone to a happier world. Ever, dear Miss Goldsmid, most affectionately yours,

M. R. MITFORD.

To Miss Goldsmid, *Whiteknights.*

Swallowfield, June, 1853. Tuesday afternoon.

Sorry as I am to have missed you, I am yet glad that you should have seen Whiteknights this year in its flowery beauty, and that you should have shown it to Miss Toller—the most interesting of American women, and one whom I should so much like to have met and known. Some day, perhaps, that pleasure may yet happen—I may grow stronger—at least so I will hope. I do all I can to become so by sitting out of doors, to have as much as possible of the summer air, which is, Mr. May says, the best tonic. A very pleasant seat it is, at the corner of my little dwelling, under a great acacia-tree, now loaded with snowy tassels waving like the green leaves, and wafting their rich perfume with every motion. Underneath is a syringa-bush, also in full flower—the English orange-tree, so charming in the open air; and on the table pinks and roses. I quite lament when this showery weather prevents my being transported to that shady seat, or sends me in before my time.

I have a real passion for sweet scents, and like even perfumes, when I can not get flowers. I suppose it is to this love of flowers that I owe a singular visitor that was found in my room last night. As K—— was putting me to bed, she broke forth in a series of exclamations, all of which ended in a desire that I would look in the candlestick. At first I saw nothing but a dull-looking caterpillar, till the creature moved, and then came a tiny reflection of green light. It was a glowworm. I could not go to look after it, bright star of the earth as it is! There were two jars of pinks and roses from the garden, and there had been one of wild honeysuckle from the lane. Of course it must have entered with the flowers. We extinguished the light, and Sam deposited the candlestick on the little plot of grass before the door, and in ten minutes it had crawled out upon the grass. I hope it will live out its little life in comfort. Was it not a singular circumstance?

So you do not go into Kent? Ah! I can not help hoping that we may meet this year. Adieu, dearest Miss Goldsmid.

Ever faithfully yours,   M. R. M.

Did you know Grace Aguilar? I am reading her last vol-

ume of tales. How affecting they are! And how healthy
and true is the pathos—springing, as it does, from our best
affections—from generosity, from self-sacrifice, and sometimes from a gush of joy. She was a great loss to female
literature, and must have been a charming and admirable
person.

To Mrs. Hoare, *Monkstown, Ireland.*

Swallowfield, Autumn, 1853.

It is not because Mr. —— is a Tractarian, dearest Mrs.
Hoare, that Mrs. —— dislikes him, but because she considers
him (truly enough, I think), as a mere smooth versifier, without an atom of poetry in him. In these days there are thousands such:

> " I trust we have within our realm,
>   Five hundred good as he "

would be an under-estimate of our present affluence of versi-
fiers of that calibre. Of course Mrs. —— likes him none the
better for remaining a Puseyite; because all the honest and
earnest and really clever men of that school go immediately
to Rome; Puseyism being nothing more nor less than pope-
ry in black and white—without the poetry, without the
painting, without the music, without the architecture—without the exquisite beauty which wins the imagination in the
ancient faith. For my own part, I hold too firmly to the
true Protestant doctrine (which so many Protestants forget)
of freedom of thought—complete liberty of conscience—for
others as well as myself—ever to become a Roman Catholic;
but I have many friends of that persuasion. My favorite
young friend is a Catholic convert, and I can quite understand the process: what I do not understand is the claiming
for the Church of England all that is repudiated in the
Church of Rome. In Reading we have a clergyman who,
whenever he can, gets around him seven assistants, and prac-
tices all the forms and ceremonies of the mass, without any
of the prestige; and every now and then one meets in society bilious-looking young men, with coats as long as my gown,
doucereux, mielleux, and wanting nothing of being real Jesuits
but the instruction and the knowledge of human nature by
which that society is commonly distinguished. The Angli-
cans, as they call themselves, have commonly a large female

following; and, indeed, of nothing is one more ashamed than
the way in which single women, old and young, run after
curates.   Living within thirty miles of Oxford, and the sons
of all one's acquaintances belonging to that university, I
have of course seen much of them, and have observed that,
from Dr. Newman downward, all men of any intellect have
either quietly drawn back from their peculiar tenets or have
gone over to the Roman Catholic Church.   Newman's last
book, "Lectures to the Brothers of the Oratory," is a capital piece of writing, better, because less recondite and more
popular, than those admirably written "Tracts for the
Times," in which we always recognized his masterhand.
Of course I see the fallacies, the onesidedness, and the soph-
istry; but as mere writing—to read as a high intellectual
treat, as one reads "Junius" or "Les Lettres Provinciales"
—I know nothing finer, especially the travestie of an Exeter
Hall speech put into the mouth of a Russian general, where
"Blackstone's Commentaries" is substituted for "Dens' The-
ology."

I suspect that you, my friend, from your Irish training,
will be a little shocked at my allowing to Roman Catholics
exactly the same freedom of conscience which I claim for myself; and I can understand that also—not merely because you
have been trained, in an antagonism of sects, to dwell upon
differences amongst Christians, whilst I have looked chiefly
to the great accordances; but because, with us, Roman
Catholics are almost universally persons of ancient family
and very high breeding, accustomed to a certain high tone
of manners and morals—as if, in days of persecution, it was
needful for them to be better than their neighbors.   You
can hardly imagine how finely this tells in a great north
country house, for example, with the chapel and the chaplain, and the regularity of the family worship—so apart from
ostentation, that it is, as much as it can be, concealed from
Protestant guests.   You, on the other hand, see none but
the least cultivated and the poorest; and, I suppose, as a
rule, that the Irish Catholic priest is very inferior to the accomplished men, trained at Prior Park or Ascot and then
sent to a foreign college, whom we see in England; although, here and there, Banim and Gerald Griffin have given
magnificent pictures of pastoral devotedness and simplicity.

God grant the day may come in which good men of all shades of doctrine may command the love and respect of all!

As a rule, Puseyism is a mere transition state for the many fine intellects who have passed through it. Dr. Pusey himself appears to me a very ordinary man. The great light was Newman. I do not know him, and probably never shall; but I know one trait of his character whilst still at Oxford which struck me much. It happened that a distant connection of my mother's, the eldest son of a chaplain in the navy, was seized with a violent fancy to go to Oxford. He was a plodding lad of Greek and metres—with singular good conduct, but no shining talents—likely to get on by classi-cal knowledge as a tutor or professor. There was a large family, and little money; and his father told him at once, "Frank, I can not afford the necessary allowance." "Just give me a little to begin with, father," returned Frank, "and I will get on as my betters have done before me, by teach-ing others, while learning myself." His schoolmaster being sure that he could and would do this, Frank was sent to Ox-ford, taking, amongst other recommendations, letters from me, in which I openly told this design. One of my letters was to an old friend of Mr. Newman's, to whom he showed it; and, when next I saw Frank, he told me—somewhat to my alarm (for it was in the very height of the controversy) —that he owed to me the kind notice of that great scholar. "I breakfast with him once a week," quoth Frank, "and he gives me the best advice possible." "What about?" I in-quired. "Every thing," returned Frank—"the classics, history, mathematics, general literature. He thinks me in danger of overworking myself at Greek"—he, such a schol-ar!—"and tells me to diversify my reading, to take exer-cise, and to get as much practical knowledge and cheerful society as I can. He questioned me about Shakspeare's poetry, and the prose writers after Lord Bacon. In short, he talks to me of every sort of subject, except what is called Tractarianism, and that he has never mentioned."

Now this seemed to me most honorable. Here were a mind and heart plastic in his hand to mould as he liked; but doubtless he saw that it would have been bad for the poor boy's prospects, and abstained. The end has been, that the lad became Low Church, and would have done well as a tutor, only he fell in love with a girl of some small fortune, and was, when I last heard of him, married on a curacy; but with so much scholarship and so high a degree and so good a character as will insure him private pupils if he wants them. Was not this very honorable in Dr. Newman?

I have just been reading another volume of Poe, with additional tales—very painful. Mr. Fields says he arrived at Boston to give a lecture so drunk that they got him to bed. Before evening he got drunk again, and requested to read.a poem instead of giving a lecture, as he had forgotten to bring the lecture with him. The permission was given of course, and the poem turned out to be "The Raven." That night he told Mr. Fields that "there was yet no drama—Shakspeare was nothing; but there should be one if he lived. He had it all in his head."

Of course you know his story—how he died of delirium tremens, in the prime of life, after throwing away more opportunities than ever man had before. His countrymen were most generous and kind to him. It is a terrible contrast, in that point of view, to the story of Gerald Griffin and Chatterton, and doubtless many other men of genius in England.

How long the above has been written, dearest Mrs. Hoare, I can not tell. Between ill health, an overwhelming correspondence, and an incredible number of visitors, my best and oldest friends accept me upon the condition of uncertainty as to letter-writing; but, if I be forgetful as to epistolary debts, I am not, I assure you, forgetful of friends or neglectful of friendship. Latterly I have been so much engaged, for one still so weak, that that would in itself be an excuse. But there are many things that I have to talk to you about when I have time. Ever faithfully yours, M. R. Mitford.

I feel very much the pressure of the work that I have undertaken—the long tale. I never write any thing without going over it three times; and the mere act of writing—the position—when it comes to four or five hours of continuous work, is very trying indeed. One can hardly bear the pain. But the booksellers, who have behaved exceedingly well in every way, are so unwilling to give up the story, that I feel bound to go on with it.

"Hypatia,"—I have been reading that. It is full of vigor

and power. Mr. Kingsley takes your old friends Cyril and
Augustine down from their pedestals, and lowers them into
human beings. He animates that whole mob of Alexandria
—animates and individualizes Greek and Roman, Egyptian,
Goth, and Jew. He puts life into the very sands of the desert. But there are some strange things, and I half dread
what the bishops may say, though he is so excellent as a
parish priest, and so much beloved in his parish, that I hope
they will take his bits of truth, and his vivid description of
scenes which doubtless occurred, as parts of a picture ; they
will if they have sense. It is certainly a work of great power.

To Miss Goldsmid.

Swallowfield, Winter of 1853.

If you have time for reading, do look at De Quincey's Autobiography, now republished in England. The truth and
life of those Lake sketches is something wonderful. Of course
the blind worshipers of Wordsworth quarrel with him ; but
there is quite enough left to praise and admire in the bard of
" The Excursion," after accepting Mr. De Quincey's portrait.
Two or three of my friends have visited Mr. De Quincey at
Lasswade, where he now lives (did Miss Caroline see him
when with poor Dr. Mainzer ?), and they all say that it is the
strangest mixture, of an appearance so neglected that he looks
like an old beggar, of manners so perfect that they would do
honor to a prince, and of conversation unapproached for brilliancy. He confessed to one of my friends, who saw him on
a bad day, that he could only quiet his nerves by a semi-in-
toxication with opium—so that he has not left it off. His
daughter Margaret, my correspondent, whose letters are as
charming as her father's books, is going to be married to a
young Scotchman who has bought land in Tipperary ; a venture ; but a genial young couple may, I think, find and make
friends amongst the Irish. I should not be afraid, should
you ? Adieu, dear friend. Ever most gratefully yours,

M. R. Mitford.

To Mrs. Browning, *Florence.*

Swallowfield, Nov. 10, 1853.

My very dear Friend,—I can not enough thank you for
your most affectionate letter. I am still just as I was ; but I

have no sort of faith either in homœopathy or mesmerism. Indeed my friend, Dr. Spencer Hall, the great mesmerist, gave
up the one, which had nearly killed him, and has taken to the
other, which, I suppose, does less harm to the physician if not
to the patient ; so that I have got to believe them grown-up
toys, the skipping-ropes and battledores of elderly people ; and I now cling obstinately enough to the quiet rational
ways of established practitioners. My present ailment is rheumatism, which has been long coming on—" a highly rheumatic condition," to use the medical phrase, upon which that terrible overturn, just at the beginning of a wet winter, fell like a
spark among gunpowder. I don't think there is the slightest chance of any improvement, and must be content with
what remains to me—the use of my intellect, and to a certain extent of my right hand, a comfortable cottage, excellent servants, kind neighbors, and most dear friends. And
this is much. We must not forget, in thinking of my case,
that for above thirty years I had perpetual anxieties to encounter—my parents to support and for a long time to nurse
—and generally an amount of labor and of worry and of care
of every sort, such as has seldom fallen to the lot of woman.
I had not time to take care of myself, or of my health ; and
that, beyond a doubt, laid the foundation of my complaints.
When I see you in the summer, my own beloved friend, if it
please God to spare me so long, you will perhaps find me sitting under my acacia-tree ; and I hope to get a garden chair
and be wheeled about in the open air. It is a great thing to
have a man like Sam, at once so strong and so gentle, who
can bear me along by putting his hands under my arms, and
even lift me down stairs step by step—only that that is so
painful a process that I avoid it whenever I can, and see as
few strangers or mere acquaintances as possible.

I have had a most interesting account of Miss Brontè and
a charming letter from her. She is a little, quiet, gentle
person ; the upper part of the face good, but something
amiss in the formation of the mouth ; her conversation full
of power and charm. She lives with her father—the only
child remaining out of six—in a most secluded Yorkshire
village amongst the moors. He is a gentlemanly and amiable man. I suppose the living is very small, for Miss Brontè
went to France for two years ; and the *debùt* of Lucy Stowe

(*vide* " Villette ") in Brussels was literally her own. She also speaks to me of coming to London without necessity, as a thing hardly warrantable ; and seems to me exceedingly un-affected and unspoiled. I like both " Shirley " and " Vil-lette."

Remember me to your dear Robert and Mrs. Trollope. Ever most affectionately yours,   M. R. MITFORD.

CHAPTER XXIII.

LETTERS FOR 1854-5.

To the REV. WILLIAM HARNESS, *Kensington Gore.*

Swallowfield, March 26, 1854.

MY DEAR FRIEND,—I do indeed rejoice to hear that that sweet child is recovering. Poor Mr. and Mrs. Hope ! What a winter of anxiety this must have been to them !

Heartily glad shall I be to see you. For half an hour, or perhaps a whole one, you will find the old good spirits ; but strength is quite gone ; and any fatigue brings a tenfold ac-cession of the terrible neuralgic pain over the chest and un-der the arms. Between three and four, previous to the dreadful operation of getting up, is my best time. K—— and Sam will tell you all about me. By-the-by, be so good as to bring the will. I wish to leave that five hundred pounds to them, feeling sure, that, even were K—— to die, Sam might be trusted implicitly. They have been every thing to me this winter.

Poor Talfourd ! He came to see me the Sunday he was in Reading, and we talked with the old friendship, and parted with the old cordiality. Both felt that it was a last parting, although neither dreamed which strand of the cord was so soon to give way. I am very glad to have seen him, and that our last interview should have been so affectionate. He spoke with a glowing thankfulness of your kindness, in prom-ising his son a title, and of the advantage of his being your curate. Lady Talfourd is just the woman to bear this trial well ; there is a great deal of stern stuff in her character.

" Atherton " has twice nearly killed me—once in writing —now, very lately, in correcting the proofs. The original printer having failed, they sent the whole volume in four consecutive days. Don't read the shorter stories, only "Atherton," and tell me how you like it.

Poor Lady Russell is very anxious about Sir Charles, who forms one of the expedition now at Malta. She is as faithful to me as ever. Love to dear Mary. Ever, my dear friend, most affectionately yours,   M. R. MITFORD.

To MRS. BROWNING, *Rome.*

Swallowfield, March 29, 1854.

Weaker and weaker, dearest friend, and worse and worse; and writing brings on such agony that you would not ask for it if you knew the consequences. It seems that in that overturn the spine was seriously injured. There was hope that it might have got better; but last summer destroyed all chance. This accounts for the loss of power in the limbs, and the anguish in the nerves of the back, and more especially in those over the chest and under the arms. Visitors bring on such exhaustion, and such increase of pain, that Mr. May forbids all but Lady Russell. Perhaps by the time you arrive in England I may be a little better. If so, it would be a great happiness to see you, if only for half an hour.

May God bless you, my beloved friend, and all whom you love!   M. R. MITFORD.

To JOHN LUCAS, *Esq.*

Swallowfield, April 11, 1854.

Thank you, dearest Mr. Lucas, for liking "Atherton," and, above all, for telling me so. Other people are so good as to like it also. William Harness, John Ruskin, Henry Hope, and persons of that class; so if you mistake, you err in good company. Every body detests the portrait; William Harness says that it represents "a fierce, dark, strong-minded woman." Mr. Hope says that "not only is it utterly unlike the author of 'Atherton,' and 'Our Village,' but that it was morally impossible that it should have been like her, although it might very possibly be a striking likeness of the author of 'Uncle Tom.'" This is killing two birds with one stone, after the fashion of that thrice-charming person.

I am almost confined to my bed, and so weak as to be exhausted by half an hour's conversation; but there is a chance

that, if I and my bed can be transplanted into my little sitting-room (say six weeks or two months hence), I may have
a charming garden-chair which has just been given to me,
wheeled to my bedside, and through the window.   This is,
at all events, a delightful hope.   God bless you all !   Ever
yours,   .   M. R. MITFORD.

To MRS. JENNINGS, *Portland Place.*

Swallowfield, Monday [in May, 1854].

Ah ! dearest friend ! how glad I should have been if you
could have come to see me before leaving London, and how
sad it seems that another year should pass away without my
meeting you and dear Mr. Jennings.

An avalanche of kindness has come from America, where,
as in Paris, my book has been reprinted.   Letters to me, or
for me, addressed through my friend Mr. Fields, have arrived, I think from almost every man of note in the States :
Hawthorne, Longfellow, Holmes, etc., etc.   And one lady,
Mrs. Sparks, wife of Jared Sparks, President of Harvard University, Cambridge, gravely invites me, with man-servant and
maid-servant, pony and Fanchon, to go and take up my
abode with them for two or three years ; an unlimited hospitality, which, as she could not know with how much impunity invitations may be sent to me, seems to English ears as-
tounding.   Cambridge is close to Boston, where most of the
literary men of America live ; and, if I were not such a miserable, helpless creature, really one would be tempted to go
and thank all these warm-hearted people for their extraordinary kindness.

Mr. Hawthorne has just finished another tale, which an
acquaintance, who has seen the MS., speaks of as even finer
than the works we know.   I suppose it will be printed as
soon as my friend Mr. Fields (whom I am expecting here on
Wednesday) returns to the United States.   He is a partner
in the greatest publishing house of America, and the especial
patron of Hawthorne, whom he found starving, and has made
almost affluent by his encouragement and liberality ; for the
great romancer is so nervous that he wants as much kindness of management, as much mental nursing as a sick child.
I have never known a more charming person than Mr. Fields,
quite a young man, who has been in France and Italy all the

winter to recover from the shock occasioned by the death of his young wife. He has brought me no end of memoirs, portraits, and busts of Louis Napoleon, for whom I have a passion. Mrs. Browning (a stanch Republican, who went to Paris with a bundle of letters of introduction from Mazzini) is quite as enthusiastic about him as I am; so is Mr. Fields, who has spent the last month there, only they are less frank, and pretend to be cool judges. Ah! I should just like to tell you a few stories about him which I know to be true!

It is not only "Faust" that Longfellow has made free with, but an old German poem, from which he has taken the story, much improving the catastrophe. The "Evangeline," if you remember, was taken from Goethe's "Herman and Dorothea." I am glad you like the "Golden Legend;" I do heartily, especially the Sermon on the Bell; it is so racy, and so full of spirit and of life. There are three new American poets whom you would like—Bayard Taylor, Stoddart, and Reede—young men, quite. If I should live, and recover to write another book, I shall give some specimens of these writers, although a new book of mine would have perhaps few specimens, except the quite forgotten and the quite new.

All happiness to you both! Believe me ever, dearest friends, most faithfully and affectionately yours,

M. R. MITFORD.

To MRS. JENNINGS, *Portland Place.*

Swallowfield, May 22, 1854.

DEAREST MRS. JENNINGS,—Thank you for your kindness in liking "Atherton." It has been a great comfort to me to find it so indulgently, so very warmly received. Mr. Mudie told Mr. Hurst that the demand was so great that he was obliged to have four hundred copies in circulation. I do not think the story would have been the better for being longer; and as for alterations and additions, after two editions of a work have been sold (to say nothing of those in Paris, Leipsic, and half the cities in America), they are out of the question. Katy is too young for love; and I could not have lengthened the story without letting the secret ooze out and spoiling the effect of the last scene. In all my suffering I yet took such pains with "Atherton," that every page was written three times over.

The days, or weeks, or even perhaps months (very few) that I may last, will be entirely a question of the duration of my power of receiving nourishment, and that is in His hands who knows what is best for us. I feel all your kindness, and can only send you my thanks and blessings.

I am sitting now at my open window, not high enough to see out of, but inhaling the soft summer breezes, with an exquisite jar of roses on the window-sill, and a huge sheaf of fresh-gathered meadow-sweet giving its almondy fragrance from outside; looking on blue sky and green waving trees, with a bit of road and some cottages in the distance, and K——'s little girl's merry voice calling Fanchon in the court.

Yes! the Emperor is a great and wonderful man; greater, I think, than his uncle, because he can command himself, and looks to the happiness of his people rather than to the soldier's glory. My young neighbor, Sir Charles Russell, is with his battalion (Grenadier Guards) at Aladyn. One of his letters amused me much. He said that the French soldiers passed their leisure time in catching frogs. Does not this carry us back to the days of Hogarth and Smollett? Say every thing for me to your own Robert and to Mrs. Trollope. Ever, my most beloved friend, your affectionate,　　M. R. MITFORD.

To the REV. HUGH PEARSON, *Sonning.*

Swallowfield, July 22, 1854.

MY VERY DEAR FRIEND,—Will you forgive my inconsistency if I beg you to defer the administration of the sacrament till we have met again? The thought agitates me more than I can express, especially as the time approaches. I am quite sure that it would prevent my getting any rest for at least two nights, and do me more harm physically than any one not acquainted with my nervous temperament could possibly imagine. In great part this is the fault of the body; but it can hardly be the desirable state of mind for the reception of that holy ordinance.

Be sure, dearest friend, that I do not fail in meditation, such as I can give, and prayer. It is my own unworthiness and want of an entire faith that troubles me.

But I am a good deal revived by sitting at the open window, in this sweet summer air, looking at the green trees and the blue sky, and thinking of His goodness who made this lovely world. And I doubt if it be even right to give my-self so great a shake as I know would be the result of any agitation or emotion.

Let me have one line, and forgive my hesitation. I know what the physical effect of emotion, or even the fear of emo-tion, is upon me. It was merely the visit of a dear friend—a mere pleasurable excitement—which brought on the strug-gle for breath and the consequent exhaustion. Ever most affectionately yours,   M. R. MITFORD.

To the REV. WILLIAM HARNESS, *Kensington Gore.*

Swallowfield, Aug. 25, 1854.

MY VERY DEAR FRIEND,—I received on Monday, with Sam and my dear old friend, Mrs. C. Stephens, sister of Sir W. P. Wood, the sacrament at Mr. Pearson's hands. I wish you had been here also. I think you will approve of my having done so, not merely as a Christian, however unworthy, but as adhering to the Church of England, which, with all its faults, is the most large and liberal of the many English sects. For my own part, I fully believe that this long visitation has been the greatest mercy of the gracious God, who has been very good to me all through life. I firmly believe that it was sent to draw me to Him. May He give me grace not to throw away the opportunity ! I have twice gone through the Gos-pels, and once through the whole of the New Testament, since we met ; and I *believe* with my whole mind and heart that di-vine history. Still, dearest friend, I find it difficult to real-ize ; and I am troubled in prayer with wandering thoughts. Pray that He may quicken my faith and deepen my repent-ance. I feel fully my own unworthiness, and that my hope must be in His mercy. Pray for me, dear friend !

You would love Hugh Pearson. I have no words to speak of his piety, his tenderness, and his charity. He is just a younger Dr. Arnold, fully worthy to be your friend.

I have had the kindest possible letter from Dean Milman ; and I do not think there is an authoress of name who has not sent me messages full of the kindest interest. It is one of the highest mercies by which this visitation has been softened, that I can still give my thoughts and time and love and sym-pathy, not merely to dear friends, but to books and flowers, and the common doings of this work-a-day world.

I hope Miss Hope continues well, and her father and mother happy, and that you are enjoying yourself. When do you return to the Deepdene? Ever affectionately yours,

M. R. MITFORD.

To MRS. BROWNING, *Florence.*

Swallowfield, Aug. 28, 1854.

I am still spared, my beloved friend, still lingering here, wasted to skin and bone, and in such a state that a week ago my beloved friend, Hugh Pearson, took leave of me for three weeks, hoping, but evidently not expecting, that we should meet again here below. I wish you knew Mr. Pearson. He is a man as beloved as any I have ever known—of exquisite taste and the keenest sympathy. I went to him for spiritual comfort, being persuaded that this visitation has been sent most mercifully by the Great Father to draw me to Himself and to the Divine Mediator. May He grant me His grace that the opportunity may not be lost! But I am troubled by wandering, fluttering thoughts—an impossibility of fixing the mind in prayer. I long for a quicker, livelier, more realizing faith. Pray for me, my beloved friend.

Well! this being my state, and intellect still granted, and actual writing less difficult (the pen being filled with ink and my paper fixed for me) than it often has been, I have often thought that I would write one more letter, such as I used to write. Sometimes persons in my state linger longer than might be expected; and I should like to hear that you, and especially that your sweet boy, has not suffered from the heats of Florence during this splendid harvest, which has been tryingly hot in England—although never, for crops or for weather, has been known such plenty so gathered in—a national mercy of the most blessed kind, for the poor suffered grievously last winter from high prices. Now either bread must be cheaper or wages higher, perhaps both. Tell me that you are all well, and that your darling has regained his roundness and his roses.

I have had bad news about the poor Talfourds. About a month ago a Reading solicitor, who had been long living much above his income, ran away with between twenty thousand and thirty thousand pounds belonging to various persons—amongst the rest with four thousand pounds of

Lady Talfourd's, forming a considerable part of what the judge had saved. Is it not strange that since the poor judge's death not one copy of his works has been sold? But we all know how soon the world forgets.

Mr. Tom Taylor is re-appointed Secretary to the Board of Health, with a salary of one thousand pounds a year. I suppose there is not in English literature a young man so truly admirable in mind and in conduct. Dear Mr. John Ruskin was, when I last heard from him, at Geneva, with his parents, sending me every thing that he could imagine to help or amuse me. His last gift was a French volume, "Scenes et Proverbes, par Octave Feuillet." Do you know it? "La Clef d'Or" is very pretty. Farewell, well-beloved friend, farewell! May Heaven bless you, and all whom you love!

M. R. MITFORD.

My young neighbor Sir Charles Russell is with his battalion of the Guards at Varna. His account of the mismanagement of our troops is fearful. In all matters of administration the French are generations before us. There is nothing but sickness, and neither medicines nor surgeons.

To the REV. WILLIAM HARNESS, *Blaney Castle, Ireland.*

Swallowfield, Sept. 4, 1854.

MY VERY DEAR FRIEND,—I have always believed with a calm conviction in that divine history and that divine mission; but I used to worry myself about the manner of it. Now I am reading the Gospels for the third time within two or three months, and accepting the whole of the holy mystery as I find it. Mystery there must be; and it is wiser to take humbly the relation of eye-witnesses than to seek to reconcile what we can not comprehend by our own feeble intelligence. But still it is a calm conviction—quite without the lively and vivifying illumination which I hear people talk of—and greatly troubled by wandering thoughts. However, dear Mr. Pearson (who is just such another as yourself) did not seem to mind that; and I throw myself humbly, hopingly, fearingly, on the mercy of God.

I wish you were sitting close to me at this moment, that we might talk over your plans. . . . Swallowfield churchyard, the plain tablet, and the walking funeral have only one objection—that my father and mother lie in Shenfield

church, and that there is room left above them for me.   But
I greatly dislike the place where the vault is—just where
all the school-boys kick their heels—and I doubt the room.
After all, I leave that to you—I mean the whole affair of the
funeral.   It is very doubtful whether I shall live till October.
At present I am better; but since I have been better, Mr.
May would not answer for my seeing Mr. Pearson again
three weeks hence.

Before talking of other things, let me say that I now put
up my feet upon *your* chair.   You will not like it the less
for having contributed to my comfort.   I am still as cheerful as ever, which surprises people much.   Is it uncommon?

What a royal demesne Mr. Hope's must be, and how admirably he will rule over it.   I remember your saying that
justice was the distinguishing virtue of that fine mind—
large, with all its fineness; add, what I am sure of, great
sagacity, and you get the two qualities most wanted in that
station and that country.   He and Mrs. Hope will do immense good there.   Long may they live, and happy be their
reign!   I hope the dear little princess is really recovered.
Say every thing for me to them all, and to your own dear
people.   God bless you all!   Ever yours,

M. R. MITFORD.

Your letter has been a great comfort to me, because you
do not seem to think that rapturous assurance of acceptance
necessary.   My hope is a trembling one, from the consciousness of my many sins; but yet it is a real though fearful
trust in the infinite mercy of God and the promises of the
Gospel.   Is this enough?   I am a real skeleton.

To MRS. JENNINGS.

Swallowfield, Sept. 20, 1854.

I can not help answering your most charming letter, dearest Mrs. Jennings, which has given me the highest gratification—first, from its affection, which I most truly recipro-
cate—next, for its spiritual views, which are exactly my own.
I am now reading the Gospels for the third time within the
last two months; and I see in them such love, such mercy,
such charity, that it is impossible to weigh the rare threats
against the constant promises.   My friend, Mr. Harness, never
mentions faith in his letters without interpolating confidence.

So—" faith (confidence)." And the other dear friend, Hugh Pearson, who has been so much to me, and who is just returning from Switzerland, where he has been with Arthur Stanley, is just a younger Bishop Stanley, or Dr. Arnold himself.

For my own part, I hold this visitation to have been sent in mercy by that most merciful God to draw me to Him. May He grant His grace that the opportunity be not cast away! I have none of the " holy joys " that I often hear of, nor even your " home feeling," dear friend; nothing but a trembling, fearful, humble hope, and a full sense of my own unworthiness. Nay, I have much to strive against in wandering thoughts, which often beset me in prayer. But I strive against them, and, through Christ's infinite love and mercy, I have hope. Pray for me, dearest friends, as, all unworthy as I am, I have prayed for you and yours.

I have now somewhat better news to tell you of my health; so far better that, though still in imminent danger, there is now (humanly speaking) a probability that my life may be for some brief space prolonged. I am obliged to sit on an easy-chair day and night, sitting on a wool cushion, sometimes propped by air-cushions, sometimes with my feet on another chair. About three weeks since an amendment took place. I fluctuated—better one day, worse the next; still, at the end of every week, I was better than the week before; and two days ago my friend Mr. Barrett coming to see me from London, and Mr. May arriving at the same time, the latter said, in answer to his inquiries, " that he could answer for nothing—that he should be very sorry to give false hopes—that the danger was still great, though there did seem now a possibility of such an amendment as might prolong life—but that any cold, over-fatigue, or over-exertion—any thing, in short, which affected the breath, would certainly carry me off in a few hours." The case simply is, that I am no longer utterly given over. But this is much, and, under Providence, I owe it entirely to the unwearied friendship of Mr. May, who, with his enormous practice, and I being six miles off, and, as he thought, in a hopeless state, instead of abandoning the stranded ship, continued to watch every symptom, and to try every resource of his noble art as anxiously as if fame and fortune depended upon his success. May God bless and reward him! I can not tell you what alleviations have been brought to my sick-room.

Forgive my not writing again for a long while; I am ordered not to write. Tell dear Mrs. Dupuy what Mr. May says. But do you come and see me as soon as you return to town. Ever yours,   M. R. MITFORD.

I have just heard from Miss Manning, who is suffering from a severe illness. Nothing can equal her piety and resignation.

To the REV. WILLIAM HARNESS, *Kensington Gore.*

Swallowfield, Oct. 30, 1854.

MY VERY DEAR FRIEND,—I write to you, having just read Mrs. Opie's Life, and experiencing a desire to talk of it. What a miserable hash they have made of what might have been so interesting! What a miserable hash *she* made of her own existence! Nothing is clearer than the hankering she had after her old artistic and literary world. She even contrived to mix gay parties with May meetings to the very last. But the want of congruity jars in the book, and must have jarred still more in actual life; more especially as those Fry and Gurney people—popes male and female in their way—seem to have taken upon them to lecture the dear soul. How she declined in taste and in intelligence after joining the Friends! wasting so much good enthusiasm on that bag of wind, Lafayette,—taken in by that humbug, as he, in his turn, was taken in by Louis Philippe!

The most satisfactory thing in the whole work is a letter to her from Mrs. Inchbald—whose "Simple Story" is worth a wilderness of Mrs. Opie's slipshod tales. I had not a notion how bad her English was till this reading. I suppose that one grows more and more fastidious till the power of judging deserts us altogether. But it is not merely the good writing that strikes me in Mrs. Inchbald's letter; it is her loyalty to the great Emperor—the womanly fidelity with which she clings to her admiration for Napoleon—then our most formidable enemy. She fights the ground inch by inch, and never retreats a single hair's breadth from the first line to the last. I wish I had known her! An old friend of mine used to tell me how, being her neighbor in Leicester Square, it was edifying to see her order and regularity in putting her room to rights—doing all the work to save money for a sister, sufficiently unthankful. She was a great woman, and faithful to greatness. Do you remember how Benjamin West, on a lord-in-waiting being sent to tell him of the Emperor's escape from Elba, stole off to the farthest corner of the house and gave three cheers. I wish he had been a better painter, if only for that true story.

Another person to whom this work does huge injustice is Mary Wollstonecraft. Of course I don't.go along with her extreme opinions, although they are but pale, not to say faded pink, compared with the dashing scarlet of American and French audacity; but she was an exquisite writer. Madame de Staël stole much from her; but *her* French is miserable bombast compared to Mary Wollstonecraft's charming English; and Georges Sand—approaching her in the pure and perfect style—is wide as the poles apart from her in purity of feeling; for, married or not married, Mary Wollstonecraft wrote like a modest woman—was a modest woman.

To come back to Mrs. Opie; as her life was a double one, so should have been her biography—one book rose-color for the world, another drab for the Quakers. I doubt, too, if it be permissible to ignore so entirely the absolute engagement she was under to marry Lord Herbert Stuart (I forget names, but surely it was Lord Herbert, a lame man). My good old friend Sir William Elford was invited by her to meet him at dinner; at that time all was arranged and the time fixed for the wedding. It went off on agreement, because each had enough to live on—he as a bachelor in lodgings, passing eight months of the year in the country houses of kinsfolk and friends, and she as a poor authoress without the encumbrance of rank,—but they could not muster enough to keep house and preserve a certain appearance in days when broughams and pages were not, and horses and men were, essential to an establishment, however modest. Then things are so smoothed over. All her friends knew how hard it was that the furniture for which she had worked should be sold for the benefit of her coarse sister. In short—besides the omission of quantities of anecdotes, like that you told me respecting Sir Thomas Lawrence and the Siddons sisters—I have seldom seen a biography which suppressions on the one hand, and glossings over on the other, have rendered more unfaithful,

more untruthful, than this Quaker biography.   Mrs. Opie was
herself so kind and excellent a woman, that she could well
have afforded to have the truth told respecting her.   But as
you say—or rather as my correspondent the curate of Tod-
ley says—these people, who are good *ex officio*, do contrive
to be no better than their neighbors, and sometimes to be a
good deal worse.

Only think of their having stereotyped " Atherton " in
America !   It is a beautiful edition, with a fine American engraving from John Lucas's portrait—the only engraving like
what I was three years ago.

I have hardly been well enough lately for the bed experiment.*   The first cold night I shall try.   God bless you !

M. R. M.

To the REV. HUGH PEARSON, *Sonning.*

Nov. 24, 1854.

I am so sorry, dearest friend, that I worried you by writing yesterday, but Mr. Bennock's kindness to me is so much
that of a son that you will pardon my desire not to keep him
in suspense.   I shall write to him by this post, fixing Dec.
9th for our meeting.   I most gratefully accept your and Mrs.
Stephens's offer, to come here on St. Andrew's Day to receive the holy communion.   I was most unwilling to defer
that sacred and comfortable rite until illness should pros-
trate me mind and body.   At present I am clear enough
mentally, and not too weak physically, to give my whole faculties to the blessed office.   I had a most kind note from
Mrs. Stephens, informing me of its being her birthday.   I
write to her by this post.   I trust, by God's blessing, I may
still hope for some prolongation of existence ; at least so I
argue from Mr. May's manner and the change of medicine.
Remember, Saturday the 9th, the engagement is peremptory,
because Mr. Bennock can not come on any other day ; and I
want you to know each other.

To-day brought me a most delightful note from dear Mr.
Ruskin ; he is suffering from an obstinate cold and inflammation of the throat.   You shall see all his letters : they are
charming.

I can not think from whom I long ago gathered my notion

* Trying to go to bed, instead of sitting up all night in an arm-chair.

of the good archbishop.* Somebody who knows him, for it corresponds exactly with your account. Those are the men for high places. I have always thought the working clergy contained many of the best and most cultivated men in the kingdom; but to keep the Church in the affections of the people, the bishops should, as a body, resemble him who is at their head. This book of Maria Norris—which is a dissenting novel full of artistic faults, and not quite so good in the last volumes as in the first—gives a picture, only too true, of high church and low church excesses, not excluding those of dissenters. It is a most honest book, from which all extreme parties might learn much good, if red-hot partisans ever would admit plain, naked, unadorned truth.

This war is sickening! Lady Russell received a telegraphic message, at two o'clock on Wednesday, to tell her that her son's name was not in Lord Raglan's fatal list; and yesterday she had a letter, dated the 7th, from Sir Charles himself, partly, I believe, written on the 6th. A terrible history of the Grenadier Guards. Of those officers, his tent-mates, two were killed and one mortally wounded; of the battalion, one thousand strong when they sailed, only two hundred remained. But, my dear friend, think of those savage Russians! they went about killing the wounded. One officer, a friend of Sir Charles, was stabbed in three places as he lay on the ground, after being shot through the body. It was a complete butchery. Of course the poor mother has already begun to fear again; although, being now too weak to defend their old post, they will be, I trust, in a less exposed position. Nothing can exceed the good feeling between the French and English armies. Heaven bless you!

Ever most affectionately yours,   M. R. MITFORD.

To MRS. JENNINGS.

Swallowfield, Nov. 29, 1854.

This war is terrible to think of, especially its mismanagement—the worst of surgeons and hospital dressers and orderlies; for between ourselves, I have no faith in the lady nurses. Mr. May says that the whole faculty are unanimous in distrusting their power of being of real use. They will probably sicken and die, and certainly be in the way and give

* Sumner.

trouble. Men are required. Even the female hospital nurses of London wards would be of small avail amongst those sights and sounds and smells. Besides, there are things which even a sister and a daughter should not see, only a mother or a wife. But those ladies wanted excitement and notoriety, and they have got them. I wonder who published Sidney Herbert's letter, which certainly could not have been intended for publication? I suppose the Nightingales; for it is certain that Miss Florence's sister has written a poem in her glorification. Our men are, as you say, admirable in their valor and their devotedness. Did you know Mr. John Whatle, the Catholic priest? With a very considerable fortune, which he always spent in charities, making no difference between Papist or Protestant, and a very frail body, he devoted himself in a cause in which he was sure to perish, because sure not to spare himself. Our men are admirable, whether surgeon or chaplain, or officer or private soldier; but I have no patience with our incapable government, or our notoriety-seeking women. It is just like the Mrs. Stowe fever. She is here forgotten now like a gone-by fashion—forgotten everywhere but in her own land, where they always knew her. As you say, it is fearful to read names that one only knew as gay, kind, genial young men, shot down in this fearful manner. I try to get away from the thoughts as often as I can, but they always cling to me. May it please God to spare your cousin!

Have you a mind to read a dissenting novel?—a rarity, because there is a distaste for works of fiction among the sectarians; and one seldom gets a truthful view of the habits of a dissenting family. One has just been dedicated to me. The book (by name "Philip Lancaster") is so clever that the writer ought to be ashamed of herself for having sent it into the world as full of artistic faults as an egg is of meat.

I have been also reading some old novels which I loved in my youth. I remembered a library in Bristol rich in such rarities, and got a friend to ask for some and hire them for me. The bookseller, finding who wanted them, wrote me a charming letter putting his whole stock at my disposal; I never read so graceful a note. Since then I have been revelling in old associations and good English. Did you ever read any of Charlotte Smith's novels? Except that they want cheerfulness, nothing can exceed the beauty of the style. Whenever Erskine had a great speech to make he used to read her works, that he might catch their grace of composition.

Heaven bless you, dear friend! I am much as I was; that is, I have been worse, but have again revived. Heaven bless you all! Ever most gratefully and affectionately yours,

MARY RUSSELL MITFORD.

The Duke of Devonshire, having heard of my illness, sent, through Mrs. Dupuy, a most kind message.

To the REV. WILLIAM HARNESS, *Kensington Gore.*

Swallowfield, Dec. 7, 1854.

MY VERY DEAR FRIEND,—I am so glad that you agree with me about Fielding. Of course there are good things in "Tom Jones," such as Partridge's criticism upon Garrick; but take it for all in all, I know no book so much overrated. I am now reading "Humphry Clinker." How very superior that is! How much fuller of gayety! The one thing that has provoked me is Smollett's pleadings against York Minster. But the characters are capital, and the *laisser aller* perfect. The expedition might have taken place, and the letters might have been written, which is more than one can say for any of Richardson's books, wonderful as Lovelace is—a perfect inspiration, which the prig who wrote it never understood. *That* might have been dictated by some spirit, say of Congreve, only I believe he was not dead. After I have finished "Humphry Clinker" I shall try "Peregrine Pickle" and "Roderick Random," and then go to "Gil Blas" and "Don Quixote." It is a long while since I read "Gil Blas." This is going the round of the famous comic romances; but some, not so famous, are much better. I assure you there is no comparison between "Tom Jones" and "Hemsprong," whether for cleverness or as a matter of mere amusement; allowing always for what, sixty years ago, was called the mad philosophy. Scott thought of it pretty much as I do.

Just now I have been reading the *feuilletons* of the "Presse," that contain the *Mémoires* of Georges Sand— very kindly sent to me by Henry Chorley. Bits are charming, especially some bird stories, which have great interest for me now, because some weeks ago a robin tapped at my window, and finding himself supplied—a tray fastened outside the window-sill for his accommodation, and kept well stored with bread crumbs for his use—he has not only been constant in his own visits, but has brought his friends and kinsfolk, to my great content. Her love of birds and her skill in taming them was hereditary, her mother being the daughter of a little *oiseleur* upon the Pont Neuf, whilst her father was a grandson of Marshal Saxe. Is not this a charming pedigree? Marshal Saxe being an illegitimate son of Augustus, King of Poland, it follows that Madame Sand was amongst the nearest relations of Louis the Eighteenth and Charles the Tenth—much nearer than the Orleans branch. Some of the correspondence between her father and her grandmother is delightful. Of course she has touched it up —and there are traits of jealous fondness in the old grandmother's letter, equal to any thing in Madame de Sévigné. Still there is a want of truthfulness all through. You feel that you are reading a *plaidoyer* for the exceptional woman, and not a true narrative of her life—or rather the lives of her ancestors, for as yet she is not born.

What a grievous thing this war is! And how wretchedly incompetent our miserable Government! God bless you, dearest friend! Love to dear Mary. Ever yours,

M. R. M.

To MRS. JENNINGS, *Portland Place.*

Swallowfield, Dec. 9, 1854.

Ah! dearest friend, how very, very much too kind you are. The packet arrived in excellent condition—a brace of pheasants, a brace of partridges, and a hare. Game is the only thing I take, or can take. Even that I only suck as largely as I can, but do not swallow. I thus obtain the nutriment without oppressing the digestion. This is my meal at one o'clock. Then, at night, I have a teacupful of actual essence of game, the juices being drawn out in a jar, into which the hare and grouse are cut, without water. The jar is put for three hours into an oven, and then, when the essence is poured off, the rest of the meat is just, so to say, rinsed out with the least possible water, some of this strongest of extracts being added to the noontide meal. But although this mode of dealing with your magnificent presents is most wasteful, you send too large a supply, dear friend. How can I ever thank you half enough! I suppose the best thanks are, the being kept alive by it. I have been very ill since I wrote last, in consequence of a tornado of wind which filled my room with smoke; but gradually and slowly I am getting round to my former state. Thanks, once again, to your family.

I have been much affected by a letter from Miss Manning, the author of the pretty account of Milton's courtship, "Mary Powell." I know her only by correspondence; but in her letters was so much to love and admire, that when, after a long silence, I heard this week that she was dangerously ill, and had resigned herself to death, without incurring the expense of consultations, I was deeply moved, and have tried to prevail on her to reconsider her determination. Mrs. Walter (the dowager) has recovered completely under judicious treatment.

To Mrs. Jennings.

Swallowfield, Dec. 13, 1854.

That book of Judge Edmonds's is an abomination. It came into my house by accident. An old friend, who was desirous of getting the work, requested me to procure it for him from America, and the agent whom I employed sent it to me. The writer has no reverence for any thing, divine or human. Daniel Webster having died on the 24th of October, one of these circles summoned him, through their medium, and represent him as " dark and suffering," because of his not having believed this new faith of theirs, and print long dialogues (false, of course, but which they call true), without regard to the sacredness of death or the feelings of the living. Thank you, again, a thousand times. Ever, dear friend, most gratefully yours, M. R. MITFORD.

To the Rev. William Harness, *Kensington Gore.*

Swallowfield, Dec. 16, 1854.

MY DEAR FRIEND,—Judge Edmonds's book arrived Saturday afternoon, just before Messrs. Pearson and Bennock, and I sent it off on Monday by Mr. Chorley. Before this time Mr. May had called; and I wish you had seen how much

VOL. II.—Q

these two men (I mean Mr. May and Mr. Pearson), both accustomed to death-beds, were frightened to find me reading it.
Of course they did not suspect me of believing, but they say
that the hold which such subjects take on the nerves is extraordinary.   Bulwer is in the hands of a set of mediums, and
passes his time in conversation with his dead daughter.   Mrs.
Browning believes every word, and referred me to that very
book for facts and proofs.   The madhouses in America are
overflowing with the victims of the delusion.   Young George
R——, a gay barrister, full of levity, went to Ireland last
year (this year I mean), and met with an American family
called Ram, or something like.   He and others of his set
acted in private theatricals with the Ram daughters, who
are pretty, and got acquainted with the governess. · She,
being a medium, persuaded the young man to allow her to
summon his dead brother and his poor father, and well-nigh
drove him crazy.   He so far believes in his father having
desired him to thank his widow for her prayers for his soul,
that he delivered the message, and has believed in purgatory
ever since.

I shall be very curious to see "The Hermit of Malta."*
It can hardly be worse than " Voltigern and Rowena," which
took in half the learned people—or, indeed, than a great
many of the wretched abortions which now pass under that
greatest name.

A year or two back I read in a New York magazine (I
think "Putnam's") some verses, said to have been dictated
to one of the mediums by the spirit of Edgar Poe.   The
writer had caught the peculiar chime of that extraordinary
genius, and other peculiarities—in short, just what a clever
imitator can catch of such a writer.   And although Shakspeare is too great for any real deception, yet I have no
doubt that certain turns of phrase will be caught up, and a
better play concocted than " Voltigern and Rowena," which
was poor beyond all poverty.

Mr. Chorley is gone away under the impression that I
have nothing the matter with me—because he and his sister
grumble and fret and whine—which you know is not my
way.   You must come soon, for a little while may settle all

* A play published in America, as having been dictated by the spirit of
Shakspeare.

with me. Mr. May can not get the pulse up. And yet I take six or eight doses of brandy—old Cognac brandy—always without water, every twenty-four hours. And, by-the-by, this is a day which I never expected to see—my sixty-seventh birthday. God bless you! Ever yours,

M. R. M.

[The three following notes were written in the last week of Miss Mitford's life.]

To the Rev. William Harness, *Kensington Gore.*

Swallowfield, Jan. 4, 1855.

My very dear Friend,—So frightful an attack of retching came on Monday, after writing, that my notes must be limited to the fewest possible words.

I did not know Mrs. Calmudy personally, but I know quite enough about her to understand all that you will have felt on her death. You are left, dear friend, to be the one green oak of the forest, after the meaner trees have fallen around you. May God long preserve you to the many still left to grow up under your shade!

If I live till to-morrow, you will receive with this a certificate of my existence which I never thought to send; for on New Year's Day I thought myself going, so did every body.

Little Mr. Rennett is as kind and good a creature as lives. God bless you, my beloved friend! I hope to see you as soon as you can come. Write to say the day and the hour. K—— will get your dinner. Ever yours, M. R. M.

[Extract.]

To a Friend of Mrs. Hoare's.

Swallowfield, Jan. 7, 1855.

It has pleased Providence to preserve to me my calmness of mind, clearness of intellect, and also my power of reading by day and by night; and, which is still more, my love of poetry and literature, my cheerfulness, and my enjoyment of little things. This very day, not only my common pensioners, the dear robins, but a saucy troop of sparrows, and a little shining bird of passage, whose name I forget, have all been pecking at once at their tray of bread-crumbs outside the window. Poor pretty things! how much delight there is in those common objects, if people would but learn to enjoy them : and I really think that the feeling for these simple pleasures is increasing with the increase of education.

To the Rev. HUGH PEARSON.

Sonning, Jan. 8, 1855.

MY BELOVED FRIEND,—May I fix definitely with Mr. Bennock the time at which you will dine with him here? Let me know whether it is to be the 20th or the 27th. I shall not trouble you long.

This day week I had a terrible shake, being New Year's Day. I had many letters to answer, which brought on exhaustion of the brain, and such an attack of retching, that both Sam and K—— thought me dying; so did Lady Russell and Mrs. Hunter, who called and would come up. I got over it through ten doses of brandy, a wine-glass each, not more watered than it would be for sale; but it has left me much weaker; and yesterday I had a return of those terrible neuralgic jars running through every limb, from which I have been latterly free. To-day I am better; but if you wish for another cheerful evening with your old friend, there is no time to be lost. God bless you, my dear friend! Ever affectionately yours,   M. R. MITFORD.

On the 10th of January, two days following, the generous and ardent spirit, by whom the above lines were written, passed away. Her friend, Lady Russell, had been with her during the whole day, and at five o'clock in the afternoon, as she was holding her hand, saw her expire so peacefully that she hardly knew which moment was her last. And as she lay in her coffin the features of the face, undisturbed by any trace of the cares, the vicissitudes, the exertions, the illness that she had undergone—still bearing their resemblance to the miniature that was painted of her in childhood—were overspread by an expression of intense repose and peace and charity such as no living face had ever known.

Her simple funeral, attended by her executors, the Rev. W. Harness and G. May, Esq., and by her faithful servants

Mr. and Mrs. Sweetman (better known to the reader of these letters as "Sam" and "K——"), took place on the 18th of January. The coffin was laid in a place in the churchyard of Swallowfield which had been selected by herself; and the spot is marked by a granite cross, which was erected to her memory by the contributions of a few of her oldest friends.

THE END.

Printed in the United States
103399LV00006B/75/A

9 781428 633315